The NZSO National Youth Orchestra Joy Tonks

The NZSO National Youth Orchestra: Fifty Years and Beyond

Joy Tonks

Victoria University Press

VICTORIA UNIVERSITY PRESS
Victoria University of Wellington
PO Box 600 Wellington
victoria.ac.nz/vup

First published 2011

National Library of New Zealand Cataloguing-in-Publication Data

Tonks, Joy, 1939-
The NZSO National Youth Orchestra : fifty years and beyond /
Joy Tonks.
ISBN 978-0-86473-609-3
1. NZSO National Youth Orchestra—History. 2. Music and youth—New Zealand.
3. Musicians—New Zealand—History.
784.20830993—dc 22

This book was written with the generous assistance of a grant from The Fame Trust.
It is published with the generous assistance of a grant from the Lilburn Trust.

Editing, typesetting and index by
Ahi Text Solutions Ltd, Wellington

Printed by PrintLink, Wellington

Dedicated to
NZSO National Youth Orchestra players, past and future
– and to Lucia, Harriett and Lilli.

Contents

Foreword *by John Hopkins* *viii*

1. Prelude – 'The impossible dream': 1959 *1*
2. Realising the Dream: 1906–1959 *10*
3. Into Orbit: 1958–1959 *25*
4. 'A Harvest Rich Beyond Our Knowing': 1960–1974 *36*
5. The Grand Tour: 1975 *69*
6. In the Aftermath: 1975–1978 *102*
7. Guest Conductors – and an Australian Tour: 1978–1988 *123*
8. 'Cast Adrift': 1988–1998 *155*
9. 'What a gift!': 1999–2004 *181*
10. 'A Taste of the Real Thing': 2004–2009 *196*
11. Celebrating 50 years, plus: 2009–2010 *213*
12. Future Proofing *by Peter Walls* *232*

Acknowledgements *241*

Appendices:

A. Members of the National Youth Orchestra *245*
B. Leaders/Concertmasters/Co-concertmasters: 1959–2009 *261*
C. Conductors: 1959–2009 *262*
D. Soloists and groups: 1959–2009 *263*
E. Sponsors *265*
F. Awards and scholarships *269*

Notes *277*

Bibliography *301*

Index *303*

Colour sections following pages 118 and 214

Foreword

In 1958 I heard several young musicians play who were keen to become members of the National Orchestra. They were very talented and were young and enthusiastic, but still at school. Among these were Coralie Leyland in Timaru, Angela Connal in Christchurch and, in Wanganui, Ted and Ross Pople. I knew there must be more, and it seemed to me that if the National Orchestra was going to have New Zealanders trained to the level necessary, two things could help to bring this about.

I discussed the formation of a small training group alongside the National Orchestra, but this seemed to worry the Musicians Union, and the idea for this, and a youth orchestra on a national scale, seemed to worry Broadcasting even more. I mentioned the idea to Walter Harris of the Education Department, and together we went to see Arthur Harper, who was then the head of Internal Affairs. We must have made a convincing case, as we left his office with his agreement to provide money to bring an orchestra of young players from every part of the country for one week of the May school holidays in 1959.

So the National Youth Orchestra came together at Wellington East Girls' College, rehearsed with me every day and played a short concert on Saturday morning. That which was considered impossible was actually happening! It was all very exciting! The many radio stations throughout New Zealand had announced the proposal and all agreed to make recordings of the young musicians for selection in Wellington. The program that year included Handel's *Occasional* Overture, Beethoven's First Symphony and *Carmen* Suite no 1 by Bizet. I still remember Ron Webb's beautiful oboe solo in the Handel. With the first week such a success, Broadcasting agreed to bring the Orchestra together again in the August holidays and to present public concerts in Wellington and Lower Hutt with two young international soloists, Ilse von Alpenheim and Igor Ozim.

I remember the feeling of apprehension showing on faces on the young musicians when we started to play together for the first time. But it all began to come together remarkably quickly as everyone got down to serious work, and by the end of day one I went home feeling a great sense of relief. I don't remember the schedule except that as well as full rehearsals there were sectional rehearsals with leading members of the National Orchestra. At these, many of the details and tricky passages were worked over and improved so the second rehearsal was already much better than the first day when those naturally unused to playing in such a large group, and those who were wayward and not watching the conductor, quickly learnt the precision skills required when playing as part of a large section and not as individuals. I felt more and more optimistic each day of the week. When it was decided to present two public concerts in the August session I felt we would be up to playing Mozart's Piano Concerto in E flat major (K482) with Ilse von Alpenheim and Mendelssohn's Violin Concerto in E minor (op 64) with Igor Ozim. These concerts were so successful that I was immediately thinking of a more challenging program for the next year. When I last conducted the National Youth Orchestra in Christchurch in 2000, Ravel's *Daphnis and Chloe* complete with the National Youth Choir was just one of the many works we performed! I remember it with much pleasure. Recently I was sent some CDs of the orchestra which are truly impressive and certainly comparable to the Australian Youth Orchestra which I have conducted on many occasions since moving to Australia in 1963.

As well as many of the players becoming members of professional orchestras, it is particularly moving to me when people come up to me and tell me what it has meant to them to have been in the National Youth Orchestra, that their children are now members of the orchestra, and that they themselves are still playing in the home and in the community. I've come to realise that this is one of the most valuable aspects of the whole idea of youth orchestras around the world. It is one of the greatest forces for good because of the collaborative team spirit it generates.

Before I came to New Zealand I had only heard part of a rehearsal of the National Youth Orchestra of Great Britain, but since 1960 I have conducted youth orchestras in many parts of the world such as South Africa, Canada, China and Venezuela, as well as throughout Australia. I'm very grateful for all I have learnt through this over the years. It has shaped my life in the most fulfilling way.

I'm grateful, too, for the support of the players in the National Orchestra who have been so generous and helpful in the realisation of this 'impossible' dream. I wish the National Youth Orchestra every success in this its 52nd year, and much joy in making music in the future.

John Hopkins OBE
Founder, National Youth Orchestra of New Zealand
April 2011

INSTRUMENTS OF THE ORCHESTRA

(NOT DRAWN TO SCALE)

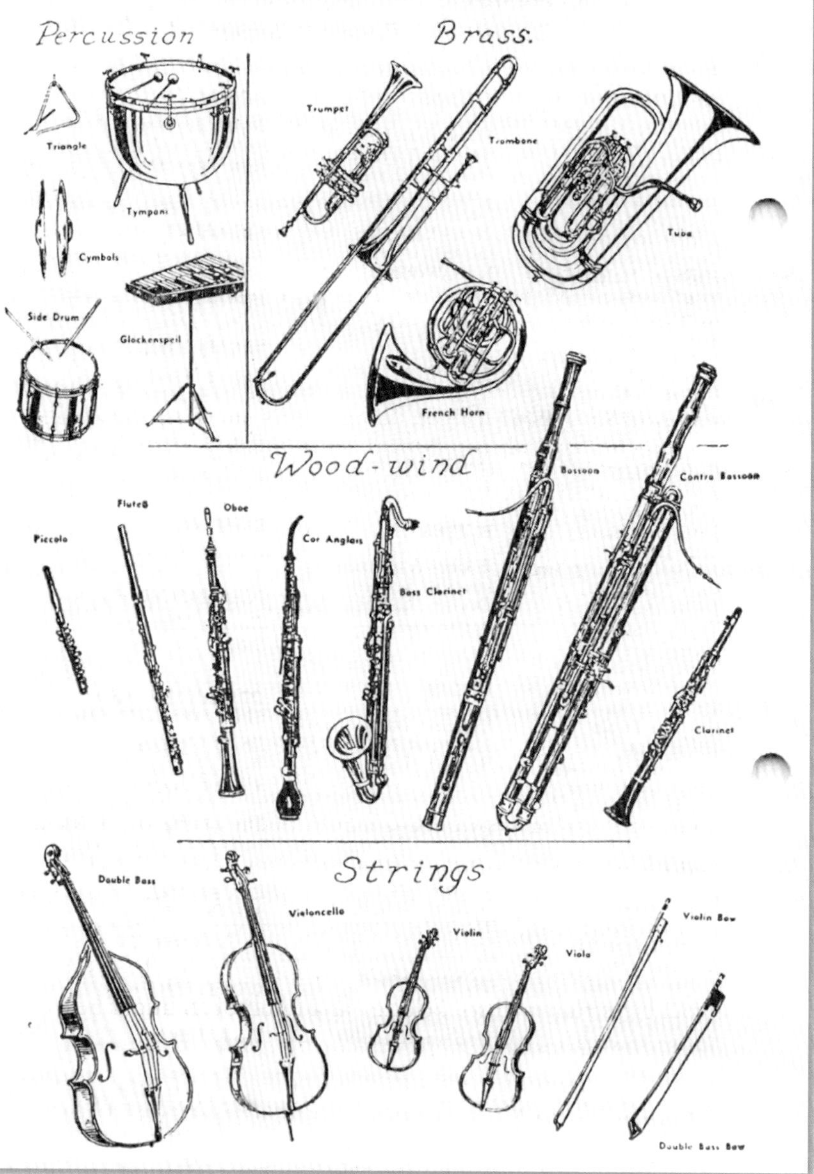

Programme illustration, 1959

1 Prelude

'The impossible dream': 1959

'I was sixteen, still at school, and it was a big adventure ... The NYO changed the direction of my life, really, and once I became involved and hooked, I could only go on and take a chance on becoming proficient enough to earn a living...'

– *Angela (Connal) Lindsay, NYO 1959–61*[1]

It begins, like any other successful musical journey, with a rehearsal – a challenging rehearsal for an orchestra in which most players are strangers.

It's a Monday morning, 11 May 1959, the first official day of the New Zealand National Youth Orchestra. School holidays have begun, but it's a back-to-school day for seventy-nine pioneer young players, thirty-nine boys and forty girls, gathered in the assembly hall of Wellington East Girls' College, on a high hillside overlooking central Wellington.

Among them are some of New Zealand's most accomplished and up-and-coming young instrumentalists. Selected as a result of auditions held around the country from a total of over 250 hopeful applicants, they have come here from all major cities and towns: Auckland twenty-two players, Wellington sixteen, Christchurch fourteen, and Dunedin thirteen, with others from New Plymouth, Hamilton, Wanganui, Napier, Palmerston North, Nelson and Invercargill. Stefan Palliser, a thirteen-year-old percussionist, is the youngest and Vincent John Aspey, the leader, is nineteen.

Most are teenagers – a new word then. They are dressed conservatively, as if in uniform, and no-one wears jeans. The boys have buttoned shirts and trousers, sports jackets or blazers, and some wear ties. The girls wear ballerina-length dresses or skirts, with cardigans, and a few have used make-up: a dash of lipstick, some powder, and maybe mascara – all discreetly applied.

They may seem somewhat formal and respectful, but the world is changing. It's the rock'n' roll era and someone called Elvis will soon be 'The King', although those here today may not agree. It's not Elvis or Bill Haley they have come to hear, or rock 'n' roll they want to play – it's classical music that has drawn them here, to this hall full of young musicians. They are strangers and yet linked by a common interest in music that most others of their 'hip' generation would consider 'square'.

The sound is indescribable: a cacophony of many different instruments, all being played at once, but not together. Snippets of scales, exercises, excerpts and difficult bits in the music that now sits open on the stands in front of them – a piece that few have played, or even heard before, but one that few will forget.

Three violinists, who are meeting for the first time this day, will become NZSO colleagues for the next five decades: Juliana Adams (Radaich), fourteen, Robin Perks, fifteen, and Jane Freed, nineteen.[2]

Looking back over fifty years it all seems 'terribly formal' to them now, with everyone coming well-prepared, bringing their own pencils and rubbers to mark the score as they were told to do. 'It was drilled into us then', they recall, 'but it doesn't happen now'.

Jane (NYO 1959–62) thought it quite 'thrilling',[3] meeting so many other musicians, and she did not mind the sight-reading. 'It was exciting and I loved it; I think we very quickly achieved the standards.'

'Just coming to Wellington was exciting', for Juliana (NYO 1959).[4] 'I travelled down from Auckland on the steam train with two sixth-formers, Bryce Bartley (horn) and Ron Granwal (bassoon), and Miriam Carr (double bass). The people who billeted me were waiting at the station. They lived in Mt Victoria, not far from Wellington East Girls' College.'

Robin Perks (NYO 1959–63) came up from Christchurch on the overnight ferry, and that too 'was an adventure'. He is one of very few here today who plays regularly in a large orchestra (the CSIM, Christchurch School of Instrumental Music, founded by his father, Robert Perks, in 1955). Robin, although then the leader of that orchestra, remembers feeling nervous but exhilarated on that first day; 'the NYO was formidable, but fantastic', he says.[5]

Vincent Aspey, founding leader of the National Orchestra, is here also, as coach to the first violins. A professional musician from the age of twelve, Aspey began his career playing violin at the Huntly 'pictures' and now, aged fifty, he is acknowledged as the most outstanding orchestral musician of his generation in New Zealand.[6] 'A most gifted violinist and a very skilful handler of human beings. He had natural diplomatic gifts and a brilliant sense of fun and humour.'[7]

The first rehearsal. Conductor John Hopkins, sub-leader Michael McIntrye, Jane Freed, principal second violins, and Robin Perks at Wellington East Girls' College, 11 May 1959. *Green & Hahn Photography Ltd*

The time has come. There is a hush in the hall as the instruments fall silent, and then a beaming John Hopkins, principal conductor of the National Orchestra, steps up to the podium.[8] He has only been in New Zealand for eighteen months but is already so 'famous', with his photograph so often in the newspaper, that everyone – even those people with no interest in classical music – knows who he is. The National Youth Orchestra was his idea and he will conduct it. Some members of the audience at his National Orchestra concerts may consider that he does not 'look old enough' to be a proper conductor, and he does not have the requisite white hair, but as they and these new players will soon discover, although disarmingly young and friendly, John Hopkins is always serious about the music.

Seventy-nine young faces look expectantly towards him as Hopkins takes up the baton and says, with little preamble, '"Let's begin with some music, because that's what we came here for …" The oboe provides an A. There is a last spate of tuning, and the National Youth Orchestra launches itself, somewhat raggedly, into its first chord'.[9]

Two pieces are to be played this morning. Handel's *Occasional* Overture is on the stands and, as the orchestra's leader remembers, it was 'pretty difficult'. Vincent John Aspey[10] – or 'Vincent Junior', or 'Young Vince' as he was called then (and sometimes still is) – has followed in the footsteps of his father. A month before his eighteenth birthday he had been appointed by John Hopkins to the second violins as the National Orchestra's first 'cadet player', and now, aged nineteen, Vincent John has been seconded to lead the National Youth Orchestra.

'I like it, it's great', he tells the *New Zealand Listener*. 'Even though I like the atmosphere of the National Orchestra, I miss being with people of my own age. Here there are plenty.'[11] In his new role, Vince will receive coaching from Anthony Bonetti, third desk player in the National Orchestra.

After a few bars Hopkins stops his players and tells them, 'One of the most important things about playing together is not just playing in tune together ... but playing as one ... My beat may be still up here and I get a rat-rat-tat as people come in before they should ... there are also a few who wait too long and are then too late. We'll try it again ...'[12]

'The first big explosion of sound, with all of us young people playing, was absolutely wonderful', Juliana remembers, 'but terrifying for me because sometimes, in the midst of the throng, I have to swop from the violin and play the harp'.

The Walk to the Paradise Garden, the next work on the stands, is lyrically described by the *Listener* reporter present: 'Delius's warm, rich, sunlit music soon filled the hall and muted the pelting of the rain outside ...'[13] It's a poignant story of doomed young lovers that will resonate with youthful players, most hearing and playing it for the first time. It may be a 'wet and windy day outside', according to the article, but the music and excitement of this first rehearsal remain fresh in the memory of its players fifty years on. As Robin Perks recalls, 'It was magical'.[14]

A full and comprehensive programme has been set for the week, ensuring that not a minute is wasted. After a short break for morning tea it is the turn of Dr Charles Nalden,[15] professor of music at Auckland University, to take the string sectional rehearsals, and for Mr William Walden-Mills,[16] the new advisor to the Department of Education Music-in-Schools section, to rehearse the wind and percussion sections.

The course is rigorous for the young musicians. They are required to work the same five-and-a-half hour day as professional players in the National Orchestra at that time: from 9 am to 12.30 pm, and 2 to 4 pm.

Beatrice Hill sits at the back of the first violins. She admits to finding it a struggle at first, but enjoys tutorials with Vincent Aspey senior who seems like 'a good-natured Hoffnung character: "take it easy, you can do it eh?"'. She finds she can 'do it'.[17]

Rehearsing in the full orchestra is only a part of the course, and sections are sent off to receive tuition from the relevant National Orchestra section principal.

They will also watch that orchestra in rehearsal in St Paul's schoolroom, Thorndon, and, 'to help the players really get the "feel" of being in a big orchestra, they will rehearse sitting opposite their equivalent in the National Orchestra'.[18]

One hour each day has been set aside for relaxation – 'musical entertainment' – with chamber music concerts provided for the young musicians by Auckland string quartets and woodwind and brass ensembles from the National Orchestra.

Media coverage of the National Youth Orchestra has been fully supportive since its first announcement. Local and national press have turned out in force for this first rehearsal, only to be turned away, not by Broadcasting (which always welcomed and encouraged publicity), but by Education. The two government departments have dual responsibility for the orchestra. Later, undeterred, the press return in significant numbers to capture something of the special atmosphere: 'Beside the players' obvious enjoyment John Hopkins looked as if it were arranged for his delight … even the photographer and the reporter, stayed to listen'.[19]

Wellington-based newspapers and journals provide the biggest coverage, as might be expected of a host city. Some provincial papers publish full lists of those accepted, often supported by interviews and photographs of players who are already destined for distinguished music careers, such as Wanganui brothers Ross (cello)[20] and Edward (Ted) Pople (violin).[21]

After rehearsals, players have time to socialise. They get to know one another in those heady days of making music by exploring Wellington's milk-bars and fledgling coffee bars. Among these, as Juliana remembers, was Mary Seddon's Monde Marie, in Majoribanks Street, where there was 'goulash, in pottery bowls, and weirdos playing guitars'.[22] There were also the Picasso Coffee Bar in Farish Street, Parsons Bookshop on Lambton Quay, and Casa Fontana on Victoria Street. 'It seemed dangerous and exciting then', Jane says, 'and I learnt to drink Pimms, in a long glass, somewhere in Central Terrace'.

As the week progresses John Hopkins acknowledges that he is 'well satisfied with progress … The somewhat out-of-tune sound and the ragged entries have disappeared … now everyone comes in on the beat, and the composers' marks are faithfully followed … some difficult passages have stuck them, but a fragment here and there has been played quite up to professional orchestral standards ... It is a wonderful thing to have started this orchestra – as wonderful in a way as was the start of the National Orchestra. Apart from the players we shall undoubtedly get for [that] Orchestra this venture will also give some 80 young musicians quite a new conception of symphonic music …'[23]

On Saturday morning the orchestra demonstrates what it can do by presenting an informal two-hour performance of the music they have worked on all week, for the 'benefit of interested persons'. It is a little disappointing to have reached this level of accomplishment and not have an opportunity to perform for a much wider audience, but the impression made on this small, elite group will be instrumental in deciding the ultimate fate of this National Youth Orchestra. No public performance will be possible without this approval. John Hopkins knew that: 'This was the deciding point. If it was a success they would be brought back together again in August.'[24]

For the young musicians the week closes on a high note of optimism. Contact phone numbers and addresses are supplied, and all players are encouraged to 'keep in touch', and where possible, to practice together. Some who were strangers a week ago have already forged friendships that will last a lifetime, and while at this stage there can be no confirmation that the orchestra will continue, everyone is hopeful that they will all meet again soon, 'fingers crossed'.

Delight at the progress and achievements of these past few days is evident in a flurry of glowing official reports received in the week that follows from Broadcasting and Education Department organisers. One Broadcasting staff report acknowledges 'very helpful co-operation' extended to them by the school authorities, and a week's work that was, 'marked by keen enthusiasm, and a remarkable improvement ... shown by the young players'. It's estimated that the costs of the session, 'will not exceed the approved amount of £800'.[25]

William Yates, director of Broadcasting, writes more formally to his Minister, and confirms that, 'in accordance with approval given by Cabinet ... a National Youth Orchestra ... was duly selected and rehearsed during the week ending 16 May 1959 ... The general opinion was that the experiment was a remarkable success and the opportunity for the young people to play in a professionally organised group will no doubt be most beneficial to them, and should have a considerable effect on the general appreciation of orchestral music'.[26]

Approval and funding are quickly confirmed, and a determination is made to reassemble in the next school holidays. John Hopkins recommends

Peter Glen, the National Orchestra's founding principal horn, taking a sectional rehearsal with National Youth Orchestra horn players John Schwabe, David Smale, Neville Cudby, and Bryce Bartley. 1959. *Weekly News*

that engagements be offered to two international recitalists then touring the country, Swiss violinist Igor Ozim and Austrian pianist Ilse von Alpenheim, as soloists – as this would provide 'excellent experience for the young orchestra'.[27]

It will be four months before a now 'official' National Youth Orchestra can meet again, in September 1959, to perform with these soloists; an impatient wait for the young players. For John Hopkins, the startling results achieved in this first week of rehearsals have already exceeded his or anyone else's expectations.

'I was very pleased with the work at this session', Hopkins said. 'I considered some of it was well up to professional orchestral standard and was confident, even then, that public performance would present no difficulties to these young but accomplished players.'[28]

As Michael McIntyre recalls, 'Above all there was the sheer wonder of being catapulted from the musical outback straight into the middle of something marvellously new and mind-blowing, the thrilling sound-world of an excellent symphony orchestra able to do real justice to the great classics. Adding to the magic of it was the feeling of a shared experience ... So there we were, in the NYO, that magical, newly formed group of young, switched-on human beings, working and playing together like crazy.'[29]

The 'impossible dream', as Hopkins will later call it, is on its way to becoming a reality.

The National Youth Orchestra assembled for rehearsal, with assistant conductor Dr Charles Nalden, professor of music, Auckland University. Dominion, *12 May 1959*

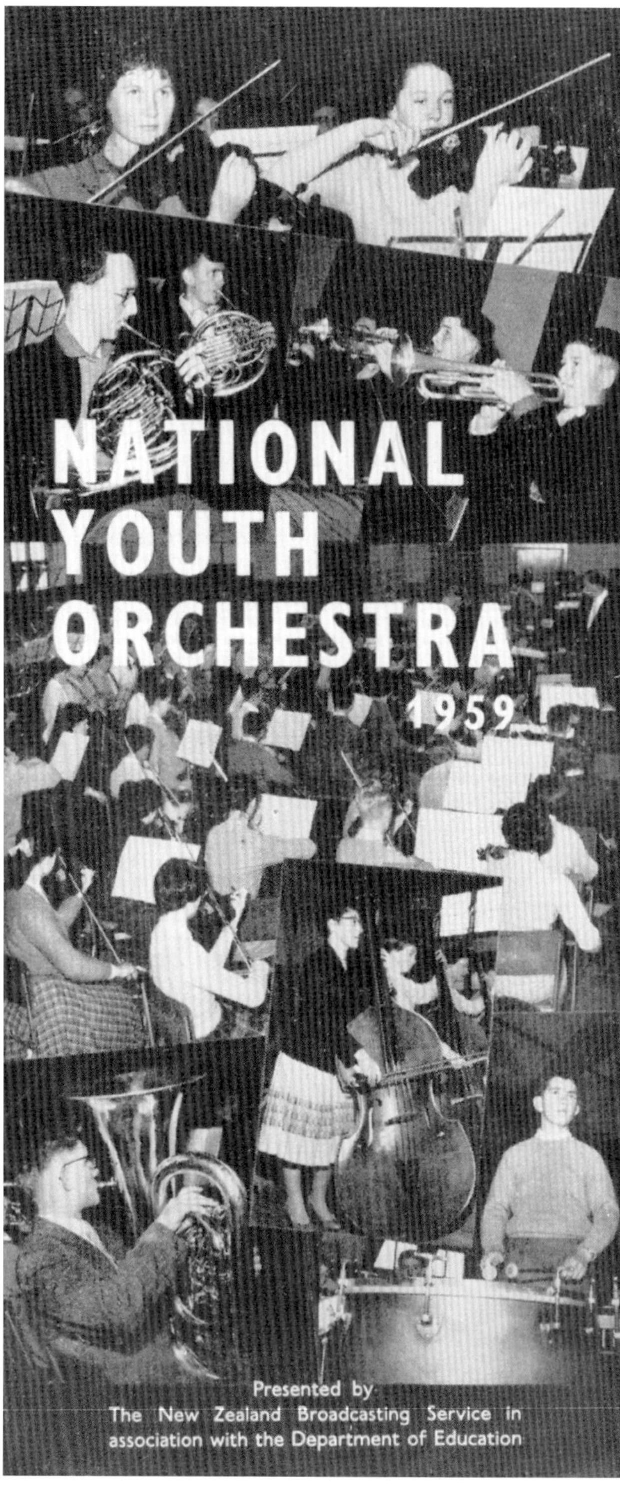

National Youth Orchestra first brochure cover, 1959

The National Youth Orchestra

Jointly organised by the N.Z.B.S. and the Education Department, the National Youth Orchestra was first suggested last year by John Hopkins. The idea was to give talented young players a chance to meet each other, to work together, to gain orchestral experience, and, says, Mr. Hopkins, "to see what hard work it is to play professionally—to play not just when you want to, but to be disciplined and work in a team".

All secondary schools and colleges were circularised, applications from those under twenty-one were called for, and auditions arranged at radio stations throughout New Zealand. 250 applied for the 70 to 80 places available, and were screened by an auditioning committee consisting of John Hopkins, W. H. Walden Mills of the Education Department, and Ashley Heenan of the Broadcasting Service.

The organisation involved in auditioning, arranging transport and accommodation, rehearsal times and halls, culminated in these young people meeting for a week's rehearsal in Wellington in May of this year. Full orchestral rehearsals were conducted by John Hopkins, and section rehearsals taken by Dr. Charles Nalden, Professor of Music at Auckland University, and Mr. Walden Mills. In addition, the players were given special tutorial instruction by the leaders of their particular sections in the National Orchestra.

By the end of the week, enthusiasm was even greater than when rehearsals had started. All of the players, from the youngest, a thirteen-year-old percussionist, to Vincent Aspey Jnr., leader of the Youth Orchestra, had settled like veterans to the special techniques of orchestral playing.

John Hopkins was very pleased with the work at this session—some of it he considered was well up to professional orchestral standards—and he expects the week of concentrated rehearsal in early September to produce outstanding results at the Lower Hutt and Wellington concerts.

Youth orchestras are already well established in England, Wales and Australia, and some have been set up in New Zealand cities. The formation of an orchestra on a NATIONAL basis will not only help the existing groups, but will, it is hoped, provide a fund of experienced players on which the National Orchestra can draw. It will also give some eighty young musicians, and those who in time succeed them, a new conception of symphonic music.

LOWER HUTT — TOWN HALL

THURSDAY, SEPTEMBER 10th — 8 p.m.

Occasional Overture .... Handel

The Walk to the Paradise Gardens .... Delius

Symphony No. 1 in C .... Beethoven

Violin Concerto in E minor .... Mendelssohn

Polonaise (Life for the Czar) .... Glinka

Soloist: IGOR OZIM

Conductor: JOHN HOPKINS

WELLINGTON — TOWN HALL

FRIDAY, SEPTEMBER 11th — 8 p.m.

Occasional Overture .... Handel

The Walk to the Paradise Gardens .... Delius

Symphony No. 1 in C .... Beethoven

Piano Concerto in E flat major, K.482 .... Mozart

Polonaise (Life for the Czar) .... Glinka

Soloist: ILSE VON ALPENHEIM

Conductor: JOHN HOPKINS

Special Youth Concert Prices: 9/-, 6/6, 3/6.

Schoolchildren's Concessions: 4/6, 3/6.

There was a good deal to be considered in the choice of works for the inaugural concerts by the National Youth Orchestra. The Handel "Overture" was chosen, not only because this year is a Handel tercentenary, but also because it will give the audience the opportunity of hearing the full orchestra at the beginning of the programme. Evocative music is represented by the Delius piece, while the Beethoven Symphony serves as a good introduction for the young players to the classical orchestral repertoire. In the "Polonaise", they all have a chance to demonstrate the brilliance of Glinka's orchestration. The composer makes technical demands on the full orchestra, particularly the strings, and all players will be able to show the high standard they have reached.

COVER BY SPENCER DIGBY STUDIO

National Youth Orchestra first brochure, inside pages, 1959

2 Realising the Dream

1906–1959

The National Youth Orchestra had a dream run in its first year, thanks to John Hopkins. It had been first discussed in February 1958, initial rehearsals were in May 1959, and the first performances four months later. In contrast, a national symphony orchestra was a dream deferred for four decades, its first performance in March 1947 preceding that of the National Youth Orchestra's by a mere twelve years.

Orchestras began to spring up in main centres of New Zealand from the mid to late 1880s. Their players – 'a mixture of amateurs and teachers, with a sprinkling of paid professionals'[1] – were limited by the availability and quality of instruments at the time, and faced competition not only from the more traditionally acceptable choral societies, but also from popular brass bands, for which instruments were more readily available.

Among Auckland's orchestral music pioneers were the conductors Karl Schmitt, who gave early orchestral concerts and was the first professor of music at the Auckland University College (appointed in 1888), Arthur Towsey of the Auckland Orchestral Union (1889), Johannes Wielaert of the Auckland Orchestral Society (1903), and Colin Muston who ran the Bohemian Orchestra (1914–36) and the Auckland Symphony Orchestra (1939–47).[2] The Wellington Orchestral Society was formed in 1875, with some members from the 65th Regimental Band, and had its 'most distinguished regime under a young Alfred Hill'[3] in 1892–96.[4] It later gave way to the Municipal Orchestra, conducted by Maughan Barnett, and the Wellington Professional Orchestra, conducted by Leela Bloy.[5] Belgian émigré Leon de Mauny[6] founded the Wellington Symphony Orchestra in 1928 'to give the people of Wellington some flesh and blood music'.[7] Australian pianist John Bishop conducted the Royal Wellington Choral Union from 1928 to 1934. He also formed a 25-piece chamber orchestra, the Guild of Music Makers, in 1929, and the following year the Wellington Philharmonic Society with seventy-five players.[8] Both of these included many players from the rapidly disbanding theatre ensembles.

After early activity in the late 1870s, orchestral music in Christchurch was centred in two spheres: the Christchurch Orchestral Society, re-established in 1908 and active until 1939 under conductors Benno Scherek, Alfred Bunz and Angus Gunter, and the Christchurch Symphony Orchestra (1916–20) conducted by Alfred Worsley. A third significant group in Christchurch was the Laurian Club, a fine string orchestra of twelve players, founded by cellist Harold Beck, in 1932.[9] Dunedin's first orchestras were George West's fifty-piece Philharmonic Society (1865), and the New Zealand and South Seas Exhibition Orchestra, conducted by Arthur Towsey with leader Signor Squarise (1889). The latter was the forerunner of the Dunedin Philharmonic Orchestra, also led by Squarise, which lasted from 1904 until 1933. Violinist James Coombs's Orchestral Society (1888–1930) attracted large audiences to the Garrison Hall, and the well-known Gil Dech, the former director of Columbia Recording Studios in NSW, became conductor of the Dunedin Symphony Orchestra in 1936, and of the 4YA Orchestra.[10]

New Zealand's first professional orchestra

The New Zealand Government chose to mark the country's important change in status from colony to dominion, in 1906, with the New Zealand International Exhibition held in Christchurch. In conjunction with the six-month exhibition, an orchestra would be assembled and funded by Government for the duration. Alfred Hill was named conductor, and given the added responsibility of recruiting players for the 53-piece orchestra. Some of those he selected had played in the orchestra of the Melbourne Exhibition of 1880–81. For six months the orchestra gave two concerts each day, one classical and one popular. 'Its programmes of symphonies, overtures, incidental music and concertos played by New Zealand soloists aroused much enthusiasm and won excellent reviews', with increasing attendances that, 'reached a peak as the exhibition drew to a close'.[11] After the exhibition ended, the *Triad* wrote that although it 'could claim no phenomenal mechanical excellence, no profundity of thought in expression ... the greatest achievement of the orchestra was the conversion of the public; it was a veritable triumph for instrumental music of the highest type'.[12] Buoyed by this reaction, the orchestra embarked on a national orchestral tour for a further six months financed by independent sponsors, John and Lena Prouse,[13] with hopes it might be sustained. But, despite much goodwill and pressure put on the Government to retain this successful established ensemble as New Zealand's first permanent professional orchestra, a unique opportunity was lost. The orchestra disbanded and many of its musicians, including Alfred Hill, departed New Zealand.

It was fourteen years before New Zealanders heard another professional orchestra. In 1920 the 100-piece New South Wales State Orchestra toured under its Belgian conductor Henri Verbrugghen, the first director of the Sydney Conservatorium (appointed in 1915).[14] As the first symphony orchestra ever to visit New Zealand, it was 'declared to be the finest orchestra ever heard in this part of the world [and] its performances aroused great enthusiasm'.[15] Verbrugghen himself had expressed the wish to make the orchestra 'Australasian in concept, and practice',[16] and the suggestion was supported by several newspapers. In Christchurch, the *Press* encouraged 'those in musical positions to confer with Verbrugghen and form a deputation to wait on the Prime Minister'. Recalling the fate of the Christchurch Exhibition Orchestra – 'disbanded and not retained' – it urged: 'Opportunity knocks again at our door, and should not this time be denied.'[17] But denied it was, despite a second successful tour by the New South Wales State Orchestra to New Zealand, in 1922. On its return home, a deficit of £2,019 9s 6d led to acrimonious exchanges between the New South Wales State Government and Verbrugghen. As a result, Verbrugghen resigned and left Australia to become conductor of the Minnesota Symphony Orchestra, and the New South Wales Orchestra later disbanded.[18] New Zealand had lost a second chance for a ready-made professional orchestra, and it would be two decades before another opportunity presented itself.

Such was the continuing interest, however, that when international musicians arrived in New Zealand to perform – or just passed through – their advice on starting an orchestra was eagerly sought. Conductors Malcolm Sargent, Antol Dorati and others made helpful suggestions for choosing a conductor, but Alfred Hill had a better understanding of what was required in New Zealand. On 17 June 1936, he wrote to Prime Minister Michael Savage to advocate 'a New Zealand Conservatorium of Music',[19] a suggestion first made by Roland Foster, a well-known singing teacher. Hill envisaged an institution 'so good, that your students will not have to come to Australia or go abroad to study' that could be made to pay if New Zealanders, 'not London musicians', examined all New Zealand [music] students. 'Untold wealth had left New Zealand in the pockets of English Examination Boards', he claimed, but if the 'New Zealand Government backed its own examinations and made music compulsory … in the Public Schools, an immediate income of thousands of pounds would result. New Zealand should leave the Mother strings, and stand on her own feet musically … All good musicians could be absorbed in the work of a Conservatorium', and an orchestra could be developed, 'for broadcasting symphonic concerts, operatic performances and chamber music… This would give employment to many of your finest people and put New Zealand on the map, musically…' Thirteen days later, Hill wrote again with a new suggestion, 'a Conservatorium could well take charge of Maori culture and music' – a matter close to his own heart. Hill, having pledged his help and advice, was considered with others for the role of director of the New Zealand Conservatorium, but as the war clouds gathered, both it and a national orchestra were deferred, and only one would be realised.

New Zealand broadcasting

Alfred Hill's advice was well meant, but he could not foresee that, when eventually a professional orchestra was established, the impetus would come from an unexpected source: radio broadcasting. The transmission of vocal and musical items in New Zealand started in 1921, and by 1925 several broadcasting companies had been formed. Gordon Coates (then Postmaster-General, later Prime Minister)[20] having reached agreement with the Radio Broadcasting Company of New Zealand Ltd,[21] a national broadcasting system of radio stations was established in all four main centres.[22] The service was initially limited to two hours' programming per night, and with the broadcasting of recorded music restricted, musicians, singers, actors and other entertainers performed in the studio, without a fee. By 1928 the novelty had worn off and the policy changed. Artists were paid to perform, and live music was relayed into the studio over a standard telephone line from Auckland theatre orchestras and cabarets.

The first director of music, WJ Bellingham, was appointed in 1927, and stated his philosophy: 'Do not under-rate the capacity of the audience to appreciate good music, well played. I believe in a varied programme with a major proportion of standard works. The essential feature is that what is done, whether a foxtrot or a symphony, must be well done.'[23] Bellingham thought it necessary, 'to develop a number of highly trained professional players who will be able to read at sight and intelligently and artistically interpret the whole range of music from classical to modern time'. He encouraged the engagement of better artists, formed permanent instrumental trios and quartets at radio stations in the four main centres, and from 1928, National Broadcasting Service studio orchestras. Bellingham considered that he had a 'duty' to music as well as the Radio Broadcasting Company, and as 'custodian of musical standards within the company' he particularly 'wanted to broadcast a substantial proportion of high-quality music'.[24] Bellingham's insistence on high standards and a repertoire of classical works was not appreciated by Ambrose Reeves Harris, whose priorities were said to be, 'programmes that would encourage people to buy radio sets, pay the license fee, and listen'.[25] A clash between the two was inevitable. Bellingham returned to England, but the popularity-versus-quality debate continues to engage broadcasters and listeners – and remains unresolved.

In 1931, new legislation gave responsibility for the development of a national radio-broadcasting service to the New Zealand Broadcasting Board, under which jurisdiction, 'broadcasting' activities were extended in an unexpected direction. Four years later, in 1935 a tour was organised by the Broadcasting Board for the international Australian musician Percy Grainger, as 'guest conductor, solo pianist, organist, ukulele player, composer'. From this small beginning, 'Broadcasting' steadily increased its commitment to engage many of the world's most important artists – conductors, instrumentalists, singers, and entertainers – to perform as soloists in New Zealand concert halls, or to record for radio, and later television. It had become a de facto patron of the arts. 'A new impresario entered the field.'[26] The New Zealand Broadcasting Board existed for only five years before it too was abolished. Under the Broadcasting Act 1936, its rights, property, liabilities and assets were transferred to the Crown, to become the National Broadcasting Service (NBS). Professor James Shelley, the first professor of education at Canterbury University, was appointed the first director of broadcasting. A year later, on the passing of the Broadcasting Amendment Act 1937, NBS split into two new government departments: a National Broadcasting Service with twelve non-commercial stations under Shelley, and a National Commercial Broadcasting Service with four commercial stations under a controller.

Within his first year, Professor Shelley was outlining government proposals for a National Broadcasting Centre in Wellington, to include a conservatorium of music and the spoken arts. 'A National Symphony Orchestra will naturally be associated with such a conservatorium, and it is hoped that within a few years the employment of musicians will no longer be the casual thing that it has been in the past ...'[27]

The centennial of New Zealand

Almost simultaneously, a deputation from the Royal Wellington Choral Union led by AR Wright, MP, together with British conductor Dr Malcolm Sargent, called on the Minister of Internal Affairs, Hon WE Parry, to discuss suitable celebrations to mark the centennial of New Zealand in 1940. Of considerable interest was a proposal 'to set up a Musical Festival', with choirs and orchestras in each of the four main centres, 'such festival having as its objective the establishment of a Musical Scholarship Fund to be devoted to the encouragement and assistance of younger musicians'.[28] A high-powered committee comprising Joseph Heenan[29] and AW Mulligan from Internal Affairs, James Shelley from Broadcasting, and George Sinclair from Treasury, met to consider the proposal. When they eventually reported back to their respective ministers, the proposition was considerably changed and expanded, and the cost had spiralled to £30,000. An accompanying statement frankly acknowledged, 'that, as a community, New Zealand has not developed culturally, as it has in other directions, and we feel that the advantage should be taken by the Centennial, with its two-fold objective of celebrating the past one hundred years and laying a foundation for the next hundred years, to make a special feature of the musical and dramatic side of the celebrations'.

On 1 March 1939 a Centennial Music Festival was approved by Cabinet, under the direct control of the National Broadcasting Service, with Professor Shelley as chairman of a centennial music committee, which included Joseph Heenan and other prominent representatives: Professor Horace Hollinrake of Auckland, Mr William Page of Wellington, Professor James Hight of Christchurch, and Dr Victor Galway of Dunedin. A stated aim of this committee was to 'eliminate the petty jealousies existing among the several music and dramatic societies throughout New Zealand', and its most significant new addition was, 'the establishment of a full time Centennial Orchestra, to be continued as a permanent, professional national symphony orchestra of New Zealand'.[30] At last!

Festival preparations were already well advanced when, in September 1939, the New Zealand Government – walking slightly ahead of Britain – declared war on Germany. Despite the uncertain international situation, the national celebrations went ahead, albeit on a reduced scale, and two months later the Centennial Exhibition of New Zealand opened on 8 November, in Kilbirnie, Wellington.

As Shelley had promised, a twelve-piece National Broadcasting Service (NBS) String Orchestra was formed and directed by British musician, Maurice Clare.[31] Launched on 1 December, its musicians also formed the nucleus of the Centennial Orchestra of thirty-four players, led by Clare, and conducted not by Malcolm Sargent as originally planned, but by another British musician, Andersen Tyrer, best known then as a concert pianist – 'the high priest of polish in pianoforte playing' – and a visiting music examiner for Trinity College of Music, London.

The Centennial Orchestra, augmented by players from National Broadcasting Service studio orchestras, and Wellington Symphony Orchestra, toured for the Centennial Music Festival, taking opera, oratorio, and orchestral concerts to cities and towns around the country. Shelley, an outstanding festival director, was indefatigable and expected much of his staff and artists. Four international singers, among them New Zealand bass Oscar Natzke and English soprano Isobel Baillie, travelled 2250 miles by car, giving fifteen performances in twenty-five days. A reluctant opera singer, Baillie claimed to have been 'tricked by the small print in her contract', and, persuaded by James Shelley, sang 'Marguerite in *Faust*, in 16 New Zealand towns'.[32]

The Centennial Festival Symphony Orchestra, conductor Andersen Tyrer, with (l–r) Maurice Clare, leader, Vincent Aspey, sub-leader, Haydn Murray, principal second violins, Winifred Carter, harp. 1940. *Charles P S Boyer*

New Zealand provided a peaceful haven for these artists at that time, but when the Centennial celebrations ended six months later, the war still continued. Work stopped on the foundations of the impressive five-storey Broadcasting building in Bowen Street, which was to have included New Zealand's first National Conservatorium of Music and Dramatic Arts, and it would be twenty-three years before a very different building, Broadcasting House, would open on this site. The Centennial Orchestra was disbanded. Its players returned home, or joined the armed forces, and plans for the new National Orchestra were put on hold. Only the NBS String Orchestra, the 'Royal Strings', as players called it, was retained and its members eventually became the inaugural string principals of the National Orchestra.

In 1943 the two broadcasting services were amalgamated under the Director of Broadcasting, but it was two years before Professor Shelley, on 11 September 1945, could submit his proposal to the Minister of Broadcasting 'to establish a fulltime national orchestra under the control of the Broadcasting Service, for the purpose of giving public and broadcast concerts'.[33] As Shelley waited for approval, 'Broadcasting' underwent yet another change of name, becoming the New Zealand Broadcasting Service (NZBS) on 1 April 1946. There would be more such name changes in its long, chequered history, most coinciding with a change of government, or April Fools Day, or both. Confusion was largely avoided because, irrespective of variations in the official title, it was always referred to as 'Broadcasting', a sobriquet that not only identified and defined it, but provided continuity from 1925 to 1975, when it became Radio New Zealand, and that name 'stuck'.

A national orchestra for New Zealand

Official confirmation of the orchestra came on 25 June 1946, but was pre-empted by the revelation that Andersen Tyrer had been appointed 'Musical Director and Conductor of a national orchestra'. This was a position never advertised, which nevertheless received Cabinet approval, on 21 February 1946, four months before the official announcement.

The appointment was contentious because Tyrer, although by now well known as conductor of the Centennial Orchestra, was not considered suitably qualified for the position. In an attempt to justify this action, Prime Minister Peter Fraser revealed the text of a cable from distinguished British conductor Sir Thomas Beecham who affirmed that Tyrer was 'just the man for the job'. This was an ambiguous remark, which some attributed to Beecham's 'cynical wit'.[34] It failed to change public response to a deeply unpopular decision, evidenced in the number of letters sent to newspapers and questions raised in the House of Representatives, to which Fraser replied.

It was all to no avail. Andersen Tyrer kept his job, for which he had unique advantages; he was still resident in New Zealand, and having worked closely with many of its best musicians for six months in the Centennial Orchestra, he knew their strengths and weaknesses. Tyrer in fact was a conductor ideally placed for a New Zealand Government impatient to establish a symphony orchestra without further delay.

For some months before the orchestra was confirmed, Tyrer had begun the long process of travelling the country to interview or audition over 300 musicians. Not able to impart any definite information, he was restricted to whispers and dropped hints, often telling successful players that they could 'expect to receive a contract, but please don't tell anyone'.[35] Now he had to set off again on a final round to complete the process, and offer contracts to a fortunate sixty-five players – a tiring schedule, but to give him his due, Tyrer managed to deliver an orchestra in a remarkably short time.[36] On 24 October 1946, in the broadcasting studio in Waring Taylor Street, Wellington, the National Orchestra of New Zealand (or 'Nat Orch' as it was sometimes affectionately known) was launched by New Zealand's distinguished war hero, Governor General Sir Bernard Freyberg VC. There were speeches[37] but no music until after all the officials had gone, when Tyrer and his newly assembled orchestra began rehearsing repertoire for the inaugural concert season. The first work, appropriately, from Dvořák's Symphony no 9 *From the New World.*

Like their leader Vincent Aspey, most of these foundation members of the orchestra had played in the 1940 Centennial Orchestra, as members of the NBS String Orchestra, NBS studio orchestras, the Royal New Zealand Air Force Band, brass bands and cinema orchestras. Several were highly trained musicians from Europe – émigrés and refugees, and sub-leader Alex Lindsay had most recently been on active service in the Pacific with the Royal New Zealand Navy.[38]

Intense rehearsals followed for a couple of weeks, and then players dispersed to their homes around the country, returning four months later for another round of rehearsals. The culmination came on Friday 7 March 1947, in the Wellington Town Hall, with the first concert by the National Symphony Orchestra of New Zealand, given to extraordinary acclaim from its public,

The first official photograph of the National Symphony Orchestra, prior to its first performance, with conductor Andersen Tyrer, Wellington Town Hall, February 1947. *Photo News*

and a few picky remarks from academics and critics. This event was followed a few days later by some rather formal school concerts in a Town Hall packed full with children, and then the first concert tour, to Christchurch, Dunedin, and Auckland.

Recruitment

As New Zealand's first permanent, professional orchestra, there was no precedent to follow, and since it was administered by Broadcasting – a government department – the orchestra initially was run on public service lines, and players worked office hours. When that was later found to be unsustainable, it changed to six hours per day, and later, five.

The first tours were to main centres, but before long the orchestra was also required to perform in smaller centres, travelling by trains, boats, or bus (but not by planes until the mid-1960s). Concerts were given in a variety of venues in cities and small towns, and some were broadcast live on air. Players stayed in hotels and boarding houses. For many older musicians, or those with young families, the novelty of travelling away from home, often for several weeks at a time, very soon wore thin. Especially trying was the nine-week tour by the Italian International Opera Company in 1948. Long extended tours during the winter months increased the risk of players succumbing to seasonal ills and having to be replaced at short notice – if indeed there were any other suitably qualified players available at the time.

The orchestra was based in Wellington. Most of its rehearsals were held there, and players living in other centres spent much of their time travelling back and forth between home and the capital. Some antagonism was evident from cities which complained, with some justification, that the orchestra had taken all their best players. To placate them, a 'group scheme' was introduced to enable players to live in their own region, play in their local orchestra for part of the year, and receive an allowance when required to play in Wellington.

Recruitment became a cause for concern when, within the orchestra's first year, several players resigned and a new round of auditions proved unsuccessful. New Zealand had very few musicians of professional standard, and no formal tertiary training available, and so, although the Musicians Union disapproved, Tyrer set off to seek replacements in Britain. He returned with several respected musicians, among them, Eric Lawson, who would become the orchestra's long-serving deputy leader, and James Hopkinson, principal flute. But still numbers continued to decline as many players, including several Auckland musicians, opted to remain in their home base, despite the incentive of an extra allowance.

Andersen Tyrer's three-year term ended in 1949. He was followed by Irish conductor Michael Bowles, 1950–53, who was almost immediately faced with demands from the Musicians Union. The Union wanted less rehearsal time in relation to concerts, a limit on tours to duration of three weeks, and the retention of the 'group scheme'. When Broadcasting, as a cost-cutting exercise, threatened to reduce the orchestra to fifty-five players, Bowles countered with a suggestion of having the orchestra fully based in Wellington, and the abolition of the 'group scheme', 'to gain stability, and provide the opportunity for higher standards'.[39]

Broadcasting agreed, although more resignations resulted, of players who refused to move to Wellington and others who regretted their loss of allowances. When only fifty-eight of sixty-nine players started the 1951 season, Bowles, with Broadcasting approval, set off to recruit players in Sydney, with disappointing results. Some thirteen had looked good on paper, but only three passed the audition, and these were offset by a further three resignations in New Zealand.

It was Bowles who introduced the orchestra's subscription season, conducted the first Proms and outdoor concerts, and arranged a rather unbalanced exchange of conductors: Sir Bernard Heinz conducted the National Orchestra in New Zealand for four weeks, and Bowles conducted for thirteen weeks in Australia. After this, Bowles took an early departure from New Zealand.

British-based New Zealand conductor Warwick Braithwaite was engaged to fill this gap. Recognising that a more experienced orchestra no longer required constant rehearsing, he used the spare time gained to completely reorganise the orchestra's music library. He would later conduct a triumphant first Royal Concert for Her Majesty Queen Elizabeth II, in 1954.

In that same year, Braithwaite was replaced by James Robertson, who, shocked by constant complaints about the 'cost' of the orchestra, made it his mission to 'sell' it to the public, and succeeded. An English opera conductor whose symphonic repertoire was not then extensive, Robertson found the then fifteen-day tours and the requirement to perform so many different programmes – for a live broadcast each night – a nightmare. He talked to the audience (a novelty they loved, and the players endured), then alienated some string players by insisting on re-auditioning them all, for the first time since the orchestra's establishment.

Each resident conductor added his unique contribution to the orchestra's development. Robertson raised its profile, and under his direction, it became increasingly professional. He held the first workshops for composers, initiated 'concerto' days for orchestra members who had never played one, and 'conductors' days for players, who had never conducted. He also introduced 'Youth Concerts', for 'the young in heart', in one of which leader Vincent Aspey and his teenage son Vincent John Aspey performed the Bach Double Violin Concerto in D minor, in June 1956.

A year before that, Robertson conducted a massed school orchestra of over 100_players at a music seminar, and was heard to express interest in forming a 'Youth Orchestra for the whole of New Zealand'. This suggestion was greeted with enthusiasm, but nothing came of it at that time.[40]

John Hopkins

As James term was coming to an end in New Zealand, John Hopkins, conductor of the BBC Northern Orchestra, was working on scores in Manchester's Central Library. Filling in time between a lunch-time and evening concert, he wandered into the reference room, and, noticing an advertisement in *The Times* – 'Principal conductor, National Orchestra, New Zealand' – he jotted down the details on the back of an envelope. The idea of warmer weather and the adventure of travelling so far away were attractive, he remembers. 'I later drove back to our home, fifteen miles out of Manchester, through thick fog; and getting lost two or three times on the way. When I got home I jokingly asked my young wife, Rosemary: "How would you like to live in a decent climate?" I think most people would think I was going to say "the South of England," there was the Bournemouth Symphony there, and Rosemary said, "yes, I'd rather like that", but I said, "there's a job going in New Zealand!"'[41] Interviews for this position were held at New Zealand House in London, where (under a long-standing arrangement) the comparatively inexperienced New Zealand Broadcasting Service received assistance from a sister organisation, the British Broadcasting Corporation (BBC) when appointing a new conductor. A committee of three members had assembled for the interview, at which John Hopkins was surprised to find himself facing two senior BBC executives: the BBC controller of music, and the BBC Orchestra manager. 'They were quite surprised to see me too', John remembers, 'because I was a BBC employee, working with them, and under contract to them!'[42]

Thirty-seven applications had been received for the position, from which twelve were selected for interview and three eventually short-listed. John Hopkins was placed third on that list. The London Committee deemed the other two finalists 'better qualified' than the 29-year-old Hopkins, who, in their opinion, 'was too young and inexperienced, for such a responsible position'.[43]

This was not the result expected by Broadcasting executives waiting back in New Zealand. John Hopkins was known as one of the BBC's rising stars.

Aged twenty-two, he had been appointed assistant conductor of the BBC Scottish Orchestra. Two years later, aged twenty-four, he had replaced Charles Groves[44] as conductor of the BBC Northern Orchestra. Hopkins was then the youngest person in that orchestra – and the youngest conductor of any major orchestra in Britain.

The Broadcasting Committee thanked its counterpart in London, and politely requested that it 'reconsider' its recommendation. The committee did so, and then wrote to reiterate its original decision. John Hopkins' youth, it claimed, 'was against him'.

'He is still very young and probably unfortunately for himself as a conductor, looks younger still', a committee member explained. He then expressed his personal opinion that, 'Hopkins's youthful appearance, would come as somewhat of a shock' to audiences.

John Schroder, the NZBS's assistant director, was frankly sceptical. The New Zealand Committee was 'not at all disposed to take very seriously the deprecation of Hopkins' youth', he wrote to New Zealand House, 'or even of his unhappy trick of looking younger still, when it was observed that our BBC advisers, who objected so strongly to his youthfulness … belonged to an institution which had made him a conductor when he was five years younger'.[45] Convinced that John Hopkins was 'the man for the job', the New Zealand Committee rejected the recommendation of their London colleagues, and appointed him principal conductor of the National Orchestra. It was an unprecedented decision, but one that they never had any cause to regret. Now with new confidence in its own decision-making abilities, the NZBS no longer sought the BBC's assistance for subsequent appointments, although the usual close co-operation continued for many more years when engaging guest conductors and soloists to perform in New Zealand.

Unaware of the controversy concerning his appointment, John and Rosemary Hopkins, and their new baby daughter Clare – then only a few months old – set off for New Zealand. An unusually eventful five-week journey on the *Rangitane,* with a fire on board followed later by a collision with another ship during a storm in the Gatun Lake and repairs in Panama, caused a delay of five days to their arrival.

'It was quite a journey', John Hopkins recalls, 'and then one morning I remember waking up and seeing Wellington Harbour. It was a lovely day and quite extraordinary to see this incredible beauty.'[46] John Hopkins' youth – considered a 'disadvantage', by the BBC – would prove a significant advantage to New Zealand Broadcasting, with its youthful National Orchestra then just eleven years old. Full of ideas and energy, Hopkins charmed New Zealanders with his contagious enthusiasm and ready smile, from the moment that he and Rosemary stepped off the boat in Wellington, on 2 November 1957.

Two men waited on the wharf to greet the newcomers that day: James Hartstonge, the National Orchestra's concert manager, and its departing principal conductor, James Robertson. It was a first meeting that Hartstonge would always remember with great pleasure: 'Here was this fair-haired, young man with his vast repertoire ... He was naturally adventurous, unassuming, friendly, and a good PR man; he brought a new dimension to the orchestra in the form of a spirit of adventure. The BBC had a habit of sending him music, and saying, "John, please play it", and he did. It was one of the great things he did for this orchestra: extending the repertoire; and a great deal of modern music.'[47]

A 'golden era' for music in New Zealand

Arriving some months before the beginning of the new season, John Hopkins had an unprecedented advantage over all previous resident conductors – the opportunity to see and hear his new orchestra rehearse and perform two end-of-year choral concerts, and also, to briefly meet his predecessor, and to compare notes in passing.

'It's not like England', John Hopkins remembers James Robertson saying. 'You really are the one they all look to, here, whether it be the brass band world, the choirs, massed choirs, or the opera company'.[48] This was so, as Hopkins would very soon discover when he in turn became the 'Mr Music' of New Zealand.

Aged twenty-nine, John Hopkins was the youngest principal conductor of the National Orchestra: twenty-four years younger than Andersen Tyrer, eighteen years younger than Warwick Braithwaite, and respectively eleven and twelve years younger than Michael Bowles and James Robertson. 'Charisma' was a word not generally used in the 1950s, but it applied to John Hopkins, and coupled with his enthusiasm it proved a powerful tool. When he shared his vision for music in New Zealand, musicians, administrators, and audiences were swept along with him – together with some of the orchestra's most entrenched critics. He became known to the public in general, and arguably generated more publicity and goodwill for the orchestra than any other of its previous conductors.

John Hopkins soon became aware of the vulnerability of the National Orchestra. 'It had brought everyone together in one place and, like a skyscraper in a desert, drained other areas. New Zealand had no conservatory, and there was no university training programme for orchestral players ... James Robertson told me that the players, were, "always marvellous and would play if they possibly could", but in those days you literally had seventy players who were utterly essential, and if one was unwell, there was no-one to replace them.'[49]

The same problem had confronted all previous principal conductors of the National Orchestra since 1947 when, following its first season, Andersen Tyrer had travelled to London to recruit more players. Young New Zealand musicians were starting to return home after studies in that city made possible by New Zealand Government bursaries, but more were needed, and the recruitment of players for certain instruments would remain an ongoing problem, for decades.

More players, better training, and higher standards were essential, Hopkins realised. At one of his first meetings with the Broadcasting Orchestral Consultative Committee, he referred to the 'grave shortage of players good enough to fill the Orchestra's vacancies' and made three far-reaching recommendations: 'to establish a conservatorium, a youth orchestra, and the institution of cadet players'.[50]

The new conductor, John Hopkins, attends a rehearsal of the National Orchestra under the baton of his predecessor, James Robertson, in St Pauls Schoolroom, 1957. *Spencer Digby*

3 Into Orbit

1958–1959

'A new musical satellite was put into orbit last night ... an astonishingly successful debut ... by the National Youth Orchestra'

– *Owen Jensen,* Evening Post, *1959*

Some two months after his arrival in New Zealand John Hopkins marked his first visit to the South Island with what seemed a remarkable claim: 'New Zealand may have its first national youth orchestra by the end of this year ... I have had informal discussions on the subject ... with the Director of Broadcasting, and he is very interested in the idea ... It would not mean that New Zealand would have two orchestras ... the youth orchestra would be a training ground for future members of the National Orchestra.'[1]

Two months later in Auckland, elaborating on his earlier remarks, Hopkins explained that the orchestra would be, 'based on similar lines to the enormously successful British orchestra ... and [would] bring the best young players of the country together for instruction and ... ensemble playing, as one of the surest ways of having adequate replacements available for the National Orchestra'.[2]

Hopkins' views were always widely reported, but those concerning a youth orchestra were possibly misunderstood initially. 'It is still only an idea, but I definitely intend to pursue it', he reiterated.[3]

It was a new concept to the New Zealand public, and while the response from musical circles was enthusiastic, others were wary, perhaps suspecting another frivolous use of taxpayers' money so soon after the National Orchestra was itself established.

There had been many complaints about that in 1946, so soon after World War Two. Ten years after its establishment, the newly arrived James Robertson had been greatly shocked to read letters in local newspapers which criticised his appointment and demanded that he be 'sent back'.[4]

The announcement of the formation of a national youth orchestra prompted a strongly critical letter to the *Otago Daily Times*:

> Sir, It is well known that widows, with their pension of £4.17.6d a week, have a tough time … therefore I was disgusted to read in your newspaper that a youth orchestra is training in Wellington. It seems to me an outrageous waste of public money … bearing in mind that the National Orchestra is costing the tax-payer £80,000 a year in operating loss, it would be interesting if the Broadcasting Service would tell me just how much this dream costs … If Mr Nash is so interested in the welfare of older folk, why does he not disband the National Orchestra and put the resultant money saved into increasing the widow's pension …?[5]

The *Otago Daily Times*' editor had taken the precaution of 'submitting' this letter to the NZBS in Wellington first, and then published both the complaint and response together. It was a letter 'based on inaccurate understanding of the financing of both orchestras', the NZBS responded. 'The National Orchestra does not cost the tax-payer a penny, let alone £80,000 a year. It is financed by the Broadcasting Service out of regular broadcasting revenue. Members of the youth orchestra were not paid for their playing, and they paid for their own accommodation in Wellington. The cost of their travel was met wholly without calling on the taxpayer'.[6]

This answer may have reassured others with similar doubts, and certainly John Hopkins was a very passionate and persuasive advocate on behalf of a national youth orchestra. As James Robertson predicted, Hopkins quickly made his mark on the local music scene. Indeed within a matter of days he recalls, 'meeting people from all these different areas, all coming up and wanting to do things. I felt that this was right – that one should at least involve oneself, and help as far as one could'.[7] It was a policy that saw Hopkins's musical influence in New Zealand reach far beyond symphonic repertoire, to embrace opera, ballet, choral, brass bands and contemporary music.

The lack of a suitable training programme was brought home to John Hopkins on this first visit to the South Island. 'In Christchurch a father brought his young daughter, Angela Connal (now Lindsay) to play for me, and ask my advice; and then in Timaru, I heard another young girl, Coralie Leyland, who had played in amateur orchestras, but had no idea of what it was like to play in a symphony orchestra. She auditioned for the National Orchestra, but I could see it was useless, she would be lost.'[8]

Angela Lindsay remembers her father taking her to play for John Hopkins, 'and to ask his advice as what to do for the best as regards a career in music. There wasn't a great deal happening at that time, to make one feel confident that it would be a sustainable career in New Zealand. Our school orchestra was just a motley collection of instruments, and we wouldn't have any brass for instance in a girls school in those days. Lesley Anderson, my French teacher, was an original violinist in the National Orchestra, and she took the small group of instruments that there were, and tried to coach us.'[9] As Hopkins said, there was no national conservatorium, no advanced training nor any course available for these two talented young New Zealand violinists. Later, both would become members of the National Orchestra – Coralie Leyland briefly, before going overseas,[10] and Angela Lindsay for sixteen years, following three years as an inaugural orchestra trainee, from 1961 to 1963.

The idea of a national youth orchestra may have seemed radical to New Zealanders in 1958, but the precedent had been set in 1945, when Irwin Walters founded the Welsh Youth Orchestra, the first in the world. The National Youth Orchestra of Great Britain assembled for the first time soon afterwards (in Bath in 1947) under its 25-year-old founder, Dr Ruth Railton (later Dame Ruth King). Ten years later, the Sydney Youth Orchestra gave its first performances, with both the Melbourne, and the Australian Youth Orchestras established the following year, 1958. The national youth orchestras of all three countries – Great Britain, Australia, and New Zealand – have not only survived but thrived, the NZSO National Youth Orchestra being the last of the three to celebrate its 50th anniversary.

The first youth orchestra in New Zealand was the Auckland Junior Symphony Orchestra, founded by Gordon Cole, in 1948. Charles Nalden took over its conductorship in 1950, and held the position very successfully, until the early 1970s.[11] Two other youth orchestras would appear on the scene in 1959: the thirty to forty member Napier Junior Orchestra (formed at the Secondary Schools Festival of Music on 2 May) became the second after Auckland, and Peter Zwartz's Wellington Youth Orchestra closely followed the National Youth Orchestra, and gave its first performance, with sixty members, on 12 July 1961.

John Hopkins's youth orchestra initiative was underway in a matter of months, it having proved remarkably easy for him to persuade the Broadcasting hierarchy that this was a worthwhile undertaking. 'Mr Yates, the Director General, and Mr John Schroder his deputy were both marvellous', Hopkins remembers. 'They supported me enormously, every idea I came up with; in fact I cannot think of anything [for which] they did not give me their whole hearted support.'[12]

Walter Harris, music advisor for the Department of Education, and representative for schools concerts performed by the National Orchestra, was one of the first to whom John Hopkins mentioned his idea of forming a national youth orchestra, in early 1958. According to John Thomson, Harris had 'inveigled James Robertson into conducting one hundred young players at a musical seminar ... [with] high hopes that this would be the precursor of a "national" youth orchestra',[13] and as might be expected, he became 'an enormous partner in this', John Hopkins remembers. 'He was very keen, on this idea of bringing together all the finest young people.'

Broadcasting's approval having been given by Yates and Schroder, the NZBC's director and deputy director, Hopkins and Harris then went together to discuss the matter with Arthur Harper, director of Internal Affairs. Harper too was receptive to this idea, and encouraged by his offer of support, Harris prepared a formal proposal for Dr Clarence Beeby the influential director of Education, on 23 May 1958, advising that this orchestra should be, 'a permanent part of the cultural life of the country...'[14]

As a result, at Broadcasting's suggestion, an executive committee was formed, comprising John Hopkins, Walter Harris, William Yates, and John Schroder, and extended to include Dr Beeby and Arthur Harper. This committee met several times between July and October, and responsibilities were allocated: publicity would be shared between the two departments, selection would be the responsibility of the NZBS, and Education would cover the assembling of the orchestra. Bernard Beeby along with Arthur Harper not only agreed to starting the orchestra in the 1959 May holidays, but to providing a grant of £770 for that first session. That sum, they decided, would appear in the 'estimates of the Education Department, which would also arrange clerical assistance, hall bookings, accommodation and travel'. Broadcasting would provide 'the conductor, tutors, music and day-to-day supervision'.[15]

On 7 October 1958 representatives of the three government departments gathered around the table. With evident good will they determined to hold two public concerts, and to establish a national youth orchestra of New Zealand that would 'not be a flash in the pan, but a permanent addition to the country's cultural life'. Walter Harris summed up the committee's aims as being:

1 to provide opportunity for the most talented players in the country to play together in an orchestra.

2 to give an incentive to young people to acquire greater skills with orchestral instruments.

3 to discover young players of outstanding talent who might be encouraged to make themselves proficient enough to become members of the National Orchestra.[16]

> We are concerned that it should not be just a flash in the pan. We should like it established in such a way that a National Youth Orchestra will continue as part of the cultural life of the country long after we cease to take an active part in it…'[17]

The original plan was for the orchestra to meet twice a year, in the May and August school holidays, and to perform one concert each session. It was further agreed that 'for political reasons' the orchestra would not appear in the budget of the National Orchestra, as it was 'still contentious to some tax-payers'. Instead, like that orchestra, the National Youth Orchestra would also receive direct funding from 'Broadcasting'.[18]

There was some difference of opinion about age. John Hopkins favoured 'up to 25 years' but John Schroder's shrewd suggestion that 'under 21 would have much greater appeal' carried the day with the age set from twelve years to twenty years inclusive. The cost was estimated at £800 per week, to include £7 per player, together with payments to the deputy conductors and tutors, the cost of music, travel and transport. Players could choose their own accommodation in Wellington, or for £6 it would be provided for them in hostels, or billets would be found. A suggestion from concert manager James Hartstonge[19] that, 'public concerts to a paying audience would be a spur and a reward to players … and would help offset costs' was fully endorsed by the committee.[20]

There was no dissent from the music community this time, and the proposal was greeted with unanimous enthusiasm. On 14 October 1958, a deputation to the Ministers of Broadcasting and Education was led by Ormond Wilson, New Zealand Federation of Chamber Music Societies, with Hugh Temple White, Registered Music Teachers Registration Board, a representative of the Post Primary Teachers Association, also Dr Beeby, John Hopkins, John Schroder, and Hartstonge, 'to request a sum of £1600 be provided, for the annual estimates to establish a National Youth Orchestra'.[21]

Cabinet approval was initially received for one public concert per session, but later considered that it was 'too risky to assume that this could be achieved in one week', and amended approval to 'May holidays for rehearsals and … September for further rehearsals and two public concerts'. All costs were again divided amicably between Broadcasting and the Education Department.[22]

Auditions

Before presenting its submission to Cabinet on 15 December 1958, the NZBS prepared an audition sheet and plan, for the use of audition committees throughout New Zealand. An application form was also prepared, with dates arranged for the next rehearsal sessions. Concerts were proposed for both Lower Hutt and Wellington, and in recognition of Dr Charles Nalden's 'great deal of experience with the Auckland Junior Symphony Orchestra', he was invited to attend as deputy conductor.

Applications duly arrived from an astonishing 255 young musicians. All were invited to attend auditions at their nearest radio station, where they were handed sight-reading selections of music, prepared especially by John Hopkins and Ashley Heenan (then a member of the NZBS's programme staff).[23] Once recorded, all audition tapes were returned to Wellington, where another programme staff member, Peter Averi,[24] became an inaugural member of the National Youth Orchestra's audition panel.

It was the start of an association with the National Youth Orchestra which lasted almost thirty years for Averi. 'I clearly remember that Geoffrey Newson[25] and I were the only ones on that panel. We listened to tapes recorded by applicants in their local radio stations, and the final assessments were made by the selection panel – Ashley Heenan and William Walden-Mills (the Education Department's advisor on school music) – or referred on to John Hopkins, who settled any doubtful cases.'[26]

Seventy-eight young players and a leader were invited to join the orchestra, but as one rehearsal overlapped the Auckland University term, two students were not able to accept and were replaced. A third student, David Smale (French horn NYO, 1959–60), says, 'I pressed my Professor of Geology for a "personal rather than professional opinion", and he said "It might be better to develop the individual rather than the specialist", and so I attended NYO, thank goodness!'

'I was horrifyingly casual', David recalls. 'I combined the rehearsal week with train tours, and little practice. As I had paid for a month on rail, I spent some nights on the train from Wellington to Taihape and Ohakune, to save on accommodation. I overslept once and had to go on to Taumarunui, and so I was late getting to rehearsal! I remember Weir House fondly, YMCA in Willis Street less so, as we had four to a room instead of two.'[27]

Since the first mention of a national youth orchestra was made by John Hopkins, its debut was warmly anticipated and welcomed by the New Zealand Press, often in quite stirring tones. In Wellington, a long leader in the *Dominion*, under the banner 'Concord of Sweet Sounds Swells in New Zealand', praised the orchestra as 'another important step in the advance of music ... [that] will strengthen the foundations of musical performance and taste ... [and] provide wider opportunities for training and public playing among gifted young people ... a person of real cultural leanings will be interested in the march of music in New Zealand, not only in itself, but as a link with the great world'.[28]

John Hopkins was 'not one to let grass grow under his feet', the *Christchurch Star* observed in its similarly long leader. He had, 'launched his intention for a national youth orchestra in Christchurch, and now little more than a year later, it has been formed … 255 applicants for seventy-eight places [is] an encouraging indication of the active interest in good music taken by many of New Zealand's youth … more enlightened teaching of music in New Zealand schools has resulted in a musical renaissance in the Dominion …

'If it receives the permanent blessing of the Government it will become a training ground for future members of the National Orchestra, and in the words of the sponsor, not only improve the playing of young players, but will, "widen their musical horizons…" Although the concept of a junior orchestra is not new, the enthusiasm of Mr Hopkins has led to what may ultimately prove to be a new era in the history of music in New Zealand'.[29]

First performances

The glow of the National Youth Orchestra's first rehearsals had not diminished when four months later the orchestra reassembled, this time at the Waring Taylor Street studios, scene of the National Orchestra's historic first rehearsal in 1946.

Some players had, as suggested at the first gathering, met to practice together during the term. No longer a gathering of strangers, section members greeted one another and the now-familiar faces in other sections around the room. Only a few 'reserves' had been hastily brought in for this September session, as replacements for the few unable to attend this time.

Brent Southgate was one of these replacements. A fourteen-year-old Dunedin boy, he was one of the youngest players, and says that his seat was 'appropriately humble, at the back desk of the second violins. Most of the other members seemed impressively mature, and I remember feeling uncomfortable at being the only one wearing short pants. I did have a pair of longs in my luggage, but had been instructed to "keep them clean" for the concerts.'

Brent's music having failed to arrive in Dunedin before he left home, he had to go and collect it from the Broadcasting studios on his arrival in Wellington before he could start practicing. 'It all meant a good deal of extra pressure, but people were friendly, and I soon found myself swept up in the joy of collective music-making. The experience gave me a better understanding of the hard work and attention to detail required for any worthwhile achievement, and forced me to do some rapid growing up.'[30]

Final rehearsals began on Saturday 5 September. They continued through the week on the same four works rehearsed during the May sessions, but with the addition of a violin concerto and piano concerto to be performed by the two international soloists.

Once again the press attended a rehearsal. 'The atmosphere was light-hearted and friendly as National Orchestra conductor John Hopkins led his players through the rich melody of the Beethoven (Symphony no 1). The youngsters obeyed his instructions with sensitive skills.'[31]

Michael McIntyre vividly remembers John Hopkins' 'firm but gentle way with the orchestra. "Coom on", he'd cajole in what I took to be a Yorkshire accent, "YOOO can doo better than the woons who didn't get in!"' He also remembers Vincent Aspey: 'During section coaching sessions the deep musicality that permeated his demonstrations took us close to the heart of the music in a way I'll never forget.'[32]

Lower Hutt Town Hall, Thursday 10 September, 1959. Conductor: John Hopkins. Handel – *Occasional* Overture; Delius – *The Walk to the Paradise Garden*; Beethoven – Symphony no 1 in C major, op 21; Mendelssohn (soloist Igor Ozim) – Violin Concerto in E minor; Glinka – Polonaise (from *Life for the Czar*)

'There was a good deal to be considered in the choice of works chosen for the inaugural concerts', John Hopkins wrote in the small brochure advertising the National Youth Orchestra's inaugural concerts. In his article Hopkins discussed the repertoire to be played, and why particular works were chosen, information that was repeated in the two printed programmes issued for each historical performance, which had identical repertoire, apart from the two concertos.

'The Handel Overture was chosen not only because this year is a Handel tercentenary, but also because it will give the audience the opportunity of hearing the full orchestra at the beginning of the programme. Evocative music is represented by the Delius piece, while the Beethoven Symphony serves as a good introduction for the young players to the classical orchestral repertoire. In the Polonaise they all have a chance to demonstrate the brilliance of Glinka's orchestra. The composer makes technical demands on the full orchestra, particularly the strings, and all players will be able to show the high standard they have reached.'[33]

Special youth concert prices were offered for admission to the concerts: nine shillings; six shillings and sixpence; three shillings and sixpence, and schoolchildren's concessions: four shillings and sixpence; three shillings and sixpence.

Owen Jensen, the Wellington musician and music critic well-known for his acerbic reviews, wrote a report on the orchestra while it was still in the rehearsal stage. Although he had not yet heard it play at that time, Jensen urged his readers to attend its concerts. 'From all reports', he said, ' the work of the youth orchestra is so astonishingly good that there can be little doubt that it will grow into one of our most cherished musical organisations'.[34]

A week later, Jensen gave his verdict: 'A new musical satellite was put into orbit last night when the National Youth Orchestra gave its first concert at the Lower Hutt Town Hall. It was an astonishingly successful debut ... when some of the ... publicity talked about "professional polish" one could have been excused for regarding this as an extravagant fancy. Not a bit of it ... many professional ensembles would have been proud to acknowledge the National Youth Orchestra's superb aplomb ... It must have been clear to Mr Hopkins and all concerned with the project that New Zealand has a significant addition to its musical resources of which we can be well proud'.[35]

On the following night, Friday 11 September, the same programme was repeated in the Wellington Town Hall, but with the violin concerto replaced by Mozart's Piano Concerto in E flat major (K482), with soloist Ilse von Alpenheim.

'The National Youth Orchestra put the seal on its success with a second concert ... before a large and enthusiastic audience', wrote Jensen.[36] The

The National Youth Orchestra performs its second concert, its first in Wellington Town Hall, conducted by John Hopkins, 11 September 1959. *Archives New Zealand AAQT 6418/1, R1440*

Mozart concerto had offered 'the greatest challenge to the young players of the two programmes', he said. 'If they all discovered, as I am sure they must have, Mozart is not always as easy as sometimes seems, this programme would have been an invaluable lesson.'

A second hearing of the rest of the programme confirmed the 'fine impression' made at the orchestra's first concert, Jensen said, but with the impact of the first excitement of its first performance a little diminished, he thought it 'time to take stock'. In doing so, he drew attention to weakness in the wind and percussion, and warned: 'gratifying as these first performances were, and hopeful as we may be for more polished ones, the concerts are only the end to the more important aspects of the youth orchestra, the practice and rehearsals. For the work they have done in these last six days, the players deserve nothing but praise.'

RWB (Russel Bond), music critic for the *Dominion*, who also attended both concerts, had praise in plenty for the performance of the orchestra in Lower Hutt, which he said 'marked an important advance in New Zealand's musical development'. This was 'a thoroughly successful debut from the musical point of view, and that of the audience reaction', he said, although the audience itself was 'not as big as the occasion warranted'.[37]

It was Wellington's 'privilege' to hear the orchestra, the following night, RWB wrote after the second concert, 'and gratifying to record that its concert-goers, although not attending in full-force, had at least done so in sufficient numbers to testify adequately, to their faith in music-making in New Zealand'. They had given their testimony in 'unstinted applause for this fine band of players, and by inference showed their appreciation of the efforts of those responsible … John Hopkins, the Broadcasting Service, and the Education Department ...

'When Mr Hopkins expressed the hope last night that the orchestra would go on from strength to strength, he was certainly echoing the sentiments of all who heard it.'[38]

The first hurdle was over. The first performances had been successfully given, and suitably exhilarated players in the first National Youth Orchestra returned home.

For leader Vincent John Aspey, 'My best memory of the 1959 NYO was playing the solo in Handel's *Occasional* Overture and the Mendelssohn Violin Concerto with the violin soloist Igor Ozim and having some violin lessons with Ozim afterwards'.

For Juliana Adams (Radaich), it had seemed the 'most exciting thing ever, to walk out on that stage in Lower Hutt and look out on that audience. But the second night was even more exciting, to see even more people in the audience, and the beautiful ornate plaster-work in the Wellington Town Hall. I was wearing my white lace ballerina-length frock, and on the radio next day, Aunt Daisy[39] said, "the little girl playing the harp looked and sounded like an angel." And that was me.'[40]

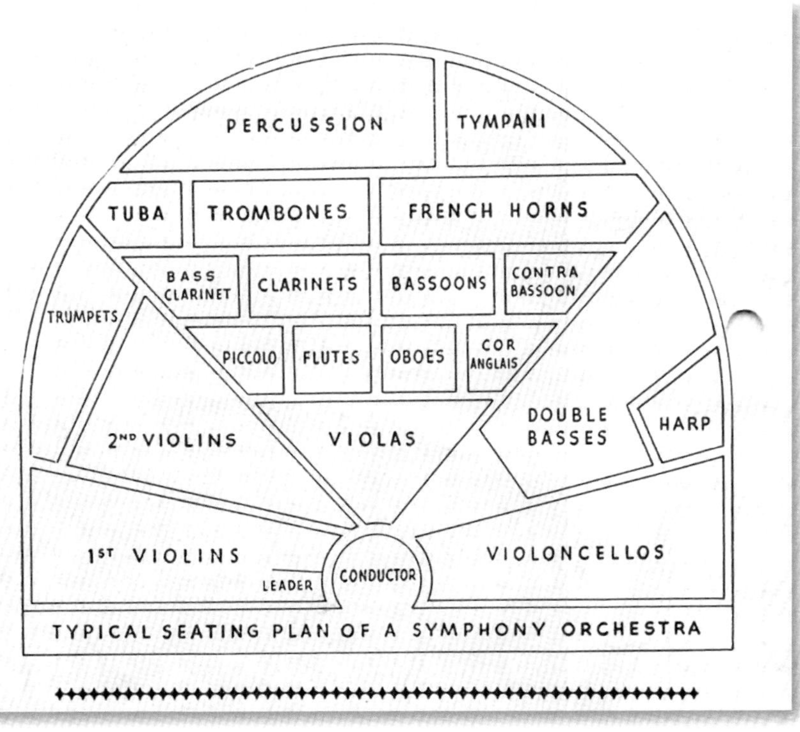

Seating plan from the National Youth Orchestra's first programme, 1959

4 'A Harvest Rich Beyond our Knowing'

1960–1974

National Youth Orchestra rehearsal, Lower Hutt Town Hall.
David Smale, 1960.

The National Youth Orchestra's first season had succeeded beyond expectation. Performance standards, audience numbers, and enthusiasm were high, and all reviews, excellent. Financially too the result was good. The budget had been set at £1600, but with fewer tutor fees to be paid in this session – and a higher return than estimated from the proceeds of the first two concerts – the net cost was only £966. John Schroder reduced his budget accordingly. He requested £1000 from the Broadcasting account, 'for the establishment of a National Youth Orchestra in 1960', and this was granted by Cabinet, the next day.[1]

There was much to celebrate – and a few lessons to be learned, mainly arising from inadequate communication between the two government departments. In a situation without precedent some problems could be expected, and these soon became apparent. One was the attitude to young people: the Education Department was more used to dealing with younger students and was inclined to refer to all the players as 'children' and to treat them as such.

Although Broadcasting was more experienced in transporting musicians, the administering committee had assigned the responsibility for travel arrangements to the Education Department. Travel warrants were issued too late for bookings to be made. As a result expensive airfares had to be provided at short notice for half the orchestra.

A tendency of the committee to make arbitrary decisions became evident on the first official rehearsal day when some members of the press were turned away by Education Department staff and the *New Zealand Listener*'s photographer was 'obstructed'. There appears to have been no prior discussion on this subject, or that of a dress code for girls for public concerts. Players were told to wear 'white blouses and black skirts' by Education – a directive hastily countermanded by Broadcasting, which advised 'pastel coloured evening frocks'. This and other inside stories were passed on by local youth orchestra players to the *Taranaki Herald* and *Hawke's Bay Herald Tribune*,[2] and reported rather gleefully, to the embarrassment of the orchestra's organisers.

The National Orchestra's concert manager, Maurice Glubb, elaborated on some of the problems in an internal report to NZBS Director John Schroder. 'The general approach of the Education Department nominees was that the National Youth Orchestra was an extension of school music, even though more than half the players were beyond secondary school age. We, on the other hand, were anxious that professional standards of instructions and rehearsal should be maintained to give the young players experience of actual playing conditions in a professional orchestra. The paternal attitude adopted by the Education Department representatives did not accord with this objective.'[3]

1960

A few glitches in the first year could be expected. Through the experience and success of 1959, systems became more efficient and audition requirements and procedures more streamlined. Applicants could now prepare a work of their own choice and only two of their three sight-reading passages were recorded by the audition panels at each radio station. All auditions for the same instruments were recorded on one tape with each individual applicant graded for suitability by the panel, which now also provided additional comments to assist the selection committee in Wellington. Nevertheless selection remained a lengthy undertaking, with Ashley Heenan and William Walden-Mills estimating that it took them over twenty-four hours to listen to all 200 applicants.

Michael McIntyre was selected as leader. 'As a shy myopic teenager I had no personal charisma whatever', he recalls. 'But I did play the violin quite well and I did care passionately, and indeed obsessively, about excellence in music-making. So I was well in tune with John Hopkins' ambitions in founding the orchestra. Once the rehearsals got going, I found a self-confidence that I'd never dreamt of beforehand. It might never have been unlocked had it not been for the NYO experience. Of course whether or not I did a good job as leader is for others to say.'[4]

National Youth Orchestra players arrive on New Zealand Railways buses outside the Dominion Museum, for rehearsals at Wellington Technical College. *David Smale, 1960.*

It soon became obvious to the committee that standards had risen, with several players from the previous year unable to retain their seats against increased competition. Where there was little difference between competitors, the audition committee reported that they 'tended to give the nod to younger players, aged 14–15, [who] they considered would receive more benefit from membership than 20-year-olds, [who would be] eligible for only one year'. John Hopkins was delighted by these results. 'It was obvious', he said, 'that here [lay] the field of potential players for the future'.[5]

The format for the 1960 season mirrored that of the previous year: a first concert at Lower Hutt Town Hall on a Thursday, with a second concert again in Wellington but, at John Hopkins' canny suggestion, not scheduled for Saturday but Sunday. It would be broadcast live to 'ensure nationwide publicity'.[6]

The drawback was that there was a long-standing booking for the Wellington Town Hall on the chosen day. It was the school holidays, and the Wellington Competition Society had scheduled a full programme of activities for young people competing in various categories of music, dance, speech, and other performing arts. The matter was amicably resolved with the cooperation of the Society, which quickly vacated the hall allowing the concert to take place.

Lower Hutt, Wellington, 1 and 4 September 1960. Conductor: John Hopkins. Glinka – Overture *Russlan and Ludmilla*; Schubert – Symphony no 8, *Unfinished*; Weber – Concertstück for piano and orchestra; Delius – *Over the Hills and Far Away*; Mahler – Adagietto, Symphony no 5; Bizet – *Carmen* Overture; Intermezzo, *Les Dragons d'Alcala*; *Danse Bohème*

Janetta McStay (one of a small group of professional pianists in New Zealand at that time) was the soloist for the 1960 season, and the first New Zealander to perform a concerto with the National Youth Orchestra.[7]

The attendance at Lower Hutt was 656, and in Wellington the orchestra had its biggest attendance yet, reportedly 'over 2,000 with hundreds turned away'.[8]

Dress rehearsal with audience, Wellington Town Hall. 1960.

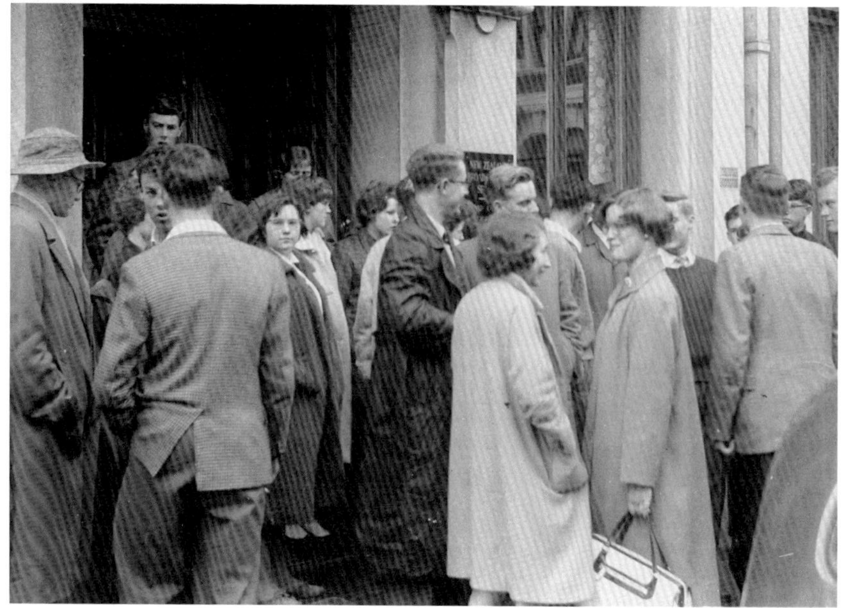

NZBS Waring Taylor St Studios. Among the players waiting for their bus is a young horn player (left) wearing a hat – the now-noted conductor and composer Sir William Southgate. *David Smale, 1960.*

Full house or not, the requirement at that time – and one strictly enforced – was that 'no profit' could be made on a Sunday. The NZBS was therefore left out of pocket to the tune of £250, while the Social Club for the Blind benefited from a very large, unexpected donation from the concert proceeds.

Afterwards John Schroder, now director of Broadcasting, was so pleased with the response from local newspapers that he took the unusual step of writing personal letters to thank them all for their support. To the *Evening Post* he wrote, 'I regarded it as a high compliment that Mr Jensen took the occasion, the programme and the performance so seriously as to mix some measured reproaches with his praise … and, in particular let me thank you for … devoting a leading article to the orchestra'.[9]

It was the first year for flutist Lois Belton (NYO 1960–67), who says her most striking memory, 'was on the very first day in 1960 when John Hopkins said "We will begin with the *Russlan and Ludmilla* overture." I recognised the score immediately: it was the one we had as the sight-reading part of the audition. Terribly easy: D major, simple values, nothing faster than passages of sedate quavers, but … it just went like the wind! *Alla breve* and fast!!! No-one had ever told me about double-tonguing. I was then at the beginning of my fourth year of flute-playing and had [had] a lot of trouble getting started at all, because my mouth was definitely not the right shape; and, with the benefit of hind-sight, I would say my Saturday morning flute teachers didn't really know

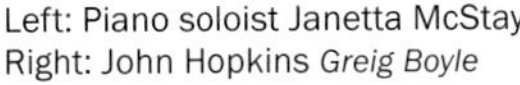

Left: Piano soloist Janetta McStay
Right: John Hopkins *Greig Boyle*

much about teaching. Right through the second term it was a race against time to get those quavers out fast enough … and I only just managed.'[10]

Alex Cowdell (violin 1960–63) also remembers the Glinka overture: 'Never having played in any kind of orchestra before, the impact of the full orchestral sound around me as we launched into the brilliant and exciting music of the overture for the first time was a revelation to me. To be part of the incredible power and energy of this music literally changed my life. I realised that this was what I wanted to do.'[11]

1961

Lower Hutt, Wellington, 2 and 3 September. Conductor: John Hopkins.
Elgar – *Introduction and Allegro* for string quartet and string orchestra; Dvořák – Symphony no 8; Holst – *A Somerset Rhapsody*; Saint-Saëns – *Introduction and Rondo Capriccioso* for violin and orchestra (Vincent Aspey, violin); Borodin – 'Polovtsian Dances' from *Prince Igor*

'The youth orchestra has already its quality in rehearsals … It not only has the breadth and solidarity of tone that comes with numbers, but a surprising degree of buoyancy and liveliness. Above all it has exuberance, that admirable quality of young people playing for the love of playing, an exuberance which the conductor, John Hopkins, at once controls and exploits. Conducting an orchestra like this is rather like handling a team of partly schooled horses. Maintain control and the result is an exciting exhibition of driving. Lose control and anything can happen. But conductors like John Hopkins do not lose control…. to hear this orchestra play the '*Polovtsian Dances*'…is to know what Walter Scott meant by the "fiery vehemence of youth …" and to hear the cellos shape so bravely and broadly the opening phrase of the Dvorak G major symphony is to know that these players will not be like Tennyson's sober man, "whose youth was full of foolish noise".'[12]

This was bass player Gerald Newson's first of six years (NYO 1961–66). 'One's early years in music, and indeed life generally, are marked in such vivid colours, as often this is the period when major changes and directions are made and set. In my case this was the turning point and I became determined to be an orchestral bass player in a symphony orchestra. A great playing moment in the first year was the Elgar, *Introduction and Allegro* for strings, which I spent hours as a 17 year old practicing and then getting it right, only to realise in later life that I never, ever, played it again.'[13]

Gillian Witton (now Roberts, NYO violin 1960–62) also remembers thinking of the Elgar that, 'I have never heard anything so beautiful. It was a new work for me, as was the Borodin, a challenge which I enjoyed. It was very inspiring to play under John Hopkins. I was quite nervous as many players appeared to be more talented and self-assured than I was, but [looking back] I think I was not the only one who thought that.'[14]

The Orchestra Training Scheme

Writing in an internal memo, James Hartstonge, the National Orchestra's concert manager, revealed that he was 'becoming frustrated at constantly having to read audition reports that stated, "... with orchestral experience this player may develop into a suitable candidate"'.[15]

As Hartstonge pointed out, there were almost no opportunities to gain 'orchestral experience' in New Zealand, at that time. To try and redress this problem, an attempt was made to integrate 'cadet' musicians into the orchestra, to receive individual coaching and experience on-the-job training similar to that given to unqualified 'cadets' in Broadcasting and the Public Service. Vincent John Aspey became an unofficial 'cadet' in the orchestra, in 1958, and a year later, Gail Jensen, a double bass player, joined as the first official 'orchestra cadet, in February 1959'.[16]

The scheme was considered suitable for string players, who could be 'passengers' and not upset the orchestra's 'real work', but it was deemed unsuitable for wind and brass players. After much debate the Musicians Union agreed reluctantly to a trial scheme but submitted a long list of restrictions. A cadet could not take part in rehearsals, studio recordings, tours, or public concerts with the National Orchestra, fill temporary vacancies in the orchestra, or augment it. Broadcasting had proposed up to ten cadets, but although Jensen completed her year as 'one lone cadet', the scheme did not succeed. According to Maurice Glubb,[17] cadets would need to 'possess almost superhuman qualities of enthusiasm and diligence to maintain a steady attack on the work required, without some definite incentive'.[18]

Fred Turnovsky, who had arrived in Wellington in 1940 as a refugee from Czechoslovakia, was president of both the New Zealand Opera Company and the New Zealand Federation of Chamber Music Societies, and a foundation member of the Arts Advisory Council. Turnovsky was interested in building up orchestra numbers to provide an opera orchestra. He suggested that 'student' membership of the National Orchestra be offered to gifted National Youth Orchestra players whose careers otherwise might end when they were obliged to seek a living. 'Students would not lower standards', Turnovsky said, 'they would add vitality of a young orchestra in a young country'.[19]

The Musicians Union and the NZBS, unable to proceed on their own, requested assistance from the Department of Internal Affairs. Secretary JV Meech declined, on the grounds that the department's funds were used to 'support students studying overseas, not in New Zealand'. The Music Bursary Committee considered the arrangement 'necessary and beneficial', but 'a matter for Broadcasting, not Internal Affairs'.

It was 'not the impression the NZBS had initially been given', John Schroder grumbled. A cadetship of one or two years would not necessarily end in an orchestral appointment. It was like a Government Bursary, intended to provide an 'educational and professional advantage to the National Orchestra', but not to be a guaranteed outcome of the time and skill devoted to the cadet. 'A token contribution was all that NZBS should be expected to make.'[20]

'I do appreciate your position as I am sure you do my own', Meech replied. It was obvious that this time Broadcasting would have to act alone.Three months later Schroder presented a submission to Ray Boord, then Minister of Broadcasting. In the absence of a conservatorium, the submission said, players had to be imported from overseas. This shortage also affected the opera and ballet companies. The proposal was to 'attack the problem' with ten 'apprentice players' who would work under similar conditions to those in the 'cadet scheme' – performing in local concerts with the orchestra, but not touring. The idea of a national conservatorium had not yet been abandoned and, as it was consistent with the scheme, 'each would serve the other'. The cost was estimated at £500 per apprentice – £5000 in total.

John Hopkins' comments added authority to the proposal. 'The gap between promising young players and the orchestra's requisite standard had widened', he wrote. 'Twenty-three players from the last National Youth Orchestra (1960) had expressed interest in an orchestral career but their potential could only be realised through extra experience … Proficiency as an orchestra player can only be achieved by daily work in an orchestra [and] built up gradually as the result of experience in ensemble and orchestral playing. One does not suddenly qualify as with an examination ... The stepping stone of experience that an apprentice scheme would offer will provide incentive for the young musician at the threshold of his musical career.'[21]

The Minister gave his approval in three days, but the Musicians Union continued to quibble over designations: 'apprentice' was contentious; 'bursar' inappropriate; but 'trainee' was acceptable. There was agreement on 'performances in Wellington and Lower Hutt only, and no touring'. Finally, on Sunday 11 September 1960, the latest addition to Broadcasting's orchestral empire was announced on the nine o'clock radio news as 'the National Orchestra Trainees'. They would come to be known variously as the 'Orchestra Training School', the 'Trainees', 'Schola Musicum', and finally 'Schola Musica'. Ashley Heenan was appointed officer-in-charge, and later, musical director.

Heenan's father, Sir Joseph Heenan CBE,[22] played a pivotal role in the Centennial Music Festival of 1940, and was instrumental in the establishment of the National Orchestra in 1946, and government arts bursaries in 1948. He once generously told government bursars in London to please see him if they needed assistance. 'No New Zealand government would ever like to think that any of you came home with aspirations unfulfilled for lack of money.' His own son was a musician, and yet, despite all this, in a letter to the Prime Minister and his Minister, Heenan senior expressed an apparently poor view of musicians, which he considered, 'a quarrelsome, intolerant section of the community, split into a number of mutually antagonistic cliques'.[23]

At his father's suggestion Ashley Heenan entered the public service straight from school, aged seventeen, to ensure that if 'called-up' for military service overseas, that would count as 'service'. As a broadcasting cadet, he was placed in the NZBS music library, where he built up his knowledge of music in combination with his music studies at Victoria University, 1944–47. Heenan was granted leave to study at the Royal College of Music in London for two years, 1948–49.[24] He returned to the NZBS in 1951, this time in the music section, assisting successive resident conductors Warwick Braithwaite, James Robertson and John Hopkins with programme planning for the

The first orchestra trainees, 1961 (l–r): Angela Connal, Jane Freed, Wendy Pitt, Helen Gold, Sheila Riches, Gloria Findlay, Sonia Smyth, Lars Johnasen. *Spencer Digby. Reproduced from Tonks,* New Zealand Symphony Orchestra, *p. 125*

THE GLAMOROUS YOUTH ORCHESTRA

Six attractive members of the National Youth Orchestra enjoying some Wellington sunshine during the morning tea break of the orchestra's rehearsals today. Members of the orchestra have come from all over New Zealand to take part in the first of this year's rehearsal sessions. For six hours a day, under the baton of John Hopkins, the young musicians practise in the recreation hall of the Wellington College. The girls are (from left), back: Misses K. Evans (Christchurch), R. Harris (Auckland). Front: Misses J. Collins (Auckland), S. Smyth (Wellington), A. McKenzie (Wellington), J. Freed (Wellington).

'The Glamorous Youth Orchestra'. Caption reads: 'Six attractive members of the National Youth Orchestra enjoying some Wellington sunshine during the morning tea break of the orchestra's rehearsals today. Members of the orchestra have come from all over New Zealand to take part in the first of this year's rehearsal sessions. For six hours a day, under the baton of John Hopkins, the young musicians practise in the recreation hall of the Wellington College. The girls are (from left), back: Misses K. Evans (Christchurch), R. Harris (Auckland). Front: Misses J. Collins (Auckland), S. Smyth (Wellington), A. McKenzie (Wellington), J. Freed (Wellington).'

National Orchestra. Heenan resumed his music studies, and graduated BMus from Victoria University in 1956. From 1959 he was increasingly involved in auditioning candidates for the new National Youth Orchestra.

New Zealand's first full-time orchestra trainees began work on 6 February 1961. All were members of the National Youth Orchestra: Angela Connal, Jane Freed, Wendy Pitt and Helen Edwards (violins), Sheila Riches (viola), Lars Johansen (cello), Sonia Smyth (bass), Gloria Findlay (clarinet) and Noeline Kloogh (bassoon).

'Nine aspiring, hopeful, but inexperienced young musicians assembled; complete with instruments, youthful idealism and ambition', as Heenan would describe them later. As NZBS employees, they were now bound by Public Service regulations, which, as Heenan noted, stated, '37 hours 35 minutes a week' and dutifully for the next eleven months the trainee day commenced at 8.30 am.'[25]

The scheme had been set up specifically to train young musicians for a career in the National Orchestra. It was always intended that trainees would participate in rehearsals with the orchestra; but the scheme evolved in a different direction. The first rehearsals were held in the cavernous old Winter Show Buildings in Newtown,[26] and then in various locations around Wellington, including church halls and an empty cottage waiting to be demolished in Sydney Street.

Trainees worked a six-hour day in the studio and also received individual lessons from tutors (generally principals) from the National Orchestra. Over the years the relationship with the professional orchestra evolved, with trainees sometimes called in to perform when extra players were required. The trainee group gave performances in schools and in public. They toured, and were recorded (commercially and in the studio), becoming known as 'Schola Musicum', a performing ensemble in their own right.

A year after he was given responsibility for the trainees, Ashley Heenan travelled to Europe and the United States to take up a UNESCO fellowship in composition (1962–63). In his absence, trainees completed their year in the National Orchestra, playing in recordings, studio broadcasts, public concerts, and for the NZBC Concert Orchestra.[27]

In 1963 the new Broadcasting House opened in Bowen Street and Broadcasting staff, housed in various buildings around Wellington, moved in. Some months later, the NZBC Symphony Orchestra, concert section staff, and the orchestra trainees converged on now-vacant Broadcasting studios and offices at 38 The Terrace. This building, originally a Masonic lodge, had a large studio at ground level for the orchestra, staff offices on a mezzanine floor, and a former Masonic temple on the second floor that became a rather grand rehearsal and performance studio for orchestra trainees. It would be the orchestra's home for thirteen years, from 1964 to 1977.

On Ashley Heenan's return in 1963 it was decided to continue the trainee scheme on a limited basis, now in direct association with the National Orchestra, and no longer separate. From 1963 to 1965 only six trainees were accepted, four of whom were appointed to the National Orchestra. Heenan singled out violinist Robin Perks and Gary Brain, timpani and percussion,[28] for their 'infectious enthusiasm and dedication' which 'contributed immeasurably to the *esprit de corps* of the youth orchestra at that time'.[29] These two were the last individual trainees, and when they left, the scheme went into recess.[30]

1962

Broadcasting

Broadcasting by now was adept at using income received from its commercial radio stations to support its non-commercial operations – a juggling act which operated quite successfully for some decades. As a part of the 'Broadcasting family', the National Orchestra also benefited from a new addition: television, the experimentation for which began in New Zealand in 1959. In 1961 limited television broadcasting commenced, and a year later (on 1 April 1962) with the passing of another Act of Parliament, the New Zealand Broadcasting Service – radio, television, the National Orchestra and the *New Zealand Listener* – were removed from direct government control to become a public corporation, the New Zealand Broadcasting Corporation, or NZBC.

As the 1960s progressed, profits from television rose along with those of the *Listener*, whose sudden rise in popularity was attributed to its status as the only publication permitted to publish television programme details. These profits helped to offset the growing costs of Broadcasting's non-profit-making activities, which, along with the YC stations, now included the renamed NZBC Symphony Orchestra, the National Youth Orchestra, and the NZBC Orchestra Trainees.

There were more changes for the National Youth Orchestra in 1962 when the New Zealand Federation of Chamber Music Societies sponsored free master classes in violin, viola, cello and clarinet for National Youth Orchestra members. These were held before the May rehearsals. Then in August the orchestra travelled south to perform concerts in Christchurch on its first tour outside the Wellington region. This major departure was a result of 'constant complaints' from other centres, all clamouring for a turn to host this popular orchestra.

The *Christchurch Star* of 15 August 1962 welcomed players with an obviously proud headline: 'Youth Orchestra to Honour City with 2 Concerts'. The article noted: 'That Christchurch should be chosen for the orchestra's first performance outside Wellington suggests a confident opinion of the city's musical life'.

Christchurch, 30, 31 August. Conductor: John Hopkins. Lilburn – *Aotearoa* Overture; Fauré – Pavane in F Sharp minor; Franck – Symphony in D; Mozart – Piano Concerto no 16 in D; Tchaikovsky – *Nutcracker* Suite

The initial 1962 National Youth Orchestra concert was significant. Not only was it the first given outside Wellington, it was both the first South Island performance and the first performance of a New Zealand composition. *Aotearoa* Overture, by Douglas Lilburn, would be performed regularly by the orchestra from then on. Swiss pianist Bela Siki, then making his third of four visits to New Zealand to perform with the NZBC Symphony Orchestra,[31] was the National Youth Orchestra's first international soloist. Siki expressed generous praise for the orchestra, which he said, 'has reached a high standard. New Zealand can be proud of these young people.'[32]

'[A] tour de force full of ebullient good things', said the *Press* reviewer, CFB, and 'while it was thrilling to hear some 90 or so young New Zealanders playing in an orchestra there was no call to make any allowances musically on the score of age'.[33]

Bass trombonist Ron Adams (NYO 1962–63) found the first rehearsal under John Hopkins 'an electrifying experience. We opened with the third movement of the César Franck Symphony and although I had many bars rest before I had to play, this was my first time I had actually felt orchestral music in a physical way. After the dramatic opening by the strings, the searing melody from the full bank of cellos literally sent ripples down my spine.'[34]

During the final rehearsal of the *Nutcracker*, the brass played a memorable trick on their departing conductor, as Warwick Slinn relates: 'At the final rehearsal for the last concert Bill Southgate rewrote the parts for the horn section, so that when the horns entered after the harp introduction to the *Waltz of the Flowers*, they played "Now is the Hour", in perfect harmony'.[35] As Ron remembers, 'The "Now is the Hour" persisted until John Hopkins had to stop conducting – because he and the rest of the orchestra collapsed with laughter'. But Warwick Slinn is certain that, 'John Hopkins stopped conducting at the first chord, although the orchestra generally went on for several bars. I used to watch Hopkins a lot (a tuba player has time for that) and he was always quick to notice very small details, through the whole orchestra sound.'

'I can still see John Hopkins leaning back against the rostrum railing, baton across his chest, and grinning broadly from ear to ear', Ron says. 'It was a great moment to remember.' On that point, they both agree.

A master class by the Allegri String Quartet drew National Youth and National Orchestra players, Catholic Sisters, and local musicians, among them: front row (l–r) Marian Stronach, Helen Newman, Olga Nash, William Pleeth, cello and Eli Goran, violin (Allegri), John Hopkins, conductor, James Barton, violin and Patrick Ireland, viola (Allegri), Jane Freed, Wendy Pitt, Evelyn Kolloh. Middle row: Margaret Tibbles, Olywn Castle, and back row: John Bonifant, Kathy Evans, Joyce Collins, Robin Perks, Alexander Cowdell, Margaret Diprose, Christopher Salmon, Donald Best, Farquhar Wilkinson, Kenneth Hoy. Wellington, 1963.

1963

Wanganui and Wellington, 6 and 8 September: Conductor John Hopkins.
Wagner – *Rienzi* Overture; Rachmaninov – Piano Concerto no 2; Haydn – Symphony no 104 in D, *London*; Kodály – Suite *Háry János*

A steady rise in the National Youth Orchestra's playing standard over four years meant that it was no longer deemed necessary to hold two separate rehearsal periods each year. No rehearsals were held in Wellington in May 1963, although some preparatory work was done in regional rehearsals in the four main centres between May and August. The orchestra then reconvened to rehearse and perform as usual, on dates timed to fit in with the then mostly synchronised school and university holidays throughout the country.

Wanganui became the fourth venue in which the National Youth Orchestra performed, and the city showed its appreciation with a civic reception and luncheon to welcome the orchestral party. Afterwards, John Hopkins thanked the mayor, RP Andrews, and said that to his knowledge 'no other orchestra had had a civic reception in New Zealand although it was customary overseas'. The mayor in turn expressed his 'great pleasure to meet the players' and noted with some pride [that] 'there were four from Wanganui'.[36]

Viola player Linda Roberts (NYO 1964–67) from Wanganui attended the mayoral afternoon tea and remembers asking John Hopkins '"How can I become a member of such an amazing orchestra?" and he said, "Fiddles are two-a-penny. Learn the viola!"' Linda followed his advice. 'I unearthed a small viola from the depths of the Girls' College music store and began a wondrous musical journey, wholly influenced by John's acuity.'[37] For the sight reading at her audition Linda was given the opening of Brahms' D major symphony. 'In those days there was no prior knowledge of the excerpts … and I played the open C string, thus demonstrating a considerable lack of knowledge of the alto clef! Regardless of this major glitch, I was accepted as number 12, rank and file, for the 1964 season. What joy!'[38]

Many musicians who would become well-known faces in New Zealand music joined the orchestra this year, among them, Christchurch twin brothers John (violin) and Alan (cello) Chisholm, and also violinist Peter Walls (1963–66).[39] An exotic addition was Dam Xuan Linh, a nineteen-year-old Colombo Plan student from Vietnam who was living in New Zealand at that time. A second violinist, he became a very popular member of the orchestra and always featured prominently in articles and press photographs. Robin Perks, back from studying overseas, was once again leader, a position he would hold for the next three years.

In the Wanganui concert David Bollard, a twenty-year-old Auckland pianist, provided additional drama to his exciting performance of the Rachmaninov. According to the reviewer, Bollard 'showed great fortitude ... when he split his finger on a key at the start of the long number, but kept on playing ... when he had the opportunity David wiped the blood from the keys of the piano and from his finger. In spite of the discomfort and the handicap, David's playing was magnificent'.[40]

There was an interesting link to the composer Zoltán Kodály, whom Ashley Heenan had met in Jerusalem during his UNESCO fellowship. When he heard that the National Youth Orchestra would be playing his work in New Zealand, Kodály expressed his pleasure and asked Heenan to deliver his 'personal best wishes'.[41]

The performance of the Kodály suite was poignant for Keith Hunter whose brother Clive, a foundation trombone player (NYO 1959–63), featured on the cover of the LP recording of the orchestra's 1960 concert. The two brothers were to sit together for the first time as principal trumpet and principal trombone in August 1963. 'I was particularly looking forward to playing alongside Clive in Kodály's *Háry János*', Keith Hunter says, 'however he was involved in a car crash three days before the orchestra assembled and died in Auckland on the first day of the rehearsal period, Monday 26 August. I arrived [for] rehearsal several days late – a very sad time for me.'[42]

The Wanganui concert was the end of an era for many National Youth Orchestra members when they learned that they would play under Hopkins' respected baton for the last time. It seemed unthinkable that the towering force in New Zealand music would soon leave the National Orchestra, and the country, enticed away by the ABC's general manager Charles Moses and assistant general manager Charles Buttrose.[43] John Hopkins, an 'infectious enthusiast with unquenchable energy', according to Buttrose, was to become director of music at the Australian Broadcasting Commission in Sydney, with responsibilities for serious music on radio, television, and in concerts throughout Australia, and as administrator for six state symphony orchestras.

In his six years in New Zealand John Hopkins had invigorated the music scene in an extraordinary way, fulfilling all but one of the three major goals he had set himself on arrival: a national youth orchestra, an orchestra training scheme for young musicians, and a conservatorium.

Only the last eluded him, and that now seemed an increasingly unlikely possibility with plans to introduce schools of music into New Zealand universities. As part of his legacy, John Hopkins had installed an awareness of the importance of a high level of specialised training to meet ongoing demands for suitably qualified New Zealand musicians for the National Orchestra.

John Hopkins conducting, 1964

Hopkins returned to this topic in one of his last interviews, revealing his concern to the *Auckland Star*: 'New Zealand music [is at a] crucial stage of development … a national school of music must be considered urgently'.[44]

A tribute to John Hopkins in the *New Zealand Herald* said, 'there can be no real sense of loss when he leaves us the rich and enduring legacy of his talents', citing the disciplined enthusiasm and style he had imparted to the orchestra. 'His work for the festivals, for opera and ballet, and particularly the Youth Orchestra, has planted good musicianship over a wide and fertile field from which the harvest can be rich beyond our knowing'.[45]

1964

Hamilton, 28 August and Auckland. Conductor: John Hopkins. Tchaikovsky – Ballet Suite *Swan Lake*; Rachmaninov – *Rhapsody on a Theme of Paganini*; Brahms – Symphony no 2

Two significant new conducting appointments were made in New Zealand in 1964: Juan Matteucci,[46] an Italian-born conductor from Chile, became the National Orchestra's principal conductor, and the Hungarian László Heltay,[47] the orchestra's first associate conductor. It may have been expected that either of these men would inherit John Hopkins' role as conductor of the National Youth Orchestra. Instead, John Hopkins returned from Australia to conduct two further concerts with New Zealand's youth orchestra. Since taking up his position with the Australian Broadcasting Commission Hopkins had extended his role in youth music, conducting the Australian Youth Orchestra at the 1964 Adelaide Festival. Many had feared that his departure would see him lost to New Zealand music (in a pattern familiar in New Zealand–Australian relationships). However, his leaving was not the end, but the beginning of a different relationship between the NZBC and Hopkins, one built on a background of shared achievements over almost seven years, and a mutual respect which would continue and endure for decades to come.

The soloist in 1964 was pianist Maurice Till from Christchurch, one of New Zealand's best known and most celebrated concert pianists: soloist, recitalist, chamber musician, broadcaster, teacher and highly esteemed accompanist for a variety of international artists.[48]

Maurice Till, 1964
Brynly Keith Ltd

Stephen Guest was on a reserve list for the orchestra in 1964, and 'was offered a place – way at the back of the 2nd violins … I was in the fifth form and I think the only person in Dunedin that year to get a place. I was blasted into another world …

'It was very intense. I was billeted with Vincent Aspey, who within an hour of my arriving entertained me by giving me an hour-long lesson on the violin part of the Brahms … My experience in the orchestra made me grow up slightly faster … I discovered just how talented people could be. Some of the players were not only highly talented at music but talented in other ways. I became aware of an intensity of emotion – in the music and the musicians … At any rate I felt I learned something better about how people could be.'[49]

The Heenan Years

After weeks or perhaps months of conjecture, the new man at the helm of the National Youth Orchestra, the replacement for John Hopkins, was revealed as one who had been involved with the orchestra from its beginning. Ashley Heenan was named conductor in 1965. Heenan's close association with the youth orchestra was an advantage. He had been involved in assessing auditions, and served his apprenticeship under the direction of John Hopkins, and as the officer in charge of the orchestra trainees since 1961 he had a vast knowledge of youth music and musicians in New Zealand.

It would be difficult for anyone to attempt to fill John Hopkins's shoes. The two men had very different personalities and very different philosophies in dealing with young people – as would become obvious.Writing his first introduction to a National Youth Orchestra programme as its conductor (in 1965) Ashley Heenan gave credit to John Hopkins' vision, which he said went beyond his stated objects '"to give 90–100 players the opportunity of concentrated orchestra playing at a high level . The hope that through the Youth Orchestra we should find some potential players for the National Orchestra [and] that young instrumentalists would go back to play in groups in their districts with increased experience, a new sense of values and added incentive."

'His vision was wider than this, for he saw in the organization and presentation of the Youth Orchestra an assured future for orchestra musicians in New Zealand. The profession can survive only when there is a strong and flourishing community of young musicians on whom to draw in replenishing the ever-changing personnel of orchestras … Today not only the NZBC Symphony but also semi-professional orchestras in different parts of the country include in their own personnel young musicians introduced to orchestral playing through Youth Orchestra activities …

'This year the NYO takes the stage for the first time without John Hopkins. But the orchestra remains as a monument to his musical sojourn in this country. It is more than that. The orchestra is a musical legacy to the youth of New Zealand, a legacy ever dependent on the continued support of music lovers throughout the country.'[50]

1965

Wellington, 4 September. Conductor: Ashley Heenan. Beethoven – Overture *Coriolan* op 62; Mozart – Piano Concerto no 16 in D, k451; Stravinsky – *Scherzo à la Russe*; Tchaikovsky – Symphony no 5 in E minor

Ashley Heenan's first programme as conductor of the National Youth Orchestra was led by Robin Perks. Owen Jensen, writing in the *Evening Post*, said that it was 'some of the best playing from the youth orchestra [and] a personal triumph for this year's conductor'. Josephine Burry, a nineteen-year-old Auckland pianist and the youngest soloist to play with the National Youth Orchestra, was 'an outstanding young talent' and 'the Mozart Concerto was the best performance of 18th century music we have had from the National Youth Orchestra … for Ashley Heenan, who has been a sort of foster father to John Hopkins' baby, these concerts … must be a source of considerable personal pride. His players have rewarded him well.'

Ashley Heenan, 1965

Playwright and reviewer Bruce Mason wrote, 'The first thing to say about this concert as a whole was the astonishing sense of ensemble in the playing, yet the orchestra has been a body for only a week of intensive rehearsal. Ashley Heenan's beat was clear and the musicians as apt to it as he could have wished; his interpretations were equally clear and utterly sound. The tone of the orchestra had a collective ring, very different from that of the NZBCSO, less rich, less authoritative, but often making statements of simplicity that the adult body does not achieve … [In the Mozart Concerto] Ashley Heenan remarkably

Josephine Burry, soloist, 1965

elicited some of the delicate interplay between piano and orchestra, he did not ever to my ear swamp the woodwind with a mass of fudgy strings … Tchaikovsky Five … the great old tunes came out splendidly articulated … of emotionally expressive violence there was little, but I must say that I like my Tchaikovsky as simple and direct as this … A fine concert, a moving experience, the best Youth Concert I have heard. Ashley Heenan spoke warmly of John Hopkins's child, born in 1959, and the child is growing up.'[51]

Neil Shepherd (violin NYO 1965–72)[52] travelled from the small rural town of Ruawai on the Northern Wairoa River to record his violin audition in Whangarei, and remembers feeling very embarrassed later. 'One of the sight-reading pieces was the slow movement from a Mozart piano concerto, and I played it three times the tempo it should have gone. My excuse is that you didn't have much opportunity to listen to Mozart in Ruawai in the 1960s; the 1YC programme signal didn't reach that far North then. My excitement at being accepted soon changed to trepidation on receiving the part for Tchaikovsky's 5th Symphony. It seemed rather too daunting a step up from Grade VII. However after the 14-hour journey to Wellington on the Limited Express I was soon swept away with the excitement and challenge of playing in a full symphony orchestra for the first time. I also discovered (since confirmed by professional violinists) that "faking it" is a very important orchestral technique.'

Linda Simmons remembers early morning rehearsals at Wellington College were 'bitterly cold … until our collective enthusiasm and body mass brought some heat into the place. Glynne Adams[53] was to have been our tutor, but at our first viola sectional rehearsal in walked a Michael Caine look-alike,with parted, tight wavy hair, and large horn-rimmed glasses.'

Although the resemblance was indeed striking, this was not the well-known British actor, but Vyvyan Yendoll,[54] principal viola of the NZSO, who, Linda says, 'became a dear mentor and friend'.

Yendoll, then in his middle twenties, says, 'I felt able to relate to my own experience of being in the British Youth Orchestra a mere decade previously … John Hopkins was so innovative as far as programming was concerned [and] we were introduced to many of the 'latest' contemporary works, by New Zealand and international composers … a thing which any orchestra should be endeavouring to do'.

Ashley Heenan rehearsing the National Youth Orchestra, Wellington Town Hall, 1966

1966

Royal Youth Concert, 4 September. Conductor: Juan Matteucci. Vaughan Williams – 'Spring' from *Folksongs of the Four Seasons*; Jenny McLeod – *Cambridge* Suite; Edwin Carr – *A Blake Cantata*; Bruch – Violin Concerto no 1 (Michael McClellan, violin); Ashley Heenan – *A Maori Suite* especially commissioned for the Royal Concert (Ashley Heenan, conductor, Donna Awatere and Laurette Gibb, sopranos); Glinka – Overture *Russlan and Ludmilla*

A special honour for some members of that 1965 group was being recalled six months later to play in a prestigious special royal youth concert in the presence of Her Majesty Queen Elizabeth The Queen Mother in Wellington Town Hall on 26 April 1966. The concert was presented by the Government of New Zealand and, in an introduction to this performance, Owen Jensen wrote: 'One of the NZBC's most spectacular contributions to youth music has been the National Youth Orchestra launched in 1959. In these few years it has become a focal point of incentive and experience for the country's more talented orchestral instrumentalists.'

Juan Matteucci, then principal conductor of the NZBC Symphony Orchestra, conducted the Royal Concert Orchestra, which combined young players from all major orchestras: the NZBC Symphony, Auckland Symphonia, Christchurch Symphony, Dunedin Civic and the 1965 National Youth Orchestra. Robin Perks was the leader, and the programme began with 'God Save the Queen'.

Viola player Hugh Townend (NYO 1964–67)[55] remembers this time well. 'We'd gathered in Wellington for rehearsals in the old Broadcasting House and I was staying in a boarding house somewhere off Molesworth Street. At 6.49pm on April 23rd the guy upstairs appeared to be jumping up and down vigorously and making the whole 2 storeyed wooden building shake. It was the Seddon earthquake, a magnitude 6.1 earthquake about 22 km deep in Cook Strait. I don't think Her Majesty was affected as I believe she was on the royal yacht, *Britannia*. However, fellow musicians still practising in the basement of Broadcasting House said that the walls rippled before the lights went out.'[56]

Many years later, as a GP in Rotorua, Hugh met Elsie Awatere and discovered she was Donna's mother. 'Her delight was obvious when I said that I'd been part of that 1966 concert and what a lovely voice Donna had.'[57]

A few months later, the National Youth Orchestra players met for their usual annual rehearsal week, again in Wanganui. Writing in a foreword to the printed programme, Ashley Heenan drew attention to 'the rapid rise in semi-professional orchestras in New Zealand in the past two years'. Prominent in the personnel lists of these three orchestras (Auckland Symphonia, Christchurch Symphony, and the Dunedin Civic) he noted, were the names of young players from not only the National Youth Orchestra, but also from similar orchestras in their regions. The National Youth Orchestra is 'no longer a singular example of national youth activity, but now the apex of a pyramid of youth orchestral activity throughout the country.' Heenan credited Dr Charles Nalden and the Auckland Junior Symphony Orchestra, the 'established existence of which in 1959 ensured the effective inauguration of the NYO … and [which is] a main contributor of key players'. He also mentioned the Wellington Youth Orchestra, the Christchurch School of Instrumental Music, the Manawatu Youth Orchestra, and the New Zealand Secondary Schools Orchestra (directed by WH Walden-Mills).

Wellington, Lower Hutt, Wanganui, 27–29 August. Conductor: Ashley Heenan. Niccolai – Overture *The Merry Wives of Windsor*; Lilburn – Suite for Orchestra; Sibelius – Symphony no 3; Tchaikovsky – *Variations on a Rococo Theme for cello and orchestra* (Ross Pople, cello); Stravinsky – 'The Shrove-Tide Fair', from *Petrouchka*

Soloist Ross Pople, 1966

The third concert of 1966 was significant on several counts. Cellist Ross Pople, an emerging artist at the start of a long and distinguished career, was the first National Youth Orchestra player to perform as soloist. His brother Edward (Ted) led the orchestra for the first time, the current leader Robin Perks having generously ceded his position to allow both brothers to take centre-stage for this special performance in their home town of Wanganui. All three were orchestra foundation members.

'The National Youth Orchestra goes from strength to strength', wrote Owen Jensen in his review in the *Evening Post* following the Wellington concert of this same programme. 'It was splendid playing in what was the most challenging programme any National Youth Orchestra has presented … It is a good orchestra and it could be and deserves to be better', said Jensen, making a plea for 'at least two weeks' rehearsal instead of a hard week's grind. Instead of one repeat concert … it should be given a short tour during which it would have the opportunity of stretching itself to the full.' It was time for a new look at the orchestra. 'It is too valuable a musical asset to be left to freewheel itself to success.'

At the end of that year, Linda Simmons says, 'Ashley Heenan suggested I come to Wellington every other weekend to play in the Wellington Youth Orchestra to gain more orchestral experience. He personally met my travel expenses, for which he will be gratefully remembered, and with increasing exposure to orchestral playing in all its many guises, it became very clear that this was the life for me.'[58]

1967

Hastings, Lower Hutt, Wellington, 30 August–2 September. Conductor: Ashley Heenan. Walton – Overture *Johannesburg Festival*; Debussy – *Prelude à l'Après-midi d'un faune* (Lois Belton, flute); Schumann – Symphony no 3 in E flat, op 97, *Rhenish*; Tchaikovsky – Piano Concerto no 3 in E flat (Christine Cumming, piano); Khachaturian – Ballet Suite *Gayaneh*

Paula Ryan, 1967 cover design competition winner

In 1967 a competition was instigated to encourage interest in the National Youth Orchestra. The NZBC Students' Art Contest was open to all 'bona fide students, aged between 15–20', who were called on to submit designs suitable for the cover of the orchestra's annual printed programme. The judges were graphic designer 'Mrs Kate Coolahan,[59] Mr Geoffrey Nees, industrial designer,[60] and Mr Raymond Boyce, theatrical designer for New Zealand Opera and Ballet'. All expressed themselves 'impressed with the high standard of entries, a high proportion of which were from post primary school students...[who] skilfully captured the spirit of both youth and music'.

The inaugural winner of this competition was an eighteen-year-old graphic designer working in the art department of the United Box Company, Paula Ryan, who was studying art with the International Correspondence School, and is now a fashion guru, designer and publisher. The competition ran annually for the next three years, and subsequent winners were Ralph Davies (1968), Jane Boyes (1969), and Ferila Leaso (1970).

Fiona Knight (clarinet NYO 1967–69) remembers the friendship and camaraderie of 1967. 'We were rehearsing at Wellington College, and Peter Wilton,[61] the principal oboe, was taking Lois Belton, the principal flute, for a ride on his scooter around the college grounds as we lazed about one lunch break. It was the days before compulsory helmets so it was youthful hi-jinks, but a lot of fun. Peter had the best oboe tone I've ever heard, all at the age of 16. ... Vincent Aspey was simply lovely, a pleasure to know and work with. He had been tutoring the first fiddles, and sat at the back desk playing away with us, with a look of sheer delight on his face. Years later ... he also remembered that with pleasure, and said that he, "loved joining in and feeling the exuberance of young players."'[62]

Christine Cumming, piano soloist, 1967 *John Tudhope*

1968

Hastings, Palmerston North, Wellington, 28–31 August. Conductor: Ashley Heenan. Beethoven – Overture *Leonora* no 3; Stravinsky – *Danses Concertantes*; Saint-Saëns – Piano Concerto no 4 in C minor, op 44 (David Galbraith, piano); Dvořák – Symphony no 6 in D

A guest editorial in the 1968 programme, written by Malcolm Rickard, NZBC controller of programme (sound), provided interesting statistics for this, the orchestra's tenth season: the total membership was 105 players, with 28 making their first appearance, and representation from Auckland (22) Wellington (28) Christchurch (26) and other places (29). 'The NZBC is proud to include its 16 orchestra trainees', Rickard noted. 'Thirteen players were now in their ninth consecutive year, and 20 per cent of NYO members from 1959 to 1963 had subsequently become professional members.'

Oboist Ronald Webb and timpanist Gary Brain, two of the first former youth orchestra players to become principals in the NZBCSO, were the first ex-players to return as tutors. Pianist David Galbraith was soloist, 'a brilliant interpreter'.[63] Galbraith performed with the National Orchestra/NZBCSO over nineteen years in a 23-year period, 1955–72. The orchestra appeared on television for probably the first time this year, as Fiona Knight recalls. 'We were being filmed and got rather tired. Ashley Heenan finally gave up on us and we were sent home to conclude the filming next day. They forgot to tell us to wear the same clothes, so when you watched the show it seemed that some of the orchestra had changed clothes between movements.'[64]

'It was in the prime time 8 pm slot, and I was seated in the second desk of the second fiddles', Neil Shepherd remembers. 'I was seen right in the middle of the television screen for much of the broadcast, thus finally achieving my 15 minutes of fame in my hometown.'

The National Youth Orchestra rehearses in the NZBC Symphony Orchestra studio at 38 The Terrace, before embarking on its first summer tour, 1969–70. *John O'Neill*

Peter Daly and Belinda Bunt,[65] violins, and Richard Prankerd, trombone, 25 August 1969
Evening Post *Collection, Alexander Turnbull Library, Wellington New Zealand. E/P/1969/3576*

1969

Wellington, 31 August. Conductor: Ashley Heenan. Rossini – Overture *The Italian Girl in Algiers*; Kleinsinger – *Tubby the Tuba* (Christie Hendy, tuba; Craig Pollock, narrator); Copland – Ballet Suite *Billy The Kid*; Tchaikovsky – Piano Concerto no 1 in B flat minor, op 23 (David James, piano); Gershwin – *An American in Paris*

Gisborne-born pianist David James was soloist. A student at Auckland University, he was already recognised as an outstanding young player, having given his first performances with the NZBCSO in the 1969 Proms. The National Youth Orchestra's 10th anniversary concert may have seemed low-key, but it served as the prelude to an event that would break spectacularly with tradition. The orchestra had travelled to several centres in its first decade, but never more than three a year, and always in spring during the August–September school holidays. This summer tour would be twice as long and cover a far greater distance. Players would travel over a thousand miles by bus and visit ten centres in fourteen days, performing two programmes in venues that ranged from Levin's Regent Theatre to Rotorua's Sound Shell Auditorium and the Auckland Town Hall. This would be the orchestra's biggest undertaking yet.

1970

NYO Summer Tour, 15–27 January (10 centres). Conductor: Ashley Heenan. Wanganui War Memorial Hall, 15 January (piano); New Plymouth Opera House, 17 January (violin); Te Puke High School, 22 January (piano); Napier Municipal Theatre, 27 January (violin). Rossini – Overture *The Italian Girl in Algiers*; Kabalevsky – Symphony no 2 in C minor; Tchaikovsky – Piano Concerto no 1 in B flat minor op 23 (David James, piano); Or/Mendelssohn – Violin Concerto in E minor, op 64 (Edward Pople, violin); Gershwin – *An American in Paris*

Family programme. Auckland, 19 January (piano); Tauranga QE2 Youth Centre, 21 January (violin); Whakatane War Memorial Hall, 23 January (violin); Rotorua Sound Shell Auditorium, 24 January (violin); Hastings Municipal Theatre, 26 January (piano); Levin Regent Theatre, 28 January (violin). Quilter – *A Children's Overture*; Kleinsinger – *Tubby the Tuba* (Christie Hendy, tuba; Craig Pollock, narrator); Tchaikovsky – Piano Concerto no 1 in B flat minor, op 23 (David James, piano); Or/Mendelssohn – Violin Concerto in E minor, op 64 (Edward Pople, violin); Gershwin – *An American in Paris*

Five months after the 1969 National Youth Orchestra, the same eighty or so players were reunited in Wellington for three days of rehearsals in the NZBC Symphony Orchestra's studio on The Terrace. On 15 January the entire tour party – players, conductor, orchestra manager Trevor Gane, and other assistants from the concert section – hit the road in a convoy of three New Zealand Railway buses and a truck carrying the heavier percussion instruments.

The first concert was in Wanganui, where players met their billeting hosts, rehearsed, had a meal, and performed – all in the same evening. It was a pattern that would continue for the next two weeks: travel, rehearse,

Backstage, Wanganui, during the 10th anniversary tour – the first summer tour *John O'Neill*

and perform. There were two programmes. One, specifically designed for younger audiences, featured Quilter's *Children's Overture* and the always-appealing *Tubby the Tuba,* with soloist Christie Hendy, and former singer and NZBC announcer Craig Pollock as narrator.[66]

The repertoire list for the tour contained seven items plus encores. Most of these works had been performed in the Wellington concert the previous year. The soloist for the Tchaikovsky Piano Concerto in 1969 and 1970 was again pianist David James. A second concerto soloist was Edward Pople, who played the Mendelssohn Violin Concerto in the family programme. A major work of the tour, performed in the 'other' programme, was the Second Symphony by Kabalevsky.

The tour made its way around the country, from Wanganui to New Plymouth, where the group received a whakatau – a Māori welcome – and then to Auckland, Tauranga, Te Puke, Whakatane, Rotorua, Hastings, Napier, Levin, and back to Wellington.

It was a demanding schedule. The eighty players, aged from twelve to twenty-six years, were expected to work and rehearse hard, but were also given time to let off steam, to swim, and to enjoy the summer. For Fiona Knight it was 'a fabulous experience to finish my time with NYO. It was the first tour, and a lot of fun being billeted around the country, not to mention the interesting concert venues. I remained friends with some of the billets for some years after the tour … Ashley's choice of music always ensured he extended the abilities of players – we had some hairy rehearsals and some difficult ones, but the end results and performances were magnificent, for youngsters at that time'.[67]

Backstage, Wanganui. National Youth Orchestra 10th anniversary tour. *John O'Neill*

Oamaru and Dunedin, 27 and 29 August.
Conductor: Ashley Heenan. Kabalevsky – Overture *Colas Breugnon*; Saint-Saëns – Cello Concerto in A minor (Ivan Andrews, cello); Stravinsky – Suite *The Firebird*; Beethoven – Symphony no 7

Soloists (l–r): David Galbraith, 1968; David James, 1969–70 (*Blyth Studios*); Christie Hendy, 1969–70 (*Tom Shanahan*); Craig Pollock, 1969–70

After touring the North Island so extensively in January, the National Youth Orchestra headed south for its traditional concert season in August. The orchestra was in its 11th year and, as Ashley Heenan pointed out in his annual programme note, musical activities in the community were now more numerous and sophisticated than they were in 1959.

'These together with some criticisms, have tended to obscure the real benefits of the National Youth Orchestra. I still believe that the achievement of performing at a high artistic standard a piece of established repertoire is more meaningful, stimulating and beneficial than an inadequate presentation of music technically and intellectually beyond the resources available … Encouragement is a great tonic to youthful aspirations. It arouses a sense of purpose and this in turn, generates the urge to seek and achieve higher standards … Our form of encouragement should be to give their musical requirements top priority.'

Twenty former youth orchestra players had now gone on to become members of the National Orchestra. Heenan himself had benefited from his work with youth in New Zealand. He had, in that year, conducted the Australian Training Orchestra, in Sydney, and in the following year, 1971, would join John Hopkins as a conductor at the Australian Youth Orchestra Summer Camp.

The first NYO manager

Various members of staff had travelled with the National Youth Orchestra on tour, but the position was not formalised until 1971, when Alwyn Palmer, NZBC radio manager in Tokoroa, was appointed assistant to George Perry, concert manager of the NZBC Symphony Orchestra. 'I was in the job for a week, when Peter Nisbet[68] asked me also to take over the National Youth Orchestra', Palmer recalls. 'It was never mentioned in the interview, or [as] part of the job specification, and in true New Zealand fashion then, it was run almost by the "seat of the pants."

'Touring often meant ten days. There was a small allowance paid for penal rates, but no compensation for time away. Only two management staff went on tour, me and Bev Malcolm, the assistant manager. Bev had been on many previous tours, as chaperone or "Camp Mum", and I was expected to do everything else: stage management, looking after artists, organising travel, the movement of instruments, and arranging accommodation. I had worked with choirs previously, but had had no experience with orchestras, and there was no one around to tell me what to do. Later, I had the sense to appeal to the players for stage assistance, and over the years a number of them helped with the physical work. I recall Nick Sandle (NYO, double bass 1969–74)[69] being stage manager on several occasions.'

Alwyn Palmer took up his appointment in July 1971, and one month later he went on his first National Youth Orchestra tour. It comprised three concerts, in Auckland, Tauranga and Hamilton, conducted by John Hopkins, but 'by then everything had been basically organised – all players selected, and all halls booked, etcetera. There was nothing to do', Palmer says. 'I just picked up touring and management as a going concern.'[70]

Images from 1970 (l–r): Ashley Heenan conducting; soloist Ivan Andrews; piano soloist Rosemary Mathers. *Georg Kohlap.*

1971

Auckland, Tauranga, Hamilton, 26, 27, 28 August. Conductor: John Hopkins. Lilburn – *Festival* Overture; Grieg – Two Elegiac Melodies for Strings; Rachmaninov – Piano Concerto no 2 in C minor, op. 92 (Rosemary Mathers, piano); Dvořák - Symphony no 7 in D minor, op. 70

In between his last visit from Australia and this one in 1971, John Hopkins had conducted the Australian Youth Orchestra at Expo '70, and at the World Festival of Youth in Japan, and had received an OBE for his services to music. His concertmaster was again John Chisholm[71] (NYO 1963–66, concertmaster

In rehearsal, 1972. Stephen Managh, leader 1972–73, and Edward Barry. *NZBC Television photograph*

Musical families. Brothers and sisters in the National Youth Orchestra (l–r): Mark and Antony Walton; Jane, Susan and Jeremy Thompson. 1972.

1967). Chisholm had become a member of the NZBCSO in 1970, and was seconded back to lead the youth orchestra in 1971. Rosemary Mathers from Matamata was soloist in the Rachmaninov. A pupil of Janetta McStay, she had performed as soloist with the Auckland Junior Symphony Orchestra, had given many recitals including for the Auckland Festival, and had toured as a member of a chamber music group.

This was Bruce McKinnon's last year in school. 'I was very excited to be selected. I packed my drums in my van and drove from Auckland down to Hamilton. I remember the buzz of that first rehearsal at the Teachers' Training College. It was fairly standard repertoire but of course it was my first time, and I recall playing the famous cymbal part in the 2nd Rachmaninov Piano Concerto and realising there was more to this orchestral percussion playing than I thought. All of us were staying in the residence halls, so there was a great social scene and a real sense of camaraderie amongst all the players.'[72]

Piano soloist Jacqueline Stone, 1972

1972

Wellington 27 August. Conductor: Ashley Heenan.
Walton – Overture *Portsmouth Point*; Bach – Brandenburg Concerto no 6 in B flat; Mozart – Piano Concerto no 23 in A (Jacqueline Stone, piano); Grainger – *A Lincolnshire Posy*; Beethoven – *Battle Symphony* (Wellington's Victory)

Pianist Jacqueline Stone from Wanganui was the soloist. On completing her studies at the Royal Academy of Music in London, she was appointed sub-professor, and performed as a solo and duo recitalist before returning to New Zealand in 1966.

Bruce McKinnon had by then moved to Wellington to study at Victoria University, where he became the first percussion student to graduate. 'Gary Brain was my teacher and one of the things we decided was that I would play timpani in the French manner with the large drum on the left, as opposed to the German system, in which it was on the right. Gary had studied in Berlin, and did play the German system.

'Youth orchestra audition time came around and I turned up at the Terrace Studio where Ashley Heenan was running the auditions. The timpani were set up German style, so I started to change them around. "Mr Brain plays them this way; you play them this way," said Ashley. I explained that it was my teacher Mr Brain who had recommended that I play them the *other* way round. I continued to change them around and played the audition. I thought I played reasonably well.

'At our next lesson Gary told me that Ashley said I was "a very arrogant young man."

'The music arrived. I had got into the orchestra but was only to play the triangle in Beethoven's *Battle Symphony* (for which 15 percussionists were required) so I would do almost nothing in the whole concert. The musical *Hair* came to town and I was playing percussion in the (fantastic) backing band. The last performance of the show clashed with the first rehearsal of the youth orchestra. I asked if I could be excused, as I was not doing much in the concert. "Definitely not!" was the reply. So I withdrew from the orchestra. Later I learned that the *Battle Symphony* had not been rehearsed at all during the first rehearsal. I did not apply for the NYO ever again.'[73]

1973

Christchurch, 25 August. Conductor: Ashley Heenan. Beethoven – Symphony no 8; Ravel – Piano Concerto in G (Michael Houstoun, piano); Tchaikovsky – *The Sleeping Beauty* (scenes from the ballet)

This was the National Youth Orchestra's first visit to Christchurch since 1961, and the orchestra included thirty young players from that city. Ashley Heenan's *Maori* Suite had been performed in the 1973 NZBCSO Proms. He was periodically conducting the Australian Training Orchestra and, from time to time, the NZBCSO in studio and schools programmes.

Pianist Michael Houstoun with the youth orchestra in 1973
Tom Shanahan

Soloist Michael Houstoun, then at the start of a distinguished career, joined the youth orchestra for the first of many performances together.[74]

'It was a strange experience', Michael remembers. 'I had been warned about Ashley Heenan's nasty personality, and didn't know what to expect. It turned out he was extremely nice to me, and horribly sarcastic and destructive to some individuals in the orchestra. I found it compromising and unpleasant, even though I loved playing the Ravel.'

1974

Piano soloist Margaret Lion, 1974

Invercargill, Dunedin, 29 & 31 August. Conductor: Ashley Heenan. Brahms – *Academic Festival* Overture; Beethoven – Piano Concerto no 4 (Margaret Lion, piano); Mahler – Symphony no 1, 'The Titan'

Newly returned from the Schola Musica's ground-breaking tour to Australia, Heenan conducted the National Youth Orchestra's first complete Mahler symphony.[75] The pianist for the Beethoven concerto was Margaret Lion from Dunedin, 'a pupil of Maurice Till, and a regular prize-winner at Dunedin, and other main centre competitions ... who also regularly performed as soloist and accompanist.'[76]

Concerts were still usually held in one place in the 1970s, Alwyn Palmer says. 'Later they tended to be two or three in different centres, held over a weekend, which meant having to adapt from small halls in smaller centres to bigger halls and practice rooms in main centres, where players were either billeted, stayed with family, or in hostels. Accommodation was a problem in some places, although many others welcomed us. The Logan Hall in Dunedin was particularly good, and we used Lincoln University halls of residence in Christchurch more than once.'[77]

Palmer made twenty-three tours with Ashley Heenan, from 1972 to 1994. 'I personally experienced no major difficulties with Ashley Heenan', Palmer says. 'All conductors have their moments, and he occasionally threw a bit of a wobbly, but towards me he was nothing but professional on tour. There was a perceived favouritism of the Trainees, and other players were adamant that there was a professional bias towards them; it was one of the things brought up from time to time. The Trainees were always in the front desks, and that rankled.'[78]

John Hopkins, portrait in 1971 programme, artist unknown.

5 The Grand Tour

1975

'Long Live National Youth!'
'I owe my complete development as an orchestral player to the opportunities presented to me at NYO courses.'

– *Grant Cooper, principal trumpet, NYO World Tour 1975*

To New Zealand artists comparatively isolated at the far edge of the world, a challenge to perform and prove themselves on other shores to other audiences can be irresistible. In the early 1970s, when such opportunities were almost unknown, there was considerable excitement when, one after the other, within twelve months, all three Broadcasting orchestras received invitations to perform internationally.

Schola Musicum tour, Australia, August 1974

The orchestra trainees, then thirteen years old and performing as the Schola Musicum, was the youngest of the three, and the first to test the water. The group had been a performing ensemble in its own right since 1970, giving Baroque concerts on Sunday afternoons. Now it had the honour to be invited as guest artists at the 11th International Conference of the International Society for Musical Education (ISME) in Perth, Western Australia, a gathering of 2000 performers and 1500 music educators from forty countries.

'New Zealand's foremost performing baroque music group', as it was termed, comprised musical director Ashley Heenan, leader Julie Taylor, first violins Anthea Secker and Donald Armstrong, second violins Eleanor Houtman, Simon Miller and Glenda Craven, violas Charles Mountfort and Alison Bowcott, cellos Julia White and Roger Brown, double bass Judith McKenzie and harpsichord Anthony Jennings (director of music, Auckland Cathedral).

At the opening concert in Perth on 6 August, the New Zealanders performed a work attributed to Pergolesi – Concertino in G minor – as well as the Vivaldi Violin Concerto in A major (soloist Julie Taylor), Hindemith's *Five Pieces for Strings*, and Mendelssohn's Symphony no 9 in C minor. Two more concerts followed, but a planned fourth – an all-New Zealand programme with pianist David Bollard[1] – was abandoned on advice from the New Zealand consul. To avoid becoming stranded by an escalating airline strike, the party flew out a day early, on the last flight to Melbourne where they were initially accommodated at Monash University.

The group gave four concerts in Melbourne, the first to its largest audience (over 600) at Blackwood Hall. Next day they performed to a student audience at Hawthorn State College, and that evening gave a Soirées Musicales performance in Coppin Hall. The venue did not have stage lighting, so standard lamps had to be hastily borrowed. The final concert was in St Peters' Church, Eastern Hill, a performance praised by one of the city's 'most feared critics'.[2]

In Sydney, on the last leg of this acclaimed tour, the players joined in a three-hour rehearsal with the ABC Training Orchestra, and gave their last concert at St Thomas's Anglican Church in North Sydney.

NZBC Symphony Orchestra Australian tour 1974

The tour by the Schola Musicum had been good value at $8239.04. It provided useful experience for the NZBC, taking its first touring group overseas, and served as a curtain-raiser for a longer, more significant and infinitely more demanding tour just two months later.

In comparison, the NZBC Symphony Orchestra's Australian Tour in October 1974 was a major undertaking. It had a touring party of 125 comprising ninety-four players, five management, two soloists, the conductor Brian Priestman, his wife and infant daughter, sixteen orchestra family members, a television crew of five who would make a documentary on the tour, and four tonnes of orchestral equipment.

The invitation for this tour came from the Sydney Symphony Orchestra. It was a request for its New Zealand counterpart to replace it in six subscription concerts at the Sydney Opera House and three other concerts, while the Sydney Symphony Orchestra made a thirty-three-concert, eight-week tour to Great Britain and to six countries in continental Europe.[3] The NZBC Symphony Orchestra would have a demanding workload in Australia, performing nine concerts in eleven days between 11 and 21 October, with seven different programmes, two repeats, and only the two Sundays off.

Misplaced cross-Tasman rivalry may have deterred some Sydney subscribers from the initial concerts, and it was unfortunate that most reviews were not published until after the visitors returned home. The juxtaposition of house-full signs and empty seats was bewildering to the New Zealanders but, as concert manager Peter Averi explained, unlike New Zealand, 'the ABC and Opera House then had no facility for re-selling unoccupied seats'.[4]

'Audiences were really impressed by the outstanding international quality of the New Zealand soloists', Averi recalls, and cites 'the soprano Kiri Te Kanawa singing the "*Four Last Songs*" of Richard Strauss, pianist Michael Houstoun playing the Prokofiev third Piano Concerto, and NZBCSO principals Vyvyan Yendoll (viola) and Wilfred Simenauer (cello) performing Strauss's *Don Quixote*. New Zealand composers were also to the fore: [they played] Anthony Watson's *Prelude and Allegro for Strings*, Edwin Carr's *Twelve Signs for Woodwind, Brass and Percussion*, John Rimmer's *At the Appointed Time* and Symphony no 3 by Douglas Lilburn.'[5]

Australian critics responded warmly, deeming the tour an artistic success. Said *The Australian*: 'The NZBCSO endeared itself to Sydney audiences during a gruelling whirlwind visit [performing/giving]... seven concerts in eight days with five changes of programme ... At its best it was quite thrilling. At other times its arduous schedule seemed to catch up with it in mid-concert ...'[6]

Kiri Te Kanawa, already acclaimed for her performances at Covent Garden and recent sensational debut at New York's Metropolitan Opera, ignited audiences, but as the *Mirror*, Sydney, acknowledged, the orchestra 'was not only first class, but gave a far more interesting programme than many from our own orchestra'.[7]

The final performances were in Canberra and in Adelaide's new Festival Theatre, where the orchestra received '20 minutes of applause, cheering, and also a standing ovation'.[8]

It had been a demanding twelve days and many players returned home probably more exhausted than exhilarated. Results were excellent but in retrospect it was acknowledged that there had been too much to prepare in the short time available. Conductor Brian Priestman had been unable to join the orchestra in New Zealand until shortly before the tour started. In his absence an additional strain was placed on concertmaster Alex Lindsay, who had the onerous responsibility of preparing and rehearsing the orchestra for seven different programmes.

Alex Lindsay's sudden death, aged fifty-six, came six weeks after the tour, and it will always be irrevocably linked to that important milestone in the orchestra's history. The pressure on Lindsay, as many of his colleagues still believe, caused the untimely death of a much-loved and respected concertmaster.[9]

A remarkable achievement of this tour was that the main criticism levelled by the Australian press was not about the orchestra's performance. Its name – the New Zealand Broadcasting Service Symphony Orchestra – was less than successful. 'Clumsy in name alone',[10] wrote one reviewer. 'What a mouthful', sniffed the *Sunday Telegraph*.[11] The next restructuring of Broadcasting would see the NZBC shuffled around to become the BCNZ in 1977, but the 'NZBC' disappeared from the orchestra's title within months of this tour, in 1975, when it became, and remains, the New Zealand Symphony Orchestra, or NZSO.

National Youth Orchestra on the world stage

It was now the turn of the sixteen-year-old National Youth Orchestra to step out onto the world stage. The touring party for this orchestra would be far smaller than that of the NZSO, although the scope of its touring and performance schedule would be longer and even more demanding.

It would become a 'world tour', although that was not foreseen in 1975 when the National Youth Orchestra was invited to attend the International Festival of Youth Orchestras in Aberdeen and London. This was its second invitation to this festival, which had been established in 1968 to 'bring together with a common cultural purpose, youth from different countries, socio-economic backgrounds, religions and races'.[12] This time the message was made more difficult to refuse since it was delivered in person by Joy Bryer, the festival's secretary-general and the wife of Lionel Bryer, the festival's chairman. As Alwyn Palmer, the National Youth Orchestra's touring manager reported; it was 'a matter of some prestige and honour that an international jury had considered our group to be of acceptable standard'. However, in his opinion, the costs – including travel to Scotland, London, and to include Long Island in the United States,[13] an estimated $148,000 for a seventy-piece orchestra – were 'beyond the bounds of Broadcasting's responsibility'.

Assistance with funding was immediately sought from the Ministry of Foreign Affairs, the Ministry of Defence (for transport by the Royal New Zealand Air Force), the Department of Internal Affairs (for a dollar-for-dollar subsidy on the NZBC's expected $50,000), and from the Queen Elizabeth II Arts Council (for direct assistance) – but the results were disappointing.

Foreign Affairs offered $3000. The Arts Council questioned 'the value to be derived at such expense, from one trip?' and then it and all the other institutions declined, expressing surprise that, 'NZBC had not accepted full responsibility'.[14] The NZBC then dropped its pledge to $45,000; a sum that head of music, Peter Nisbet,[15] said was 'inadequate'. Nisbet then made the announcement, 'I cannot recommend that we go ahead with this proposal'.

Grant Cooper, 1975

Grant Cooper, the youth orchestra's principal trumpet, heard of this development and took up the challenge, determined not to give up a once-in-a-lifetime opportunity. 'People would be disappointed', he wrote. The lack of support 'reflected an incredible lack of understanding of the implications the trip would have on the future of orchestral growth in New Zealand ... from my own point of view, I owe my complete development as an orchestral player to the opportunities presented to me at NYO courses, and I'm sure this is very true of many others too, all of whom would feel that NYO fills a very important need for young orchestral musicians in New Zealand ... We should all adopt as our slogan, "Long Live National Youth!"'[16]

Players responding to this rallying call began a campaign to save the tour and, as Grant recalls, 'each of us later paid an incredibly modest amount – $500 – to go on the trip. I accepted responsibility for the "Auckland contingent", and we were lucky to have a critical mass of people from the region going on the tour, [some of whom were] beginning their professional careers with the then Symphonia of Auckland. Indeed some young musicians who were not going wanted to participate also, and equally importantly, conductor Juan Matteucci[17] offered to conduct, gratis, a series of fund-raising concerts that we put on as a chamber orchestra around the Auckland region.

'What really stands out is after writing to the Auckland Savings Bank asking for support, we were turned down on the basis, "we only sponsor activities that benefit our depositors."' In his reply to the bank, Grant persuasively outlined the benefits to Auckland Savings Bank depositors of having 'all these young people gain this incredible experience in the larger musical world, and then bring it back to the cultural life of New Zealand'. The success of this persistent approach, he says, 'gave me the confidence to navigate the market-driven financial landscape of US orchestra funding throughout my post-NZ life!'[18]

In the face of this enthusiasm, Broadcasting which had initially agreed to subsidise the tour on a 2:1 basis, somewhat grudgingly agreed to increase its funding to $55,000, on the proviso, as Grant has noted, that players each contribute $500 and the orchestra be reduced to thirty-nine players. Peter Averi, receiving this message in London where he was meeting orchestral managers, immediately cabled back 'Considerable disappointment about size of orchestra ... Funds being sought from Commonwealth Youth Exchange but amount of grant much reduced if we send only 40 ... I strongly urge decision be reconsidered and send full band of 70. My recommendation: 1. Forget Long Island … 2. Travel direct NZ–UK–NZ … I believe wonderful opportunity for New Zealand orchestral music we should not miss …'[19]

'No hope of increasing size of party … lucky to have got funds for this group', replied Peter Nisbet, who was then in the midst of another 'restructuring' of Broadcasting. The timing was unfortunate, with the NZBC about to be replaced by yet another organisation, and the subsequent fate of all three orchestras unknown. Although two 'final deadlines' had passed, the continuing support of Joy Bryer and other festival organisers ensured that National Youth Orchestra's late application was warmly accepted. The orchestra would go to the festival in Aberdeen and, as a new itinerary issued in early January 1975 revealed, that would be followed by additional performances through England and Wales, before returning home via London, Holland, Sydney, and Christchurch.

An energetic fund-raising effort was by now well underway. On sale was a souvenir recording, *The Best of National Youth Orchestra 1972–74*, a boxed album featuring works by Bach, Brahms, Beethoven, Mahler, Tchaikovsky, and Ravel, conducted by Ashley Heenan with pianist Michael Houstoun, who generously donated his fee. Bags of coal were sold – a Christchurch initiative – a raffle was held in conjunction with a record company; there were bring-and-buy sales; and house concerts and recitals were given. An official Players Fund-raising Committee was formed, with Ashley Heenan (chairman), Peter Averi and Bert Ridding (NZBC), Farquhar Wilkinson (NZSO), Grant Cooper, Susan Thompson and Anthea Secker (NYO players), Professor John Ritchie, and conductor Juan Matteucci. No formal meetings were held, but through this group Ashley Heenan was able to stimulate fund-raising efforts.

Additional funding of $12,000 was received from the Arts Council as the direct result of a personal request from Joy Bryer, and a personal application for twelve more players from Ashley Heenan. This enabled an increase in the touring group number from forty to fifty-two players, but even after a reassessment of costs and several changes to programming and repertoire, finance remained an issue.

As the tour hung in the balance help arrived from a most unexpected quarter – the New Zealand Women's Club of Great Britain – which offered 'financial help to cover a nine-day tour in Britain, plus all expenses for fifty-five musicians'.[20] To the relief of everyone the tour was assured, but then came another twist to the story.

Peter Averi and Ashley Heenan received an unexpected invitation to meet the Chinese Ambassador. 'Tea and pleasantries were exchanged', as Averi recalls, and the two answered many questions about the youth orchestra: 'How is it structured? Where do its players come from? How are they chosen? What are they going to play?' Then an hour or so later 'everyone shook hands, and we walked down the street wondering "what was that all about?"' A few days later the answer came by way of a formal invitation for the National Youth Orchestra of New Zealand to perform in the People's Republic of China. 'Well, of course that really threw everything into chaos', Averi says. 'This was an exciting proposal and all the more attractive because costs would be met by the Chinese hosts. The only cost for players was $112 each, to cover airfares and hotels in Hong Kong and Tokyo. We had to ask if they were prepared to stay on, and of course nobody demurred, even if it meant another three or four weeks'.[21]

The National Youth Orchestra's straightforward return trip to Aberdeen had become a full-scale world tour with the inclusion of the People's Republic of China. This was a particular honour as the youth orchestra would be one of the first western orchestras to perform in China since the Cultural Revolution. Three months before the tour was due to start the schedule had to be amended again, with two concerts in Amsterdam and Sydney being replaced by two others in Hong Kong and Tokyo. More funding was required, and this time the suggestion was made, that if brass bands can receive funding to tour, why not the youth orchestra?

The National Band of New Zealand was then touring North America; a previous tour by the National Band, under leader Ken Smith, had won the brass band section of the 1962 World Music Contest in Kerkrade, Holland.

It was a valid argument, and Foreign Affairs eventually agreed to increase its assistance with a grant of $3000 from its Cultural Exchange budget, and a further contribution, to bring its total contribution to $6500. This sum had still not been paid when the orchestra departed, and an advance from Radio New Zealand had to be sought to cover the temporary deficit.

The National Youth Orchestra's world tour 1975

Thursday 24 July 1975 was day one of the youth orchestra's great adventure, and the touring party had converged on Christchurch. At 5 pm 'tea' was served in the Durham Street Methodist Hall,[22] followed at 7 pm by the first rehearsal in three days of intensive rehearsing, to prepare for the concerts ahead. In the official party were musical director Ashley Heenan, Peter Averi, orchestra manager, and Beverley Malcolm, known to everyone as Bev, the official assistant manager and unofficial 'mum' for players. Sandy Whyte, the Qantas Airways representative, was tour escort and would join the group for the latter stages of the tour.[23]

There were fifty-two young players who would travel from New Zealand, and another four currently living overseas would join the group in London. The average age was eighteen, and the youngest, Sharon Gadd, fifteen years old. Nine players had undertaken to assist management by taking on special responsibilities as 'marshals' on tour (Schola Musicum members are denoted by an asterisk): Tony Walton (first violins); Peter Barber* (second violins and violas); Roger Brown (cellos and basses); Keith Spragg (woodwind and horns); Grant Cooper (brass and percussion). The equipment and stage managers were Donald Armstrong* (violin),[24] and Alan McKenzie (trombone); the librarians were Eleanor Houtman* (violin) and Alison Heenan* (viola). All players were instructed to 'note their respective Marshal and co-operate fully when given instructions, both at concerts for stage directions, and also at travel times when players will assemble for buses or aircraft'.

This message was printed in the tour diary – a forty-page booklet featuring a stylised image of cellist Julia White (NYO 1967–74) on a distinctive red cover. This was packed with essential details such as rehearsal calls, travel, repertoire, concerts and accommodation, as well as general information, suggested clothing and basic travel advice. Radio New Zealand chairman Patrick Downey's foreword said the tour was 'another notable "first"' in the musical life of New Zealand … Now it is your privilege to venture into the Northern Hemisphere to participate in the first overseas tour by the National Youth Orchestra … Radio New Zealand is proud to be the organisation coordinating the tour. We are all very conscious of the great effort … and I must congratulate you on the magnificent … fund-raising to match the cash subsidies you have received … on behalf of the Corporation I wish you all a most enjoyable and rewarding experience, both musically and socially.'

In Christchurch players rehearsed solidly, often with three sessions a day, for five days from Thursday 24 to Monday 28 July. They had a day off for final packing and then on Wednesday 30 July the travel party began its epic thirty-hour journey to London – the first New Zealand orchestra to travel to the Northern Hemisphere.

At a time before budget travel made the world more accessible, for most young players, this was their first experience of overseas travel. Stopovers in Sydney, Singapore and Kuala Lumpur went without incident, but in Bahrain a National Youth Orchestra member was apprehended by police for carrying a knife. Although he tried to explain that it was for 'sharpening pencils and cutting string', his boy-scout knife was confiscated before the plane was permitted to leave for Frankfurt.

The long international flight ended at Heathrow in London. It was here that four ex-pat National Youth Orchestra members joined the group:

Members of the National Youth Orchestra wave farewell at Christchurch Airport today.

'Members of the National Youth Orchestra wave farewell at Christchurch Airport today.' *Christchurch Star*

Julie Taylor (viola), Elizabeth Turnbull (violin), Julia White (cello) and Rupert Bond (double bass). A strike by baggage handlers was then in progress, Peter Averi recalls, and the airport was in such confusion, that 'the connecting flight to Aberdeen took off without us, and we faced the rather gloomy prospect of a very long bus ride, after flying 30 hours'. Fortunately, after consulting with airline staff, the group was allocated a special flight north via Glasgow and a short time later were instructed to board. 'There were some very tired people by the end of the day', Averi reported in the first of his daily broadcast reports to Radio New Zealand, 'but in Aberdeen, in contrast, pipers and Highland dancers greeted the orchestra and everyone was made to feel welcome'.[25]

The party was taken by bus to Dunbar Hall at the University of Aberdeen, where over 1000 participants from fourteen countries had converged for the festival. Orchestra members would have three days in which to rest and recover from their journey, and enjoy their surroundings and the atmosphere. Aberdeen's streets were bedecked with flags, and trees hung with colourful musical motifs, in celebration of its Seventh International Festival of Youth Orchestras.

Elizabeth Turnbull, viola soloist, 1975

Claudio Abbado rehearses Mozart for International Youth Orchestra concerts in Aberdeen and London
Kevin Currie

The opening ceremony on Monday 4 August was held in Aberdeen's Music Hall and featured the Young Musicians Symphony Orchestra of Great Britain. Leading youth orchestras, choirs, dance troupes and opera schools were welcomed like Olympic teams, by the playing of each country's national anthem. Taking part were groups from Denmark, Germany, Ghana, Great Britain, Italy, Luxembourg, New Zealand, Poland, South Africa, Sweden, Taiwan, the Philippines, Turkey, and the United States of America. There were massed choirs, and the Aberdeen City Police Pipe Band.

Peter Averi recalls 'Blyth Major, the Festival's music director, conducting a deafening fanfare by Eric Ball, and a young Simon Rattle conducting a forgettable piece by Zděneck Lukáš, but it was interesting to see the 21-year-old displaying talent that would take him to the heights of conducting fame and a knighthood a few years later'.

On that first evening the National Youth Orchestra was honoured to present the first formal concert of the Festival at the Music Hall, playing Lilburn's *Aotearoa* Overture, Mozart's Symphony no 39 in E flat, *Scottish Dances* by Ashley Heenan, Vaughan Williams' Suite for Viola and Orchestra (soloist Elizabeth Turnbull), and the Kodály *Dances of Galanta.* Guest conductor Avi Ostrowsky conducted the Mozart. Ashley Heenan conducted the other four works, and took the opportunity to introduce both New Zealand

Ashley Heenan conducting, 1975

compositions: his own *Scottish Dances*, written especially for this tour, and Douglas Lilburn's *Aotearoa* Overture, the work most frequently played on the tour, and the best received.

'Tonight New Zealand musicians have shown their calibre to a wildly enthusiastic audience of over 1200…with a superb concert', Peter Averi told his listeners, and this was confirmed next day in the eagerly awaited Aberdeen *Press and Journal* review.[26] 'The NYO of New Zealand set a cracking standard for their fellow participants to emulate … indeed I am prepared to say that unless my memory is playing tricks, they are one of the best to appear in the festival since its inception in 1973'. This was praise indeed, and the high standard of New Zealand players was further confirmed a few days later when twenty-three players successfully auditioned for places in the International Festival Youth Orchestra. This total rose to twenty-four when a keyboard player was required and first violinist Martin Lamb took on that role.

This total was almost half the orchestra's full complement of players, without the orchestra trainees, who did not audition. They were considered professional players by their director, who required them to perform chamber concerts on tour as the Schola Musicum.

Keith Spragg in Aberdeen
Kevin Currie

The festival had scheduled two recitals by the Schola within its first few days. The first, a programme of Boyce, Handel, and Bach on Sunday 3 August (pre-empting the official opening of the Festival) drew an audience of 350 in the fifteenth-century Cathedral of St Machar in Old Aberdeen. Two days later a second concert, in the Aberdeen Art Gallery, was also well-received.

Concerts and performances by the festival's various participating groups were given every evening and there were also seminars and other activities. But the place to go, as the Aberdeen *Press and Journal*[27] revealed, was the youth disco entertainments, 'where over 600 young people gathered each evening after the official events'. Several jazz groups played there, but the 'main attraction at the disco' according to the paper, was the 'NZ Beer Band,[28] which entertained with tunes from the 30s and 40s'. An accompanying photograph revealed its members as Alan McKenzie and Paul Morris (trombones),[29] Ken Young (tuba), Graham Johns (percussion), and Norman McFarlane (trumpet); the group also included cellist Josephine Harris, who played the tambourine.

'"We're only here for the beer" joked some members of the National Youth Orchestra of New Zealand, who have formed a small brass cabaret group', as the newspaper reported. It was intended as a light-hearted comment, but Ashley Heenan, 'wasn't best pleased!' Ken Young recalls,[30] when he read that next morning!

The popular New Zealand Beer Band, Aberdeen. Left (l–r): Alan McKenzie and Norman McFarlane. Right (l–r): Norman McFarlane, Ken Young, Josephine Harris, Alan McFarlane, Graham Jones, and Paul Morris.

'The beer band was such fun', says Ken. 'There was a party every night back at the university campus where we were staying with all the various Youth Orchestras in attendance. There was a lot of beer and laughter and so we decided to play some beer band music we had brought with us to add to the tumult.'[31]

Eight days of preliminary rehearsals for the International Festival Orchestra began on 6 August at the Elphinstone Hall, under a young and up-and-coming British conductor, James Judd. As a nineteen year old, Judd had formed and conducted the Young Musicians Symphony Orchestra of Great Britain (1968–71); and the same orchestra was present here, as the festival's resident host orchestra. As assistant conductor for the International Orchestra, Judd spent several days rehearsing the 120-strong International Festival Orchestra in the lead up to its first performance. Then, two days before the concert, the orchestra of young players had its first rehearsal with Italian maestro Claudio Abbado, on 12 August. James Judd would later renew his acquaintance with some of these young festival musicians many years later, when he became music director of the New Zealand Symphony Orchestra (1999–2007) and now, music director emeritus.

Nicholas Braithwaite was another festival conductor with a strong New Zealand connection as the son of an early conductor of the National Orchestra, Warwick Braithwaite.[32] Nicolas Braithwaite would become a guest conductor of the New Zealand Symphony Orchestra himself from 1977 onwards, and the guest conductor of the National Youth Orchestra in 1992.

A feature of this international festival was a parallel series of performances by festival artists, in twenty or so large and small venues around Scotland. On the National Youth Orchestra's first venture outside Aberdeen, players were driven through thick fog down the East Coast to Stonehaven, through Montrose at the mouth of the South Esk River, to the fishing village of Arbroath, near Dundee.

The orchestra performed that evening at Arbroath's Webster Memorial Theatre, to the accompaniment of hundreds of screeching seagulls flying around the roof of the theatre as the fishing boats returned with their catch. This was an evocative sound, that seemed to add to the atmosphere of Douglas Lilburn's *Aotearoa* Overture and, after returning home, Peter Averi wrote to tell the composer that the work had 'never sounded better, the sound of many sea-birds adding a nostalgic touch to the music', almost as if he had 'composed a special part for them'.[33] The sound of those seagulls crying overhead became an integral part of that performance, and it remains a still-vivid memory for many of the players.

At a time when their colleagues were preparing for the biggest concerts of their lives, members of the Schola Musicum performed a concert in the village of Tarland, near Braemar. Proceeds from this concert were to help the Blind Committee raise funds for guide dogs, and with many of these dogs seated beside their owners in the front row it made for an unusual audience. At their next performance, an open-air concert in Aberdeen a few days later, there was an equally unusual audience, as the headline in the *Press and Journal* indicates, 'Orchestra have parrots in audience'.

'When rain began to lash down during the Schola Musicum's open-air recital in Duthie Park yesterday, the artistes simply picked up instruments and headed for the Winter Garden, where they continued their performance – not in the least bothered by inquisitive baby parrots circling around them.'[34]

In fact rain and baby parrots were of less concern to players on that, their last performance in Scotland, than the humidity and sweltering heat under the Winter Garden's glass.

Parrots notwithstanding, the newspaper also noted that this was 'the first time any New Zealand orchestra has toured the Northern Hemisphere'.

The 1975 International Festival Orchestra

The Music Hall, Aberdeen, 14 August, 7.30 pm. Conductor: Claudio Abbado.
Stravinsky – *Le Roi des Etoiles* for Male Chorus and Orchestra (Men's Chorus of the Haddo House Choral Society); Tchaikovsky – Violin Concerto in D op 35 (Kyung-Wha Chung, violin); Berg – Three Orchestral Pieces op 6; Richard Strauss – *Tod und Verklärung* op 24, *Death and Transfiguration*

An audience of 2000 attended the International Festival Orchestra's Aberdeen concert, which was praised in the following day's *Press and Journal* as having 'easily outdistanced its predecessors in the overall quality of the concerted music-making'.

'I felt fortunate to be among those selected for the combined festival orchestra of 120 players', says violinist Simon Miller.[35] 'I remember Chung's playing as being so perfect that I was afraid to play in case I spoiled something! The programme was highly challenging, but a colourful and varied experience of symphonic repertoire far beyond my horizons, with musicians I could only aspire to emulate.'

The next morning an early start was required for all participants in the festival, as 1000 or so players and officials prepared to leave Aberdeen. Breakfast was at 5.30 am, after which all were to assemble at the Aberdeen railway station, to catch two trains to London. It was a relaxing, ten-hour journey through Scotland and England, by courtesy of British Rail, before the group arrived in London. Accommodation there had been arranged for them at the Penta Hotel in the Cromwell Road which, as Peter Averi discovered, was 'a huge tourist factory, with tasteless mass-produced food of such poor quality, we had to negotiate a special price for cooked breakfasts for the group from the "contingency fund".'

Ken Young, wearing a tam-o'shanter and puffing a pipe
Kevin Currie

The extra expense was justified for a day in which players would be required to rehearse and perform their second concert in the 1975 International Festival Orchestra. The programme was the same as that given in Aberdeen two nights earlier, but performed to a much larger audience at the BBC's Henry Wood Promenade Concert in the Royal Albert Hall in London, where the anticipation and excitement in the auditorium was raised several notches higher.

Royal Albert Hall, London, Saturday, 16 August 1975, 7.30pm. Conductor: Claudio Abbado. Stravinsky – *Le Roi des Etoiles* for Male Chorus and Orchestra (Men's Chorus of the Haddo House Choral Society); Tchaikovsky – Violin Concerto in D op 35 (Kyung-Wha Chung, violin); Berg – Three Orchestral Pieces op 6; Richard Strauss – *Tod und Verklärung* op 24, *Death and Transfiguration*

Violinist Ursula (Ruthchen) Evans, aged sixteen, watched from the audience. One of the NYO's youngest players, Ursula had elected to not be in the International Youth Orchestra, and says, 'I remember feeling a little giddy, sitting up the top of the Royal Albert Hall, looking down at the tiny figures so far below on the stage, busy as mice on their instruments. I'd never experienced such a huge concert hall…'[36]

'It was an outstanding performance under [Claudio] Abbado's direction', Peter Averi reported, later that night. 'There was much pride in the New

Soloist Keith Spragg, 1975

Zealand participation, especially for Marya Martin principal flute, and Keith Spragg clarinet, who were given a special ovation … We were proud to see such a large group from the New Zealand NYO represented in this 1975 International Festival Orchestra, amongst players from Luxembourg, the Federal Republic of Germany, Poland, Tacoma USA, South Africa, Taiwan and Italy.'

For a young Wilma Smith, sitting in the first violin section:[37] 'the concert had a profound effect. *Death and Transfiguration* by Richard Strauss affected me particularly, and I remember that at the end of our performance Abbado too was obviously deeply affected, with tears rolling down his face. It was that performance and all the experiences leading up to it that convinced me of the power of what we were privileged to be doing, and set me on my course to becoming a professional musician.' Wilma and Mary Allison were stand partners at that time, and are now colleagues in the Melbourne Symphony Orchestra. 'We both feel the same way', Wilma says, 'and whenever we play that Strauss tone poem, we share reminiscences of that pivotal point in our lives and careers'.[38]

'The quality of the New Zealand players had surprised even the most experienced musicians', as Averi reported. 'Conductors from the Tacoma Symphony, a South African Youth Orchestra and the Vivaldi Academy in Rome in particular sought us out to express their enthusiastic appreciation of the highly professional performances by our orchestra … One critic in summary … placed New Zealand in the top three to appear since 1973.'[39]

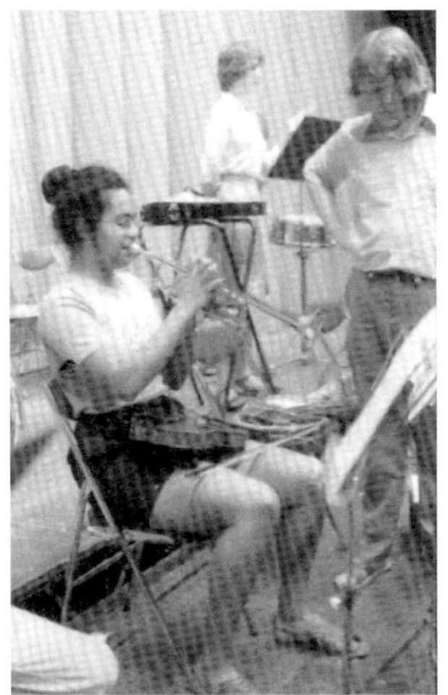
Violinist Wilma Smith tries a new instrument *Kevin Currie*

Afterwards, there was an end of festival party at which an announcement was made that was said to have brought 'great cheers from the New Zealand contingent'. The Harry Dexter Cello Scholarship for six months' study with Professor William Pleeth at the Guildhall School of Music in London had been awarded to Roger Brown, whose progress 'they had all followed, with bated breath, from finalist, to semi-finalist, and finally, winner!'[40]

Grant Cooper, too, was congratulated. Abbado had been so impressed by Grant's playing that he had offered him a 'bench' in his orchestra at La Scala. 'We both expected this would be "next month"', Grant recalls, 'but La Scala advised it would not be open until the following year, and Maestro Abbado suggested I either wait a year, or go to Vienna'.[41] Grant decided to wait.

Trumpeter Grant Cooper warms up. *Kevin Currie*

He started studies with Bernard Adelstein of the Cleveland Orchestra, and when they next met, Abbado was about to resign from La Scala, 'which he did – then later retracted', says Grant. 'By then I was doing so well in New York, I decided to stay. Had I gone to La Scala chances are I would never have had the opportunities [I have had as a conductor], so no regrets!'[42]

A day after their BBC Proms concert the New Zealand group presented a concert of their own, on a somewhat smaller scale, to a much smaller audience at New Zealand House. The function was hosted by Deputy High Commissioner Denis McLean, and as Peter Averi remembers, 'some of the players found the playing of "God Defend New Zealand" particularly emotional'.

The tour of England and Wales

There were a few free days after the concert, and while most players were happy to sight-see around London, a few others took the opportunity for a day trip to Paris. Despite some misgivings from management, all returned safely to resume the next phase, a concert tour through Wales and England. Travel was by coaches with two tour guides who came as 'part of the deal' and seemed more accustomed to tourists – they referred to the players as 'children'. The final straw came when these two women announced on the coaches that as 'the children' had been 'very good all day', they could have 'tomorrow off!' This comment provoked an angry reaction from both conductor and manager, who pointed out that a rehearsal had been scheduled for next morning, and that orchestras take orders from their management – not tour guides.[43]

Players packed into a small carriage on a narrow-gauge railway train in Aberystwyth, Wales. In the front seats are Ken Young, Josephine Harris, and Greg Hill. *Kevin Currie*

The orchestra stayed overnight at the University of Cardiff and travelled next day to the seaside town of Barry in the Vale of Glamorgan. A concert had been scheduled in its Memorial Hall, but because of a fire a few days earlier this was transferred to the Students Union Hall of the College of Education. This may have explained the small audience but nevertheless, the orchestra was given an enthusiastic standing ovation. Travelling north to Aberystwyth, they were accommodated at the university hall of residence. Next day, after rehearsal, the whole party spent an enjoyable afternoon riding on a real steam engine – the narrow-gauge railway (only fifty-eight centimetres wide) which climbed eighteen kilometres through the Rheidol Valley to the scenic terminal at Devil's Bridge.

The concert that evening was in the Great Hall at the University of Aberystwyth to a large audience. A press report later called this 'a polished performance', although Ashley Heenan had deleted some repertoire which he considered was 'under-rehearsed'. The *Aotearoa* Overture was substituted for a Wolf-Ferrari overture, and the Ritchie Clarinet Concertino replaced the Vaughan Williams Viola Suite; perhaps significantly, as Averi suggests, 'well-known works were replaced with unknown New Zealand compositions'.

Leaving Wales, the party was driven through winding country roads and small villages to Chester, where they all stayed overnight in a local youth hostel in Kendall, Westmoreland. Next morning, they had a short stop to visit Wordsworth's cottage at Grasmere, in the Lake District, before continuing on to the coastal town of Whitehaven. This was their next venue, and they performed there that evening, to a large audience in the Civic Hall.

Travel next day took them from Whitehaven to the city of York, where there was a chance to visit the famous York Minster and to stroll through the nearby Shambles in the lunch break. The whole party stayed in the Kesteven College of Education at Grantham that night, and spent the evening watching a replay of the International Youth Orchestra concert at the Royal Albert Hall, on BBC television. 'Everyone sat in rapt attention around the set, and it was good to see the 24 New Zealand players were clearly picked out by the cameras, and everyone was proud to see that Mary Martin in particular was singled out during her very fine solo flute playing.'[44]

It was a short trip from Grantham to Cambridge, where the orchestra stayed at St Catherine's College. A large marquee had been set up at the Midsummer Common Leisure Fair on the bank of the River Cam, and folding chairs were set out for a huge crowd already gathered for the orchestra's 6.30 pm performance. Playing was preceded by the release of fifty-nine named balloons which were bought by the orchestra in aid of a local charity. 'It was a sweltering hot day, and acoustics were far from ideal, but the audience appeared to enjoy the music', although Averi himself thought some of it, 'a little too esoteric for a summer carnival'.

The final performance on this section of the tour was an informal concert in Essex to honour eighty-year-old composer Gordon Jacob, Ashley Heenan's former teacher at the Royal College of Music, London, where he had studied

Left: A couple of local 'yokels' – Rupert Brooke and Peter Barber. Right: Punting on the Cam in Cambridge. *Both images by Kevin Currie.*

from 1948 to 1950. Gordon Jacob, who lived in Saffron Walden, was brought down to the small Saxon village of Thaxted by his daughter to hear the National Youth Orchestra perform in its medieval parish church. The composer Gustav Holst had also lived in Saffron Walden, and played the organ as director of music at this church from 1916 to 1925, so there were significant links made with British composers that day.

Composer Gordon Jacob greeted by his former student Ashley Heenan and youth orchestra members, who performed a concert to celebrate his 80th birthday. Thaxted, Essex. *Kevin Currie*

Heenan, in introducing the programme, remarked that this could be described as, 'a little 20th century extravagance, in that it is rare these days for a symphony orchestra to travel specifically to give a concert for one person'. The vicar too had expressed his doubts that there would be any audience, 'in the middle of a week-day afternoon', and in fact it was the smallest audience of the tour, about

Performing a concert in a marquee at the Midsummer Common Fair, in Cambridge *Kevin Currie*

forty people, including tour guides and drivers. The orchestra nevertheless gave their best, in a programme featuring two of Gordon Jacobs' compositions – *Sketches for Strings* and *Fantasia on the Alleluia Hymn* – and compositions by two of his pupils, Ashley Heenan's *Scottish Country Dances* and Douglas Lilburn's *Aotearoa* Overture.'

As afternoon tea was being served in the Recorder Tearooms, there was an outburst from the driver engaged to transport the orchestral equipment. He had locked himself in his truck, and was refusing to move the gear, apparently frustrated at being treated like a 'second-class' citizen by the tour guides. His complaint, as relayed to Peter Averi, was that they never included him in any meal breaks and left him to buy his own meals. The 'final straw' was when he was told that he was 'not welcome' at the Thaxted concert; and he had 'boiled over'.

'It was the English class system at work', Averi realised, and with the driver still refusing to budge from his cab, he rang New Zealand House. 'Tell the man that his contract will be honoured and to bring the equipment to New Zealand House in London', the Deputy High Commissioner Denis McLean advised, and Averi did so. The orchestra made the two-hour coach journey back to the Penta Hotel and, as it transpired, on the arrival of the truck, staff at New Zealand House grabbed the keys and locked it in The Haymarket.

Loading the bus (again)
Kevin Currie

Storage space for the equipment was provided at New Zealand House, and everyone had three well-earned days off to relax and enjoy the hot summer weather. There was a Thames cruise to Greenwich and other sight-seeing, with some players hiring bicycles to get around the city. Rehearsals began again on 30 August for the next stage of the tour: Asia.

A farewell concert given at New Zealand House on 2 September was attended by Denis McLean, and representatives from the People's Republic of China. The programme included Lilburn's *Aotearoa* Overture, the Ritchie Clarinet Concertino (with Keith Spragg), and *The White Haired Girl* – a revolutionary ballet suite which would be a feature of concerts in China. A representative from the Chinese Embassy made a speech of welcome to the players, and presented an orchestral score to Ashley Heenan. A supper afterwards was attended by a number of New Zealanders and artists associated

New Zealand House, London, a home away from home for National Youth Orchestra players, who performed their last concert there before leaving for China. *Kevin Currie*

with New Zealand. Among them were James Robertson, former principal conductor of the National Orchestra,[45] and the New Zealand-born opera conductor, John Matheson.[46]

'Performing the *Aotearoa* Overture at New Zealand House still stays in my mind', Marise White (percussion 1974–77),[47] recalls. 'I was proud to be a New Zealander, but I was also very aware of just how far away from New Zealand we were.'

It was a day off for the orchestra next day, but not for the Schola Musicum which performed its final London concert at the Church of Notre Dame de France, in Leicester Square. There the group played a programme of Boyce, Handel, Vivaldi, and Bach, as one of forty-three concerts and recitals performed simultaneously in London that day.

It was then time to farewell the players who had joined the tour in London, who would not be accompanying the orchestra to Asia. Julie Taylor, Elizabeth Turnbull, Julia White and Rupert Bond[48] would resume their places respectively at the Royal College of Music in London, Trinity College, the Conservatoire of Music in Brussels, and London University followed by the Royal Academy of Music.

The Asian adventure

Another long journey lay ahead. Six weeks earlier the New Zealand party had flown into Heathrow in the midst of a baggage-handlers' strike, and now as they arrived for their departure they were caught up in a bomb scare. Qantas flight QF6 then flew from London to Belgrade, where many Yugoslavian emigrants joined the flight, and then on to Athens where they were delayed for three hours. The Syrian Government would not permit the plane to fly over its territory to Damascus, and passengers could not leave the plane at any of the places they landed during this fourteen-hour flight. Finally, arriving late in Bangkok after many delays, players were issued with boarding passes by flight attendants waiting on the tarmac, and they went straight to their flight to Hong Kong without entering the terminal.

On their arrival in Hong Kong, Bart Finney, the New Zealand High Commissioner, was waiting to greet them alongside Sandy Whyte, the Qantas representative who would accompany them on this Asian stage of their tour, becoming an integral member of the management team.

The first performance was a matinée concert given on 6 September in the 1500-seat City Hall on Hong Kong Island. A capacity audience heard Lilburn's *Aotearoa* Overture, the Haydn *Drum Roll* Symphony no 103, Heenan's *Scottish Dances, The White-Haired Girl* Suite by Chu Wei, and Kodály's *Dances of Galanta.* Afterwards, the orchestra's playing was praised in both the *South China Post* and the *Hong Kong Standard* newspapers, and its high standard was still recalled five years later, when the New Zealand Symphony Orchestra became the featured orchestra at the Hong Kong Festival over three weeks in February 1980.

The next day the youth orchestra was taken by bus to Kowloon Railway Station, and then by train to the border station of Lo Woo – a one-hour journey. After a short walk to a military post, they were advised that customs formalities were waived, and they were free to cross into the People's Republic of China at a point where a British flag was flying on one side of the border, and the red flag of China on the other. At the railway station, the party ate its first genuine Chinese meal with chopsticks, which was a new experience for most of the group.

The group, travelling in a modern air-conditioned train through rice fields, arrived in what was then known as Canton (now Kwangchow), where it was greeted by over 100 children in brightly coloured dress, holding paper flower posies, dancing, and chanting a welcome. When the train arrived at the station the official party was quickly told not to disembark. Moments later it moved forward a few metres, to ensure that the leaders were directly opposite the welcoming party when the train stopped. The Chinese wanted to ensure that protocol was strictly observed. Ashley Heenan had to alight first, Peter Averi to follow, then Beverley Malcolm, Sandy Whyte, and the orchestra leader Anthea Secker. This was the set procedure, for every occasion.

Visiting a commune in Canton (clockwise l–r): Michael Cuncannon, Marise White, Alan Stapleton, Peter Barber, Alison Heenan, a commune resident, Greg Brown, Kevin Currie, and the interpreter. *Official tour photograph*

A moving welcome was accorded the group as it walked past waving crowds through the station concourse, into the motorcade waiting to take the orchestra to the East Wind Hotel. After a brief rest they were all then driven to see the concert hall where the orchestra was to perform, and then returned to join a procession of buses 'through crowded streets, with bicycles everywhere, car horns sounding continuously, and traffic police in cubicles at intersections shouting instructions over loudspeakers'.[49]

A formal reception in the banquet room of the hotel was held that evening at which music was performed 'very brilliantly' by Chinese artists, and officials were very attentive, superb hosts, with strict observance of protocol.

On arrival everyone in the tour party were given gifts of money (yuan notes, equivalent to about NZ$12) to spend in the Friendship Store so that it went back into circulation very quickly. They were also given copies of the *Little Red Book*, containing the quotations of Chairman Mao Tse Tung. Everywhere they went the visitors were accompanied by bilingual interpreters, without whom they would have been 'totally lost', as Averi says.

'The weather was hot and humid, with no rain, and walking in the streets provoked much curiosity, as Chinese people looked at our European faces. A banner hanging over the gallery in Chinese proclaimed "Long live friendship of China and New Zealand". At the first concert the New Zealand managers, as official guests, received a standing ovation from a capacity and noticeably very noisy audience, which reacted when something appealed to it, with a buzz of conversation. When the percussionist raised her cymbals to give them a mighty crash, there was a round of applause.'

Afterwards Peter Averi was unable to call in his New Zealand radio report from the hotel and was escorted through empty streets by the interpreter, 'only to learn that the telex was closed until 10 – which I discovered, meant "October", and it was then 9 September!'

'The New Zealand National Youth Orchestra received an enthusiastic reception from a capacity audience when it opened its tour of the People's Republic of China, last night', wrote Derek Round, NZPA staff correspondent, in a review published in the *Evening Post*, Wellington. '[Its] playing of *The White-haired girl* ... was a big hit with the Chinese who stood applauding for several minutes ... Earlier a ripple of obvious approval ran through the audience in the 1400-seat Kwangchow Friendship Theatre when the New Zealanders played a selection from the Chinese ballet *Children of the Grasslands* ... The orchestra is the first Western Orchestra to play in China since the Philadelphia Orchestra was here in 1973 ... Chinese musicians from the Kwangchow Philharmonic Orchestra joined the New Zealanders ... including a harpist, flautist and Chinese fiddle players ... People's Liberation Army soldiers in their olive green uniforms rubbed shoulders with factory workers and peasants from nearby communes ... [as] the Orchestra ... opened the concert with the Chinese National Anthem, and then *God Defend New Zealand* – the first time it has been played in China ...'[50]

On leaving Kwangchow the New Zealanders received another rousing farewell from more than 100 children waiting at the airport as the orchestra arrived to board the plane. After a first aborted landing at Peking (now Beijing) the party landed safely and were afforded the sort of reception 'one might expect for leading dignitaries or heroes', as Peter Averi recalls. 'The New Zealand Ambassador, Bryce Harland, was standing on the tarmac alongside leading Chinese officials, and behind them were hundreds of children waving coloured ribbons. Two bands played rousing music as we were escorted past the lines of waiting children, as if it was a military inspection, and then into cars waiting to take us to the hotel, on the edge of Tiananmen Square ...

'As in the hotel in Kwangchow, we were not given room keys. The doors were left open all the time, Chinese porters were on constant vigil, and replaced each item once it was used – face cloths, sweets, and fruit – nothing was ever taken.'[51]

The National Youth Orchestra performing one of its most significant concerts of the tour, in Peking (Beijing)

Musicians from the Shanghai Philharmonic Orchestra played traditional instruments alongside National Youth Orchestra players in Peking (Beijing)
Kevin Currie

On their first evening in Beijing, players were taken to the Friendship Association theatre to see a ballet film, *Red Detachment of Women*, 'a long and rather tedious performance, during which several players fell asleep', according to Averi. The next day, while rehearsals were underway at the Theatre of the Nationalities Palace of culture, he made another attempt to send his radio report, but on a keyboard that had only Chinese characters 'it took two hours to laboriously type it out, letter by letter'.[52]

The concert party were taken as tourists on a tour through the Forbidden City. They had lunch at the New Zealand Embassy, where players were delighted to find a large swimming pool and tennis court, and made the most of their visit. Afterwards they attended the opening ceremony of the third Chinese National Games, with 100,000 in the audience, 10,000 athletes, and 20,000 children who presented a series of coloured picture tableaux from their seats, with swift changes of coloured cards.[53] That same evening, the orchestra known in China as the 'New Zealand Philharmonic Society', gave its first performance in Beijing.

As Derek Round reported later, in the *Evening Post*, 'The conductor... Ashley Heenan, said that the reception accorded the orchestra, "far exceeded my wildest dreams ... It was a thrilling experience for all of us to be made so welcome, and to know the capacity audience appreciated the music ... a few players from the Shanghai Philharmonic Orchestra played traditional instruments in the Chinese pieces, and the curious mix of their sound with the other orchestral instruments added a unique dimension to the music..."'[54] Keith Spragg was again the soloist. Playing in NYO gave him confidence, Keith says, but his 'worst memory' of the tour occurred at this concert. 'I was on stage, listening to the orchestra and thinking what a wonderful sound they were making, and then realising that they were waiting for me to come in!'[55]

Special guests at both concerts in Beijing were Ambassador Bryce Harland, and Rewi Alley, the legendary expatriate New Zealand writer and teacher who had lived in China since 1927. At the following concert, on 13 September, the Second Vice-Premier Chang Chun Chiao (Zhang Chun Qiao)[56], and other members of the Chinese Government, were present, says Greg Hill. 'My memory is of the players at the end of a concert, bunched in a line a few people deep, at the front of the stage, clapping at the audience while they clapped at us. A delegation of official-looking Chinese walked along the line, and the man who seemed most important shook many players' hands. I remember pushing my arm through from behind and he shook my hand. Of course he was wearing a Mao suit, everybody was!'[57]

The Great Wall of China. Standing (l–r): Sharon Gadd, Ken Young, Graham Johns, Ruthchen (Ursula) Evans, Judith McKenzie, Keith Spragg, Paul Morris, Dean Major, Judith Williams, Jennifer Young, Simon Miller, Marise White, Donald Armstrong, Ross Radford, Mark Thomas, Greg Hill, Murray Rogers, Tony Walton, Norman McFarlane, Peter Barber, Vicki Philipson, Peter Watt, Michael Cuncannon, Wilma Smith, Anna Salamonsen, Gail Thomas, Jeremy Thompson, Warren Wiggins. Seated (l–r): Jane Wilkinson, Glenda Craven, Kevin Currie, Alison Heenan, Eleanor Houtman, Gillian Ansell, Martin Lamb, Josephine Harris, Roger Brown, Ann Hunt, John Ure, Alan Stapleton. *Marise McNeill*

At the Canton Museum

After each concert the official party was escorted up to the stage and presented with flowers. 'We soon learned the courtesy of applauding at the same time as the audience', Averi explains, 'a curious gesture but one which was a compliment to our tour hosts'.

Four concerts had now been performed by the National Youth Orchestra in China, two each in Kwangchow and Beijing. Each time the concert halls were filled to capacity, as the party learned later, because most of the audience had been given tickets as a reward for their 'consistent hard work'.

The orchestra's hotel in Beijing was on a wide main road, overlooking Tiananmen Square. It was 'like another planet, then', Ken Young remembers. 'There were very few cars and two million bicycles, and there were always a lot of people. We thought it would be fun to give them an impromptu concert from the 11th floor balcony of the room I was sharing with Greg Hill. Well! By the time we had played two numbers, the second of which was 'Slow Boat to China', there were hundreds and hundreds of people gathered below our balcony, staring up and causing considerable consternation for the dozen or so Red Guards trying to move them all along. The music that the Chinese were permitted to listen to in those days before the death of Chairman Mao, was seriously restricted and controlled (the orchestra was not permitted to perform the Sibelius third symphony), so I guess we created a bit of an incident. After about ten minutes we figured that for the sake of international relations, we'd better desist!'[58]

'It was chaos!' Greg Hill says. Next day, the entire touring party was taken on a two-hour drive to the Great Wall of China. This was a major highlight of the tour, a timeless place with extraordinary views, which everyone wanted to climb, and photograph. It was here that the whole group sang 'Happy Birthday' to Peter Averi;[59] which was 'an unforgettable experience' he says. Afterwards they were driven to the valley of the Ming tombs, dated 1584, where a picnic was held alongside life-size carved stone elephants.

A final performance was given at the New Zealand Embassy, after which 'a delicious banquet was served and a big birthday cake wheeled out, inscribed "Happy Birthday Peter". This was their last night in China, Averi remembers and 'a happy occasion with singing and dancing. We were royally entertained by Ambassador Bryce Harland and the Embassy staff, who seemed reluctant to let us go at the end of the evening.'

The time set for the group's departure from China was 8.30 am. Fortunately, Peter Averi and Sandy Whyte had made an early start. They arrived at the airport at 4.30 am, and experienced their only brush with officialdom in China. 'At the Pakistan Airlines counter there was a swarthy, sinister-looking character with a thick black moustache and a cap pulled low over his eyes,

China, full orchestra, 1975

who struck fear in our hearts', Peter Averi recalls. 'He grudgingly issued tickets and boarding passes, and then, looking closer at this man's uniform, Sandy Whyte whispered "My God, I think he's the pilot as well!"'

The orchestra had been welcomed by singing children on their arrival, and now they were farewelled by more children, singing and dancing along beside the players as the group walked across the tarmac. It was the end of the marvellous hospitality of the Chinese, who, Averi says, 'charmed us with their hospitality, delighted us with their generosity, and at times frustrated us with their quiet insistence on obeying protocol. At all times the expression of "goodwill between our two countries" was a recurring theme and I believe it was a genuine desire to restore good relations with the Western world, so long denied access to this amazing country.'

Despite their reservations, the Pakistan Airlines flight was comfortable and uneventful, if slightly longer than the three-and-a-half hours scheduled. Korea denied permission for the plane to travel through its air space, so a route south over the China Sea was taken, and then they headed north to Haneda Airport in Tokyo.

The VIP treatment afforded the orchestra in China was not repeated in Japan where, like any other plane-load of tourists, they had to join a very long queue at the immigration counter. The players then went off by bus to the hotel, while Peter Averi and Sandy Whyte spent an 'infuriating couple of hours, arguing with Customs officers, to try and convince them that the orchestra was there to perform in Japan – and to allow the instruments into the country'. This involved, a 'great deal of shouting and telephoning in a language we could not understand', as Averi recalls, 'but when we saw the truck, packed with instruments, parked in the hot sun I had to insist that it must be driven into the goods shed, otherwise the instruments will be ruined!'

Fortunately, that was agreed, but the battle continued until, after a final round of negotiations, papers were stamped and the truck was permitted to proceed. It had been a long, stressful confrontation, but it ended on a lighter note when a Japanese officer came rushing in calling frantically for 'Sandy Wong! Sandy Wong!' after which Sandy Whyte became known as 'Mr Wong'

The New Zealand Embassy hosted a reception that evening, and a day off followed, in which players could go sightseeing or relax. A refreshed orchestra reassembled next morning to travel to Chu-O-Kaikan near the Ginza, for a shared concert with the Tokyo Youth Symphony Orchestra. This was held at 6.30 pm, in the modern 900-seat concert hall, where the Tokyo orchestra played Bizet's Symphony in C and *Jeux d'Enfants* Suite, and the National Youth Orchestra played Lilburn's *Aotearoa,* Haydn's Symphony no 103, and Heenan's *Scottish Dances.*

A by-now-weary orchestra reported for the final flight home on 18–19 September, and after just one brief stopover at Sydney Airport, flew on to New Zealand. But the tour was not yet over. One final concert had been scheduled for Wellington, but it was now replaced by 'Welcome Home' concert in Christchurch Town Hall, on Saturday 20 September. On arrival it was discovered that a box of music had been left behind at Sydney airport – incredibly, the only such mishap of the two-month tour. Fortunately the box was quickly located and sent on and it duly arrived safely in Christchurch in time for the pre-concert rehearsal.

It was not 'a happy event', as Peter Averi remembers. 'The element of excitement generated by the overseas concerts was missing, the conductor was tired, and the players exhausted, although they made a superb final effort.' Violinist Glenda Craven, an orchestra trainee, had a different impression, and says, 'by that stage, our playing had matured tremendously [and] despite tiredness, we managed to give perhaps our most exciting concert'.[60]

Critic C. Foster Browne was full of praise. 'Saturday evening's concert was one of those heart-warming experiences which will rekindle a glow every time it is remembered ... reports came back from many places saying how excellently the orchestra played, and we have now been given the same thrills and can verify that what was told us was true'.[61]

Members of the orchestra had been away from their homes for two months during which twenty-four concerts were performed in forty-eight days – National Youth Orchestra (seventeen), International Festival Youth Orchestra (two), Schola Musica (five) – in seven countries: Scotland, England, Wales, Hong Kong,the People's Republic of China, Japan, and New Zealand.

Some younger ones had become homesick, and it would be a sad homecoming for one young woman, whose mother passed away during her absence, while she bravely chose to carry on, knowing that it would have been her 'mother's wish', Peter Averi says. All were tired, which was not surprising given the length of the tour and its demanding concert schedule, but 'at no stage was there any lack of co-operation, or animosity between them'.

Postscript

The National Youth Orchestra Return Concert

In recognition of the tour's success, a recording of the 1975 NYO World Tour Orchestra's final performance, conducted by Ashley Heenan with soloist Keith Spragg (clarinet) in Christchurch, was made and issued by Radio New Zealand, 'to ensure that the high standard [of the orchestra] will not be forgotten'.[62]

Thirty-five years later, the high standards and achievements of that ground-breaking tour continue to resonate in the achievements and subsequent careers of its players, many of them professional musicians in New Zealand and around the world; among them: Wilma Smith and Mary Allison, Melbourne Symphony Orchestra; Grant Cooper and Marya Martin, United States; Julie Taylor, Elizabeth Turnbull, Julia White and Rupert Bond, who remain overseas, and others, including Keith Spragg, who have returned to live in New Zealand.

Twelve players became NZSO members; Donald Armstrong; Ursula (Ruthchen) Evans, Dean Major and Simon Miller, violins; Peter Barber and Michael Cuncannon, violas; Roger Brown, cello, and Greg Hill, horn, are current members. Four have since moved on: Wilma Smith, Glenda Craven (van Drimmelen) and Philip Jane, violins, and Ken Young. The orchestra included several family members, the Thompson siblings Jeremy (bassoon), Susan (violin), and Jane (double bass); Walton brothers, Tony (violin) and Mark (clarinet); White sisters, Julia (cello) and Marise (percussion); Heenan father and daughter, Ashley and Alison. Twelve members of the tour party married, subsequently, or were in long-term relationships, and four couples remain together.

Mark Walton, clarinet soloist, 1975

National Youth Orchestra world tour, 1975

Conductor Ashley Heenan (unless otherwise stated). Soloists: Elizabeth Turnbull (viola); Keith Spragg and Mark Walton (clarinet).[63]

Scotland

Sunday 3 August, 5 pm. Schola Musica. St Machar's Cathedral, Aberdeen

Monday 4 August, 7.30 pm. NYO. Avi Ostrowsky (guest conductor) and Ashley Heenan. Elizabeth Turnbull (viola), Music Hall

Tuesday 5 August, 3 pm. Schola Musica. Art Gallery

Friday 8 August, 8 pm. NYO and Keith Spragg (clarinet). Webster Memorial Theatre, Arbroath

Tuesday 12 August, 7.30 pm. NYO and soloist. McRobert Hall, Tarland

Thursday 14 August, 3 pm. Schola Musica. Duthie Park, Aberdeen

Thursday 14 August, 7.30 pm. The 1975 International Festival Youth Orchestra (including 24 New Zealand National Youth Orchestra players). Claudio Abbado, conductor, Kyung-wha Chung (violin), Music Hall, Aberdeen.

London

Saturday 16 August, 7.30 pm. The 1975 International Festival Youth Orchestra (incl. 24 New Zealand National Youth Orchestra players). Claudio Abbado, conductor. Kyung-wha Chung (violin). BBC Proms, Royal Albert Hall.

Sunday 17 August, 7.30 pm. NYO, Elizabeth Turnbull (viola). New Zealand House

Wales

Tuesday 19 August, 7.30 pm. NYO, Keith Spragg (clarinet). College of Education Hall, Barry

Thursday 21 August, 8 pm. NYO, Elizabeth Turnbull (viola). Great Hall, University of Aberystwyth, Aberystwyth

England

Saturday 23 August, 8 pm. NYO, Keith Spragg (clarinet). Civic Hall, Whitehaven

Monday 25 August, 6.30 pm. NYO, Elizabeth Turnbull (viola). Midsummer Common Leisure Fair, Cambridge

Tuesday 26 August, 3 pm. NYO, Mark Walton (clarinet). Concert for Gordon Jacob, parish church, Thaxted

Tuesday 2 September, 8 pm. NYO, Keith Spragg (clarinet). New Zealand House, London

Wednesday 3 September, 1 pm. Schola Musicum. Notre Dame church, London

Hong Kong

Saturday 6 September, 3 pm. NYO. City Hall

People's Republic of China

Monday 8 September, 7.30 pm. NYO. Concert Hall, Peking (Beijing)

Tuesday 9 September, 7.30 pm. NYO & musicians from Kwangchow Philharmonic Orchestra. Concert hall, Peking (Beijing)

Friday 12 September, 7.30 pm. NYO, and musicians from Shanghai Philharmonic Orchestra. Concert Hall, Peking (Beijing)

Saturday 13 September, 7.30 pm. NYO. Concert Hall, Peking (Beijing)

Japan

Wednesday 17 September, 6.30 pm. NYO and Tokyo Youth Symphony Orchestra, joint concert. Concert Hall, Tokyo

New Zealand

Saturday 20 September, 8 pm. Welcome Home Concert. NYO, Keith Spragg (clarinet)

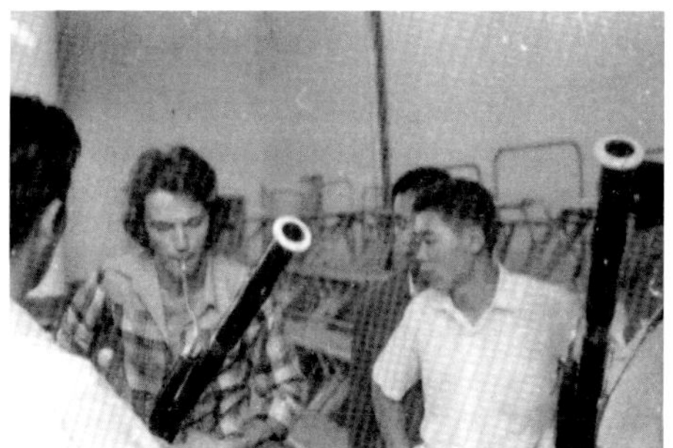

Clockwise from top: National Youth Orchestra players stroll along the Great Wall of China; Jeremy Thompson and Chinese colleagues compare bassoons; Ruthchen Evans received enthusiastic cheers and applause, in China, whenever she beat the large gong.
All images Kevin Currie

6 In the Aftermath

1975–1978

'Music, to create harmony, must investigate discord' – *Plutarch*

'There were occasions when I had to defend Ashley Heenan. He was inclined to blow his top, becoming very angry, and his face turning fuchsia in colour … my view, which I passed along to Ashley, was that one had to work within the system, I saw nothing wrong with doing that.' – *John Hopkins*[1]

In the aftermath of the National Youth Orchestra's triumphant return home disturbing rumours emerged that its conductor Ashley Heenan had 'spoilt what could have been a much more pleasant tour, for many people'.[2]

Peter Averi's first inkling of problems to come was on the flight from New Zealand, as he recalls. 'Ashley was seated beside me, and started to express concern about certain "factions" in the orchestra. "The old hands" as he called them were "seeking more power in the running of the day-to-day affairs of the orchestra, and had made a proposal to set up a players' committee," he said. Ashley was "very strongly opposed" to this, but his main concern was that he suspected a "rift would develop between players from Auckland and Christchurch." Evidently there had been some tensions between players and conductor in the previous year.'

A rift *was* developing, as Averi soon realised, but mainly between National Youth Orchestra players and the orchestra trainees, who were becoming isolated within the orchestra. Several factors contributed to this situation. The leader and all string principals in the youth orchestra were trainees, and the group performed separate concerts on the tour as the Schola Musicum. It was observed that trainees tended to gather around their conductor and did not mix with other players, and Heenan's comment that he had his 'spies in the orchestra' created mistrust.

There were no trainees in the International Festival Orchestra because none of them had auditioned, and they were not permitted to do so. This was not a decision made by festival organisers, as might be assumed, but by the group's own musical director. Ashley Heenan had argued that the trainees were a special group and in a different class from other members of the National Youth Orchestra. As paid scholarship holders with the New Zealand Broadcasting Corporation, members of the Schola Musicum were 'professional' players elected under strict audition arrangements and therefore 'ineligible' for the Festival Orchestra.

Joy Bryer (secretary general) and her colleagues disagreed. 'We all feel very strongly that in the interest of the Festival you [should] allow the members of the Schola Musicum to audition for the International Festival Orchestra … we shall be forming this year a large orchestra, although each country will be represented, the final selection must be made on merit.'[3]

The same situation had existed, 'with the Dutch National Orchestra', Bryer wrote. It too had a breakaway chamber group, and its musicians, 'did audition, for the International Orchestra, and also gave separate concerts in Aberdeen … we the Festival cannot treat [the Schola Musicum] as a separate entity, thereby barring them from auditioning for the Festival …'

Despite this official reassurance, the confirmation of a precedent, and a specific request from the Festival organisers for the trainees to participate, Heenan refused. In Peter Averi's view 'he could not accept that on this occasion Trainees were considered equal in status to every other player in the youth orchestra'.[4]

This unshakeable refusal by Heenan denied this talented group of young New Zealand musicians a once-in-a-lifetime opportunity to audition for a place in the 135-strong International Festival Orchestra along with their colleagues in the National Youth Orchestra and other young musicians from around the world, and if selected, to play under the baton of Claudio Abbado in concerts in Aberdeen and London.

It was observed that Heenan seemed irritated when the international conductors Claudio Abbado and James Judd worked with the orchestra, as if he saw this as conflicting with his own requirements. His antagonism now was also directed at the festival management which he referred to as 'the Bryer mob'. Although conductors and managers were encouraged to meet for meals and socialise in the Refectory, the New Zealand conductor was noticeably absent. His refusal to attend a formal dinner hosted by the provost of Aberdeen had left Peter Averi and Beverley Malcolm in the embarrassing position of standing alone, without their conductor, to acknowledge applause for New Zealand.

'Each day brings a different problem, mostly because of the unpredictable behaviour of the conductor', Averi wrote in his diary at that time, and then added, optimistically, 'once the Festival is over no doubt tension will ease'.

'How wrong I was', he admits now, 'because it only got worse'. The tension continued even when the orchestra was sight-seeing in remote Scottish villages. Heenan apparently preferred the company of Schola players to the exclusion of everyone else. The orchestra was divided, and while those chosen for the international orchestra were kept busy in rehearsals many others felt isolated. It was fortunate, Averi says, that Beverley Malcolm 'acted most competently as the orchestra "mother." She maintained a useful medical kit and dispensed whatever was needed with a healthy dose of encouragement and kindness, almost on a daily basis.'[5]

By the time the orchestra reached China tensions had reached crisis point, Averi recalls. 'It is a matter of regret that this wonderful tour was marred by the conductor's attitude towards his players and the management team', he wrote in his diary, on 13 September. And then a few days later he wrote, 'Another storm with Heenan!'

'That Heenan was insecure and suspicious of plots against him was plain to see. As he became more isolated with the Schola players, they themselves were subjected to his ill-temper, and it became a common occurrence to find members of the group weeping outside his door in Scotland. This continued on into the next stages of the tour and put enormous strain on those young people. The inevitable result of this treatment led to hostility on their part, and I was well aware of the feelings of many of them, especially the senior players who had clearly had enough.'

In Beijing, towards the end of the tour, Averi remembers that he was 'taken aback' when a Chinese official asked him, 'How have we offended you?' 'I gained the impression that with the uncanny sixth sense of the Chinese, they had witnessed some of the tension which permeated the orchestra whose members were by now openly critical of the conductor. Tearful players could not have gone un-noticed by the tour officials, but I also think they knew that as I said, "we had no dissatisfaction with any aspects of the hospitality accorded to us", in the two weeks in China.'

Heenan had predicted a rift between players from Auckland and Christchurch, but while there are conflicting views on the extent of that rivalry, all agree that sadly the rift between NYO players and the Schola Musicum continued. The management team was also unhappy, disputes with the conductor having soured their relationships as well.

Matters came to a head on the return flight from Tokyo to Sydney on 18 December when Peter Averi was handed a sealed envelope addressed to the 'Director-General, Radio New Zealand'. Inside was a letter pre-dated 20 September 1975, signed by forty-two members of the National Youth Orchestra – everyone except the four players who remained overseas, and the

Schola Musicum players.[6] He had heard rumours that a petition was being circulated, and here it was, together with a personal letter addressed to him as concert manager.

The letter to the Director General

> As members of the 1975 National Youth Orchestra may we thank you most sincerely for all the support given by Radio New Zealand to enable our recent tour to take place. All of us have gained immensely from the experience of the tour, and we are sure that it will benefit New Zealand music greatly, well into the future.
>
> However we do feel most strongly that the tour was marred by the conduct of the Musical Director, Ashley Heenan. Because of his actions we would urge that another conductor be appointed for future Youth Orchestras. In our opinion, Mr Heenan has neither the right approach nor the temperament for the position.
>
> Many of us remember John Hopkins when he stood on the podium at Hamilton in the 1971 National Youth Orchestra session. His first statement, said with a huge smile, was that we were there 'for one reason, to enjoy playing music together, at a high standard.' This is in complete contrast to what we have experienced before and after under Mr Heenan.

To support the petition several examples of Heenan's conduct were cited. In the Festival of Youth Orchestras in Aberdeen he was said to have, 'made himself very unpopular with officials … with his insulting rudeness'. In London it was alleged that he told one player that there were '23 players in the present orchestra' that he would 'never accept again, for another NYO'. It was noted that at one rehearsal, Heenan had claimed that he had 'spies' in the orchestra … meaning the orchestral trainees, and in the next breath, 'accused us of being a divided orchestra. How can we be otherwise, when he labels several of our members as "spies?"'

> The problem of the orchestra trainees being kept apart from the remainder of the NYO has been with us for a few years now, since Mr Heenan gathers them around him, making it impossible for them to mix with the other members on equal terms. As a consequence, Mr Heenan has made very little contact with the orchestra as a whole, generating a feeling that there is a definite lack of fraternal spirit between conductor and orchestra.
>
> One can but recall Mr Hopkins again, who insisted that two different members of the orchestra sit with him at every meal. He was especially interested

in helping and encouraging the younger members of the orchestra ... The one aspect of Mr Heenan's approach which is particularly distressing is his constant threatening of individuals, and entire sections of the orchestra. His threats always relate to the musical ruination of these individuals or sections which Mr Heenan claims he will effect on the group's return to New Zealand.

Mr Heenan betrays his professional integrity by, for instance, saying to the entire brass section, that they, quote, 'had better pray that I am not on any Arts Council panel in the future.' The brass section was then assured that they would not receive any help from this body. Also comments such as, 'I may put in a good word for you at your NZSO audition', always with the pleas that we play well for him. He has often accused individuals of deliberately playing badly. Comments such as these were not only a serious slight on the musical integrity of those involved, but in every case were untrue and never provoked.

Mr Heenan seems to suddenly explode into intense personal attacks, aimed at not improving a performance by constructive criticism, but at making one play well at the threat of one's musical career being ruined.

His methods contrast sharply with those employed by other conductors with whom members of the orchestra have performed. At the Festival the orchestra had the benefit of working and performing with a guest conductor. This conductor encouraged us to 'enjoy the music, to relax, to smile a little but still be serious.' He was attacked and mimicked maliciously and unfairly by Mr Heenan at subsequent rehearsals. This had a detrimental effect on the orchestra's performance with both conductors. His attacks on individuals affect the younger members most dramatically, since they are at the stage where their whole attitude to music as a hobby, is being shaped.

Older members have developed immunity to these methods employed by Mr Heenan. They will simply wait and sit there until it is over. It is worthless doing anything else – we have tried to reason, to explain, to apologise. Mr Heenan even admitted to several senior players, after one of his 'attacks' that he was surprised after this bout of sarcasm (as he called it) that not a single member had batted an eyelid. He reasoned that this must be because we were all tired after our long trip. Not so, we have had enough!

Conductors who require their musicians to become immune to their rehearsal methods also find that the orchestra will become immune to their entire musical outlook. It becomes a vicious circle.

Future youth orchestras will not have the experience to deal with this. They must be conducted by an experienced conductor, whose aim is only to make music with young people to the best of their collective ability. This way the NYO will flourish and bring forth many young musicians; at present, it is doomed.

– (signed) members of 1975 National Youth Orchestra of New Zealand.

The letter to Peter Averi

> Please find enclosed a letter to the Director-General of Radio New Zealand; a petition on behalf of the New Zealand National Youth Orchestra 1975 players, urging that a new conductor of the NYO be appointed. We would respectfully ask you to present this letter on our behalf, for we can no longer respect Mr Heenan's musical judgments including his auditioning of orchestra members …
>
> We would like to thank you for your help and support throughout this tour. This tour was of tremendous benefit to all concerned, and we are all convinced that there must be many more tours of New Zealand musicians, particularly of the youth.
>
> Yours sincerely,
>
> (Signed) members of the 1975 National Youth Orchestra of New Zealand.

These two heartfelt letters revealed the full depth of feeling that had developed against the conductor, Averi says. It then became his unpleasant task to pass the letter on to James Hartstonge as a sad indictment on a tour for which such high hopes had been held.

Hartstonge, as a former concert manager, had worked with Heenan as a colleague over two decades, and he and his wife Jean had watched proudly from the audience when National Youth Orchestra members performed with such distinction in the International Festival Orchestra in Aberdeen. Averi confided in Hartstonge, during their visit. 'I said that I was having problems with Heenan, and Jean Hartstonge over-heard me; she prodded Jim, and said, "You're the DG (Director General), you do something about him!" But nothing was done … and I didn't know then, that my suggestion of a letter was to turn into a petition signed by all members.'[7]

At the same time as he presented the players' letter, Averi attached a covering letter of his own. This confirmed that, as the players had written, the tour had indeed been 'marred by the difficult temperament of Mr Heenan, who on many occasions gave vent to displays of ill-manners and fury which both embarrassed and humiliated members of the group'.

'Two courses were open to me, as tour manager', Averi said. 'One was to have a "major show-down" at a number of points very early in the tour.' Certain elements in the orchestra[8] had requested him to do so, but he felt that if he confronted Heenan, 'it might lead to a complete break-down of the tour, that could damage New Zealand's good name, and even force us to return home earlier. The second alternative was to "ride it out" and present the best image possible to outsiders …'

There had been many occasions when the touring group was placed under great stress, Averi confirmed, and management had also spent time 'placating people' they met including festival officials, travel guides, hotel staff, and diplomatic staff, all of whom were subjected on many occasions to vicious outbursts of temper, either directly or as bystanders.

'My chief aim throughout the tour was to keep things on an even keel', Averi said. He had done this to the best of his ability, even to 'swallowing personal insults'. It was his view, that 'Mr Heenan is not a well man and his physical pain often aggravated his behaviour … it is clear that the length of this tour has made this situation less tolerable … I have always supported him and respected his musical integrity … but regret that such attributes have been completely overshadowed by conduct which has shattered the confidence of many people in him'.[9]

In a subsequent undated report on the youth orchestra tour, Peter Averi documented details of its background, travel, accommodation, equipment, health, repertoire, publicity, and finances, together with a full list of all twenty-four performances, with estimated audience figures for each concert, which came to a total of 22,290 overall. No reference was made to the controversial aspects of the tour. As Averi later explained, 'My report was a public document, and I thought at the time that no good purpose would be served by referring to the breakdown in communication. While I felt that Heenan had acted in a very unprofessional manner … I hoped the players' letter and the in-house problems would be dealt with only at the highest level of the Corporation …'[10]

It is not known if Ashley Heenan read the players' letter, but he responded to Peter Averi's accompanying letter, and strongly denied any suggestion of fault. In a four-page diatribe Heenan addressed nineteen points made by Averi, who he blamed for all problems on tour. There were 'bound to be differences of opinion and abrasive situations', Heenan wrote, 'but with co-operation and respect between each other and a mutual understanding of issues and responsibilities involved there is no reason for an assignment not to be successfully concluded'. Because of this, Heenan claimed, he had 'accepted with tolerance and goodwill' several actions on Mr Averi's part. He had complimented him 'on his work in the area of logistics – travel, accommodation, etc …' and said, 'I counted myself fortunate he travelled with the NYO. The main difficulties appeared then and now … to lie in [his] concept of the respective differences between:

> (a) Artistic and Administrative responsibilities; (b) The relative status of Musical Director and Orchestral Manager, when certain social circumstances eventuate

> (c) the general public's attitude (rightly or wrongly) to Music Directors and Tour Managers (d) The players' opinion and those of the Artistic Director when decisions have to be implemented.'

Also at fault were the 'unreasonable demands and arrangements made by Festival organisers … Peter Averi's relevant inexperience … and failure to manage the "dissident group".[11] On the problem of personal relations … it comes back to the public's attitude to a touring group. Musical Directors by circumstances are thrown into the public eye. So that in formal Public Relations, a certain aura surrounds the Conductor. Tour managers can be placed (in these circumstances) in a less prominent position …'[12]

After this revealing observation, Averi addressed and refuted all nineteen points in Heenan's letter with a six-page letter of his own which succinctly underscored the point that Heenan's attitudes had, 'spoilt what could have been a much more pleasant tour for many people'.[13]

By then James Hartstonge, writing on the eve of his retirement from Radio New Zealand,[14] had already delivered his verdict. Having advised Ashley Heenan that he had 'completed a comprehensive investigation of the matters raised by members of the National Youth Orchestra' and acknowledging that 'while the credibility of the document to which the list of signatures was attached is in some doubt[15] there was no reasonable doubt about the impression gained by the majority of members of the Orchestra from remarks made by you overseas, which became the focus of my investigations.' Subsequently more than half of the members, on their individual evidence, confirmed that they had received the impression that there was implicit in the remarks an element of threat:

> This becomes a serious matter when it involves a mature employee entrusted with the artistic control of a large group of young musicians, particularly under the stress conditions encountered in an overseas tour. Despite the strains which undoubtedly existed for the Musical Director in such a rigorous itinerary, there is a self-discipline which is still expected of a person in your position.
>
> On the credit side there is abundant evidence that the great majority of players who received your remarks with apprehension, also appreciated very warmly what you had done to make the tour possible and to make it the artistic success it undoubtedly became. My personal experience of the tour sustains that view.
>
> I find that you acted indiscreetly in allowing the impression to be gained that you were threatening players … That there was a dissident group which was not dealt with firmly and fairly, by the tour management is also clear…[16] but the responsibility in your own case must rest with you. I am therefore impelled to

> reprimand you for a repeated indiscretion which makes it more than an isolated spontaneous reaction. You must learn to control your public reaction to people and events which displease you.[17]
>
> I have decided in your own interests and those of the Corporation that the management of the Schola Musicum is to be placed on a better organised basis. To this end, Mr E F Pople Executive Officer (concerts) is to assume responsibility for management of the Schola Musicum, and to make the distinction between artistic and administrative responsibilities clear, you will be designated Musical Director of the Schola Musicum…
>
> You are instructed to maintain a strictly professional relationship with the trainees to confirm tutorial activities within the specified hours of work for the trainees and to carry out necessary coaching and individual training within the set hours, and on the official Schola Musicum premises.
>
> With these arrangements it is expected that your contribution to the total responsibility of the Corporation will be more fully realised and with less strain to you and to those others directly concerned.

Hartstonge's letter censured Heenan's behaviour on the world tour, and put in place long-overdue provisions for the safety of Schola Musicum players, but it did not mention any other specific concerns raised by players. Glaringly absent, also, was any comment about the future conductorship of the National Youth Orchestra, from which it could be assumed that Heenan's continuation in that role was never in question.

It was acknowledged year after year that the work done by Ashley Heenan could 'not be equated with that of any other supervisor in Radio New Zealand',[18] and that was true. Heenan's role within Broadcasting was without precedent and unique, as was that of the NZSO itself. In the National Orchestra's early years, attempts to enforce public service requirements on symphony orchestra players were unsuccessful, and decades later, similar efforts to equate musicians with other professional groups in Broadcasting (to determine appropriate pay scales) had also failed. There were no groups comparable to the orchestra then, and no other musical directors of training orchestras in New Zealand, to compare with Heenan; who it seems had been left to his own devices, with a minimum of supervision.

Violinist Edward (Ted) Pople has appeared several times in these pages, as an inaugural NYO player, leader, soloist, and from 1966, an NZBC Symphony Orchestra player.[19] In December 1975, Ted Pople resigned from the now NZSO's first violin section, to become the first player to take up an appointment in NZSO management as executive officer and assistant to Ashley Heenan, a newly created position.

Peter Schaffer

'There were a lot of issues politically and upsets between musical and management', at that time, as Ted Pople recalls, 'but we (Ashley and me) got on well, and had a great rapport. I was the sort of person that he felt secure with, and there were no problems.'[20] Ted Pople's duties involved budget issues, arranging tours for Schola Musica, and assisting students. He also travelled with NZSO concertmaster Peter Schaffer to audition prospective NYO players around the country.

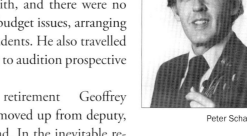

Following James Hartstonge's retirement Geoffrey Whitehead,[21] originally from the BBC, moved up from deputy, to director general of Radio New Zealand. In the inevitable re-shuffle, Ashley Heenan became responsible to Beverley Wakem, Radio New Zealand's new controller of programmes.[22]

The world tour in retrospect

Looking back thirty-five years, the National Youth Orchestra's world tour in 1975 appears an extraordinarily brave, if over-ambitious undertaking. Framed by a week of rehearsals in Christchurch and a 'Welcome Home' concert in the same city two months later, this was a very demanding schedule. Twenty-four performances given in forty-eight days, on a sixty-day tour; twenty-two of them conducted by Ashley Heenan: National Youth Orchestra (seventeen), International Festival Youth Orchestra (two), Schola Musica (five) in seven countries: Scotland, England, Wales, Hong Kong, the People's Republic of China, Japan, and New Zealand.

By today's standards, this tour would be considered severely under-resourced, with its token management team of two people, for an orchestra of fifty-five young players, many of whom were in their mid- to late teens. It was fortunate that no major incidents or accidents occurred, and 'miraculously, not too many health issues', Averi says, 'although three players were hospitalised for a time, and others suffered subsequent problems'.

Securing finance to send even a reduced orchestra on a tour of this magnitude must have seemed so uncertain, that the cost of an additional member of management could have jeopardised the entire enterprise. The conductor did not consider himself to be part of any management team, and his lack of cooperation, belligerence, and erratic behaviour[23] created most of the problems experienced. Peter Averi believed him to be 'physically unwell', but it was Heenan himself who had insisted on conducting all these concerts, although with so many disparate countries and venues, it must have placed him under immense personal pressure, which ultimately, impacted on every member of the touring party.

Despite these difficulties the musical benefits of the tour for the majority of players were obvious, and most thrived on what was a seminal experience.

'NYO 1975 was the highlight!' Marise White says. 'I still reflect on how unbelievably lucky I was to be included. NYO changed my life. Travelling overseas for the first time and in such a safe environment, with such a really friendly bunch as a 17-year-old, I felt very privileged. My overall impression of the whole tour was one of seamless clockwork … I remember the long, long bus rides around the country of Wales. We talked amongst ourselves as to what each of us was going to do after the trip finished, and it was somewhere on this part of it, that I decided to study music. One free weekend my sister Julia White[24] whisked me across the Channel to Brussels where she was studying at the Royal Conservatorium of Music … little did I know then that I would later study viola for four years in Brussels … '

Wilma Smith reflects. 'It's interesting that although there was much agitation among NYO players during our tour about conductor Ashley Heenan's inappropriate behaviour (culminating in a petition to management, and individual letters from many players including myself) my lasting memory and influence is the powerful musical experience we were so lucky to share. By not dwelling on the serious negative issues involving him, I don't wish to trivialise the pain that some of my colleagues suffered – I suppose I was lucky not to be too closely involved and so was able to escape any personal scarring, but [I] deplore the fact that some people were unable to benefit from or enjoy such a wonderful musical opportunity because of their personal trauma.'[25]

The trainee experience

Eleanor Houtman (now Elena), principal second violin,[26] and Alison Heenan (viola)[27] were the librarians.'I was responsible for looking after the music, bowings, photocopying, taping up parts, and so forth', Elena recalls. 'As Trainees we were forced into a situation where we had almost no contact with the rest of the orchestra, and I remember feeling very isolated. As Heenan became aware of the dissension … he grew totally paranoid and would spend hours ranting and raving that everyone was out to "get" him. He used to threaten particular players once back in New Zealand, and say, "Just one word from me could destroy their musical lives!" He put us Trainees in the lead positions for the obvious reason of maintaining control, even when other players may have been better suited, or more experienced. This caused resentment within the orchestra and I felt an undercurrent of ill-will towards me. It was totally exhausting having to do so many NYO and Schola concerts, and as Librarian. We all worked extremely hard, just getting on and doing the job of representing New Zealand's musical youth at this amazing International Youth Festival, and surviving! ... My goal had been to get a scholarship and do further study overseas, but Heenan's verbal abuse and bullying over three years destroyed my confidence and made me feel inadequate to the point where I almost gave up the violin. The NYO tour gave me the opportunity to meet ex-Schola and NYO graduates living the musical dream overseas, and the confidence to contact teachers at Trinity College in London, where I later studied ...'

'Missing out on the International Festival Orchestra was the sort of opportunity the trainees were denied on a regular basis', says Donald Armstrong, a trainee for four years, 1974–77. 'Musical and even social relations with musicians outside the trainees were pretty much impossible. We were not allowed to audition for the International Orchestra ostensibly because the trainees had concerts.[28]

'A youth orchestra is an *educational* organisation, and Ashley Heenan displayed no such skills, any educator would see the unbelievable benefit of the International orchestra, but he had failings as a conductor, and music educator. I come from a family of teachers. I don't know anyone who has learnt when in a constantly terrified state. He actively denigrated "soloists" and he prevented trainees from practicing virtuoso works (a staple for a developing string player). There were no outside educators brought in. As a conductor, he was not really taught and seemed to have insecurity about it. The beat was very nervous and there was little expressivity. While a high level of expertise may not be expected for a training orchestra conductor, he was not taken seriously by NZSO musicians.

'My four years in the trainees gave me exposure to the NZSO and let them know about me. My first gig with the NZSO was at age 17 to play Beethoven 9. I remember that wonderful experience to this day and it then became my dream to get a job in the NZSO. Ashley was away at the time and he subsequently told me off, for thinking I was "good enough to play with the NZSO" – well, they asked me! I think it is important for young players to have experience with the NZSO as it will attract them to audition later on … Fortunately the NYO continues to give young players that valuable association with the NZSO.'

Donald's experience as a trainee was 'not enjoyable', he says, although being stage manager on the NYO tour, 'was *extremely* enjoyable. As an eighteen year old I had no idea of the responsibility I was taking on and it was never a worry (apart from one time when an airline damaged some instruments). It was a great way to see another side of the countries away from the group, and I loved it!'

Three months after the tour, fallout had threatened the NZSO recording of Douglas Lilburn's second symphony. This was scheduled for 25 November 1975, but the day before, the NZSO Players Committee through its chairman Wilfred Simenauer[29] gave formal notice that 'members had voted not to perform under Ashley Heenan'.

Peter Averi remembers that he addressed the orchestra, next day, as directed by Beverley Wakem, and pointed out that, '"regardless of what players thought of any conductor, it was their professional duty to perform in accordance with the Players Agreement, and therefore Mr Heenan was entitled to the same courtesy, as any conductor." I then suspended the call for some minutes for players to discuss this, and soon after, the then leader John Chisholm, came to say they were ready to begin. It appears there were two petitions, the first signed by 16 players objecting to Ashley Heenan conducting the rehearsal, and 35 disassociating themselves from the others; it was not unanimous. This recording later received an industry award, and Heenan conducted the NZSO on occasions afterwards.'[30]

1976

Rotorua & Auckland, 27 & 28 August. Conductor: James Robertson.
Glinka – Overture *Russlan and Ludmilla*; Rimsky-Korsakov – Suite *Le Coq D'or*; Haydn – Symphony no 100 in G, *The Military*; Arnold – *English Dances* (set 1); Tchaikovsky – 'Tatiana's Letter Scene', from *Eugene Onegin*; Canteloube arr. – *Songs of the Auvergne* (Milla Andrew, soprano)

After an eventful year in 1975, it was fortunate that the conductor engaged for 1976 was an old friend, James Robertson, the well-regarded former principal conductor of the National Orchestra and NZBC Concert Orchestra. Robertson had returned to New Zealand primarily as musical director of two concert performances of Puccini's opera *Turandot* by the New Zealand Opera Company and the New Zealand Symphony Orchestra.[31] Milla Andrew, Angela Shaw, Tony Benfell, and Bruce Carson were the soloists in a production notable as the first for the opera in New Zealand, and the golden jubilee of the opera itself. It was an interesting coincidence when, three months later, Radio New Zealand celebrated the 50th anniversary of Broadcasting in New Zealand. Both golden jubilee concerts were held in the Wellington Town Hall,

Left: Soprano soloist Milla Andrew, 1976

Right: Conductor James Robertson, 1976

then under threat of demolition, as an earthquake risk, but ultimately saved by a vigorous public response, and strong representation from the NZSO and its visiting conductors.

During his tenure as the National Orchestra's conductor Robertson had expressed his wish 'to start a youth orchestra', but it was John Hopkins who made that wish come true. The National Youth Orchestra was already in place under Hopkins, when Robertson returned to New Zealand in 1962–64 to be concurrently conductor of the NZBC Concert Orchestra[32] and the artistic and musical director of the National Opera Company.

Conducting his first National Youth Orchestra, Robertson chose a programme that reflected his many years conducting opera,[33] and he invited soprano Milla Andrew[34] from the recent *Turandot* to be the first international singer to perform with the orchestra.

It was a relatively young and inexperienced National Youth Orchestra that assembled for Robertson in 1976. Many world tour players were no longer eligible by age, and only seventeen had re-joined, to provide 'a valuable core of experience'[35] and, for the first time since the training scheme began, there were no trainees. 'It was a difficult situation for Radio New Zealand', says Peter Averi. 'The players' petition obligated the Corporation to prevent a similar situation developing between Ashley Heenan and the orchestra, but, as a permanent member of staff, and director of the Training Scheme, the only disciplinary action that could be taken was to prevent him ever again being associated with the NYO. It was deemed untenable for the Trainees to play in that orchestra, and the easy solution was to suspend the Trainees. It was then decided to cancel the entire NYO, which would have been a rather heavy-handed demonstration that the previous conductor would not be involved, but the engagement of James Robertson as guest conductor cleared the air.'[36]

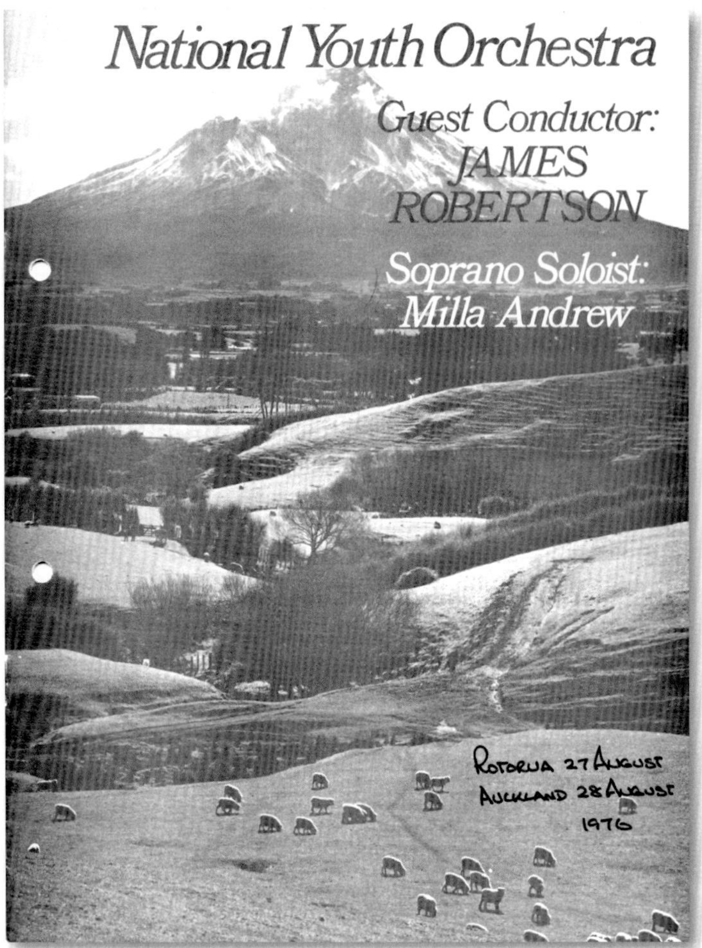

National Youth Orchestra
Guest Conductor:
JAMES
ROBERTSON
Soprano Soloist:
Milla Andrew
Rotorua 27 August
Auckland 28 August
1976

1976 programme cover

1977

The National Youth Orchestra performed to acclaim under James Robertson in 1976, and it was confidently expected to do so again, under another new guest conductor, in 1977. Instead, Ashley Heenan was reinstated. For many observers at that time (as now), Heenan's retention as musical director of the renamed Schola Musica[37] remains difficult to explain. Rumours about Heenan had persisted for some years, but it appears that few official complaints were made against him, until players returned from the world tour, and their experiences became known. Then, amid reports that some had turned away from music as a result, the announcement was made that Ashley Heenan would conduct the 1977 National Youth Orchestra – as if there were no other suitable contenders available and the problems on the world tour eighteen months before had never occurred. Anger and disbelief greeted this announcement, and prompted another wave of angry letters from all around the country. They came from prominent members of the music community, including professional musicians, academics, and music teachers, former National Youth Orchestra players, local and regional youth orchestras, and almost all condemned what many considered to be an insensitive if not arrogant decision to reinstate the former musical director. In parallel with these complaints, several players from the 1975 world tour sent passionate letters of protest to both Radio New Zealand and the NZSO. Among them, Ken Young, who said that he was 'bitterly disappointed at the apparent disregard for the sentiments expressed by those who had to cope with the totally irrational behaviour of the conductor for two months overseas … I personally still hold the same views now as I did eighteen months ago … there were numerous instances where Mr Heenan abused players to the extent they became nervous wrecks ... The orchestra's general reaction to Mr Heenan behind his back was severely hostile, certainly not to his face as that would have meant an almost certain barrage of threats and abuse … I'm concerned for the future of the young musicians in this country … so many people have been totally disillusioned by [his] approach to conducting and his general sarcastic and abusive behaviour on the platform. Surely this is not worth risking where new younger players in the National Youth Orchestra are concerned. The one point that amazes me is that in New Zealand alone there are conductors capable of training a youth orchestra and attaining orchestral discipline based upon a love of music and not fear …' Ken Young expressed his wish that consideration be given to the 'opinions of those who have previously played under Mr Heenan' before calling together, an orchestra, 'made up of those young people who have not'.[38]

Several writers said that these were not the first letters Radio New Zealand had received on the subject of Heenan's continuing intimidation, personal attacks on players, 'vitriolic sarcasm and uncontrolled outbursts'. Many others pointed out that this was something that they had 'never experienced with any other professional musicians and such tactics were not only unhelpful, but destructive and positively counter productive in achieving the best musical results'.[39]

There was disappointment that protests after the world tour were 'apparently so easily disregarded', and the recommendation of two prominent local conductors as, 'more suitable candidates'. Although both conductors wrote immediately, disclaiming any association with this protest, many others signed petitions representing most, if not all, of the country's established youth orchestras.

Some letters of support were received for Ashley Heenan and what he had achieved, but the overall anger and fall-out was such that in March, at a time when the audition process and planning would normally be in place, Peter Averi regretfully had to recommend to Radio New Zealand that, for the first time in its history, the youth orchestra should be 'abandoned'.

The decision to cancel the orchestra in 1977 was made reluctantly, but was inevitable as more and more players accepted for the NYO wrote to notify their withdrawal. Ashley Heenan's contract as conductor was revoked at short notice,[40] and the NZSO was obliged to contact remaining players, to advise them that there were 'not sufficient applications received for the orchestra this year' amid fears that it might never resume.The *Sunday News* reported the cancellation: 'New Zealand Super Music kids are out of luck. There won't be a National Youth Orchestra this year, and the official reason is there's not sufficient interest ... Not enough people have auditioned for the group so its baton in mothballs and curtain down on New Zealand's top young music makers in 1977 ... Though the orchestra will lapse in 77, Mr Nisbet said all players who were accepted will be brought together next year for a concert...'[41]

Cellist Michael Vinten was accepted for the first time for the NYO in 1977, and he recalls his 'disappointment when it was cancelled'. Michael never had another opportunity to play as a member of the orchestra, and says that he would have been very surprised to know then, that in a few years hence 'I would not only become the NYO's assistant conductor for six years, but also conductor of its second overseas tour'.[42]

After 'the aftermath'

On 11 July 1977 Pat Downey, chairman, Radio New Zealand,[43] advised a meeting of the Orchestra Advisory Committee[44] that 'Mr Heenan has stated he proposes taking legal action concerning the persons making complaints...' but there would be 'no action on the complaints until legal issues [are] determined...'

The nature of these complaints was not mentioned, but almost certainly this statement refers to letters sent to Broadcasting about the appointment of Ashley Heenan as conductor of the youth orchestra for 1977. Again, it is not known whether Heenan was shown these letters, or whether he undertook any action against the writers. Little over three months later, on 29 October, while playing croquet, he suffered a myocardial infarction and was admitted to Hutt Hospital.[45] Released on 10 November, Heenan spent almost three months recuperating although he was reportedly anxious to 'get back and conduct a full dress rehearsal' within a month or so of this acute illness.

Royal Youth Concert, conductor Juan Matteucci, Wellington Town Hall, 1966

Martin Lamb doing a Highland fling in his new kilt, in Aberdeen. 1975. *Kevin Currie.*

Arrival and official welcome in Peking (Beijing). 1975. *Marise NcNeill.*

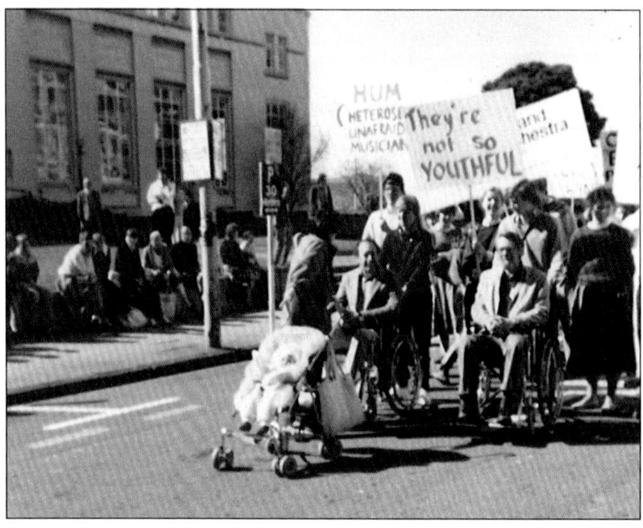

NZNYO players prepare for a march through Wellington city streets, pushing their conductor Doron Salomon and manager Alwyn Palmer in wheelchairs, because, as one billboard declares: 'They're not so Youthful!' *Palmer*

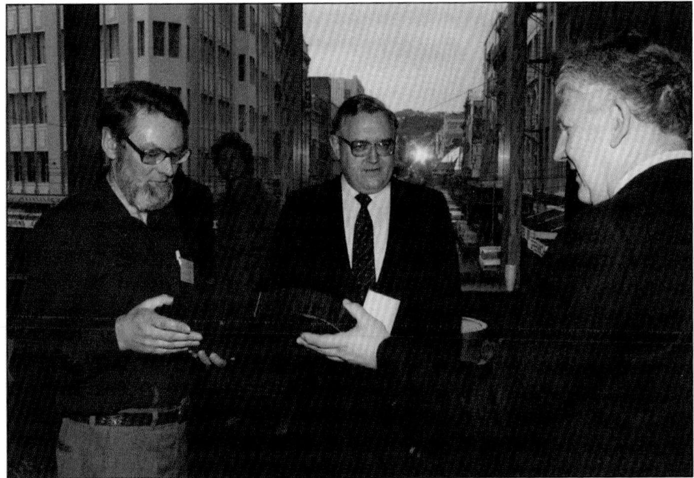

Hon Jonathan Hunt, Postmaster General, centre, Peter Nisbet, NZSO general manager, right, and Alwyn Palmer, NZPYO manager, left, with the especially-built violin case used by New Zealand Post to deliver its $20,000 sponsorship cheque to the New Zealand Post Youth Orchestra. 1985.

Players on the steps outside Hamilton Girls High School
Mark Sheppard, 1986

Jamming at NZYO *Mark Sheppard, 1987*

Michael Vinten, assistant conductor, and players in a peaceful march through Hagley Park to advertise the NZNYO's Christchurch concert
Palmer, 1987

Pius XII Seminary, Banyo, Queensland
Palmer, 1988.

Michael Vinten conducts brass players at Brisbane Expo *Palmer, 1988*.

Te Rangatahi Cultural Group performing at Brisbane Expo *Palmer, 1988.*

Leader Lisa Egen, Gudrun Scharnke, Tim Sutton, ?, Helen Polglasse at a schools performance 1988, Melbourne

In rehearsal for the 1988 Australian Tour. Leader Lisa Egen, deputy leader Marcel Trussell-Cullen.

Above: American conductor James Sedares conducted the orchestra for three consecutive years, 1993–96

Right: Susannah Lees-Jeffries, deputy-principal, double bass (successful audition, 24 May 1996). John Dodds, leader second violins, was also a member of the NYO auditioning committee with Peter Averi, and then Peter Schaffer.

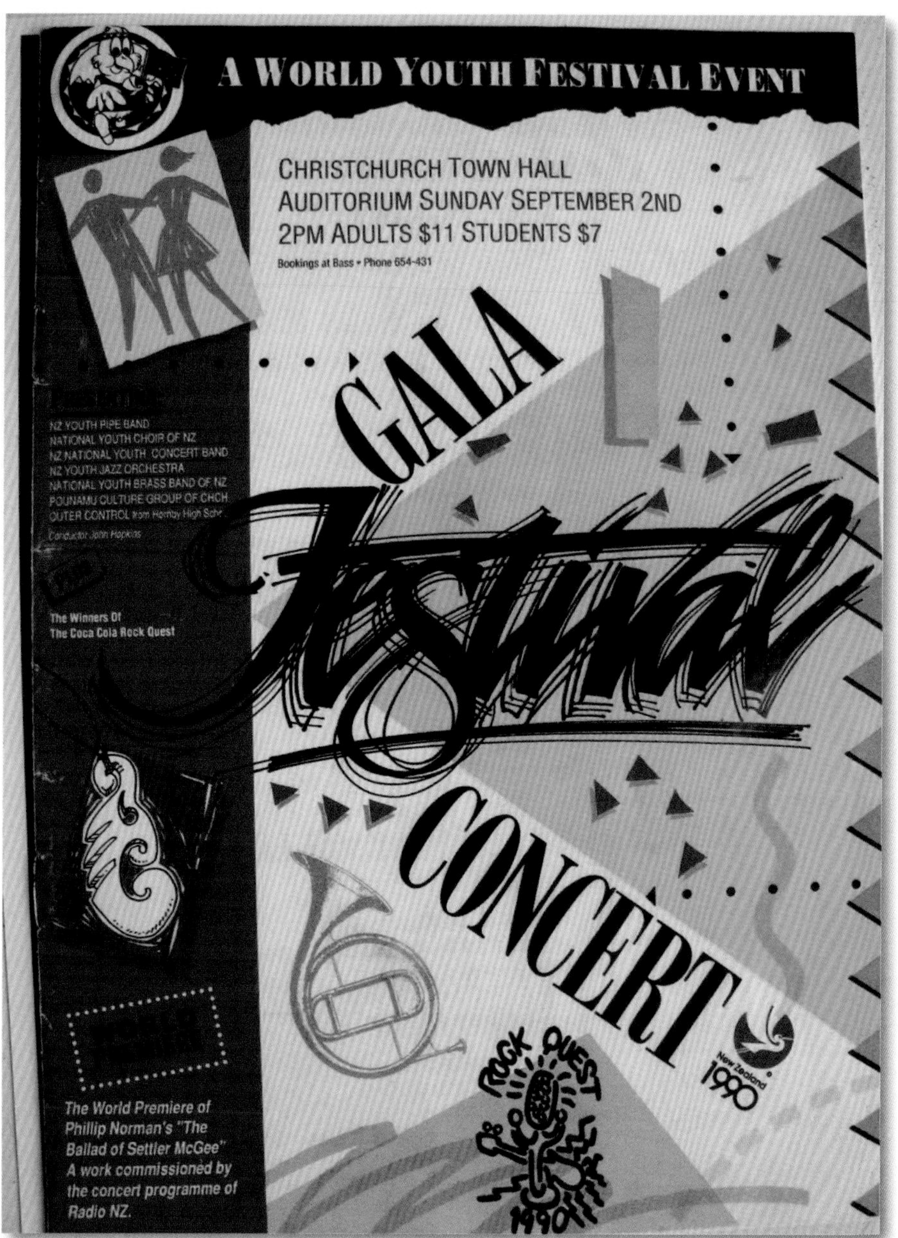

Poster for a World Youth Festival event in Christchurch, 1990

1999. Conductor Ben Zander rehearsing in the Adam Concert Room, Victoria University, before the orchestra's 40th anniversary concert.

NZSO chief executive Ian Fraser, solo pianist Justin Bird, and guest conductor Lutz Köhler, 2001
Mabel Wong

NYO manager Brigid O'Meeghan (standing far right), with five players from NYO 2003, who were seconded into the NZSO. Back: Amanda Verner, viola; Sarah McCracken, violin; Julia McCarthy, violin. Front: Christina Thompson, cello; James Andrewes, Violin.

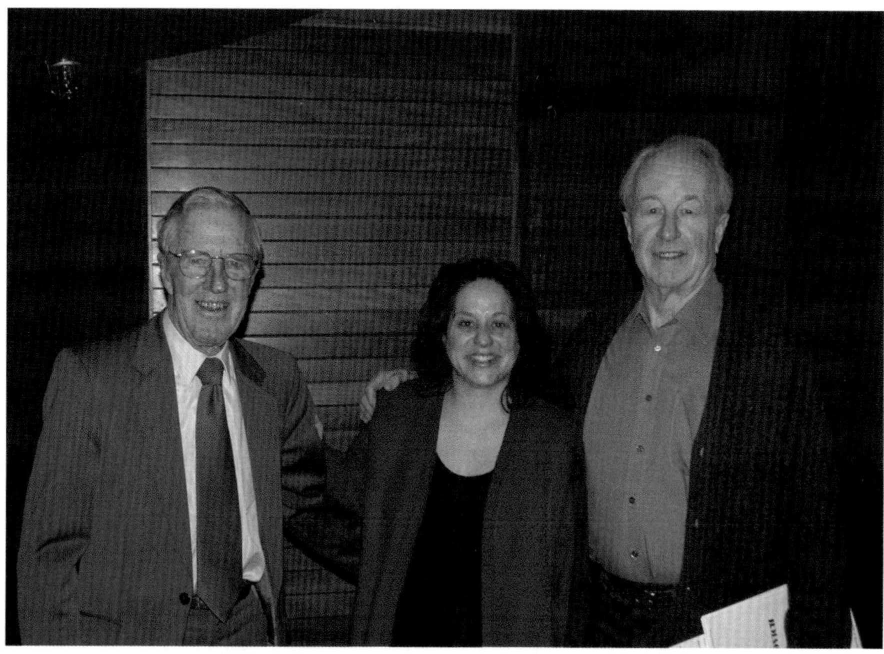

NZSO NYO tour executive David Pawsey, manager Pascale Parenteau, and conductor Simon Streatfeild
MW2006

Top: Robin Toan, the first composer-in-residence with mentor, John Psathas, 2005

Middle: Green room chaos, 2005 *Mabel Wong*

Botom: Conductor Jacques Lacombe and soprano Madeleine Pierard, in performance, Michael Fowler Centre, 2008
© Robert Catto/www.catto.co.nz

That dress rehearsal would have been for a performance by the Schola Musica in December 1977 at St Andrews on the Terrace. Instead the group was led by Donald Armstrong, and conducted by Ted Pople as acting musical director. Ashley Heenan returned to duty on 24 January 1978.

Fifteen months later, Ted Pople resigned from the NZSO, on 12 April 1979, to take up a prestigious appointment as Secretary to the School of Music at the Victorian College of the Arts in Melbourne,[46] where John Hopkins was Dean.

The position of executive officer and assistant to Ashley Heenan ceased on Ted Pople's resignation, and his other duties were absorbed by the NZSO management. Heenan, who previously was directly responsible to Beverley Wakem, had become responsible to Peter Nisbet on his appointment to the dual roles of general manager and artistic director of the NZSO.

By the end of 1977 the NZSO was packing up to leave 38 The Terrace after thirteen years. The former Broadcasting studios would soon be demolished to make way for a splendid new building that would incorporate a 'Symphony Hall' for the NZSO and trainees. When that and subsequent other plans fell through, the three-storied 1921 brick 'McDonalds' building, and another two old wooden buildings, in Willis Street, were hastily obtained and refurbished, as the first Symphony House. The music library and a common room for NZSO players were on the ground floor, and the NZSO studio in a connecting building (a former billiard saloon), with management offices on the second and third floors, on which there was also a dedicated studio for the Schola Musica.

It was to this building that Ashley Heenan returned to work, in January 1978, following his illness. One of his first actions after that was to set in motion proceedings to take the Broadcasting Corporation to court, lodging a claim for $30,000 for loss of earnings as a result of his removal as Conductor of the National Youth Orchestra in 1977.

Heenan v *Broadcasting Corporation of New Zealand* was heard in the Supreme Court on 24 April 1979. It was claimed by the defence that, in May and June 1977, 'certain groups of people attended meetings with representatives of the defendant, and made allegations against the plaintiff, and sought to have the plaintiff's appointment as Musical Director and conductor of the National Youth Orchestra terminated. The plaintiff was not given notice of the allegations or representations made … and on or about 17 June representatives of the defendant invited him to a meeting at which he was asked to relinquish his position. He refused to do so …[47]

'It is further said that he sought confirmation of the specific allegations made against him and that no such information was provided and that at no stage was he given "a fair opportunity of being heard or of giving his explanation or of putting his case in answer to the allegations made against him…'

It was claimed that as a result of this action 'the Plaintiff had been gravely injured in his character credit and reputation and in the way of his profession and office. And had suffered anxiety, stress, humiliation and concern which subsequently caused or contributed to the Plaintiff suffering a coronary attack following which he was admitted to hospital … for two weeks and unable to work for some further eight weeks. As a further result … the Plaintiff has suffered a loss of income and will in the future suffer further economic loss …[and] through loss of invitations to conduct various other orchestras that had ceased to be forthcoming.' In the judgment it is stated: 'Action dismissed with costs to the defendant: $300.00.'[48] In an agreement subsequent to that decision it was advised that Mr Heenan would not pursue his appeal if the Corporation did not pursue its order for costs in the Supreme Court and allowed the security to be refunded.' The Corporation agreed then that it 'would not pursue its order for costs in the Supreme Court, if you formally abandon the appeal … if Mr Heenan 'executes a release in respect of all claims now or hereafter arising out of the matters alleged in the statement of claim in this action and will not raise any question about the security lodged in the Court of Appeal if you undertake that this will be refunded intact to Mr Heenan'.[49]

Postscript

Ashley Heenan never conducted the National Youth Orchestra after the 1975 world tour, but he remained musical director of Schola Musica for a further seven years. In 1981 he received the CANZ award.[50] In 1983, he received the OBE, and was appointed a member of the New Zealand Croquet Council (a lifetime interest). Then, after a 42-year career in the New Zealand Broadcasting and New Zealand Symphony Orchestra, Heenan opted to take retirement leave. On 28 November 1984, he conducted the Schola Musica for the last time in a lunchtime concert at St Andrews on the Terrace, after which a small, low-key farewell was held at Symphony House, attended by colleagues from NZSO and Radio New Zealand, and current Schola Musica players.

John Hopkins, whose wife Rosemary had recently passed away, sent a gracious message. 'As the originator of the idea in 1959, I want to say thank you, from the bottom of my heart, for having cared for and nurtured the real meaning of the project…' This tribute was published in *Concert Pitch,*[51] together with another from Peter Averi, his colleague for over thirty years, while Peter Nisbet ceded his editorial space to Ashley Heenan, who in a guest editorial gave credit to Broadcasting, John Hopkins, the National Youth Orchestra, and the Orchestra Training Scheme.

It was the end of a controversial era for Radio New Zealand and its precursors; New Zealand Symphony Orchestra, National Youth Orchestra and in particular, the Schola Musica. There is no doubt that this group made many positive achievements from 1961 to 1984, but these were too often overshadowed by the controversy that seemed always to surround its musical director.

Ashley Heenan's legacy has been tarnished by negative aspects of his character, at the expense of his very real accomplishments and achievements as a musician and composer. His abrasiveness and temper tantrums have become legendary to former National Youth Orchestra players, and trainees, who it was said, observed an unwritten rule, 'to always maintain a certain facial expression known as "the Trainee look"' when he was in the room. Some still do not want to hear his name mentioned, and will not say it themselves; while there are others who say that he could be 'charming' and even 'charismatic'.

Glenda Craven (now van Drimmelen) was briefly married to Ashley Heenan and agrees that 'it wasn't all bad about Ashley, and there were things to admire about him. He was very loyal to his parents, and I don't doubt his musicianship, he was very absorbing as a teacher, and really promoted Lilburn and string music.

'But he was very stroppy, a control freak, and always a perfectionist. He pushed people into situations, making them play solos when they didn't feel prepared enough.'[52]

Violists Linda Roberts Simmons, and Alison Bowcott,[53] both former trainees and youth orchestra players, retain good memories. 'Ashley paid my travel expenses to enable me to regularly travel from Wanganui to Wellington, for viola lessons', Linda says, and Alison appreciated his assistance in buying a new viola. 'I was working in a motel on Saturdays, to earn money, and Ashley arranged for Reg Sutton[54] to sell me one of his, for a very reasonable price: $750. Ashley's training enabled me to have a fantastic career in the NZSO and music in general, and I am passing on to my students many of the things that he taught me. His temper and demanding behaviour seemed no different to me than anyone else [in those days]. I resigned three times, and he just told me to "stop wasting time", and tore up my letters. He tried to control my friends, and who my flatmates were, he was sarcastic, telling me I was "hopeless" but that only made me try harder, and I needed that. I thought I was a fantastic player because I was leading the Dunedin Youth Orchestra, but I was quite wrong! If I had known what a chasm there was between my amateur standard and a really professional standard, I don't believe I would have even attempted to be a musician. I realise that Ashley's methods did not work for everyone, but in those days there were many more autocratic conductors, and he certainly prepared us for the likes of Georg Tintner and Franz-Paul Decker. I'll always be grateful to him for giving me the gift of music at a professional level.'

Ashley Heenan and the Schola Musica were synonymous for twenty-four years, and there was speculation that Radio New Zealand would be disinclined to continue this costly and controversial institution. But then the position of musical director was announced. It attracted some high-calibre applicants, and the Heenan era ended. Within a few months, *Concert Pitch*[55] in the same issue farewelled Ashley Heenan – and welcomed his successor. A new musical director was to lead the Schola Musica in a new direction, in 1985.

7 Guest Conductors – and an Australian Tour

1978–1988

'…our Trans-Tasman cousins gave a vibrant, moving concert ... This kind of concert makes one long for many more such cultural exchanges …'

– *Newcastle Courier, 20 August 1988*

The National Youth Orchestra's new era began in 1978, its 19th season. The days of a permanent resident conductor were over and from now on (with a couple of notable exceptions), the orchestra, like the New Zealand Symphony Orchestra itself, would be conducted by a stream of international guest conductors, interspersed with a few New Zealanders.

The change was significant. Under the old system the resident conductor of the National Youth Orchestra had provided continuity, with knowledge of the orchestra's past and present players over many years. This was information not readily available to incoming guest conductors. As a result, increased responsibility would be required of the orchestra manager to provide the vital, ongoing link. The manager for this year certainly had a very good knowledge of the workings of the orchestra. He was a foundation member, had been the leader and soloist, and now Ted Pople would become manager.

Incidental oboes in Schubert's Symphony No 9

1978

Napier, 2 September. Conductor: John Hopkins. Mozart – Overture *The Magic Flute*; Ives – *The Unanswered Question*; Mendelssohn – Violin Concerto in E minor (Peter Schaffer, violin); Schubert – Symphony no 9

After the doom and gloom predictions that followed its cancelled concert in 1977, the National Youth Orchestra confounded the sceptics and bounced back with increased vigour in 1978. There was just the one concert, in Napier, but it was significant for a number of reasons. Among them were the welcome return of founder John Hopkins, and a first opportunity to hear the NZSO's new concertmaster Peter Schaffer[1] perform Mendelssohn's Violin Concerto with the orchestra. This was also Peter Nisbet's first concert in his new role as general manager and artistic director of the NZSO. In the printed programme Nisbet welcomed John Hopkins, by now dean of the School of Music at the Victorian College of the Arts in Melbourne and, quoting André Previn,[2] gave a timely affirmation of the relevance of the youth orchestra: 'The fact that the bells are supposedly tolling the death knell for the symphony orchestra seems to me to be premature. If there is in our time a twentieth-century phenomenon known as the youth orchestra, then it stands to reason that there will be a twenty-first century symphony orchestra.'[3]

Nisbet's message was unequivocal: the National Youth Orchestra was relevant, it was performing again, and, despite yet more restructuring, it was still administered by the NZSO and financed (as usual) from 'broadcasting revenue'. The mood was upbeat, with both the NZSO and Schola Musica settling into the new Symphony House, in its more vibrant location in central Wellington.

In just over two years Peter Schaffer had become 'an indispensable part of New Zealand's musical life'. He was credited with the continuing high standard of the NZSO's performance, and as an 'outstanding' soloist with the NZSO, and now the youth orchestra. Schaffer had revitalised the audition procedure, and replaced the nineteen-year-old system – by which players did their audition at their local radio station, and their tapes were then sent on to be assessed in Wellington.

1978 programme cover

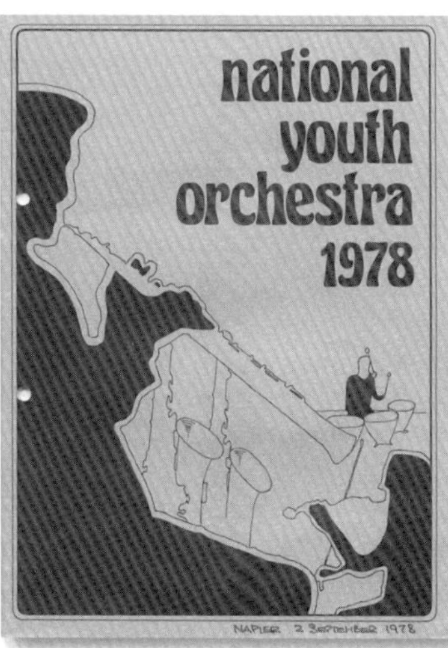

In 1978 Peter Schaffer introduced live auditions for everyone who applied for the youth orchestra. A committee of two members, himself and either Peter Averi or Ted Pople (and later Michael Vinten), would travel to each centre in New Zealand to meet between 150 and 200 young players, usually aged between thirteen and twenty-four years, and hear every audition. In this first year of the new system, Schaffer met and auditioned all 180 auditionees who were applying for sixty-eight positions available.

Violinist Glenda Rodgers (NYO 1977–80) says, 'I owe a lot to my NYO days which gave me invaluable orchestral experience. In particular I remember Peter Schaffer who taught so much with his gentle and very focused manner; the excellent conductors, but most of all the fun we all had together as young players. It really was like a big family – no, better than a family!'[4]

Georg Tintner. *NZSO publicity*

1979

Hamilton, Auckland, 25 & 26 August. Conductor: Georg Tintner. Beethoven – Overture *Coriolan* op 62; Hindemith – Symphony *Mathis der Maler* (Matthias the Painter); Rossini – 'Slander Song' (*Barber of Seville*) and Mozart – 'Within These Sacred Walls' (*The Magic Flute*) (Malcolm Smith, bass); Buchanan – *Missa De Angelis – Pro Anno Infantantum*, 1979; Beethoven – Symphony no 5

The National Youth Orchestra celebrated its 20th season in 1979 with two concerts under Viennese conductor Georg Tintner, another who fitted comfortably into both national and international categories. A member of the Vienna Boys Choir from 1927 to 1931, Tintner escaped from Vienna after the Anschluss and came to New Zealand as a refugee from Nazism in 1940. Over the next forty years he made an important contribution to New Zealand music, as musical director of the New Zealand Opera Company, and guest conductor of the National Orchestra, NZBCSO, and NZSO many times in the years from 1953 to 1995, in tandem with his international career as a conductor and composer.[5]

Georg Tintner had seemed quite frail, and players were surprised by his great reserves of energy. Mary Sewell (NYO violin, 1979, 1982–84)[6] remembers that 'he would rehearse us into the night, well beyond the official ending time of rehearsal'. Terry Gibbs (NYO double bass, 1979–83) thought Tintner was 'working the strings to death, and not seeming to be aware of any set rehearsal times'.[7] Jeff McNeill (NYO bassoon/contrabassoon, 1979) says that, 'despite studying Beethoven's 5th to death at university, Tintner brought new life to this great work for me. The NYO was something to aspire to… a confirmation that I could play at a high level. I was accepted into the Royal Brussels Conservatoire for two years, and had a great time, finally becoming a bassoonist, rather than just playing one.'[8]

Bass soloist Malcolm Smith, 1979

The 20th anniversary programme was notable for the inclusion of a new composition commissioned by the NZSO, a *Mass of the*

Top left: composer Dorothy Buchanan, 1979 *Euan Sarginson*

Bottom left: conductor Uri Segal, 1980

Right: 1979 programme cover

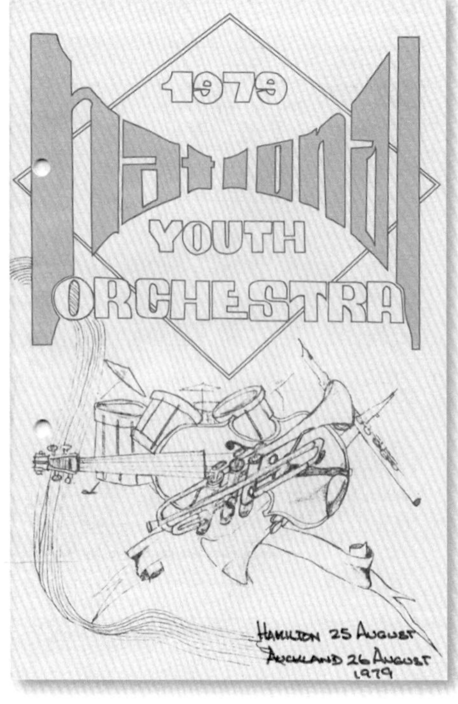

Angels for the Year of the Child by the young New Zealand composer, Dorothy Buchanan, New Zealand's first composer-in-schools. The soloist was baritone Malcolm Smith, a scientist, who was winner of the 1979 Mobil Song Quest.

The eighties had arrived, and the numbers auditioning for the National Youth Orchestra grew, with 200 hopefuls seeking places in 1980. The high standards being achieved by the orchestra were reflected by the status of its first conductor for the new decade, the Israeli Uri Segal.[9]

1980

Paraparaumu & Wellington, 29 & 30 August. Conductor: Uri Segal.
Beethoven – Overture *Leonora no 3*; Chloe Moon – *Episodes for String Orchestra*; Hummel – Trumpet Concerto in E; Stravinsky – Ballet Suite *Petrushka*

The Southward Theatre, situated in the Southward Car Museum, the home of an amazing collection of vintage cars, proved an unusual if perhaps distracting new venue for the youth orchestra's first concert on the Kapiti Coast; with a second concert held in the Wellington Town Hall. Special features of both performances were a composition by another young New Zealand composer,

Chloe Moon from Christchurch, and a performance of the Hummel Trumpet Concerto by New Zealand trumpeter Grant Cooper (NYO 1971–75). Having distinguished himself on the 1975 NYO World Tour, Grant had been awarded a Queen Elizabeth II Arts Council award to study in the United States a year later, and he has lived there ever since.[10]

'They were great days for me', says Richard Wigley of his years playing bassoon (NYO 1979–80). 'Enjoyable repertoire, interesting conductors, and plenty of contact with high quality NZSO players ... [The National Youth Orchestra experience] gave me more confidence at a key moment in my development, and brought me into contact with similarly committed musicians.'[11] This was the final youth orchestra year for violinist Catherine Jane (née Mountfort). Catherine was a member of the world tour orchestra, as was Philip Jane.[12] The couple had since married, and by now 'a mum', Catherine was enjoying her last chance to play as a member of the youth orchestra, which she had first joined eight years before, in 1973.

This was a significant year for the National Youth Orchestra, which received financial assistance from the commercial sector for the first time. The Bank of New Zealand became its first commercial sponsor, 'to help ensure that this successful showcase for the talented young musicians of this country can continue to fulfil its wide range of activities'.[13]

Conductor Christopher Seaman, 1981

1981

Nelson, 29 August. Conductor: Christopher Seaman. Heenan – *Nelson College* Overture; Arnold – *Scottish Dances*; Britten – 'The Nurses' Song' (*A Charm of Lullabies*); Glück – *Che Faro Senza Euridice*; Dona – Symphony no 8

A leading British conductor, Christopher Seaman, began his musical career with Britain's National Youth Orchestra, and later became noted for his work with young people. Young New Zealand players benefited from the experience that Seaman brought when, on his second New Zealand tour with the NZSO, he conducted New Zealand's youth orchestra in one concert at Nelson College, Nelson, for the college's 125th anniversary.

The programme began appropriately with an overture written in 1957 by Ashley Heenan, an old boy of the college, into which was woven the 'Boys College Song', and fragments from 'Willow the King', 'Gaudeamus', and the 'Girls College Song'. The soloist for the Britten and Glück was New Zealand

British conductor Christopher Seaman conducting the youth orchestra at Nelson College, in Nelson, with soloist Linden Loader, mezzo soprano.

mezzo soprano Linden Loader, winner of the 1981 Mobil Song Quest, who planned to use her prize money for study with Dame Joan Hammond, in Melbourne.

All rehearsals and the performance were held in the school hall, the heating for which, as manager Alwyn Palmer recalls, was 'only turned on by school authorities, during the winter term. As this was the holidays after that term, the heating was turned off, not to be fired up again until next winter! That August in Nelson was pretty cold, so the players, and Chris Seaman, were not so happy.'

Sandra Crawshaw (NYO violin, 1981–83) was fifteen. 'I had never played in a full orchestra before, and so I was almost overwhelmed by the experience. My best memory is probably the first rehearsal. I was a second violinist and just remember being surrounded by the incredible sound…of everything. First time away from home too, so I did a bit of growing up! I made a lot of friends and caught up with them each year.'[14]

Images from 1982. (l–r): soloist Mark Walton; conductor Meredith Davies; the programme cover.

1982

Tauranga, Te Kuiti, Auckland, 27–29 August. Conductor: Meredith Davies. Dukas – *Fanfare from La Péri*; Copland – Ballet Suite *Billy the Kid*; Malcolm Arnold – Concerto for Clarinet and Strings; Tchaikovsky – Symphony no 5

Welsh conductor Meredith Davies, CBE, President of Trinity College and conductor of the Royal Choral Society, conducted three concerts by a newly renamed New Zealand Youth Orchestra.[15]

The change of name after twenty-three years was considered 'appropriate' to 'tie in with the New Zealand Symphony Orchestra and reflect its national identity'. At the same time, 'a new phase in the orchestra's development' was announced, 'in which greater emphasis is to be placed on the potential and the advancement of players'.[16]

The role of the youth orchestra in providing experience for young New Zealand musicians was now very well established. The majority of players appointed to the NZSO were former New Zealand Youth Orchestra players, and in the past year alone six members of the NYO World Tour had joined the orchestra.[17] Apart from some principal positions, most vacancies now could be recruited within New Zealand – as John Hopkins had foreseen, all those years ago.

Winner of the Shell Youth Scholarship 1983 Caroline Cave (cello), and runners-up Peter Black (cello), and Helen Watson (violin), presented by Greg Aim, Shell NZ Holdings Co Ltd, and Peter Averi, NZSO

The Shell Youth Scholarship

The second outside sponsorship of the New Zealand Youth Orchestra stemmed from an association between NZSO and Shell New Zealand Holding Company. A Shell Youth Scholarship was announced in 1982, to be awarded annually to a string player in the youth orchestra, for three years' tuition in the NZSO Training Orchestra, with all tuition fees and a bursary paid by Shell New Zealand.

Ian Cross, chairman of the Broadcasting Corporation, distinguished author of the seminal New Zealand novel *The God Boy* and a former editor of the *Listener*, welcomed what was then an unusual commercial sponsorship of the arts as 'a heartening indication that the private sector is prepared to become involved in the cultural life of New Zealand'. Cross hoped that 'this contribution establishes another guideline for others to follow'.[18]

From a number of applications received for the scholarship, finalists were reauditioned during the youth orchestra's rehearsal week, with the winner announced at the Auckland concert on 29 August 1982. Nigel MacLean from Hamilton, a sixteen-year-old violinist, became the first Shell Scholar and would begin his orchestral training in Schola Musica the following year.

Two years after trumpeter Grant Cooper performed as soloist, his colleague on the NYO world tour, clarinettist Mark Walton[19] returned to play with the youth orchestra, in Malcolm Arnold's Concerto for Clarinet and Strings. Cooper, Walton and Mary Martin[20] had all been singled out for special praise in 1975, and since the world tour all three had gained international acclaim, after studies in the United States (Cooper and Martin) and London (Walton). Walton was awarded first prize in the Royal Overseas League International Competition.

This would have been Bev Malcolm's last tour with the National Youth Orchestra, had she not had to withdraw for family health reasons. A few months later, retiring from the NZSO after twenty-six years in various roles (her most recent as travel officer), she said: 'One of my favourite duties was my long association with the New Zealand Youth Orchestra, from its earliest days, originally as "chaperone"' [a term she disliked] and later assistant manager … Some now in the NZSO or Schola Musica still recall me looking after them as NYO members, or on the World Tour. It was a marvellous experience, although some days the three managers [including travel manager Sandy Whyte], were still at work until 2 am, and had to contend with the illnesses of several members on the tour. My best memory was in China, when some of the players began an impromptu jazz session on their hotel balcony, and a huge crowd appeared from nowhere in the street below, to listen.'[21]

Bev Malcolm was replaced as the National Youth Orchestra's assistant manager by Gae Palmer, a registered pharmacist, and the wife of manager Alwyn Palmer. Additional assistance was provided at other times by Beatrice Averill and Paddy Nash.

In 1982, the Schola Musica turned twenty-one, and celebrated this milestone by releasing its fourth commercial recording, *Canzona*.[22] This was performed by an orchestra of present players augmented by past members of the group, including some current NZSO players. At that time, twenty-one past members of the training orchestra were current NZSO players (almost a quarter of the NZSO's eighty-nine members), and each one of them had played in the National or New Zealand Youth Orchestra.[23]

1983

Timaru & Christchurch, 27–28 August. Conductor: Thomas Sanderling. Lilburn – Overture *Aotearoa*; Benjamin Britten – *Soirées Musicales*, op 9; Tchaikovsky – Piano Concerto no 1; Beethoven – Symphony no 5

Conductor Thomas Sanderling. *NZSO publicity*

Ninety-three players, including several from smaller towns, were accepted from 200 who auditioned for the youth orchestra; a slighter larger number than usual, because extra wind players were required. Pianist Michael Houstoun, himself from Timaru, was soloist for the first time with the

Conductor Thomas Sanderling. *NZSO publicity*

youth orchestra in his home town, which had good reason for pride in this famous son.[24]

The conductor for the 1983 concerts was Thomas Sanderling, who had studied at the Leningrad Conservatoire and began his conducting career in Berlin, where he became permanent guest conductor of the Deutsche Staatsoper for five years. His father, Kurt Sanderling, distinguished conductor of the Leningrad Philharmonic and Berlin Symphony, had conducted the NZSO in 1981.

Thomas Sanderling had been working throughout Europe and Eastern Europe when he made the first of two visits to New Zealand, only four months after defecting to the West, for professional reasons, in April 1983. His command of English at first was extremely limited, says Alwyn Palmer. 'We were housed with the youth orchestra at Lincoln University hostels and rehearsed in their hall, which was quite large and ideal for our use. The hostels were utilised on a "look after yourself" basis, but Thomas, who must have thought he was in a hotel, always left his shoes outside the door to be cleaned. Depending on how I felt on the day, sometimes they were and sometimes not! Thomas arrived with a pile of dress shirts to launder, which Gae spent hours pressing with a student-quality iron and ironing board. He also expected "the staff" to do his washing. We put all his clothes into the washing machine and on one occasion two black socks went in – but out came one black and one white! Thomas was very puzzled by this, and talked about it for days, afterwards. A student sock must have been left in the machine, but we never did find his missing black sock ... In those days before cell phones, the only phone in the hostel was sited on the balcony outside the rooms, and most nights Thomas spent at least an hour talking to the other side of the world. The night of the Timaru concert we bought a pavlova, as Thomas had never seen or eaten one before, so after returning to Lincoln, together with some senior players, we all sat around the common room, eating pavlova.'[25]

Derek Hopper (NYO trumpet, 1984–85) recalls another 'footwear' incident, from 1985: 'I arrived at a concert and realised I had forgotten my black shoes. Fellow trumpeter Malvin Brady lent me his black socks and then he wore his shoes without socks so nobody noticed (we think).'[26]

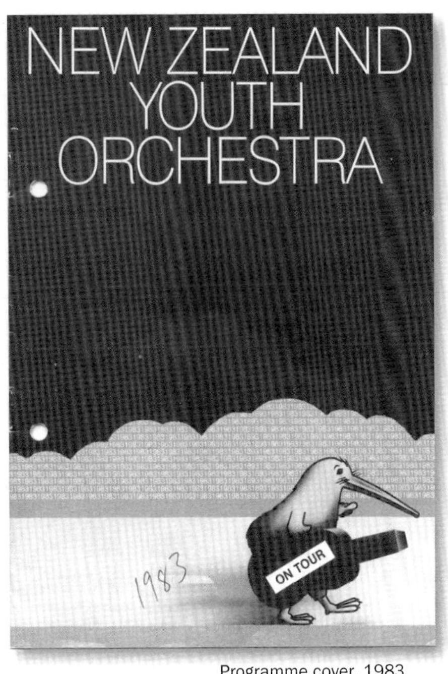

Programme cover, 1983

1984

Franz-Paul Decker, the NZSO's principal conductor, now conductor emeritus. *NZSO publicity*

Hastings & Wellington 25–26 August. Conductor: Franz-Paul Decker. Dvořák – Symphony no 5 in F; Mozart – Piano Concerto no 20 in D minor; Hindemith – *Symphonic Metamorphoses on Themes by Weber*

Announcing the 1984 audition results, Peter Averi warned that 'inevitably there will be some disappointments when out of 200 applicants only 90 are required, but the preparation that goes into an audition is a very valuable experience for any player. We should always encourage any young player to come forward, and if they are not selected it doesn't really matter. The main thing is that they have prepared a performance for a very critical test. They are gaining confidence in the nerve-wracking

Franz-Paul Decker. *NZSO publicity*

business of auditioning and hopefully experiencing something of the rigorous standards which are expected nowadays of orchestral players.'[27]

Dr Franz-Paul Decker first conducted the NZSO in 1966, and was appointed its principal guest conductor in 1984.[28] It was arranged that he should conduct the 1984 New Zealand Youth Orchestra in a concert in Hastings (to coincide with the Hastings Centennial celebrations) and also in Wellington. The soloist was New Zealand pianist Katherine Austin,[29] winner of the inaugural TVNZ Young Musicians' Competition in 1982. Katherine would leave a month after the concerts to further her musical studies in Europe, making use of the $12,000 prize money. Alwyn Palmer remembers, 'Katherine was extremely upset, when ... little time was spent rehearsing her Mozart Piano Concerto, and we and Franz-Paul Decker had words about *that*!'[30]

It seems likely that Peter Nisbet, too, had some misgivings about the formidable Dr Decker conducting the National Youth Orchestra, for he arranged for Bill Southgate (later Sir William) to be assistant conductor; a situation that Decker 'did not take kindly to', according to Palmer. Bill Southgate was himself a foundation member of the youth orchestra and, although rarely called on to conduct, during this time he provided a prayer room for players at the school in Hastings.

A Viennese waltz was scheduled for the encore. When Dr Decker discovered that the young players could not play a proper waltz rhythm, he and Gae Palmer (who had ballroom dance qualifications) danced together to demonstrate, enabling players to eventually find the right rhythm. Mary Sewell says, 'It was exhilarating and terrifying to play in the true style of a Viennese waltz under his [Decker's] eye. He had no concept of the break times, and would finish at any time it suited him ... much to the dismay of the tea ladies.'[31]

Piano soloist Katherine Austin

'I remember Decker was very enthusiastic and enjoyed the experience, with "those kids"', says Peter Shaw, writer, and music critic.[32] 'He had a considerable reputation in Canada as a conductor of youth orchestras and, contrary to rumours that he was forceful, even brusque in rehearsal, he showed endless patience with young players. Rather than using an authoritative approach he was cajoling and encouraging. What he disliked, was musical pretentiousness; talent coupled with inexperience he forgave. He was always prepared to do sometimes lengthy sectional rehearsals (even with the NZSO), piecing things together so that young players were often themselves, surprised at the professional sound he elicited from them. The performance of Hindemith's *Symphonic Metamorphoses on Themes by Weber* delighted him especially.'[33]

'Musically, Decker provided great leadership', Alwyn Palmer says, but he was 'very brusque at rehearsals, at times, and not very sociable with players. He didn't mix with them after rehearsals, sit with them at mealtimes, and had to be coerced to go to the speeches and presentations.'

Nevertheless, players seem not to have felt intimidated by the conductor or his fearsome reputation. They had even played a 'stunt' on him in Hastings that is now considered 'a highlight'. Seamus Hogan (NYO violin 1980–81, 1983–85) remembers. 'We played the first four notes of the slow movement of Dvořák's 5th Symphony, and then turned it into the Tchaikovsky Piano Concerto, which we played in Christchurch in 1983. The horns particularly enjoyed that, saying that the first Dvořák was in an easier key than the original Tchaikovsky. Decker thought our conversion was hilarious. The stunt was my idea and I had no qualms, but some of my fellow players were nervous about it, and so checked with the violin tutor John Dodds,[34] who confirmed that Franz-Paul would enjoy it.'[35] A recording of Franz-Paul Decker conducting the New Zealand Youth Orchestra, in Dvořák's Symphony no 5, was later broadcast internationally on BBC Radio 3, in a series entitled, 'Youth Orchestras of the World'.

Mary-Anne Owen and Andrew Sewell (NYO violin, 1980–84) had married just three weeks before, and became the only known newlyweds to play in NYO.[36] 'It felt strange to be a married couple there', Mary recalls. 'We were billeted with a family who had a bach out the back. We felt very naughty!'[37] A remark with which Andrew says, 'I concur'.

As a conductor, Andrew considers that, 'NYO was a critical influence, with the opportunities to work under top flight conductors: Yuri Segal, Christopher Seaman, and Meredith Davies (who invited me to observe rehearsals of *Peter Grimes* in Wellington with NZSO); also, Thomas Sanderling, and Franz-Paul Decker.'

Tim Young, principal viola NZYO (1984–86), Schola Musica (1985-1986), was the third recipient of the Shell Youth Orchestra Scholarship in 1984, and says that his impressions of the youth orchestra were: 'fantastic, great music-making, excellent camaraderie'.[38]

Michael Vinten

1985 – A new beginning

Michael Vinten was twenty-seven years old when he became the new musical director of the Schola Musica, and looked youthful enough to be mistaken for one of his own students.[39] Vinten nevertheless was well qualified, with a BMus (Hons) from Victoria University and an MMus from the University of Cincinnati, United States, and relevant experience in working with young musicians. As tutor at the New Zealand School of Dance and the Wellington Youth Orchestra, Vinten was keen to broaden and extend the scope of activities undertaken by Schola Musica, and under his enthusiastic but brief direction it was revitalised, and thrived.

Vinten signalled his intentions with a series of regular reports in *Concert Pitch*,[40] which he called, 'Jottings from the Schola'. In the first of these – radically departing from the previous regimen – he expressed the hope that 'this year you will see more of the Schola Musica performing with the NZSO'. Three members had already toured by then, and he hoped that others too, 'will get the chance to play "downstairs" (in the NZSO studio) during the year'. It was his view, Vinten said, that for 'young people being trained as orchestral musicians, one week a year at NZYO has not been enough experience for playing in large ensembles. This year as a part of the course, all members of the Schola Musica are enjoying playing in the Wellington Youth Orchestra under the baton of William Southgate. The Schola will also be getting out and mixing with other groups around town: Victoria University and the New Zealand School of Dance ... are two with whom collaboration is planned this year ...'[41]

A few months later, in conjunction with the release of a revised prospectus, Vinten outlined the benefits for prospective members in the Schola Musica, which he said 'offered the best grounding in professional playing in the country, with tuition from sectional principal players in the NZSO, the opportunity to study orchestral repertoire, aural training, singing, harmony, and music history, the chance to play occasionally with the NZSO, and to become members of both the Wellington Youth Orchestra and the New Zealand Youth Orchestra. Over and above all of this is the orchestral bursary [then, $7,200 pa]. I ask you, could you possibly turn down an offer like that ...?'[42]

For both Schola Musica and the New Zealand Youth Orchestra, this was a landmark year for several different reasons. Designated the 'International Year of Youth' by the United Nations, 1985 cried out for a special celebration and, according to Alwyn Palmer, 'the NZYO put together a great package'. For the first time, the 26-year-old youth orchestra would combine its 107 players with three other national youth organisations: over 300 young musicians would perform in three public concerts.[43]

1985

Paraparaumu, Upper Hutt, Wellington, 30 August–1 September.
Conductor: Doron Salomon. With New Zealand Youth Orchestra, National Youth Choir, National Youth Band of New Zealand, New Zealand Yamaha Youth Jazz Orchestra, Richard Chandler (piano), Shelley Alexander (contralto). Alan Broadbent – *Conversation Piece*; Stravinsky – *Rite of Spring* (Stokowski version); JS Bach – Toccata and Fugue in D minor; Constant Lambert – *The Rio Grande*; Tchaikovsky – *1812* Overture (John Ritchie arrangement)

'Usually 12 to 18 months planning went into each year, but the programme for 1985 took over two years to organise', Alwyn Palmer says.[44] 'Conductor Doron Salomon was a jazz buff who also enjoyed brass bands. He agreed to stay on after his NZSO concerts to conduct the Youth Festival, while Radio New Zealand added considerable interest to the event by commissioning a special work for jazz and symphony orchestra by Alan Broadbent,[45] who came to New Zealand for the performance, and sat-in on rehearsals.'

The participation of the New Zealand Youth Brass Band was of some concern. The band had recently toured in Australia and was financially unable to commit to another so costly undertaking. Then, fortunately, the Department of Education came to the rescue, and provided the necessary funding.

Left–right: piano soloist Richard Chandler, contralto Shelley Alexander, conductor Doron Salomon. *Evening Standard*

The week began with an official but light-hearted parade through Wellington streets. Conductor Salomon and manager Palmer led the way, seated in wheelchairs (in deference to their perceived 'age') pushed along by banner-waving young musicians. A banner behind the wheelchairs proclaimed: 'They're not so Youthful!' and noted amongst other musically themed messages were 'I'd love a DB (double bass)', 'Violas Forever!', 'Contrabasso Profundo' and 'The National Youth Orchestra is wind-powered'.

'It caused quite a stir, with that whole group parading through the city', Palmer remembers. 'The public was not used to seeing a "peaceful" march.'[46]

Michael Vinten, in addition to his role as musical director of Schola Musica, was also assistant conductor of the New Zealand Youth Orchestra. He says it was wonderful to work alongside and learn from so many and varied guest conductors over six years. 'I vividly remember my first year, with Doron Salomon. We were doing the *Rite of Spring* and as he was on tour with the NZSO, I had to conduct the first few days' rehearsal. I'll never forget standing up in front of that huge orchestra: daunting and exciting. Another rehearsal that I remember that year was Doron conducting the *1812* with the National Youth Choir. It may even have been the dress rehearsal. Jane Wright, the leader, got the whole orchestra and choir to add an extra beat into one of the opening "chant bars". Doron was puzzled, and rattled for the rest of the rehearsal because he prided himself on his accuracy. It was only as he was boarding his plane that Jane told him of the trick they'd played on him. He was amazed that the choir and orchestra were so well-coordinated.'[47]

Playing *Rite of Spring* with Salomon was cellist Mark Sheppard's 'best memory' (NYO 1985–89). 'Amazing piece; amazing conductor! Massive adrenaline burst to get to the end without a major stuff-up! Fantastic quality of performance! Not only excellent players, but also an energy that brought great excitement to the performance. I also got to play *Firebird* Suite and *Pétrouchka* over my five years, which I've loved ever since. We worked hard in rehearsal but played hard after hours too. A great balance although I always needed a week to recover afterwards!'[48]

'It was the biggest, brightest and best youth orchestra year', says Alwyn Palmer. 'The whole week and the concert in Wellington will be long remembered, and it was exciting to see the Michael Fowler Centre stage filled with over 300 players, or singers. One of the highlights of this diverse group for me was to see how they each learnt what it took to play or do some other musical discipline. Jazz players were amazed how orchestral violinists could read and play "all those notes" – and violinists marvelled at how a jazz player could improvise. It was an excellent way for them all to appreciate each other's talents and to reduce the perceived hierarchy that was obvious at the beginning ... Two years later, I met Doron in London, and he fondly remembered the youth orchestra and was very fulsome in his praise of its quality.'[49]

The cover of a large printed programme issued for this concert signalled an important new development: 'New Zealand Youth Orchestra in association with the New Zealand Post Office.' Inside, Hugh Rennie,[50] chairman BCNZ, welcomed the orchestra's new principal sponsor and announced new awards to 'enable students to further their music studies'.

The Shell Scholarship for tuition in the Schola Musica had concluded after three years, and these were now replaced by the New Zealand Post Office Awards for Excellence, of $1000 each. Four awards were to be made to string players, and three to members in other sections. The winners 'will have shown their commitment to music and potential for further musical development. They will have been fully involved in the activities of the youth orchestra during their week in Wellington.'[51] The first five recipients selected in 1985 included several who have since become well-known musicians (see Appendix F).

1986

Cambridge, Auckland, Hamilton, 29–31 August. Conductor: Thomas Sanderling. NZSO. Mahler – *Symphonic Prelude*; Khachaturian – Violin Concerto (Adele Anthony, violin); Berlioz – *Symphonie Fantastique*

Soloist Adele Anthony, 1986

Thomas Sanderling, who conducted two concerts 'down South', three years before, returned to conduct a further three, 'up North'. This was part of the plan to visit smaller centres which normally did not see the NZSO, Alwyn Palmer says. 'Cambridge was the first, as it was celebrating its century of local government, with Te Kuiti and Ashburton similarly included, in later tours.' It was an unfortunate fact that smaller centres usually meant smaller stages, and although Ashburton's local high school had 'wonderful facilities', Cambridge's very old Town Hall has, 'the smallest stage we ever played on', he recalls. 'This gave us some interesting problems, as the orchestra in 1983 was quite large.'[52]

It was noticeable that if players could get quickly into the city from the rehearsal venues, Palmer says, 'a number of them would head off during the lunch break and set themselves up as buskers. Hamilton was one centre where this worked particularly well', he discovered, 'and some players more than paid for their fees and expenses!' Horn player Erica Challis not only 'busked where she could, but hitch-hiked her way to and from orchestral weeks'.[53]

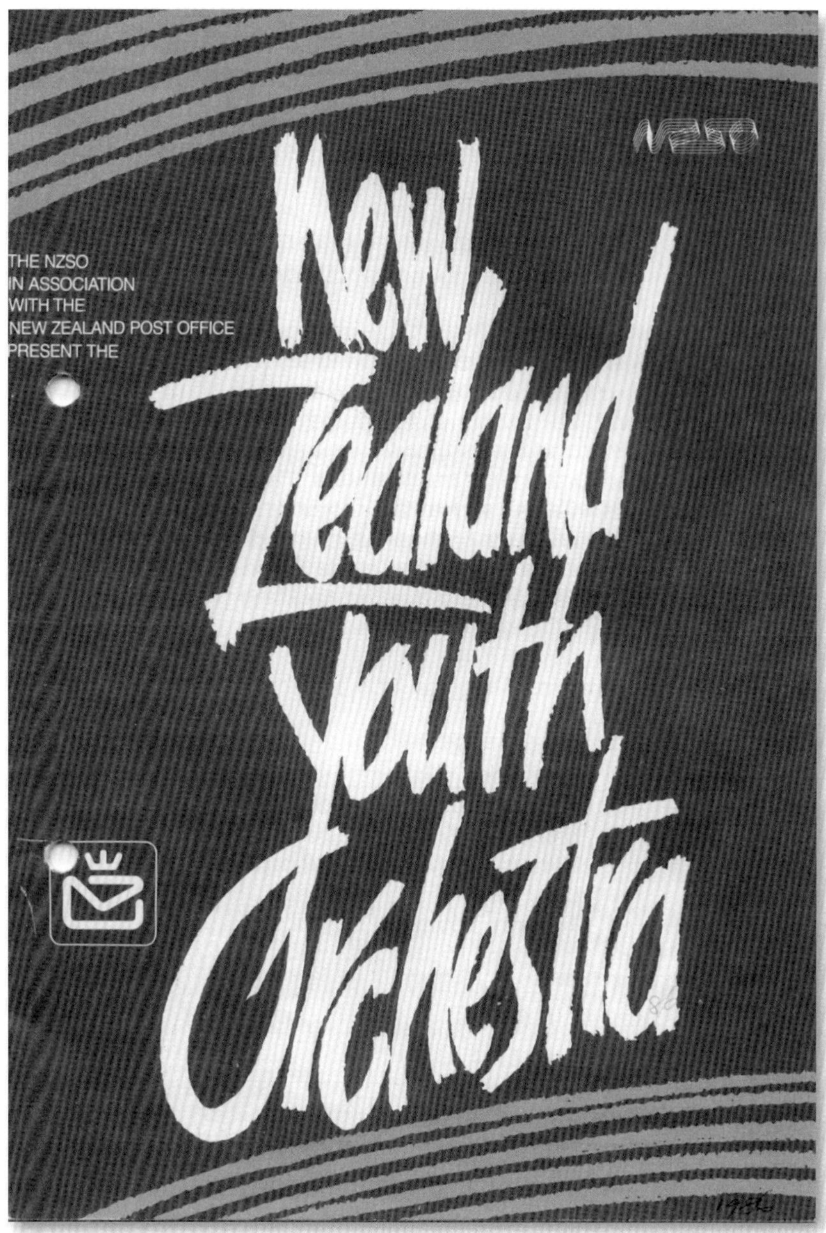
NZSO
THE NZSO
IN ASSOCIATION
WITH THE
NEW ZEALAND POST OFFICE
PRESENT THE
New Zealand Youth Orchestra

Programme cover, 1986

The piano soloist Adele Anthony, a fifteen-year-old Singapore-born Australian, was accompanied by her parents and enjoying 'a wonderful time', as Palmer recalls. 'Some of the boys "took a shine to Adele", and tossed her in the pool, but we as management were having apoplexy, imagining all sorts of disasters to her very valuable arms and hands!'

Lisa Egen, principal second violins, wrote a lively, behind-the-scenes report on NYO 1986 for *Concert Pitch*[54] that revealed the experiences of, '100-odd active teenagers and a handful of rather daring adults'. All were accommodated at Sonning, the boarding unit of Hamilton Girls' High School, which, says Lisa, 'was like a mad-house for a while: suitcases were unpacked, rooms were swapped, showers and toilets were found, the TV was booked, and of course, the kitchen checked out ... the first rehearsals were spent reading through the works and getting used to the school hall, which was rather like playing in a large bathroom. We had tutorials two or three times each day, which for many was terrifying but they soon learned that the NZSO players were not quite the slave drivers they'd imagined ... their help was greatly appreciated and [I] hope they haven't got too many more grey hairs as a result.

'Adele Anthony ... and her parents Alphonse and Grace arrived and joined our happy team. Adele quickly became "one of us" and we were all soon very fond of her. I'm sure many a budding violinist threatened to throw his or her instrument out of a 10-storey building. Boy – was she good! – and she made it sound so easy.

'Night-time in the hostel was quite an experience: some people were in bed by 10 pm, and others would crawl in somewhat later! But you soon got used to the practice going on in the next dorm, the party down the hall, the snoring across the room, and the conversation on oboe reeds in the next cubicle; and by the end of the week, most people could sleep through anything. Living in was a great experience and it really gave everyone a chance to get to know each other.'

Thomas Sanderling had added 'a little life to rehearsals', Lisa said. 'Instead of playing Berlioz, the orchestra started playing Beethoven's 5th symphony ... one of the pieces the NZYO played in 1983. [He] took this extremely well and continued to conduct the Beethoven ... we were lucky to have such a brilliant conductor and we all learnt a great deal from him ...

'All too soon the end of the week arrived, along with the concerts. Nerves were taut and people were tired, but besides this all went well, and they were a great success.'[55]

Sarah Thompson (NYO horn, 1984–87) paid credit to the organisation. 'At the time, everything just happened ... but looking back, and with a lot more thought and insight (and a fair few more years!), the organisation behind it all was remarkable – a lot of people put in a tremendous number of hours making it all come together, to create a thoroughly rewarding experience for a group of young musicians.'[56]

Conductor Piero Gamba. *NZSO publicity*

Calvin Scott (oboe/cor anglais 1986, 1988), playing for the first time in an orchestra, says that he found it 'very exhilarating; it improved my playing and brought me together with lots of people my own age with a similar interest in music. I remember the *Symphonie Fantastique* performance in Cambridge. Harpist Vanessa Souter was just about to chime the bells in the final movement, "*Songe d'une nuit du Sabbat*", when the head of her mallet fell off and rolled along the floor. It was swiftly passed back to Vanessa who stuck it back on the end of the stick and chimed the midnight bells: because they were slightly late, they seemed all the more portentous. It was really quite funny and I remember everyone at the back of the orchestra trying not to burst out into laughter!'[57]

1987

Violin soloist Mark Menzies, 1987

Ashburton and Christchurch, 29 & 30 August. Conductor: Piero Gamba. Lyell Cresswell – *Salm*; Lalo – *Symphonie espagnole*; Rossini/ Respighi – *La Boutique Fantasque* (excerpts); Stravinsky – *The Firebird* Suite

Italian Piero Gamba had conducted his first concert aged eight years, and completed formal composition studies at fourteen. Gamba was by then well-known to NZSO concertgoers through three previous tours with that orchestra, and on this his fourth NZSO tour Gamba would also conduct his only tour with the National Youth Orchestra. The soloist was violinist Mark Menzies, from Hawkes Bay, the winner of the 1985/86 Young Musicians' Competition.

Craig Utting (NYO viola 1987–89) played in the Auckland Youth Orchestra for four years, but remembers that this, his first national orchestra, 'sent shivers down my spine, big-time! I'm sure I was sitting there with a big grin the whole time. The back of the viola section is in the middle of the

From left: Peter Nisbet, general manager, Peter Averi, assistant general manager, Piero Gamba, conductor, and Peter Schaffer, concertmaster, NZSO. Averi and Schaffer auditioned hundreds of NYO players.

orchestra, and there is nothing, just nothing that compares with sitting in the middle of a large orchestral piece like *Firebird* or *Salm*.'[58]

Pianist Stephen de Pledge (NYO viola, 1987–90) writes, 'That first year was amazing ... We did *Salm* by Lyell Cresswell, which was my first encounter with truly contemporary music, with a real live composer. I was mesmerised by the piece, and it began a life-long love of contemporary music, and Cresswell too, leading to me choosing to play his works at my Wigmore Hall debut in 1999, and the commission of a new piano concerto for 2010 ... Not playing the viola any more, I really miss that feeling of being organically involved in the sound – pianos somehow are always in their own sound world, no matter how hard we try! I felt bereft the year I decided not to reapply. I look back on those years with enormous affection, for the eye-opening music-making and the great fun we all had.'[59]

Brisbane Expo 88

Thirteen years after the National Youth Orchestra's world tour in 1975, the New Zealand Youth Orchestra was invited to perform at another International Festival of Youth Orchestras. This time the duration was shorter and the destination much closer to home – in Brisbane, Australia – for the International Festival of Youth Orchestras' 21st anniversary, to coincide with the celebration of Australia's Bicentenary and Brisbane's Expo 88. Hosted by the Queensland

Youth Orchestra, for which an alumni orchestra of distinguished past players had been assembled, the festival was also attended by the Australian Youth Orchestra and other youth orchestras from Bavaria, Hong Kong, Palo Alto (United States) and Tokyo. There would be 800 players, and top international conductors and soloists.

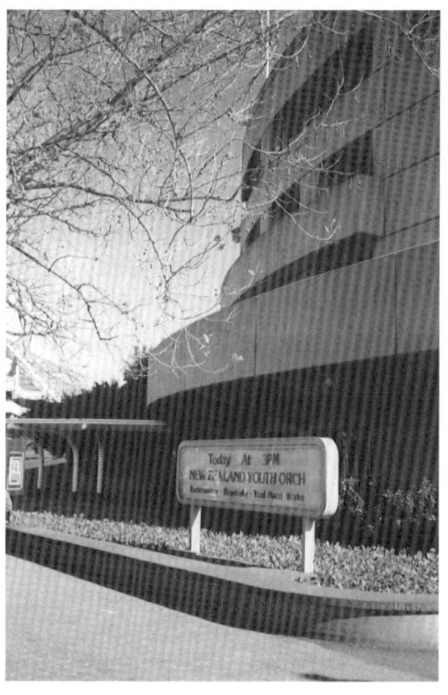

Billboard announcing the New Zealand Youth Orchestra concert, Brisbane

It was announced that, 'Generous financial assistance has been received from the Broadcasting Corporation, New Zealand Post, Ministry of Foreign Affairs, Australia/New Zealand Foundation; and each player is contributing $700'. Assistance 'to help these young musicians on their first overseas tour since 1975'[60] was requested, and later was forthcoming from Air New Zealand, the Robert Kerridge Foundation, the Electricity Corporation of New Zealand, and other public and private donations.

Michael Vinten, in his fourth year as musical director of Schola Musica, had been concurrently assistant conductor of New Zealand Youth Orchestra for three years, and he now stepped up to become conductor of the youth orchestra on its second tour. Pianist Michael Houstoun was the soloist, and Te Rangatahi Cultural Group[61] also was invited to join the tour.

'Trying to decide on the programme was a difficult task', Vinten told *Concert Pitch*.[62] 'We wanted to choose something that showed us as New Zealanders and as an orchestra to best advantage ... There was never any question but that New Zealand music would be a big part of our repertoire ... At a time when the questions of Maori/Pakeha are prevalent in our society, the New Zealand content of our programmes is a step towards the establishment of a cross-cultural relationship.'

The group would perform a new work written for it by composer David Hamilton, *A Song of Tamatea,* which combined traditional Māori instruments with European string instruments, as the programme note explained.[63] 'This work uses the most widely-used Maori instrument, the koauau – a straight hollow tube, about 10–15cm in length, with three finger-holes. Not all possible fingering combinations are used, and the effective range is only 3–4 notes. Another similar instrument is the nguru which has a curved end. The pukaea is a long hollow tube, often slightly tapered, used to produce a single note as a signal call. At one point the soloist is asked to play a traditional waiata of their own choice, which has particular significance.' Two other New Zealand works would also feature in the programme. Douglas Lilburn's *Aotearoa* Overture which, as Michael Vinten said, 'surely qualifies as our first orchestral classic', and *Te Ara Pounamu* (*The Greenstone Path*), an intercultural collaboration between Te Rangatahi and composer Michael Vinten written especially for the Australian tour.

These were 'important steps towards an even closer collaboration', Vinten said. 'Neither the tutors from Porangahau nor myself knew what to expect ... but the end result has pleased all of us.'[64]

Auditions were held by Vinten, with eighty-nine players selected. Lisa Egen, a former Schola Music player then on contract to NZSO was named leader, and she later became the first recipient of the John Chisholm Award for Leader of the New Zealand Youth Orchestra.[65] The youngest player, also a violinist, was Allan Warren who was accompanied on the tour by his father, the luthier Tom Warren.[66] Alan was only eleven, and when seated on his orchestral chair, 'his feet did not reach the ground'. A week before departure, rehearsals were held at Symphony House and the Brierley Theatre, Wellington College. This had proved difficult for Te Rangatahi Cultural Group, which had to travel down from Hawke's Bay, Alwyn Palmer recalls, and as a result, 'there were some changes of personnel, but in the end it all worked out'.[67]

Planning for the three-week tour had gone on for over a year. Every detail, from moving all the equipment and people, to providing gifts for those billeting players, had been considered and prepared for. Then, a day before departure, Palmer slipped at the rehearsal venue, and cracked a rib. The injury caused him some initial problems, he remembers, particularly when lifting the heavier instrument cases, but eventually it 'healed itself', and no permanent damage ensued. It would not be the only unanticipated event in the next three weeks.

On 31 July, the National Youth Orchestra of New Zealand met at Wellington Airport, with Michael Vinten and two of the three-member management team (the smallest at the festival), manager Alwyn Palmer and assistant manager Beatrice Averill, whose daughters Nicola (horn, 1983–86, 1989), and Joanne (flute, 1984–86, 1989) played on the tour. The other assistant manager, Gae Palmer, had travelled ahead of the main group four days earlier. Barry Muir, the NZSO's stage manager, came 'on loan', and proved indispensable on the tour. Te Rangatahi would not arrive until some time later.

The first setback was when an Air New Zealand official ruled that players could not take their precious violins and violas on board with them as cabin luggage. It was fortunate that Alwyn Palmer had anticipated this possibility and, averting a major incident, he was able to flourish a telex received in advance from airline management (no emails then), authorising that instruments 'up to a certain size' could be carried in the cabin.

A second incident, not so quickly resolved, occurred when one player discovered that he had lost his passport. As a special authority was required before he could be allowed to travel, the group had to leave without him. As *Concert Pitch* later reported, it would 'two-and-a half-days later, before he turned up, very embarrassed, having found his passport inside the lining in the sleeve of his coat'.[68]

Gae Palmer had discovered that, despite all the preparatory work, and subsequent checking and rechecking, it was apparent that some things were not up to scratch organisationally. An early indicator was that on her arrival at Brisbane airport at 12.15 am she waited two hours to be collected, before having to make her own way into the city to find accommodation. The woman who was supposed to collect Gae had got the time wrong, a mistake that she repeated when supposed to meet Michael Houstoun, a few days later.

Gae then made two discoveries. The Pius XII Catholic Seminary at Banyo (where the New Zealand group would be accommodated) was not 'only ten minutes to the hall', as they had been told, but at least forty-five minutes from the concert and rehearsal halls, and Festival organisers had provided just one minivan and a small truck, supplied by a company 'unused to orchestra requirements'.

A 'frantic few days' followed, in which Gae tried to organise more suitable transport for the New Zealand contingent. In a city where 'everything was booked out for Expo', Gae had some success, obtaining one 45-seater bus (for ninety players), one self-drive twelve-seater mini-van and 'two woefully inadequate trucks' for the instruments. Each day, Gae had to do a series of 'runs' in the van, starting very early in the morning to transport players to and from venues. On one such trip she had a puncture on a steep slope in the busy one-way system, and on another, late at night, the bus ground to a halt and a replacement had to be found to take the players back to Banyo.[69]

Postcard: Pius XII Seminary, Banyo, Queensland

International Festival of Youth Orchestras, Brisbane

A demanding schedule had been set for the twelve-day festival and New Zealand players, who all arrived on Sunday, were within hours involved in full orchestra and ensemble group rehearsals. On Monday morning, ensemble performances took place at Expo 88 and at the much admired New Zealand Pavilion. Auditions began for the International Festival Orchestra in the afternoon, and a concert by the host orchestra (the Queensland Youth Orchestra), was given that evening.

The festival opening ceremony and welcome was held in Brisbane City Hall, on Tuesday, 2 August. It began with *Aeolian Caprices,* a commission by Richard Mills, and was followed by formal addresses from the Lord Mayor and several others, and an official welcome by the Governor of Queensland.[70] A special *Festival Fanfare,* also by Richard Mills, was performed, and three local school choirs sang. The national anthems of the countries of the six participating youth orchestras were played by the Australian Youth Orchestra, and then the Australian entertainer and legend, Rolf Harris (Patron of the Queensland Youth Orchestra), played the didgeridoo. The ceremony ended with the *Academic Festival* Overture of Brahms.

Te Rangatahi performing, 1988. *Programme*

Directly after the national anthems, as violist Anita Gude (NYO 1983–84, 1986–88)[71] remembers, there was 'a very funny incident when Te Rangatahi quite unexpectedly (and certainly without consulting the strictly official programme) moved into a healthy and hair-raising haka! The poor Chinese and Japanese orchestras sitting close to us nearly literally fell off their chairs with absolute fright and with horror written all over their faces, not to mention the stunned surprise of everyone else in the auditorium. We loved it and were so proud! Our Maori colleagues were our redeemers after our *very* poor singing of New Zealand's national anthem. We all knew the first verse of 'God Defend New Zealand' but the rest? It petered out into very lame "la-la-la's!" Lucky for us the Australian Youth Orchestra played with gusto!'[72]

The next day, a special schools' concert was held in the Concert Hall of the Performing Arts Complex, featuring all six orchestras, and Te Rangatahi Cultural Group. Rolf Harris welcomed the visitors, saying: 'How wonderful it is to see the Queensland Youth Orchestra providing the opportunity for youth orchestras from across the world, to visit Australia to celebrate with us our Bicentenary in the way they know best – with fine music.'[73]

A special memory for violist Craig Utting was Michael Houstoun playing the Paganini *Variations*. 'Michael had been preparing all the Rachmaninov concertos for television, but had never played this one. He also played the orchestral part for Pétrouchka, and he said, that it was, "the first time" he had "played inside an orchestra!" I think he enjoyed himself immensely. Sitting next to Michael was Stephen de Pledge, a viola player, who is now a solo pianist!'[74] Craig also enjoyed the Expo 88 event on River Stage, on Sunday 7 August, with the Queensland Youth Orchestra augmented by players from other Australian youth orchestras, and all overseas participating orchestras. 'It was performed on a stage moored on the river, facing the riverbank, which was covered in artificial turf. The orchestra ... played the *Fountains of Rome* (I think) and also the *1812* Overture. There were six military guns which fired blanks, and on the last bang they all fired simultaneously and you could feel the air jump about a foot to one side. The concert was amazing too, many fireworks and a laser-display in the sky.'[75]

Each country represented at the festival gave its own concert in City Hall, and New Zealand's was on 9 August, two days before Expo finished. Former broadcaster Ian Fraser, then New Zealand's commissioner general to Expo 88,[76] was in the audience, and described the concert, as 'a triumph!' Fraser had particular praise for the compositions by David Hamilton and Michael Vinten which, he felt, expounded 'an important theme similar to the one embodied in the New Zealand Expo pavilion ... a statement of national identity accommodating two rich traditions ... the audience was clearly delighted by [*A Song of Tamatea*] with the haunting textures based on the sounds of two

Te Rangatahi, 1988

ancient Maori wind instruments. And they were bowled over by the exuberance and skill of the cultural group that took central stage in the work. The New Zealand pavilion is widely acknowledged as the hit of Expo 88 ... I was enormously proud that the New Zealand Youth Orchestra was here to demonstrate that we can achieve the same sort of success in all that we attempt. [It] is a national treasure and New Zealand can take pride in their performance before an international audience.'[77]

Taonga puoro soloist Mark Te Tane Hohaia, 1988

At the festival's finale on 11 August, the Bicentennial Festival International Youth Orchestra gave one performance in the Concert Hall Performing Arts Complex, Brisbane. The conductor was Denis de Coteau, and just two works were given: Liszt's *Totentanz* for piano and orchestra, with soloist Roberto Cappello, and Mahler's Symphony no 6 in A minor. This concert was the big one, with players from all participating international orchestras competing in auditions for a dream opportunity to play as a member of this huge ensemble of 140 players. Thirty-five young New Zealanders were chosen, one quarter of all players, among them leader Lisa Egen, Helen Webby (harp), and two to principal positions: Katherine Brady (principal piccolo) and Peter Black (co-principal cello).

'Brisbane's Youth Orchestra Festival ended on a glorious blaze of orchestral colour, last night', wrote John Noble. 'Here was an historic performance featuring a group of the world's leading youth orchestras coming together in one superb symphonic orchestra ... This festival has been an unqualified success musically ... Full marks to the Queensland Youth Orchestra Council.'[78]

A festival booklet provided useful details of calls and concerts specifically for individual orchestras, and it also included general information. There was a cautionary note on licensing laws, which warned international players that, 'The legal age for drinking in Queensland is 18 years of age and proof of age is often requested ... There are severe penalties in Queensland for under-age drinking and for using drugs.' And a page of helpful translations of 'English – Aussie Style': 'G'day' - 'hello'; 'Kiwi – a New Zealander, also a type of fruit'; and 'loo' – 'lavatory'. Two special disco nights were held at Rumours in Adelaide Street – 'one to welcome you to the Festival on 2 August, 10.15 to 1.00 am, and one to bid you goodbye on 11 August'.[79]

Alwyn and Gae Palmer had been surprised to find that, 'all players wanted the music turned down to a much lower level than is usual for such occasions'. It was even more surprising that the couple experienced their 'worst night with any NYO group, ever!' at the Banyo Seminary. 'There were a number of young priests in training', Alwyn recalls. 'Their manager had voiced his concern that *our* young women may "distract" his trainees, but it all seemed to be going well until one night we were woken at 3 am, by a noisy commotion in the corridor. It turned out that the young priests had invited themselves to our boys' quarters, some distance from our room, for a party; and a number of our girls had gone along too. One boy who wanted a good night's sleep, locked himself in the room of one of the partying girls, and when she, plus a trainee priest tried to get in, the commotion woke us. The poor sleeping guy opened the door and fled with us in hot pursuit. Then we discovered what was going on, and had to sort that. In the morning we faced a very angry monastery manager who said, that: "some of your guys had done the unthinkable", by sleeping in the chapel. He then of course had to deal with his own errant priests who had instigated the whole thing.'[80]

In all, forty Festival performances were given around Brisbane, after which, the eight various orchestras travelled to other parts of Australia. This new series of concerts ran from 17 July to 18 August, with performances in nineteen Australian centres in places as widespread as Cairns, Perth, Alice Springs, Sydney, Hobart, and Adelaide. New Zealand was allocated to Melbourne and Newcastle.

The arrangement to billet players in centres outside Brisbane was supposed to have been set up by festival organisers. However, when the details were queried, it was discovered that nothing had been arranged, and so while players went to the beach for their day off, Gae spent the day on the phone to the Melbourne and Newcastle Youth Orchestra managements, to try and arrange billets. Te Rangatahi also was left without accommodation, and they made their own arrangements through local Māori communities in each city.

Intense friendships had developed between some New Zealand girls and Bavarian boys as a result of the after-concert disco organised by the festival management. Alwyn recalls that on departure day, both orchestras left at about the same time, and some tearful farewells were rather evident. And there were problems getting everyone on to the plane. 'One of our party lost his boarding pass, and was not allowed through the gate. Gae who was on the second flight, had to borrow someone else's pass and go through with the first contingent, and then double back to give that pass to the player without one – security then, not being what it is today. The cultural group missed the call, altogether. There were 25 empty seats on the plane, but I located them in the airport, and we all trooped on board as the door was about to close.'[81]

In Melbourne, the orchestra and Te Rangatahi performed twice at the Melbourne Concert Hall, with an afternoon performance on Sunday 14 August, and a schools concert on Monday 15 August. The arrangements worked well, but there were 'some dramas' when transport for the players and instruments failed to meet flights at Sydney Airport. While Gae and Barry

Home away from home: Peter Black, Mark Sheppard, Heather Nicol, Stephen de Pledge, and Michael Joel, with their hosts the Chee family in Melbourne. *Mark Sheppard*

Muir headed off to arrange alternative transport, Alwyn says, 'I sat at the airport, guarding a vast amount of luggage'.

The orchestra eventually left Brisbane at 12.30 pm. It arrived in Newcastle at about 7 pm, where it was discovered that in the hall a half-size piano had been provided, when a grand piano was required. 'Efforts then had to be made quickly, to find one', Palmer says. 'Fortunately, the University of Newcastle loaned us theirs, and we got it into the hall OK, in time for the concerts, next day.'

These two concerts, at 1.30 and 8 pm, were not only the last for the New Zealanders, but the last of the entire festival. This was reflected in the atmosphere that evening, which was charged with a combination of excitement and sadness, with each performer aware that they were playing the familiar music for the last time, together.

The difference Michael Vinten thinks, 'Was that, for a change, Te Rangatahi were on the stage and we were on the floor, if I recall. Because we could see them and not just their back, there was a real frisson in that performance, we felt like we were performing for each other. That and as the last concert, everyone gave it their all, particularly in that piece.'[82]

This atmosphere seems to have been communicated to the audience as well, as a reviewer later wrote. 'Playing from the floor of the hall ... which gave immediate wrap-around sound, our Trans Tasman cousins gave a vibrant, moving concert ... This kind of concert makes one long for many more such cultural exchanges.'[83]

Programme cover for the International Festival of Youth Orchestras, 1988

It was the end of a happy tour, a contributor to which was Dog, a large black and white toy sheepdog, based on the much-loved kiwi icon and *Footrot Flats* character. As official tour mascot, Dog had attended all concerts given by the group, and appeared prominently in tour photographs.[84]

The mascot of the National Youth Orchestra's Australian tour was the *Footrot Flats* character, Dog

Amongst tour highlights, Michael Houstoun's performances rated highly with players. 'We felt fortunate to have him with us', some said, while for others abiding memories were of Michael 'performing a haka at the Aussie Barbeque Night', and 'wearing an "Aussie hat" in rehearsal in Newcastle'.

Houstoun says, 'I remember that trip particularly because in Brisbane we stayed in a seminary, and I slept in a bed usually occupied by visiting nuns. I was almost 40, and possibly one of the "oldest" soloists to perform with the NYO.'[85]

An article in *Concert Pitch,* 'Schola recall Australia', contained more random memories from returned Schola Musica.[86] Among them: 'a strong bond was formed between the orchestra and Te Rangatahi, which helped to enhance all the performances'; 'Mark Te Tane Hohaia, was really like another orchestra member'; and, 'Many new friendships were made, NZ Post have almost got their sponsorship money back ... from NZYO people buying stamps for letters to Australia, Germany, Japan and US.'

Conducting the tour was 'an obvious highlight!' for Michael Vinten. 'I remember Michael Houstoun playing not only the Rachmaninov *Paganini Variations* but also the piano part in *Pétrouchka,* the camaraderie within the orchestra, the wonderful collaboration with Te Rangatahi of Ngāti Kahungunu and the impact they had on the audience. And that last concert.' It was a shame that particular orchestra never got to do a New Zealand performance. There are still people who remember the dress rehearsal at Wellington College and ask me, "When are you going to perform that David Hamilton piece again?" [*A Song of Tamatea*] As usual at that time, the programming was eclectic and less focused on "standard" repertoire – interesting and innovative programming, that I feel has been lost in recent years.'[87]

This second overseas tour by New Zealand's premier youth orchestra was 'important in a number of ways', Alwyn Palmer comments. 'It showed that musically our orchestra, with a New Zealand conductor and soloist, was well up to international standard. It provided the opportunity for our orchestral players to meet and learn from musicians from other parts of the world; and for non-New Zealand audiences to see our young and vibrant Māori performers; and hear their music. The tour demonstrated that our young people can live and work together cheerfully and harmoniously in an unfamiliar environment; and that even though participating in the good old Kiwi way "on the smell of an oily rag", administratively we could more than hold our own.

'The major disappointment is that there have not been further international tours to build on the foundations laid by the first two.'[88]

NZYO Australian tour 1988

New Zealand Youth Orchestra concerts performed with international orchestras:

The Opening Ceremony, City Hall, Brisbane: Tuesday 2 August, 10 am; Special Schools Concert in Brisbane, 3 August, 8 pm; Expo 88 River Stage, Sunday 7 August 8 pm.

New Zealand Youth Orchestra Festival and Schools concerts: Redcliffe Community Centre, Thursday 4 August 1.30 pm (sch), NZYO & Te Rangatahi, 8 pm; Brisbane Performing Arts Complex, NZYO & Te Rangatahi, Tuesday 9 August, 8 pm; Melbourne Concert Hall, Sunday 14 August, 3 pm, NZYO & Te Rangatahi, Monday 15 August, 11 am (sch); Newcastle City Hall, Thursday 18 August, 1.30 pm (sch), NZYO & Te Rangatahi, Concert Hall, 8 pm.

Bicentennial Festival International Youth Orchestra, Concert Hall, Brisbane, Thursday 11 August. 140 players, including 35 NZYO players selected by audition.[89]

NZYO concert repertoire

Standard Programme: Lilburn – *Aotearoa* Overture; Hamilton – *A Song of Tamatea* (Mark Te Tane Hohaia, pūkaea, koauau); Rachmaninov – *Rhapsody on a Theme by Paganini* (Michael Houstoun, piano); *Te Ara Pounamu (The Greenstone Path)*, arr. Vinten (Te Rangatahi, choir); Stravinsky – *Pétrouchka* 1947 version (Michael Houstoun, soloist)

NZYO Schools Concerts, Standard Programme: Hamilton – *A Song of Tamatea*; *Te Ara Pounamu*; *Pétrouchka* (part 4); Tchaikovsky excerpts from *The Nutcracker Ballet*

8 'Cast Adrift'

1988–1998

'After 1988 NYO was cast adrift from Broadcasting, and everything changed.'

– *Alwyn Palmer*[1]

A few months after the Australian tour, the axe fell on 'Broadcasting'. Finally dismantled by another Act of Parliament, the Broadcasting Corporation of New Zealand was carved up into separate divisions: Television One, Television Two, Broadcast Communications, Radio New Zealand and the New Zealand Symphony Orchestra. The effects were final, irreversible, and devastating for the NZSO, although it would be some time before the full extent of the changes would become known.

Peter Nisbet attempted to reassure concerned concertgoers. 'When next you sit down to one of our concerts you will be convinced nothing has changed greatly since you saw the Orchestra in 1988 ... The Orchestra is still your national orchestra, the NZSO, but behind the public presentation a whole new structure has been put in place. After forty-two years under the umbrella of Broadcasting, NZSO Ltd was launched on a solo course, at the beginning of December 1988. The Company with its own Chairman and Board has only one reason for existing. That is the continuing development of the "best orchestra in the southern hemisphere" and ensuring that what Franz-Paul Decker has often referred to as "the best-kept secret in the musical world" shares its secrets with a whole lot more people as it continues to move from strength to strength'.[2]

Nisbet's article made no mention of the National Youth Orchestra or Schola Musica, and yet both were always considered an integral part of the NZSO family, or 'Company'as it was now termed. This added to the uncertainty, although it was assumed – and hoped – that for them too, the music would continue as usual.

It was left to Alwyn Palmer to relay the disappointing news: as a result of the NZSO's 'new structure and the uncertainty of major finance being available', the youth orchestra in 1989 (its 30th anniversary) was to be 'reduced by 20 players'. As Palmer explained: 'Without the umbrella of the Broadcasting Corporation which has always, up to a certain level, acted as fairy godmother to the youth orchestra, the NZSO has had to look at other ways of bringing in enough to pay the quite considerable costs.' Although players themselves, 'contributed something, this nowhere near covers even the accommodation ... it is pleasing therefore to report that New Zealand Post Ltd, which has supported the youth orchestra for the past three years, has agreed to sponsorship of $45,000 for the next four years ... The orchestra's name has been changed ... to New Zealand Post National Youth Orchestra. It is expected this generous, far-sighted sponsorship will help New Zealand's Youth Orchestra continue to develop'[3] and, despite the reduction in numbers, Palmer promised, 'with the co-operation of conductor James Loughran,[4] some testing music [will] be played'.[5]

New Zealand Post chairman, Michael Morris, wrote that his company was 'proud to contribute to the excellence in the community by its association with our nation's youth',[6] and this is confirmed by Alwyn Palmer, twenty years later. 'New Zealand Post was very good when they came on board', he says. 'They loved the association with NYO.'[7]

Sponsorship and business support will become increasingly important, Peter Nisbet accurately predicted, and, 'in the drive to sustain and develop the artistic work of the NZSO a good deal of thought and effort will go into the provision of funds ... [New Zealand Post]'s generous decision to increase financial support and undertake a four year commitment ... marked a new development in that relationship ... and the Orchestra could plan for the future with confidence'.[8] The Music Study Awards, suspended during the previous year's Australian tour, were now reinstated, while the successful collaboration between the New Zealand National Youth Orchestra and Te Rangatahi Cultural Group was warmly remembered. As a gesture of thanks, and to acknowledge the inclusion of Te Rangatahi, the youth orchestra was invited to visit Porangahau Marae, in Hawkes Bay. The invitation was accepted with some initial apprehension from management, Alwyn Palmer admits, as they were all to, 'sleep on the floor, the showers had only cold water, and it was mid-winter'. In fact, the weather was foul, the grounds very muddy, and the plumbing in the newly built marae building occasionally unreliable, but this was a 'very moving and memorable experience and we were treated like royalty'. Speeches were exchanged, on arrival and departure, and although the youth orchestra was unable to give a concert, Palmer says, 'various individual members demonstrated their instruments, and played to a small group of young people'.[9]

Members of the youth orchestra and management stayed on the marae, a new experience for most of the party, and Craig Utting remembers 'a very muddy night, when most of the orchestra slept en masse on a sea of mattresses in the meeting house'.[10] British conductor James Loughran and his wife stayed at the local hotel. It was their first visit to New Zealand, and they were reportedly, 'rather bemused, when having been promised "breakfast in their room", they were given before going to bed, two raw eggs rolling around on a tray with four slices of bread'.[11]

Conductor James Loughran, 1989

James Loughran would conduct two performances with the youth orchestra, followed by five with NZSO. Three of these would be of particular interest, as they featured Holst's *The Planets*, for which a recording conducted by Loughran had recently been awarded a Gold Disc.

1989

Napier & Palmerston North, 26–27 August. Conductor: James Loughran.
Kodály – *Dances of Galanta*; Franck – Symphonic Variations; Beethoven – Symphony no 3 *Eroica* (Napier only); Beethoven – Symphony no 4 (Palmerston North only)

'1989 was the year we started to have problems', Alwyn Palmer recalls. 'From then onwards there was not a great deal of involvement with, or interest from the radio stations. Throughout its lifetime, the youth orchestra (like the symphony orchestra), had been able to tour with a very small on-the-road team – in its case with just a touring manager and assistant (chaperone). This was possible because the Broadcasting stations around the country provided assistance with publicity, front of house, ticketing and box office, and occasional, backstage support.

'The final dismantling of BCNZ in December 1988 changed all that forever. Local stations now had different priorities, and involvement with the orchestra was not one of them. This was not necessarily the fault of local staff, but new pressures were being applied. So as well as the logistical matters I had previously been responsible for, virtually everything else was added to the list, including travelling for auditions. Initially most stations appreciated a youth orchestra visit to their patch, and for a year or two many continued to give help at concert time. I can only recall one centre where we requested help, and the manager refused to have anything to do with us.'[12]

The demise of Schola Musica

The youth orchestra was safe for now, fortunate in having guaranteed sponsorship from New Zealand Post. The Schola Musica, however, had no sponsorship and was therefore more vulnerable. One of the first actions of the NZSO's first Board of Directors, appointed by government under the chairmanship of Athol Mann, was to axe the Schola Musica in its 29th year.

It seemed surprising and sad that – considering the achievements of the scheme started by John Hopkins, the first orchestra training school in the world – few voices were raised in protest at this action. There was no official acknowledgement from the NZSO on the value of the Schola since 1961, its many acclaimed performances and commercial recordings, and the high success rate of its players. Most of them had simultaneously, been members of the National Youth Orchestra, and a considerable number had gone on to achieve significant professional careers in music, in the NZSO, New Zealand regional orchestras, and many fine international orchestras.

The demise of the Schola received no managerial comment in *Concert Pitch* magazine,[13] other than Michael Vinten's own regular column, 'Schola Notes', in which he wrote: 'This column will be the last one I write ... as Musical Director of the Schola Musica. As you may have seen in the press, the NZSO Board has decided to disband its training scheme at the end of 1989.' Vinten then reviewed an impressive list of the group's activities over the last three months. These included: 'three winter early evening concerts at Symphony House; performing at Massey University and schools concerts in Palmerston North; a performance in collaboration with Wellington Polytech's Conservatorium of Music, New Zealand Drama School and Greytown Music Group (performed in Greytown and the new Adam Concert Room[14]) involving scenes from Shakespeare's *The Merry Wives of Windsor* interspersed with scenes from Vaughan Williams opera based on the same play, *Sir John in Love*, [with] about 60 singers, actors and orchestral players ... In another collaboration the Schola performed with Wellington Polytech and the University orchestra for a Haydn Mass, conducted by Elizabeth Kerr,[15] and Shostakovich's Symphony no 1, conducted by Simon Tipping [NYO bass, 1965–68][16] of the Polytech.'

It was important, Michael Vinten said later, 'for Schola Musica to find its own niche, but we were not given time to fully settle on a "new look" before the board abandoned the scheme'. He and Flora Edwards, head of Wellington Polytechnic's Conservatorium, had been 'working on a compromise scheme and trying to find sponsorship to keep Schola alive', Vinten said, 'but time ran out and the project died before I could put my mark on the scheme and get it moving in a direction relevant for the time we were in'.[17]

This would prove a double blow for Vinten, who says, 'I saw my job as music director of Schola and assistant conductor of the youth orchestra as all part of the same job. I really enjoyed the youth orchestra side of it and was most disappointed that when Schola ended it was almost the end of my association with NYO too ... It was something that most young musicians strove to be in, in the 1980s and 90s; their only chance to play the "big" repertoire', whereas university orchestras are bigger and better, now, [and, as] the regional orchestras[18] 'rely on the equivalent young players to boost their numbers ... they have a chance to play professionally or semi-professionally'.[19]

Into the nineties

Peter Nisbet was probably right in saying that the public would 'not notice the difference' under the orchestra's new circumstances, and for New Zealand Post Youth Orchestra the new decade brought some positive new musical adventures in quick succession. The first of these was the orchestra's debut, on 13 March, at the 1990 New Zealand International Festival in Wellington. The major work was Tippett's *A Child of Our Time*, conducted by John Hopkins with the Orpheus Choir, in a programme that also included the Berlioz overture *Beatrice and Benedict*, and Franck's *Symphonic Variations*, with Romanian-born New Zealand pianist, Eugene Albulescu.[20]

Eugene Albulescu, piano soloist

The performance of *A Child of Our Time* was of special significance, being 'one of the greatest oratorios of this period', as organist Philip Walsh said,[21] and also because it would be performed in the presence of its distinguished composer, Sir Michael Tippett. Acknowledged as the 'greatest living British composer' in the festival brochure, Sir Michael was designated 'Composer of the Festival'. As such, he gave master-classes and seminars, and launched John Mansfield Thomson's *Biographical Dictionary of New Zealand Composers*,[22] written as a contribution to New Zealand's sesquicentenary, celebrated that year.

Members of the New Zealand Post Youth Orchestra had been recalled to perform in this prestigious concert six months earlier than their usual meeting time, among them violist Craig Utting. 'It was interesting to have the conductor present. He was then very elderly and wearing shiny bright yellow shoes! I told him that my beginnings as a composer were much inspired by singing in a performance of the same work, in the same venue, Wellington Town Hall.'[23]

A few months later, in June and July 1990, three former youth orchestra players, by then members of the NZSO, enjoyed the opportunity of a lifetime.

Selected to play in the Pacific Rim Youth Orchestra, in the first Pacific Music Festival in Sapporo, Japan, were violinists Lisa Egen, Sharon Tongs (NYO 1984–87),[24] and double bass player Michael Steer (NYO 1979–83, 1986).[25] Composer Gareth Farr[26] was another New Zealander among the 700 young musicians – instrumentalists and composers – brought together by the festival under the direction of two American conductor-composers – the luminary Leonard Bernstein, and Michael Tilson Thomas – and Bernstein's protégé, Eiji Oue, the festival's principal conductor. The London Symphony Orchestra was orchestra-in-residence, and young players all benefited from classes, workshops and ensemble groups with its section leaders, as well as working under the direction of the three principal conductors, and three others.

Leonard Bernstein, who was to have conducted *Francesca da Rimini* in the final concert, returned home a couple of days early because of illness. He announced his retirement three months later, on 9 October, and died of lung cancer five days after that, on 14 October 1990.[27]

𝄞

Back at home, the youth orchestra's next musical adventure was the World Youth Festival in Christchurch, a major musical undertaking for New Zealand's sesquicentenary celebrations that was even larger and more challenging than the International Year of Youth, in 1985. 'The idea of a youth festival was extended to include youth representation of all performing and visual arts as well as sports groups, to bring about New Zealand's first World Youth Festival', said Athol Mann, chairman of New Zealand Symphony Orchestra Ltd, '[which] can only enrich and enhance the artistic pursuits of the participants'.[28]

The New Zealand Youth Orchestra performed musically challenging programmes several times during this four-week festival. It was organised by Vivienne Allen and a special festival committee of the Christchurch City Council, in association with the 1990 Commission, which provided major support. Peter Averi,[29] former assistant general manager, NZSO, was its music coordinator, and had spent almost two years working with all groups on the musical content.[30]

John Hopkins, who returned from Australia to conduct the festival, was an appropriate choice for an event which combined so many diverse national New Zealand music groups: the New Zealand Post National Youth Orchestra, the National Youth Choir, the New Zealand Youth Jazz Orchestra, the National Youth Brass Band of New Zealand, the National Youth Concert Band, and the National Youth Pipe Band. Also taking part, were Māori cultural groups, and rock bands which had their own rock quests. All music groups met for the first time on 25 August in a gymnasium and, as Alwyn Palmer recalls, 'By the very nature of the building, when the combined forces got going the volume was pretty substantial, although more or less bearable until towards the end, when the pipe band joined in. If OSH had been present they would have closed us down! The string players stopped playing and blocked their ears, and John Hopkins almost fell off the podium!'[31] Hopkins recalled the festival in his autobiography *The Point of the Baton*,[32] when on arriving to conduct this work in Christchurch, he says 'I found a huge orchestra, and we played the complete *Daphnis et Chloe* by Ravel performing with the New Zealand Youth Choir. We also performed the music of Philip Norman and quite a number of other works. It was a major achievement to be able to do that.'

Four days later all music and other arts groups gathered for a great combined street parade through Central Christchurch, to promote the festival. The orchestra's first concert on 30 August began with the National Youth Choir conducted by Karen Grylls,[33] was followed by the orchestra playing Prokofiev's *Romeo and Juliet* Suite no 2, and concluded with Tchaikovsky's *1812* Overture, played by the combined forces of NZYO, National Youth Choir and New Zealand Youth Brass Band.

At a second concert on Saturday 1 September the billing was shared between the National Youth Orchestra and the National Youth Choir. The programme featured a work commissioned by the British Festival of Youth Orchestras in 1989, by New Zealand composer Lyell Cresswell: *Ixion*, Leonard Bernstein's *Chichester Psalms*, and Ravel's *Daphnis and Chloe*.

The Gala concert – 'A World Youth Festival Event' – was in Christchurch Town Hall on Sunday afternoon, 2 September. The winning band of the Coca-Cola 1990 Rock Quest began the programme, and was followed by individual performances by each of the eight participating national music

National Youth Orchestra members at the World Youth Festival in Christchurch. *Palmer*

Composer Philip Norman proofreads page 63 of his *Settler McGee* score. *Christchurch Star*

groups and the Pounamu Cultural Group (with traditional waiata). The National Youth Orchestra played excerpts from Ravel's *Daphnis and Chloe* Suite.[34]

All forces, and almost 400 young performers, combined for the final event, *The Ballad of Settler McGee*[35], by Christchurch composer, Philip Norman.[36]

The work was reviewed by Nan Anderson.[37] 'In the best traditions of A Non the nine-stanza poem tells, simply and graphically, the story of McGee's life, from his migratory voyage in 1833 to his ultimate journey on Dominion Day. Interwoven with the narrative – its jazzy rhythms clearly relished by the choir – are nine short and contrasting sections, tossed from one group to another to illustrate or symbolize the national events that provide a background to McGee's life ... Musical felicities abound: a poignant hornpipe lament as he leaves Aberdeen, gentle sounds from the concert band and Maori ensemble signifying welcome from the *tangata whenua*, predictably a brass band for Victorian pomp and circumstances, and unexpectedly a rock band[38] to express peace after the Land Wars ... Equally impressive was the "inner" control exercised by John Hopkins from the centre of a virtual stage-in-the round, working from three strategically placed stands to accommodate the massive score. 1990 is a vintage year for emotional-packed massed singing of the National Anthem, but Norman's version had little to do with jingoistic sentimentality. It was the natural culmination of all the resources – historical, cultural and national ... [used] with outstanding flair and skill ... [it] richly deserves a permanent place in our musical heritage.'

The first combined rehearsal 'was one of the most exhilarating musical moments I have experienced', Philip Norman says. 'Throughout the festival week the various groups had practiced their parts independently. I knew that each part worked in isolation and was fairly certain it would all fit together, but the power and splendour of the four hundred instrumentalists and singers unified was a revelation. I remember reeling with pleasure, astonishment, pride and a dozen other emotions, at the sheer presence of the music. One could feel and almost touch the sound – it was that immediate, that vivid ... The *Ballad* was well received and even got a standing ovation, thanks to the fact that it ended with a loud version of "God Defend New Zealand" for which the audience was invited to stand and to join in. One audience member congratulated me on my cunning in this regards, though it was of course entirely unintentional.'[39]

'It was thrilling to see everything come together without a hitch, at the festival', Peter Averi says. 'In a media-saturated world, it was refreshing to see hundreds of young performers dedicated to their art happily working together and sharing fellowship. I enjoyed my involvement.'[40] Kate Kingston (née

Hansen, NYO violin, 1990) recalls 'the number of performers that had to be squeezed in for Philip Norman's *Ballad.* I have always enjoyed musical works which span genres and involve different musical groups ... [but] playing with rock bands can be a challenge, mainly due to differing interpretations of the dynamic *forte* (or for that matter *piano*). I recall the bagpipes (an instrument I love) and the kapa haka group, and of course the fact that the work is distinctly New Zealand.'[41] Sarah McClelland, leader of the World Youth Festival Orchestra in Christchurch, her home city, says, 'I loved NYO and was so proud'. A year later, Sarah became the first New Zealander to represent this country in the Jeunesses Musicales World Orchestra (represented in New Zealand by Gary Brain). Subsequently Sarah became leader of that orchestra too, for several years. 'NYO's high standards prepared me so well for a wonderful orchestral experience with Jeunesses Musicales, and also my current position, in the Danish National Radio Symphony, since 1993', Sarah says. 'I am the only Kiwi in the orchestra, and I like to think I represent us well. NYO gave me invaluable training and wonderful memories.'[42]

1991

Invercargill, Dunedin, Timaru, 30 August–1 September. Conductor and pianist: Michael Houstoun. Berlioz – Overture *Le Corsaire*; Mozart – Piano Concerto no 24; Shostakovich – Symphony no 10

Pianist Michael Houstoun had played with the youth orchestra in 1973, 1983, and 1988, and now, in 1991, was both soloist and conductor. In the past decade Houstoun had gained conducting experience with the Auckland Philharmonia, the Wellington Sinfonia, the Christchurch Symphony Orchestra, and with players from the NZSO. This would be his first experience as conductor of the youth orchestra in three centres, including Timaru, his home town.

Alwyn Palmer had done all the preliminary work and organisation for the week of rehearsals and concerts. Eighty-five young players from around New Zealand were set up at the Studholme Hall hostel, which provided accommodation for home science students during term time. The concertmaster was Aucklander Natalie Nalden,[43] and her deputy was Matthew Ross.[44] The youngest member was thirteen-year-old Penny Taylor.

Barely had the first rehearsal started when Alwyn Palmer was recalled by NZSO in Wellington to take on another project, and Joy Aberdein,[45] the NZSO publicist and public relations manager, was sent to manage the orchestra in his absence for the remainder of the week.

'It was a baptism by fire really!' as Joy recalls. 'I was familiar with the music,

Berlioz's lively *le Corsaire* Overture, Mozart's much-loved Piano Concerto No 24 K491, chosen because of its broad instrumentation, and Shostakovich's large-scale 10th Symphony with its fierce *Allegro* said to be a musical portrait of Stalin. I'd managed concerts and chamber groups before, but never a whole 85-piece orchestra. It helped that I knew Michael, and some of the players a little, and the NZSO principals who were tutoring the sectionals. Also, Paddy Nash,[46] in her second year as administrator and "NYO den mother", fortunately was on hand to help.

'One of our first challenges, in the absence of Alwyn, was to find volunteers to move the heavy instruments, particularly on tour, but once I'd announced this at rehearsal, a group of percussion and brass players just quietly started doing it. It was a considerate and supportive group, and there was also a lot of good humour.

'As Paddy Nash said, "There was a feeling we were on our own, but everyone was well-behaved and respectful." And there was some payback for those brass players. When the buses arrived back in Dunedin after the Invercargill concert, Paddy says that some of the brass section "stood over" her. They wanted a key to get into the hostel later. They "needed a beer," they said. They got the key. Paddy knew they'd go to the pub anyway and it was probably best to stay onside. Later, in Timaru, with the final concert pending, the same group decided they really needed some staging risers. What to do? They were told that they would need to organise these themselves, which surprisingly they did in a short space of time on a Sunday afternoon.

'There was a lot of initiative in that group. Among them that year were Bridget Douglas [NZSO principal flute], Robert Orr [NZSO principal oboe], Ashley Brown [NZ Trio cello], Murray Hickman [Strike percussion] and Owen Clarke [trombone; Central Band of the RNZAF, conductor]. I enjoyed the experience.'

Bridget Douglas (NYO flute, 1991–93) remembers: 'My first NYO was truly a life-changing experience. I was doing a science degree at Otago University and had only ever played and heard the small orchestras in Dunedin. The NYO was conducted by Michael Houston. I had stars in my eyes as he was such a musical legend. I must have just scraped in as the piccolo player for Shostakovich 10 and was completely blown away by the sheer power and spine-tingling excitement of playing in a large orchestra. I spent the entire week in such a state of awe for Michael, the NZSO tutors and all the players. As a result I was inspired and encouraged to audition at Victoria University and began my flute performance degree the following year. Subsequent NYOs were also wonderful learning experiences (the partying got a little more intense too) but it was hard to beat the impact of that first time. The low point has

Four Wellington representatives of the New Zealand Post National Youth Orchestra. From left, Murray Hickman, Andrew East, Robert Orr, and Stephen Bemelman, 21 August 1991. Dominion Post *Collection, Alexander Turnbull Library EP/1991/2404/12 CA*

got to be leaving one of the NZSO's alto flutes on a park bench in Courtenay Place, never to be seen again – I felt sick for weeks after that.'[47]

Michael Houstoun says, 'I found it very satisfying to be able to play the same programme three times, each time in a different city. It was not my first soloist/conductor experience, however I had never up to that point conducted a work as large as the Shostakovich 10th Symphony, and so that was very scary, exciting and ultimately affirming for me.'[48]

Following its change of status to a state-owned enterprise in 1988, the 'NZSO Company' published a message in *Concert Pitch* acknowledging support from the 'Public Broadcasting Fee revenue' (the former 'Licence Fee') and reminded readers of their 'obligation to pay' this fee, 'which helps make this publication possible'.[49] A contemporary pamphlet, 'Public Broadcasting Fee Playing your Part, Highlights & Information', made the claim that, 'Public Broadcasting gives you a great deal for less than 20 cents a day!' and provided interesting statistics for 1987/88, for Radio New Zealand, Television New Zealand, *New Zealand Listener*, and for New Zealand Symphony Orchestra: '131 concerts in 27 centres; 11 internationally acclaimed conductors; 8 visiting soloists and a further 35 New Zealand or ex-pat soloists; major contributions to NZ Festival of Arts (including Rudolf Nureyev and Paris Opera Ballet), tours with New Zealand Ballet, film scores, backings for commercials and television programmes; further development NZ Youth Orchestra (the players of the future) and 24 Schola Musica concerts.'[50]

Michael Houstoun, 1993
Creative Services

In the first year of the new arrangement, 1988/89, NZSO received 67 percent of its funding from the Public Broadcasting Fee, and 33 percent from Internal Affairs; in the second year the figures reversed, to 33 percent Public Broadcasting Fee and 67 percent from the new Ministry of Cultural Affairs. By 1991/92 the fee, which had made so much possible for the musical arts in New Zealand, was phased out, leaving the NZSO now fully funded by the Ministry of Cultural Affairs.

A few months later, $1.3 million (15.3 percent) was slashed from the NZSO budget,[51] prompting some desperate and unpopular measures: a predictable increase in the price of concert tickets, the unannounced axing of *Concert Pitch* magazine after thirty-six issues in eleven years,[52] and the unfortunate decision to cancel both concerts for Nelson's significant 150th anniversary. These actions were made more understandable by the leak of Treasury papers obtained by the *Dominion*[53] under the Official Information Act, which revealed 'secret plans' that it claimed would have turned the NZSO into a 'part-time band', or reduced it to a regional orchestra, with parallels drawn to the fate of the New Zealand Opera Company in 1971.

The NZSO's expected move into a refurbished Shed 7 on Wellington's waterfront was no longer an option because of the dire financial situation, and as a hasty compromise, a fifteen-year-old, two-storey building and warehouse in Tory Street, off Courtenay Place, became the new Symphony House office and studio. The NZSO moved in, in January 1992, and Peter Nisbet, who had controlled it for twenty-two years,[54] retired in March. His replacement was engineer Graham Coxhead, as interim general manager, the orchestra's first non-Broadcasting manager.[55]

Conductor Nicholas Braithwaite (National Youth Orchestra 1992), pictured on an earlier visit, in 1983, beside a portrait of his father conductor Warwick Braithwaite. *Don and Beatrice Peat*

1992

Paraparaumu & Wellington, 28–29 August. Conductor: Nicholas Braithwaite. Britten – *The Young Person's Guide to the Orchestra*; Saint-Saëns – Violin Concerto no 3 (Kanako Ito, violin); Stravinsky – *Petrouchka*

Despite continuing dramas for NZSO, its offspring, the New Zealand Post National Youth Orchestra, prepared for a new season under a new conductor whose surname was well known in New Zealand musical circles. Warwick Braithwaite was chief conductor of the National Orchestra, in 1953–54, and his son, Nicholas, had followed the same path, also becoming an international conductor. Nicholas Braithwaite conducted the NZSO for the first time in 1977. He had spent some of his childhood in New Zealand, and over four previous visits he was accepted as 'one of ours'. He was the first second-generation conductor to conduct the NZSO.[56]

By the time of his fifth visit, in 1992, Nicholas Braithwaite's international career had burgeoned. He was already well known to New Zealand audiences through concerts and recordings, and this was his first time conducting the New Zealand Post Youth Orchestra.[57]

Kanako Ito, violin soloist, 1992

Appearing with Braithwaite as soloist in the Saint-Saëns' Violin Concerto no 3 was Kanako Ito, a 22-year-old Japanese violinist. Ito was the runner-up in the inaugural Lexus New Zealand International Violin Competition, which had been held as part of the 1992 New Zealand International Festival of the Arts a few months earlier. The *Evening Post*'s reviewer wrote: 'the orchestra played with the humour and zest only the young can carry off'.[58]

1993

Alwyn Palmer retired from NZSO in 1992, but in 1993 managed his 20th and final New Zealand Post National Youth Orchestra tour, organised for the first time outside NZSO offices. He had chosen a conductor that he and the country knew well: Gary Brain.

Brain had earned an enviable reputation in dual roles as the NZSO's long-serving principal timpanist and percussionist, and as the presenter of highly successful one-man music shows for school children of all ages. An exuberant performer, Brain travelled around New Zealand towing a trailer loaded with percussion instruments, both traditional and unconventional, and presenting an informative and entertaining one-man show to schoolchildren of all ages. It was in recognition of the value of these solo performances for younger audiences that Brain, aged forty in 1984, became the youngest NZSO or ex-NZYO player to receive an OBE, 'For the promotion of music and the performing arts among young people'.

Gary Brain, Champs Élysées, Paris, 1993

Brain's life had changed abruptly in 1989 when, during turbulence on an international flight, a case fell from an overhead locker, and he sustained a serious injury to his wrist. It was the end of his timpani playing, his NZSO career and schools concerts, and he retired on medical grounds.

A bleak time followed for several months as Brain assessed his career options. Then, out of the blue, he was awarded a fellowship by the French Foreign Ministry to study in Paris.[59] There he joined the graduate conductors' class at the National Music Conservatoire, and was attached to Pierre Boulez's Ensemble InterContemporain and the Ensemble Orchestral de Paris.[60] His international career as a conductor has been based in Paris ever since.[61]

Palmerston North & Wellington, 28–29 August. Conductor: Gary Brain.
Panufnik – *Sinfonia Sacra*; Pruden – *Soliloquy for Strings*; Respighi – *Fountains of Rome*; Saint-Saëns – Symphony no 3 (*Organ* Symphony)

The venues for the youth orchestra were carefully chosen: Palmerston North was Gary Brain's old home town and Wellington was where he had lived for almost all his adult life. In Palmerston North an electric organ had to be borrowed for the Saint-Saëns symphony, but in Wellington, German organist Rita Paczian had the benefit of Wellington Town Hall's celebrated Norman and Beard pipe organ.[62]

Peter Averi found the Saint-Saëns disappointing in Wellington, a fact confirmed by the Radio New Zealand recording. 'This was not a notable performance unfortunately, largely due to a lack of co-ordination between conductor, organ and orchestra, I remember sitting in the audience, holding my breath, as I heard the confusion which arose and the anxious moments before everything came together again.'[63]

Gary Brain recalls the incident: 'We had given the same concert in Palmerston North the night before perfectly, these things happen.'

A good concertmaster can play a crucial role in maintaining the cohesion of a performance, and for violinist Joe (Joseph) Harrop (NYO 1993, 1998; concertmaster 1999),[64] 'one of my best memories of six years was provided by Yid-Ee Goh's incredible leadership.[65] We had a huge orchestra, with an equally huge programme. I remember Yid-Ee's calm and friendly demeanour in what was a really challenging situation, every time I lead any kind of group.'

This performance had considerable significance for both conductor and soloist. 'Performing the Saint-Saëns Organ Symphony with the National Youth Orchestra was a great honour for me', Rita Paczian says. 'It was my first public concert in New Zealand, and I was highly impressed with the standard of performance in my new country.'[66]

For Gary Brain, conducting the NYO proved to be, 'quite overwhelming, considering that I had played in it as a kid, and that I was the first ex-member to conduct it. It was a wonderful experience to work with such gifted young musicians; and a tribute to NZSO which has the foresight to give our youth a musical future.' Gary Brain's conducting career had barely begun, then but he would soon conduct concerts and recordings with orchestras throughout Europe. Among these, the poignant 'Concert Renaissance de Sarejevo' at UNESCO in Paris,[67] various festivals, and several award-winning recordings. In New Zealand, however, he has his critics (so often the fate of our tall poppies), but his career speaks for itself, and an NZSO manager can testify to his mana at that time. Going home from the office, one wintry evening, some years after Gary moved to Paris, she was confronted by an intimidating group of young men with motorbikes in the car-park, leaning on the cars, and drinking beer. Reluctantly she asked, 'Can you please move, so I can get my car out?' but they just stared and she became increasingly uneasy. Then one pointed to the 'New Zealand Symphony Orchestra' sign and asked, 'D'you work there?'

'Yes,' she said.

'Do you know Gary Brain?'

'Yes, I know him well,' she said, and instantly, the group dynamic changed. They all became quite animated and friendly, asking her questions about Gary; and telling their stories.

'He came to our school –'

'He played all these drums –'

'He was cool, man –'

This surprising exchange lasted several minutes during which all agreed, Gary Brain was 'cool'. They moved away from the cars, opened the gate, and she drove away, awed by the power of music.

In 2009, Gary Brain returned to launch Fiona Campbell's 'Real Art Roadshow', a mobile gallery containing more than sixty original artworks (post 1945), by well-known

'Four Vic [Victoria University] students ham it up after being selected for the National Youth Orchestra. Bridget Douglas (back left) on trombone is actually a flautist; Bridget Miles trying her hand on the double bass, is a clarinettist, Jeremy Fitzsimons with clarinet is usually found on percussion, and Owen Clarke (with flute), is a trombonist.' Yid-Ee Goh, B Mus (Hons) 1992, was leader. News VUW, *16 August 1993, Les Maiden*

New Zealand artists, contained in two trucks. It unfolds to form a 64-metre gallery, and travels to secondary schools around the country. The media attention that followed this event revealed an unsuspected level of interest in Gary Brain, still remembered for his unique contribution to New Zealand music through his travelling school road-shows. Art curator Campbell had enjoyed the experience of Gary's concerts as a schoolgirl, and that had inspired her to create her own travelling show for a new generation of young people – not with music, but with New Zealand art.[68]

The youth orchestra on tour

Gary Brain's tour was Alwyn Palmer's last as manager of the youth orchestra, under its various names, from 1971 to 1993. In twenty-three years Alwyn had managed nineteen annual tours, for many of which he and his wife Gae had worked together as a management team.

'The health of the players on tour was always a concern', Alwyn says, 'but apart from the usual sore throats and colds most were blessedly free of major incidents and I can recall only a few minor problems. Once in a country town (Te Kuiti) many of the billeting farmers served duck eggs for lunch, after which a number of players suffered distressing stomach upsets. Another time, a player became so tense she hyperventilated, causing quite some anxiety, and Gae sat up all night with her.

'Having responsibility for the safety of 80 to 90 young people aged between 11 and 23 years, many of them hormonally charged, was more than a full-time job for two people. We were lucky to get four hours sleep some nights and then had to work hard next day. I don't know why we didn't insist on more help. Besides all the players' day-to-day needs, we also had to look after the conductor and often his wife. There were inevitable issues with caterers, hostel staff, carriers, hall staff, and anxious parents who would phone and ask us to keep a "close eye" on their offspring, as *they* were having "sleepless nights!"

'Generally we had very few behavioural issues. The older players adopted a very caring and responsible attitude to younger ones in their sections, and they all knew that overstepping the Palmer rules could result in an immediate return trip home. This *almost* happened to a player in Australia, and only the intervention of conductor Michael Vinten kept him on the tour.

'One of the regular brass players always had a birthday during youth orchestra week and we anxiously approached the thought of his 21st. The conductor suggested he would work the players very hard that day, and he did, so that they all collapsed into bed very early including the birthday boy! We felt rather sorry for him and somewhat guilty!

'Tours were always in winter and there were often bad colds and other ailments, but I don't recall any player having to miss the final concerts. It was not uncommon for Gae (a pharmacist) to organise a 'steaming' session for 'blowing' players, who could not take decongestants which would dry up their throats. There would be a ring of players in the common room with their heads under towels, inhaling from a steaming bowl of something that she had provided for them.

'The players worked really hard for ten days but still musical sounds could be heard around the campus surprisingly early. Being more practical than creative, Gae believed it was important that these budding musicians learnt to look after their own belongings before they headed overseas. It took some of them a while to learn this, as if they had parents that ran after them at home.

'Mostly we were accommodated in school or uni hostels which were very basic. Being holiday time the front offices were closed and of course there were no cell phones in those days, so an incredible amount of walking around the campuses was necessary, to speak to people and get things arranged. We tried to isolate any "sickies," and frequently had to take them to see doctors – which could be very time-consuming in strange towns.'

The couple were under a lot of pressure, organising the youth orchestra, each year. Both worked very hard and long hours on tour, after which, they immediately returned to their 'real jobs' (with Alwyn seldom able to get leave). But, it was always a very special time, they remember, 'to see the players finally all dressed up and hear them performing on stage for the concerts. As we come across them many years later, we always hope that even in some small way we have contributed to their success.'[69]

1994

Uncertainty about inadequate funding, and even about the survival of the NZSO itself, continued for years after Broadcasting was dismantled. The youth orchestra's chances of surviving seemed even less likely, as it was not considered 'core business' in some quarters, and without the same commitment to retain it, there was talk of it going elsewhere, perhaps to the Education Department (now Ministry), although that was no longer an option. The possibility of a closer relationship with the National Youth Choir was also explored.

In April 1994, the NZSO's new glossy magazine *Symphony Quarterly*, edited by Joy Aberdein, was launched by Helen Clark, Leader of the

Opposition. Its view of the long-term prospects for the New Zealand Post National Youth Orchestra was rosy indeed. In recent months 'the significance of its procedures has been the subject of a report by its administrators, the NZSO. Considerable research was undertaken to ensure the young students participating will achieve maximum value from it. The exciting outcome of this report is that [the youth orchestra] will take on a new impetus and meet twice a year, thus providing a greater opportunity for its participants to work with leading conductors and other youth groups ... to allow time to set these new arrangements in place, the first get together of the "new look" [youth orchestra] will take place at the end of January 1995, and not August this year (1994)'. As Alan Meek of New Zealand Post confirmed, 'we are committed to investing in long term benefits for talented young NZ musicians and we believe the new arrangements will help achieve that aim'.[70]

Anna Kominik, the *Dominion* arts reporter and a former NYO violinist (1988, 1990), covered this development: 'Youth Orchestra to take time out for revamp – The sweet sounds of the New Zealand Youth Orchestra will be taking a rest this year – the first in its 35 year history' (actually, it was the second time, following the season's cancellation amid the troubles of 1977). The postponement would allow time to plan for 'a new-look orchestra', said Mark Keyworth,[71] the NZSO's first chief executive. Keyworth drew attention to suggestions made in the new report, 'probably the most significant' of which were for the youth orchestra to 'meet twice a year in January (to coincide with Wellington's Summer Festival) as well as in August, ... to have a core number of exceptionally talented young players on a three-year tenure, and to streamline administration as part of a general revamping of both the NYO and NZSO and their combined administration ... Changes [which] would ensure that the youth orchestra would continue to grow and flourish in the future'.[72]

1995

The year 1995 began positively for the NZSO, with the announcement of its new principal guest conductor from Mexico, Eduardo Mata, and plans for its first major overseas tour, which would include performances in the BBC Henry Wood Proms in London, at the Concertgebouw in Holland, and in Germany, Austria, and Hong Kong. The tour would be a magnificent celebration of the NZSO's 50th anniversary in 1996.

Four days after the announcement of Mata's appointment came the shocking news of his death, and that of his partner, when the plane he was piloting crashed in Mexico. Then, within the month, a controversial decision was made to cancel the NZSO's world tour (hastily rescheduled under Russian conductor Alexander Lazarev) because of financial restraints.

The youth orchestra also suffered as a result of these, and other restraints. The ambitious schemes – for two seasons for the orchestra (including one in summer) and the proposed three-year tenure for talented players – did not survive the next major review. The good news announced by its new manager, musicologist Dr Allan Badley,[73] was that the orchestra would meet 'in August, after a hiatus of nearly two years. At the end of the 1993 meeting of NZPNYO it was decided to review the entire exercise in order to find ways and means of increasing the value of the experience to young musicians, and also to broaden its influence in New Zealand youth music ... Working closely in conjunction with the orchestra's loyal sponsor New Zealand Post, an exciting programme had been devised which promises to achieve many of the objectives laid down for the orchestra'.[74]

Palmerston North & Wellington, 25 & 27 August. Conductor: Isaiah Jackson. Lilburn – *Festival* Overture; Sibelius – *Karelia* Suite; Tchaikovsky – *Variations on a Rococo Theme*; Barber – *Adagio for Strings*; Elgar – *The Enigma Variations*

Conductor Isaiah Jackson, 1995

The youth orchestra was back, a fact made obvious to anyone who heard the vitality of that first concert under Isaiah Jackson, in a programme which, as manager Allan Badley had promised, would 'make no concessions to youth'. A protégé of both Leonard Bernstein and Leopold Stokowski, Jackson was the first American conductor to be appointed musical director of the Royal Ballet in London, and was the founding conductor of the Asian Youth Orchestra. The solo cellist Ashley Brown was winner of the National Concerto Competition, a prizewinner in the Adam International Cello Competition, and a former youth orchestra member and principal cellist (1989–92).[75]

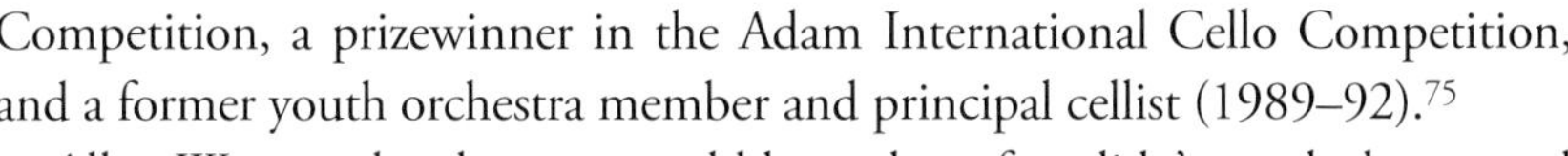

Allan Warren, the eleven-year-old boy whose feet didn't touch the ground when the National Youth Orchestra played in Brisbane in 1988, was now its concertmaster, 1995–97.

On 26 August, in between their own two concerts, members of the orchestra participated in the New Zealand Choral Federation's Inaugural Festival of Youth Choirs, conducted by the prominent English choral conductor Simon Halsey in Wellington Town Hall. The success of *Settler McGee* in 1990 had led to a further massed-item commission for its composer, Philip Norman, whose brief was to compose for large choir (the National Youth Choir and combined regional youth choirs) with an accompaniment that would include brass and percussion players from the youth orchestra. Norman says, 'I wrote clip-on interludes and accompaniments that were performed with great flair by the players at the premiere. The singers were lifted rhythmically by the crisp articulations of the brass – a vintage harvest of players, that year, as I recall.'[76]

1996

The financial woes that had beset the New Zealand Symphony Orchestra after it was set adrift in 1989 were finally addressed in May 1996 with the release of what became known as the Scott Report, prepared by former Treasury Secretary Graham Scott, who said, 'The NZSO is clearly reeling from financial pressure and its difficulties are not only about money'.[77]

As a result of this report the first NZSO board resigned en masse, and a new board was appointed, representing business and the arts, under the chairmanship of Selwyn Cushing,[78] the director of many private and state owned companies and an amateur violinist. There were six other board members.[79]

'NZSO Gets $3m Handout' said the headline that accompanied this announcement, but according to Scott, its funding from Government had dropped by $4.7 million since 1990. 'Mr Scott says the problems will not be solved by a "business as usual with a few improvements" approach. It will take a fundamental rethink to ensure the orchestra's future.'

'The orchestra has difficulties in strategy, finance, governance and management', Cultural Affairs Minister Douglas Graham confirmed in the same article.[80] 'Although the music itself has continued to improve and, at its best remains superb, the situation that has developed is beginning to affect the quality and will cause a marked deterioration unless the problems are dealt with quickly.'[81]

Much of the credit for the survival of the youth orchestra during the NZSO's financial crisis in recent years was due to the ongoing sponsorship of New Zealand Post. The 1995 programme included this recipe, under the heading 'Young musicians dare to dream': 'Take one young musician's dream ... add hours of practice, persistence, sore fingers, despondency and encouragement. Audition the very best young musicians around the country. Select the finest, and bring them together as an orchestra for five days of intensive practice. Then add internationally renowned conductor Isaiah Jackson. Recognise the outstanding promise of the top five, and help them pursue their studies with a New Zealand Post Music Study Award. Look forward to them all fulfilling their promise, but first, sit back and enjoy the concert.'[82]

That dream ended in 1996 along with New Zealand Post's eight-year sponsorship. The effect on the orchestra was immediate – although possibly the most noticeable effect to the public was the change from a professionally printed high quality concert programme, to a few pages of basic information, created in-house, without the usual list of New Zealand Post study award winners. A scheme that started with seven awards for orchestra members had been reduced to five in 1995 and was now gone for good, along with the security of funding that New Zealand Post sponsorship had provided.

Now, despite the success of the 1995 season (and a record number of almost 200 applicants for 1996), the possibility of securing a sponsor, or any type of funding, was deemed to be 'almost non-existent'.[83] The decision again was made to cancel, but then rescinded a week later, with the acceptance of a new proposal to 'proceed as a low-budget project, and to take the risk that Creative New Zealand would provide some funding'. Applicants were advised that, owing to 'an unexpected reduction in funding and sponsorship', accommodation was changed to billeting, and all meals, incidentals, and travel costs became the responsibility of orchestra members. This fortunately seemed to have 'little impact on audition turnout and applicant enthusiasm', and there had been, '100% acceptance of the low budget course'. Changing the audition system enabled further savings. In recent years auditions were held in centres to coincide with NZSO tours, and this now reverted to an earlier system, whereby two representatives, John Dodds,[84] NZSO principal second violin, and Greta Mark (NYO viola, 1990–93), NYO manager 1996–97, travelled to all centres, recording auditions for principals to assess back in Wellington. Creative New Zealand provided funding (although not to the level of New Zealand Post), and NZSO tutors provided their services free.

1996

Wellington, 31 August. Conductor: James Sedares. Barber – *Essay for Orchestra* no 2 op 17; Schubert – Symphony no 8 *Unfinished*; Tchaikovsky – Symphony no 5

The first obvious sign of change was the name. The word 'Post' disappeared and the orchestra became once more the 'New Zealand National Youth Orchestra'. The concert, subtitled, 'Youth Performing for Youth', would be in support of the Child Cancer Foundation.[85] James Sedares was confirmed as the conductor. An American then in his seventh season as music director of the Phoenix Symphony, Sedares was already known in New Zealand for his recordings with NZSO for Koch International, and had made his concert debut with the NZSO in April. His rapport with players was considered 'absolutely outstanding'.[86]

There was no soloist and, through an unfortunate clash with other events, attendance was only 1300. 'New Zealand's orchestral future depends on this orchestra', Greta Mark said afterwards 'Lack of recognition could spell its doom. It's a really difficult environment to be in. On one hand it's clean, it's green, it's youth, it's talent. On the other hand it only happens one week in the year and usually only in one city ... But if you can't look after your grass-roots, what future is there?'[87]

A few months later, in October 1996, the NZSO celebrated its 50th anniversary. Coinciding with this, an important new development was announced; the establishment of the NZSO Foundation, to support the orchestra's activities 'into the future, and beyond 2000'. Formed under a trust deed to raise funds and support specific activities and projects of the NZSO, which would contribute to its future development, the foundation aimed to raise $10 million, with support sought from 'the business sector and from all those who attend NZSO concerts'.[88]

1997

Wellington 30 August. Conductor: James Sedares. Janáček – Fanfare from *Sinfonietta*; Mahler – Adagietto for Strings and Harp, from Symphony no 5; Beethoven – Concerto for Piano and Orchestra no 1 (Christopher Hinterhuber, piano); Rachmaninov – Symphony no 2 in E minor

'This orchestra once again demonstrated its quality, verve and youthful enthusiasm', wrote reviewer Michael Vinten. The Rachmaninov Symphony no 2 had 'wowed the audience with an amazing maturity of sound, the broad sweep of its performance and attention to detail'. Subscribers had been offered free NZNYO tickets with their NZSO subscriptions, as an incentive to build up the audience, but this brought limited success, it seems. 'I have two gripes', said Vinten: 'Why weren't there more people there? The Town Hall was fairly full, but it should have been packed to over-flowing ... Every one of [the NZSO's subscribers] should be there ... the second is that a concert by a youth orchestra is not a concert for children. Once again people brought children who were far too young to enjoy what was "after all" a heavyweight programme.'[89]

Vinten's 'gripe' highlights a perennial problem when youth orchestra families bring young children to see older siblings perform. This can be distracting to others in the audience but, as records show, many of these bored or restless children will follow the family footsteps into the youth orchestra – and who would want to discourage young players of the future?

Reviewer Lindis Taylor noted James Sedares' 'warm relationship with the orchestra', illustrated when, at the end of the concert, someone 'leapt onto the stage, and put a floppy straw hat on his head'. This had 'inspired' Sedares to play an encore, Copland's *Rodeo*, although this proved 'difficult to hold together and they were indeed a bit ragged'.

'These were qualities you expect from young players', Taylor said, 'freshness, spontaneity, enthusiasm, also raggedness, lack of finesse, lack of balance, dynamics a bit unrefined, fluffed horns, timpani out of focus, shaky intonation from solo players', but at the at the end of a week's hard work with Sedares 'they had achieved the first three qualities, but none of the deficiencies remained. They were simply brilliant'.

The Beethoven Concerto, played by a young Austrian pianist, Christopher Hinterhuber, 'made us hear the work's voices', Taylor said, but he was 'curious ... at the decision to import a player [the soloist] instead of using one of our own young performers. They are given few enough chances by the principal concert promoters and surely this was an occasion for a New Zealander'.[90]

This engagement presumably was made by the NZSO's artistic manager, Austrian Dr Peter Ramsauer,[91] and among New Zealand National Youth Orchestra players also, the feeling was quite strong that soloists 'should always be young New Zealand musicians'. The opportunity to play a concerto with the youth orchestra 'is not going to do anything for an overseas artist, but would be a fantastic starting point for any young New Zealand musician'.[92] The tradition of engaging young New Zealanders as soloists resumed the next year.

1998

Napier, Wellington, 4 & 6 September. Conductor: James Sedares.
Copland – *El Salón México*; Mozart – Flute Concerto no 1 in G (Kirstin Eade, flute); Carl Orff – *Carmina Burana* (Karen Heathcote, soprano; Geoffrey Coker, counter-tenor; Teddy Tahu Rhodes, baritone)

This was the third year in a row with James Sedares, and there were two concerts, one of them out of Wellington. Flutist Kirstin Eade (NYO 1996), a finalist in the 1997 Young Musicians Competition, runner-up in TVNZ's *Showcase*, and winner of the 1996 New Zealand Post Young Musicians Award, was soloist in the Mozart Concerto.[93]

New Zealand's two leading youth entities – the National Youth Orchestra and the National Youth Choir – had last performed together in 1995. The two would now collaborate in a significant non-mainstream work which had never been performed by the youth orchestra, and few in the audience would have heard played live before.

Carmina Burana, Carl Orff's ground-breaking cantata, was based on poems found in the monastery of Benediktbeuren, Bavaria, and was first performed in Germany in 1937. Its colourful orchestration and the rhythmic vivacity Orff gave these 13th-century texts (with their universal themes of gambling, eating, drinking, love, and lewdness) remains relevant and it has enduring appeal to contemporary audiences – and to young musicians.

This was a major undertaking for the orchestra, after several years of difficult financial restraints, as the work required very large forces – 90 musicians, 140 singers, and three soloists – and it proved a challenge even to find sufficient billets.

Malcolm Mawhinney, co-principal viola (NYO 1996–2000), was impressed: 'NYO on tour! Watch out! For me, as part of the orchestra, finally having the chance to tour, even though just up the road to Napier, was exciting. We felt like a younger NZSO. The reaction from the crowd was wonderful ... it was a full house and the place was buzzing – backstage and in the hall. Playing such a powerful work with the numbers we had brought the house down. It felt like a major event, bringing so many young instrumentalists and choristers to town, and it was treated as such. Having dinner before the concert, the restaurant staff *knew* we were part of the orchestra in town that night. And did it feel great walking through the Municipal theatre car-park, before the performance and being admitted backstage, past the audience!'[94]

'We put together a superb programme', manager Lindy Tennent-Brown recalls. 'Aside from a fire alarm in the first five minutes of the concert in Napier (the Chief Fire Officer was in the audience and congratulated us for the "efficiency of our evacuation") I will never forget the feeling of satisfaction (relief) when all the people on my list disembarked from our five coaches at Wellington Railway Station – meaning we hadn't lost any second violins en route. More importantly, both concerts were well-attended and critically successful with a standard of performance widely regarded as being extremely high.'[95]

9 'What a gift!'

1999–2004

> 'NYO is definitely one of the highlights of my musical life ... Meeting other New Zealand musicians all over the world, I think that a lot of kiwi (and occasionally South Africans) feel this way.'
>
> – *Christiaan (Chris) van der Zee, NYO viola, 2000–2001*[1]

Managing the youth orchestra

The New Zealand Youth Orchestra had benefited from the consistent ongoing management of Alwyn Palmer for twenty-three years, until 1993. The orchestra did not meet the following year, and for the next four years after that it appears that its administration and management was carried out on an ad hoc basis. There was little continuity and, in an era where NZSO still grappled with major problems of its own, there was a view that the youth orchestra was 'a time-consuming distraction'.

Michael Joel (NYO violin, 1988; viola, 1990, 1992) provided continuity as assistant conductor of the youth orchestra from 1995 to 1998.[2] Grant Gilbert, the NZSO's stage manager, performed the same role from 1992, but there was no heir apparent to replace Alwyn Palmer from the downsized NZSO management. From 1995 to 1998, various people managed the youth orchestra. They came and went: musicologist and NZSO artistic development manager Dr Allan Badley in 1995; Greta Mark (NYO viola, 1990–93) was youth orchestra coordinator from 1996 to 1997; Stephen Harker (NYO percussion, 1993, 1995, 1998) was youth orchestra administrator in 1997, while doing his honours degree at the School of Music, Victoria University; pianist Lindy Tennent-Brown took over in late 1997, managed the 1998 season, and left in September to resume her studies in Manchester.

'There were some people within NZSO who were hugely supportive, generous with their skills and enormously helpful when I had questions', Lindy says. 'But I fought daily with what felt like an overwhelming disinterest in something that should have been, in my opinion, an integral, highly valued part of the NZSO's mission.'[3]

Ian Fraser, NZSO's new chief executive,[4] was not aware of this situation, when he took up his appointment, in October 1998. 'I discovered progressively, as I got my feet under the desk, that NZSO was facing major solvency issues. It was almost as if it had been pitched back into the problems of the early to mid 1990s, and was now reporting a significant deficit. When I arrived there was a sense that anything that distracted from NZSO "core" activities had to be subordinated or pushed away, while the deficit issue was dealt with. I had very warm feelings for the NYO, from my engagement with it as a younger man. I knew how important it was, that it was an icon, but by late 1998, the NZSO's education activities had fallen away, and the NYO itself, was in a state of despair. There was absolutely no doubt that the NYO might be forced to fold its tent – indeed, this prospect was openly discussed.' When the deficit became worse, in the first six months, Fraser says that he and the NZSO chair, Sir Selwyn Cushing, met with Bill Birch, Minister of Finance, and Simon Upton, Minister of Cultural Affairs, to try and persuade them to deal with the solvency issue by increasing the government grant to NZSO. 'We were assured that "the Government intended to be a reliable paymaster and that the NZSO will get this year and next year what it had got last year". Not the response we were hoping for! I made it clear to the ministers that this stance would entail having to take an axe to the orchestra's playing strength! ...

'I quite openly urged members of the orchestra and the Players Committee, to "agitate and lobby" for all they are worth, to avoid the orchestra's strength dropping from 95 or so, to maybe 75–80 members. The Players Committee was marvellous, and staged a sort of guerrilla lobbying campaign in the lead up to the 1999 general election. Building audience numbers was my number one issue, and if the relentless decline of audience numbers around the country had been allowed to continue ... well, it was obvious that even in hard times, we had to lift our game, to fill the halls.

'I remember having several conversations about the youth orchestra being a vital part of the NZSO's wider remit, and one of the keystones of its future.

'It was unacceptable that the NYO should be sacrificed because the NZSO was facing a (short-term, we hoped!) deficit and funding crisis ... The recipe for continuity was to find a sponsor and move away from the prevailing inconsistency of management. Whatever my best intentions may have been, however, I believe it could still have gone to the wall, but for Brigid O'Meeghan.'

Brigid's years

Brigid O'Meeghan, the NZSO's assistant sub-principal cello, had been watching the evolving situation with increasing concern. 'I had become aware of a high turnover of staff in the artistic department and I remember mentioning to someone that I would be "more than happy to help out, by photocopying music and stuffing envelopes for the NYO. At the end of November 1998 Professor Peter Walls who was then a member of the NZSO Board and acting artistic manager handed me the NYO project!'

The offer was unexpected and daunting. It would entail having to fit in many extra hours of work around her usual practice and playing for NZSO, but Brigid was uniquely qualified to administer the youth orchestra. A former NYO cellist (1972–74), Brigid joined NZSO in January 1977 and after two years in the cello section left to study and freelance in London. By September 1981 she had become a cellist in the Hong Kong Philharmonic, where she stayed for almost eight years.

'I was still resident there in 1989 when I was approached by Richard Pontzious who was forming the Asian Youth Orchestra [AYO]. He asked if I would be interested in joining the teaching faculty as cello coach', Brigid says. 'The AYO was loosely modelled on the highly successful European Community Orchestra, and young musicians from all over Asia were invited to audition. Sir Yehudi Menuhin agreed to be the founding Music Director and Conductor for the first summer camp, to be held in Shanghai, China, but this was postponed in June 1989.[5] I returned to New Zealand, and rejoined the NZSO in August 1989.'

In 1990, Brigid was granted six weeks' leave by NZSO to 'honour her teaching commitment'. She joined the Asian Youth Orchestra when it convened for its inaugural season in Kumomoto, Japan. 'This was hugely successful', Brigid recalls. 'Over the next ten years I attended almost all the AYO summer camps held at various cities in Asia. I also attended the celebrations in 1997 when Hong Kong was handed back to the mainland – Yo Yo Ma[6] and the AYO conducted by Sergio Comissiona performed the Elgar Cello Concerto and also a special composition, Symphony 1997, *Heaven Earth Mankind*.'

Brigid accompanied the AYO for part of its extensive tour in Hong Kong and throughout China before heading back to New Zealand. 'I knew that it was my last AYO, but over the years I had had some extraordinary experiences working with distinguished faculty from the major symphony orchestras in the United States and Europe, as well as conductors and soloists', she says. 'Whilst my role with the AYO was strictly artistic, I observed how superbly the orchestra was organised, with its small administrative staff. The daily schedule was rigorous and demanding of the orchestra members and faculty, and the results spoke for themselves. I kept in touch with many of my fellow teaching colleagues, and violinist Cho-Liang Lin, who was an AYO soloist in 1994, toured with the NZSO early in 2009.'[7]

When first offered the NYO job, Brigid remembers, 'I sat down with a large piece of blank paper, as my "blueprint," and I wrote in a box at the bottom of the sheet "concert". Gradually I worked up the page filling in the boxes with tasks and timelines. Instinctively I knew that if we found the best possible youth orchestra conductor to give the players the best possible experience, the rest would more or less take care of itself.

This is where the wonderful musicians' network came into play. 'Two colleagues on the Asian Youth Orchestra faculty recommended their colleague in Boston, Benjamin Zander,[8] a conductor and an educator. Wilma Smith, the NZSO concertmaster, had studied at the New England Conservatory in Boston, and as she knew Zander she kindly agreed to make the first phone call, and to sound him out on his availability. It was short notice, but fortuitously he was available and agreed to come in August 1999. So the conductor box was filled in, along with the date and the concert venue!'

Over the months Brigid's page filled up with more boxes, instructions and tasks, she says. 'The NZSO administration was helpful and patient and I continued as normal in the cello section.'

Benjamin Zander came with a distinguished reputation as a composer, conductor, teacher and inspirational speaker, Brigid says. 'I remember his arrival, and it was from the minute that Mr Zander bounced off the aircraft having flown directly from Boston, full of energy and enthusiasm with his infectious smile, that I knew that things were going to be all right.'

1999: The 40th birthday

Wellington, 5 September. Conductor: Benjamin Zander. Beethoven – *Coriolan* Overture; Tchaikovsky – Fantasy Overture *Romeo and Juliet*; Shostakovich – Symphony no 5

The orchestra's significant fourth decade began with a no-frills season with few sponsors, no soloist, and just the one Sunday evening concert in Wellington, held five days short of the actual anniversary date of the inaugural concert in Lower Hutt Town Hall on 10 September 1959.

The programme cover sported a new logo, combined with the old original name: 'NYO, National Youth Orchestra, a division of NZSO'.

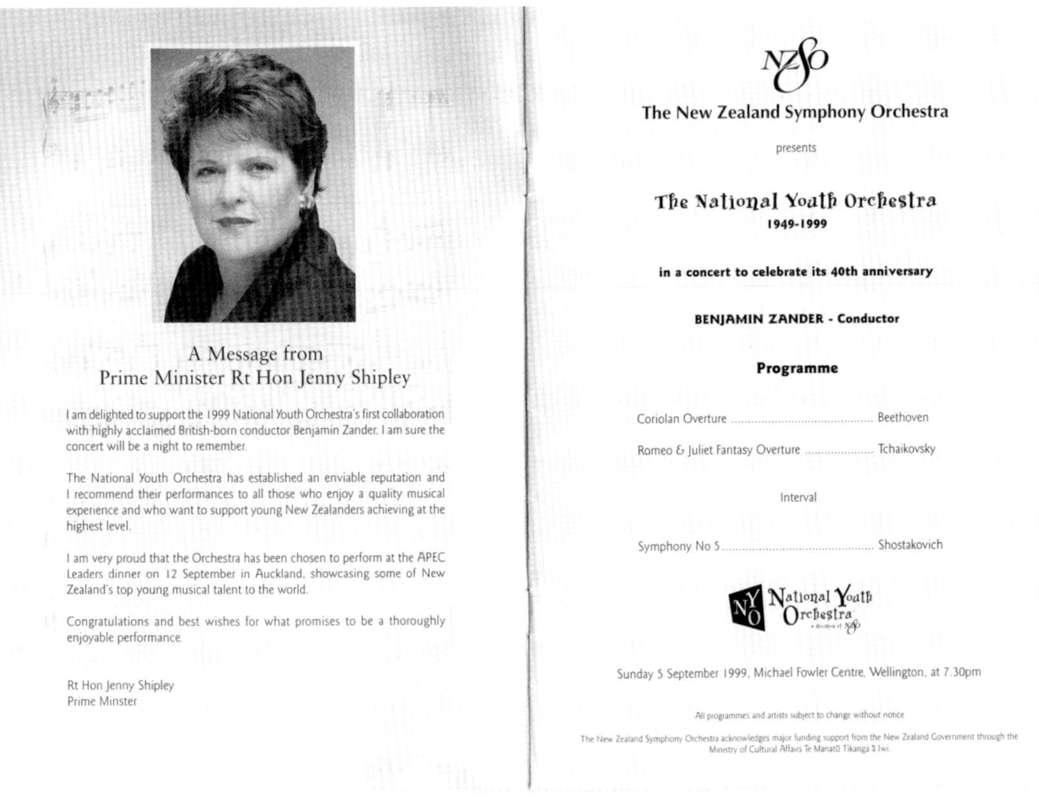

A Message from
Prime Minister Rt Hon Jenny Shipley

I am delighted to support the 1999 National Youth Orchestra's first collaboration with highly acclaimed British-born conductor Benjamin Zander. I am sure the concert will be a night to remember.

The National Youth Orchestra has established an enviable reputation and I recommend their performances to all those who enjoy a quality musical experience and who want to support young New Zealanders achieving at the highest level.

I am very proud that the Orchestra has been chosen to perform at the APEC Leaders dinner on 12 September in Auckland, showcasing some of New Zealand's top young musical talent to the world.

Congratulations and best wishes for what promises to be a thoroughly enjoyable performance.

Rt Hon Jenny Shipley
Prime Minster

NZSO
The New Zealand Symphony Orchestra

presents

The National Youth Orchestra
1949-1999

in a concert to celebrate its 40th anniversary

BENJAMIN ZANDER - Conductor

Programme

Coriolan Overture .... Beethoven

Romeo & Juliet Fantasy Overture .... Tchaikovsky

Interval

Symphony No 5 .... Shostakovich

National Youth Orchestra

Sunday 5 September 1999, Michael Fowler Centre, Wellington, at 7.30pm

All programmes and artists subject to change without notice

The New Zealand Symphony Orchestra acknowledges major funding support from the New Zealand Government through the Ministry of Cultural Affairs Te Manatū Tikanga ā Iwi.

From the National Youth Orchestra's 40th birthday programme

Inside, Jenny Shipley, New Zealand's first woman prime minister, offered congratulations, and recommended the NYO's performances to all those 'who enjoy a quality musical experience and who want to support young New Zealanders achieving at the highest level. I am very proud that the Orchestra has been chosen to perform at the APEC Leaders dinner ... showcasing some of New Zealand's top young musical talent to the world.'[9]

On the opposite page, it was stated: 'New Zealand Symphony Orchestra presents The National Youth Orchestra, 1949–1999 [*sic*] in a concert to celebrate its 40th anniversary.' As was now usual, there was an acknowledgement of 'major funding support from the New Zealand Government through the Ministry of Cultural Affairs Te Manatū Tikanga ā Iwi'.[10]

A historical note gave a timely reaffirmation of the orchestra's original and still relevant threefold aims: 'to offer concentrated orchestral playing at an advanced level to approximately 90 of this country's best young musicians, to aid in preparing potential professional symphony orchestra players, and to extend their musical experience and that of their audiences.'[11]

James Judd, then the NZSO's music director and now NZSO conductor emeritus, spoke from his own extensive background in youth music when he called the work of the National Youth Orchestra, 'a thrilling and vital part of the fabric of music in New Zealand. This is where dedication, enthusiasm, optimism and hard work combine to provide not only musicians, but also audiences of the future ... Good luck to you all and thank you all for your very good work.'

'It was a memorable week of inspiring rehearsals, master classes and hard work, which culminated in a rousing concert and a standing ovation', Brigid recalls.[12] 'The choice of Benjamin Zander as conductor had brought a wonderful response from NYO players.'

Joe Harrop, concertmaster for the 40th anniversary

This was a 'particularly inspired choice' in the opinion of Joe Harrop who was now concertmaster. 'Zander's approach to working with young people influences me on a daily basis in my work with students, now ... One of my best memories was the dress rehearsal of Beethoven's *Coriolan* Overture in the Michael Fowler centre. One of those rare, large ensemble experiences where it all works as it should. Magic.'

'Zander was an inspiration', says Malcolm Mawhinney. 'We were important. We felt professional. We performed and recorded. We have the CD. We cried as our encore *Nimrod*[13] died away. The audience was massive by NYO standards – the whole bottom level of the MFC – and we gave it to them. There was no rosin on my bow by the end of the Shostakovich, the finale played at the correct, slow tempo.'

'My best memory was Benjamin Zander's pre-concert speech to the audience, and Shostakovich 5 followed by a heartbreakingly beautiful *Nimrod* variation', says Amelia Giles (NYO violin, 1999, 2001–02). 'We all cried (a lot) and he took the time to say thank you and hug every single one of us as we walked off stage. I came home after that NYO a changed musician.'[14]

Conductor Bemjamin Zander

Performing for APEC

Auckland, APEC Forum Leaders Dinner, 17 September. Conductor: Ken Young. Mozart – *Eine Kleine Nachtmusik*; Fauré – Divertimento in D; Farr – *Te Papa*

A week after its anniversary concert sixty players from the youth orchestra and seven members of percussion group Strike performed at the prestigious APEC [Asia-Pacific Economic Cooperation] Forum Leaders' Dinner at the Auckland Town Hall, in the presence of the Prime Minister, Jenny Shipley, the United States President, Bill Clinton, and other world leaders. There had been much speculation (and possibly, rivalry) about which professional orchestra would present the concert and then Ian Fraser proposed the youth orchestra. It was a brilliant choice. 'Young people transcend the politics which often surround these sorts of decisions and New Zealand was truly represented by its most accomplished young musicians', Fraser said.

This would prove to be one of the most unusual 'gigs' performed by a National Youth Orchestra in its fifty years. Security was tight, with no one allowed to leave the Town Hall until the conclusion of the concert, and rehearsals taking most of Saturday. On Sunday evening, the performance began with the arrival of the leaders, who were entertained by the youth orchestra which played chamber music as they dined, and Gareth Farr's *Te Papa* (with an associated visual show), during dessert.

Details of the occasion were faithfully recorded by Malcolm Mawhinney in his diary: 'Our flight in was the last before Auckland International was closed for the arrival of Air Force One ... We were allowed out of the airport building and up to a perimeter fence to watch Mr President arrive on New Zealand soil ... Gareth Farr came to our rehearsals and announced that we were playing *Te Papa* "with a bloody sight more gusto than those old buggers."[15] Nice one!

'We were bussed to the top of Queen St, and dumped in the car park, having to walk into the security zone around Auckland Town Hall through the protesters. The concert was played behind a screen which lit up and became transparent to reveal the orchestra, mostly perched precariously upon the choir stalls. Only us front desks of the strings and the conductor were actually on the stage proper ... I remember locking eyes with one of Clinton's security detail – they had nine security staff watching each of us as we left ... we were then imprisoned backstage at Auckland Town Hall, until 11pm with no real refreshments, to ensure security for Bill Clinton was not compromised.'[16]

The only precedent for the APEC performance was in 1966, when members of the National Youth Orchestra played in a combined Royal Youth Concert for the Queen Mother; apparently there have been no similar invitations before, or since then. By comparison, the Australian Youth Orchestra is said to, 'enjoy a flagship status, and is proudly displayed by the federal government on important national occasions'.[17] A similar role could be equally appropriate for NZSO National Youth Orchestra, whose members, drawn from around New Zealand, unquestionably represent the cream of this country's young orchestral musicians.

The 40th anniversary was not only a significant milestone, and an opportunity to celebrate past achievements. It marked a major turning point in the fortunes of the orchestra and the way in which it was perceived. Brigid O'Meeghan provided the breakthrough when she took over the management of the orchestra, and initiated a new level of professionalism. The engagement of the inspirational Benjamin Zander as conductor was another factor in generating new confidence, as was the wider recognition of the orchestra's value which came from its engagement to perform at the APEC Forum Leaders Dinner.

Within a few weeks of the anniversary, as the icing on the 40th birthday cake, came a major announcement: Denis and Verna Adam, two of New Zealand's most significant philanthropists, became sponsors of the youth orchestra through the Adam Foundation.[18] 'I am pleased to assist because the Adam Foundation considers providing young New Zealand musicians with orchestral experience under a conductor of international standing to be imperative if standards are to be maintained', said Denis Adam.[19]

2000

The cover of the printed programme for 2000 carried a new banner, over another new name: 'The Adam Foundation presents NZSO National Youth Orchestra'. This was sponsorship initially for 'the next three years', as Brigid O'Meeghan was pleased to point out, and 'it is most gratifying to see that ten years on (in 2009), the NZYO's 50th anniversary year, Mr & Mrs Adam still maintain their support of the orchestra'.[20]

An encouraging message from the newly elected Prime Minister, Helen Clark,[21] (also Minister for Arts, Culture and Heritage), attested to her government's 'strong commitment to nurturing New Zealand's orchestral resources', and the New Zealand Symphony Orchestra's 'international reputation for excellence'. Funding measures as part of the Building Cultural Identity programme, announced in May 2000, 'will ensure that reputation is safeguarded', the Prime Minister said. The arts in New Zealand had never had such a high profile – or received such a high-level public acknowledgement of the importance of the arts and, specifically, of the NZSO, to New Zealand.

Mark Churchill, conductor, 2000. *Steven Emery*

Wellington, 3 September. Conductor: Mark Churchill.
Weber – *Euryanthe* Overture; Schumann – Cello Concerto (Ashley Brown, soloist); Bartók – Concerto for Orchestra

The engagement of a new conductor might have seemed a challenge, following in the wake of the remarkable Benjamin Zander, but Brigid O'Meeghan knew just whom to suggest next: Mark Churchill, dean of preparatory and continuing education at the New England Conservatory,[22] and his wife, Marylou Speaker Churchill, principal second violin in the Boston Symphony Orchestra since 1977.[23] Both were Brigid's colleagues on the acclaimed Asian Youth Orchestra faculty, from its first year, in 1990, she recalls, 'and they had recommended Zander to me, the previous year!'[24]

Ashley Brown, cello soloist, 2000

The youth orchestra was extremely fortunate to have for the first time, a husband-and-wife team of musicians with such impressive and relevant backgrounds. Mark Churchill was now the AYO's resident conductor, and Marylou Speaker Churchill had recently retired after twenty years with the Boston Symphony, before coming to New Zealand. Ms Churchill played a very active role as a tutor, coaching the youth orchestra's chamber music groups and giving violin master classes.Their daughters Emma and Julia accompanied their parents to New Zealand.

Malcolm Mawhinney remembers that Marylou Speaker Churchill was 'an unexpected hit. She took the entire upper string sections crammed into one of Vic's lecture rooms. She would not allow anyone in until she checked that the bridge of your instrument was straight up. What a lady! She made the string sound what it was.'[25]

Ashley Brown, soloist in Schumann's Cello Concerto, was a former youth orchestra principal cellist (1989–92), and winner of major New Zealand competitions and awards.[26] He was now an artist-in-residence at the University of Waikato, where he was also a member of the Turnovsky Trio.[27] The night before the concert, there was anxiety when Mark Churchill was hit by a food poisoning bug. The conductor fortunately recovered in time for the concert, 'much to my relief', Brigid says.

The concert was the finale of 'Youth Arts 2000', a week-long programme of young people's performing arts, including the National Youth Choir, in Wellington. 'This was a great idea and should be repeated', said Lindis Taylor.[28] 'The National Youth Orchestra concert was an inspiration. They'd been hard at work all week and it showed in a level of energy and excellence that must often be the envy of professional orchestras.'

There were two National Youth Orchestra innovations in this year, Brigid says. 'The first was the barbecue lunch at the beginning of the week, at the School of Music, and the second was the association with St Andrew's on The Terrace, in the lunchtime concert series on Wednesdays. Players were invited to submit solo or chamber works, and were coached beforehand in a master class, thus giving audiences another opportunity to hear the gifted members of the orchestra playing individually and in ensembles.'

John Button wrote, 'From the brass players who played out at the entrance to the church, to the percussion players who played a Toccata without instruments (clapping, stamping and body slapping), each and every performer was immersed in the music ... In a little more than an hour, we heard New Zealand's future – opportunities allowing, it is brighter than at any time in out history.'[29]

'Both events have become traditions of the NYO rehearsal week in Wellington', Brigid says, 'and I also began inviting NYO players to submit programme notes, which, over the years, have been insightful and interesting!'

Significant new awards for players were made. The NZSO Foundation Trust Board (through the Reeves Harris Orchestra Fund) assisted fifteen section principals towards the payment of their tuition fees; and a special prize of $500 from the Alex Lindsay Memorial Awards, to mark the year 2000, was won by oboist Stacey Dixon.

2001

Wellington & Auckland, 31 August, 2 September. Conductor: Lutz Köhler.
Mozart – Overture to *Don Giovanni*; Chopin – Variations on *La ci darem la mano* (Justin Bird, piano); Strauss – *Don Juan*; Prokofiev – Symphony no 5

It was on the recommendation of James Judd that the National Youth Orchestra, drawing from the great German musical heritage, invited conductor Professor Lutz Köhler for the 2001 season.[30] Brigid O'Meeghan says that, 'he was a marvellous musical presence, who demanded great things from the musicians whose capabilities he understood so well'.

Justin Bird, a seventeen-year-old pianist and viola player, was a youth orchestra member for both instruments (1999–2000). In 2001, elevated to soloist with the orchestra, Justin performed the 'Variations' written by Chopin

Right: soloist Justin Bird

Far right: conductor Lutz Köhler

at the same age, and wrote his own programme note, which concluded, 'Perhaps it would do the "Variations" justice in the light of Schumann's accolade ("Hats off, gentlemen! A genius!"), to observe that, while they do not themselves add up to a work of genius, they are certainly a work by a genius.'[31]

'The Orchestra's family of sponsors began to increase, at this time', Brigid says, 'and we were able to tour the orchestra to Auckland for the first time in many years. Forsyth Barr Ltd became a sustaining sponsor and awarded scholarships to five selected players to assist with their travel expenses and fees. The Alex Lindsay Memorial Award, a special prize, originally intended as a one-off award for the year 2000, was awarded again in 2001, and this continues at the same level to the present day. Also a scholarship administered through the NZSO Foundation from the Jack and Emma Griffin Trust was awarded to the soloist; and through the Reeves Harris Trust, sixteen awards were made to principal players. The John Chisholm Prize to the concertmaster continued.'

2002

Wellington, Auckland, August 23 & 25. Conductor: Benjamin Zander.
Ives – *Three Places in New England*; Stravinsky – *The Firebird* Suite (1919);
Brahms – Symphony no 4

The return of Benjamin Zander was eagerly anticipated, for his sensational first collaboration with the orchestra in 1999 was still vividly remembered. However, as Heath Lees had reported at that time, Zander had said he was 'pretty furious' and so disappointed by the New Zealand press for not publishing his interview before the Wellington concert, that he would 'never return to this country, that he'd never been anywhere with so little media interest in the arts, that all we were interested in was rapes and robberies, and as for our Kiwi obsession with sport'.[32]

'I fear Professor Heath Lees somewhat misinterpreted my reaction to the sparse coverage of the orchestra', Benjamin Zander wrote in reply to the *New Zealand Herald.* 'I was frustrated and saddened, rather than angered by the lack of attention given to the event beforehand by the media. Every seat should have been filled ... New Zealanders have reason to be extremely proud of the accomplishments of their young musicians – just as proud as they rightly are of their very fine rugby players who are rarely out of the public eye. All who attended their concert must have been inspired and uplifted by these youngsters' passion, high accomplishment and extraordinary team spirit ... I await eagerly an opportunity to continue my relationship with a group of such exemplary young people.'[33]

Benjamin Zander's remarks about media coverage of rugby would have resonated with many a New Zealand music lover and, true to his promise, three years after his first inspiring sessions he returned to perform another two equally memorable concerts with the orchestra.

Sponsorship

The growing numbers of sponsors now required its own dedicated page in the printed programme. The Adam Foundation topped a list of ten organisations who were contributing sponsors, a list that now included SSL Spotless Services as a Sustaining Sponsor in 2002. A year later, an ongoing association began with McDouall Stuart (Securities Ltd), and the Garth Williams Scholarship for ten players was initiated.

'The Wellington NZSO Friends[34] and the Auckland NZSO Friends also increased their involvement, by assisting with the annual auditions during April 2002', Brigid recalls. 'As well in Wellington the Friends took over the organisation of the barbecue lunch, which was a huge relief to me... and began their sponsorship of the annual NYO CD recording, made by Radio New Zealand from a live recording of the concert.'

2003

Wellington & Auckland, 30–31 August 2003. Conductor: Lutz Köhler.
Wagner – *Tristan und Isolde: Prelude* and *Liebestod*; Prokofiev – *The Love of Three Oranges*; Mahler – Symphony no 1

It was Lutz Köhler's second season and, says Brigid O'Meeghan, 'one of my personal NYO concert highlights was the Auckland performance of the

Vorspiel und Liebestod from Wagner's *Tristan und Isolde*. It was heartfelt and spellbinding.'[35]

A major development in New Zealand this year was the campaign for CCR – Closer Cultural Relations – with Australia. 'CCR began officially for the NYO as a result of a meeting four years earlier', says Brigid. 'Back in July 1999 I heard the Camerata of the Australian Youth Orchestra perform in Auckland. I went backstage and introduced myself as the NYO's administrator to its then manager Tony Grybowski. As a result I was invited to attend the Australian Youth Orchestra Forum in Sydney in September 1999, where I met Simon Rogers, the artistic administrator, who, like me, grew up in Christchurch. I was invited annually to attend these conferences, where I was reminded that the same issues exist everywhere: funding, competition, "endangered species" – namely violas and bassoons – and recruitment of players'.

In 2003 the Australian Youth Orchestra extended an invitation for a player to attend its Summer Camp in Perth, Western Australia. 'There was a space for a viola player', Brigid says, 'and Amanda Verner was selected to attend. As a New Zealand player she was required to pay the full unsubsidised fees, but I was able to secure special one-off funding from two private donors. Coincidentally, I was a cello tutor at the AYO's summer camp that year, in Perth. This was enormously successful and in successive years there have been two-way exchanges of players between the orchestras.'

It was during the summer holidays, 2003/2004, when Brigid was putting the 2004 NYO season into place, that she began to realise that to maintain the standard of her own cello playing in the NZSO – while continuing to develop the NYO programme – she had to make a choice. 'I fell into the role of NYO administrator quite by chance, and for over five years I was fulfilling two big but contrasting roles concurrently. For some time I would go straight to the office after rehearsals had finished, and work late into the night on NYO matters, to keep on top of the workload. It was a regime that I knew I could not keep up indefinitely.

'In early 2003 I had several months away from NZSO, recuperating from a shoulder surgery, and I found that I really missed my orchestral playing. It was one of the most difficult but necessary decisions in my life, but in January 2004 I relinquished my position with the NYO. It was very hard to let go something that I was passionate about, but the task was made easier when I handed it over to my friend and colleague Pascale Parenteau, who has taken the NYO to great heights, and who will provide the next phase in this orchestra's wonderful history.[36]

'As I reflect on my years as NYO administrator – my title later became 'Coordinator', but I was far too scared ever to accept the title 'Manager'! – I feel very privileged to have had the opportunity to serve New Zealand's most gifted young orchestral musicians, especially when I had no previous administrative background or experience. The responsibility of seeing each NYO project year through from beginning to end was challenging and hard work, but immensely worthwhile. I acknowledge all my colleagues over the years in the NZSO administration, all of whom were helpful, patient and understanding of all my blind spots. Doing the annual budget still remains one of life's great mysteries for me. Year after year the young musicians gave me so much through their enthusiasm, determination and dedication, and it was these attributes which got me through on the many occasions when things got tough. Several are now colleagues in the NZSO. Others are overseas studying or are already successful professional musicians. Some have gone into professions other than music, but retain the love of music and memories of their NYO days.

'One name in particular comes to mind from that first NYO in 1999: Amalia Hall. Amalia was ten years old, the youngest of a family of four gifted young musicians who have all been through the ranks of the NYO. In 1999 Amalia's sister Lara was associate concertmaster; and in 2003 Lara and Amalia (violins), Elroy (viola) and Callum (cello) were all members of the NYO – almost certainly a first for the orchestra.[37]

'There is something very special about a youth orchestra, whether it is a country's *national* youth orchestra, or one comprised of young kids from a small town. It's almost as if I caught a 'Youth Orchestra' bug all those years ago in Hong Kong! Seeing a group of young players completely transformed in a week from the raw material of an orchestra which has never played together before, seeing them giving their all, playing with their heart to the absolute best of their ability at any time, is a life blood to a long-time professional player such as me. The freshness, vitality and enthusiasm – like a bug – is contagious!

'The young musicians I have had the pleasure of working with over the years have given me much more than I could ever have given them – a revitalized approach and appreciation of the mystery and power of music. What a gift!'[38]

In May 2004 Brigid O'Meeghan stepped aside from the administration of NZSO National Youth Orchestra and resumed her full-time career as the NZSO's assistant sub-principal cello, having successfully juggled these two demanding dual roles for five years. Brigid's dedication and commitment had introduced a new level of professionalism to the benefit of generations of young musicians. In just five years, the profile of the orchestra was higher, its funding more widely spread, and its future seemingly more secure. Brigid's dedication and commitment has helped to save the youth orchestra for New Zealand, to the benefit of generations of young musicians and their audiences.

What a gift for us all, Brigid.

Brigid O'Meeghan recording an audition by Megan Allison, violin, for the 2000 session

10 'A Taste of the Real Thing'

2004–2009

'I wanted to give them an insight into what it would be like – to be a professional musician'

– *Pascale Parenteau*[1]

Pascale's years

Pascale Parenteau, a 'born and bred' French Canadian from Québec, was studying for a science degree in 1984, when she attended the national music camp at Orford. It was there that she met a young New Zealand violinist, David Gilling (NYO 1978–80), and decided to change direction from science to music. On completing her science degree, Pascale began a Bachelor of Music degree in violin performance at McGill University in Montréal, in 1992. David and Pascale married that same year, and by graduation, she had moved to New Zealand, where David is the NZSO's sub-principal second violin.[2]

Pascale very soon became involved in the musical life of Wellington, as a performer, teacher, and administrator, playing as a contract violinist when required by NZSO, and also principal of the second violin section of the Wellington Sinfonia Orchestra. She was the co-coordinator of the Wellington district final of the Schools Music Contest for Chamber Music New Zealand for three consecutive years, and the information services executive for SOUNZ (the Centre for New Zealand Music) from 2000 to 2004.

In 2003, Dominique Marcel, the couple's first child, was born, and ten months later Pascale became the NZSO National Youth Orchestra co-ordinator (later manager). This position, she says, 'gave me the opportunity to work with New Zealand's flagship orchestra in a capacity which combines [my] twin professional passions of orchestral playing and education'.[3]

It was a baptism of fire for Pascale, whose first few months in the job coincided with the busiest time leading up to the National Youth Orchestra course itself: 'I learned quickly the importance of entire and detailed preparation and systematic organisation, as well as the true understanding that the choice of the conductor is the crucial component on which the success of the course depends.'

This position was not fulltime, just twenty hours a week for most of the year, although this could increase dramatically, up to sixty hours, during the National Youth Orchestra week. Pascale was fortunate that, unlike previous youth orchestra coordinators, she had the great advantage of being able to call on the knowledge and generous support of her predecessor, Brigid O'Meeghan, who had not only successfully managed the orchestra over the preceding five years, but brought it to a more secure and sustainable footing.

'It was quite an honour to work on such a project', Pascale recalls, 'knowing that I was the first ever dedicated staff member to be employed to run the NYO. In the past this role was always filled by various staff members in addition to their other duties within NZSO. I was well aware of its importance, and I believe that the decision to change its status reflected a desire on the part of the NZSO to enhance the NYO experience, while maintaining the high standards already achieved. I felt quite a responsibility but at the same time, I was extremely excited by the challenge!'[4]

2004

Wellington, Christchurch, Auckland, 31 August–4 September. Conductor: Alasdair Neale. Berlioz – *Roman Carnival*; Elgar – *Enigma Variations*; Brahms – Symphony no 1

Conductor Alasdair Neale

Conductors for Pascale's first two years were already in place. The first was Alasdair Neale, music director of the Marin Symphony, who also held the positions of music director of the Sun Valley Summer Symphony, principal guest conductor of the New World Symphony and music director of the San Francisco Conservatory of Music.[5]

'The NZSO National Youth Orchestra's annual concert has become one of the city's mid-winter highlights, giving 90 young musicians a chance to show what a week of intensive work with an international conductor can achieve', William Dart wrote after the Auckland concert. 'In 2002, the charismatic Benjamin Zander thrilled us with Ives and Stravinsky. Last year with Lutz Köhler we had a Mahler First that was startling in its maturity', but Alasdair Neale 'with unimpeachable credentials ... did not quite ignite as it could have'.

Although Dart considered 'Elgar's *Enigma Variations* would make demands on the most experienced orchestra ... the NYO fared magnificently after only a week together ... and the Brahms First Symphony, with the brass coming forward in resplendent chorale ... was given the ecstatic peroration that the programme note – beautifully written by [NZSO NYO] violinist Marcel Fernandes – had promised'.[6]

In Christchurch a reviewer claimed, 'the orchestra's snappy opening bars blew me out of my seat. By the time they had finished the rest of Berlioz's *Carnival Romaine Overture,* I wondered why the NYO of about 90 hadn't toured south for some time as it is stacked to the hilt with Christchurch players. The programme hugged well-trodden romantic favourites. But when their Elgar ... and Brahms ... were dispatched so freshly under the baton of Alasdair Neale, you couldn't quibble much.'

'Youth concert – just superb', was David Sell's headline.[7] 'Let's put aside this "youth orchestra" label and consider this as a full-scale orchestral concert. In this context it rates as one of the best.'

No sooner had this successful season concluded, Pascale says, 'than I was on the lookout for the best first class conductors I could invite – within my budget of course – and avoiding the "cliché" of youth orchestra specialists. I wanted someone that could relate to the young players that would not lower their standard, but would expect their best from them. I wanted to give them a taste of the real thing, an insight of what it would be like to be a professional musician.'

New initiatives

Pascale then prepared a five-year action plan and came up with proposals for four new initiatives to enhance the youth orchestra experience. Three of these were adopted and incorporated into the following season, and the fourth, modified slightly, was added to the 50th anniversary season in 2009.

1. The Composer-in-residence Award

Drawing on her experience at SOUNZ, Pascale identified another opportunity to enhance the NYO experience, by launching a competition for young composers. This project was intended not only to find new compositional talent, but also to encourage interest in the performance of contemporary music on the part of orchestral members and audience while complementing the wider New Zealand music strategy of the NZSO.

The award is available to New Zealand citizens and residents under the age of twenty-five. It must be a 'fully original work, not previously offered to any other organisation, and must not have been performed in rehearsal, concert or workshop'. The winning composer would be appointed to the youth orchestra for the 2005 season, and spend from the 17th to the 25th of August with the orchestra. A package of prizes included Sibelius music-writing software and training, and the opportunity to work with a full-size symphony orchestra, with the winning entry performed in all three concerts in the 2005 season.

2. The Concert Artists Programme

This initiative sought to take advantage of the combined talents of the National Touth Orchestra's soloist principals to perform substantial chamber music repertoire, both in concerts at the Christchurch Arts Centre and at St Andrew's on The Terrace, Wellington – and also in open master-classes with the National Youth Orchestra's guest conductors. 'As a result of its success, NYO has been approached since to participate in both concert series', Pascale says.

3. NYO/AYO Exchange Programme

A player exchange programme between the NZSO National Youth Orchestra and the Australian Youth Orchestra enables a complete range of repertoire and allows mutual collaboration for any player shortfall. When it proved impossible to find an applicant of the required standard for tuba, Pascale had approached the AYO, which recommended its own successful tuba player from the 2004 season. In exchange, Pascale says, 'three NYO members were invited to audition for the Australian Youth Orchestra's national music camp in Canberra in January 2006. Since the implementation of this arrangement between NZSO NYO and AYO, we have had the pleasure to welcome a succession of Australian players – a French horn, harpist, and a double bass player – while a total of 13 NZSO NYO players have had the valuable opportunity to attend the Australian Youth Orchestra's national music camp.'

4. The Conductor Workshop

The last initiative was incorporated not only to develop New Zealand conducting talent but to provide a complete orchestral educational experience, through the youth orchestra, addressing 'the necessity to develop composers and conductors, in addition to players', Pascale says.

A lack of resources meant that this proposal could only be carried out on an informal basis by Simon Streatfeild in 2006, Jacques Lacombe (who provided Gemma New with the opportunity to conduct part of a rehearsal in 2008), and John Hopkins and Paul Daniel together, in 2009.

National Youth Orchestra–Australian Youth Orchestra exchange player, Mathew Seggar, tuba. *'BD'*

'It was a steep learning curve', Pascale says, ' but at the end of this first year I felt pleased with what had been achieved in such a short time. The three initiatives that stand out for me are the Composer-in-residence Award, the NYO/Australian Youth Orchestra Player Exchange, and the NYO Concert Artists Programme. Over the next four seasons I examined everything very closely, with the aim to improve all aspects of NZSO NYO – artistic, marketing, and financial matters.'

Sponsorships, scholarships and awards all increased in 2004. Awards were made available through the NZSO Foundation, with assistance with travel expenses from the Jack and Emma Griffin Trust and Reeves Harris Trust, and for performance excellence from Garth Williams.

2005

Wellington, Christchurch, Auckland 23, 25, 27 August. Conductor: Edwin Outwater. Glinka –*Russlan and Ludmilla* overture; Robin Toan – *Tū-mata-uenga 'God of War, Spirit of Man'*; Prokofiev – Piano Concerto no 3 in C major (John Chen, piano); Tchaikovsky – Symphony no 4 in F minor

Edwin Outwater, resident conductor of the San Francisco Symphony and Wattis Foundation music director of the San Francisco Youth Orchestra, was recognised for his work in musical education and community outreach. In 2004 his education programmes received the Leonard Bernstein award for excellence in educational programming. In the same year he led the San Francisco Symphony Youth Orchestra on an acclaimed tour to major European cities, and made his Carnegie Hall debut, conducting Dvořák's New World Symphony.

The soloist, eighteen-year-old John Chen, was then a master's performance student at the University of Auckland. In 1994 Chen had become the youngest-ever winner of the Sydney International Piano Competition since it began in 1977 – and was also the first performer from Australia or New Zealand, to win the prestigious competition, which was followed by a 22-concert series tour.

'The impact of the collaboration with John Chen as soloist and chamber music partner in the Concert Artists Programme, was particularly satisfying', Pascale says. The first live broadcast by Concert FM of the Auckland performance 'also represented a significant breakthrough for the orchestra'.

The first composer-in-residence

A feature of this concert was a composition by Robin Toan, the inaugural composer-in-residence, a 21-year-old composer and performer from Auckland (NZSO NYO clarinet, 2002–03),[8] who won the youth orchestra's inaugural composition prize for her five-minute work *Tū-mata-uenga 'God of War, Spirit of Man'.*

From left: 2005 conductor Edwin Outwater; piano soloist John Chen; composer Robin Toan

The Māori story of creation inspired her work, Toan said. 'It starts in the beginning when the world between Rangi-nui, the sky father and Papa-tū-a-nuku, the earth Mother was cramped and dark. Their children could not grow in this environment and were forced to take action to survive and Rangi and Papa were forced apart – creating the world as we know it today. I have portrayed the part of the story where Tū-mata-uenga struggles to tear Rangi from Papa.

'To represent the God of War there are two dominant motives ... the semitone, used to portray the frustration of his inability to separate his parents, and secondly, the militant rhythmic passages which emphasis the act of war. The second theme is more angular. It reflects another side of Tū-mata-uenga, the more complex "spirit of Man". It leaps and slides around the dissonant augmented 4th interval. Gradually another more legato melodic line is infused with the angular theme.'

As a major advantage of her award, Robin had the benefit of mentoring by distinguished New Zealand composer, John Psathas.[9] In his report, Psathas praised the award for offering Robin 'a highly stimulating, positive and encouraging experience, which is practically impossible to come by any other way'. It was a delight to witness her 'transition from a composer, unsure if her piece "worked", to a creative participant in the preparation for performance'. Psathas had found the experience very rewarding. 'Robin was an excellent choice as the young composer, and *Tū-mata-uenga* was very well suited to the orchestra, both challenging and accessible to young musicians.' During Robin's residency the two had met several times to discuss *Tū-mata-uenga* as well as listen to a range of her other compositions. 'This enabled us to engage in more substantial dialogue about her style, her strengths and weakness as a composer, and ideas for the future study and development ... I feel this degree of contact with the mentor, as well as the mentor's presence at all rehearsals, to be crucial in maximising the young composer's benefit during the residency ... the NYO composer in residence offers an accelerated education and powerful musical stimulant for the chosen young composer.'[10]

John Button praised Robin's composition as a 'superbly confident, skilfully orchestrated work'.[11] David Sell considered it, 'a securely conceived piece, aggressive in character, as its Māori story suggests. It was compelling listening.'[12] Garth Wiltshire thought it a 'rhythmically-strong piece ... very skilfully written, imaginative and well-orchestrated to utilize the qualities of the orchestra'.[13]

Satisfaction survey

A 'Satisfaction Survey', in the form of an anonymous questionnaire, was issued to every player, to ascertain their response to various aspects of the 2005 NZSO National Youth Orchestra course. This was this first survey undertaken, and players were asked several questions. Some interesting comments were received.

(1) Would you agree or disagree with the statement 'The conductor inspired me and made me play to the best of my ability' : Agree, Disagree, No opinion.

- 'Highly agree!! I was very inspired and owe a lot of that if not all, to Edwin. For me it was a life-changing musical experience!! Those are the best kind.'
- 'Agree. Something about Edwin made me want to practice lots so that I would play as well as I could, and not let the rest of my section down. Maybe his youth?'
- 'Agree. Edwin related to the players, he clearly communicated his ideas in an enjoyable, relaxed manner, in a great working atmosphere.'

(2) 'Of all the works the orchestra played, which was your favourite? And why?'

Tchaikovsky:

- 'knowing the story and passion behind this moving work made it all the more enjoyable to play'
- 'a big work with lots of detail and character'
- 'because it made me feel something I can't describe'
- 'It's big & loud & not too hard & pretty to play and listen to.'

Prokofiev:

- 'It had some extraordinary textures and amazing quirks. It wasn't as physically demanding as the Symphony (because it was shorter) and it was an excellent experience playing with John Chen.'
- 'It was a very exciting piece to play, all the instruments had moments on their own, and the piece contained a lot of different characters that were challenging to play.'
- 'The soloist was awesome.'

Glinka:

- 'GLINKA of course!! It was such a nice opening!!'
- 'Exciting and I loved the way Edwin conducted!!'
- 'the Glinka is really fun and fast.'

(3) Least favourite?

- 'My teacher says we have to be professional and love each piece the same and play each with all your effort'
- 'Glinka – I thought it was cheesy'
- 'Tū-mata-uenga, I did like this piece but not as much in contrast to the other more established works.'
- 'I find it hard to understand modern music'
- 'Tchaikovsky's Nutcracker Suite Marche (encore): 'It seemed tacky and not as tight as the other works'.

The Tchaikovsky Symphony proved the favourite, followed by Prokofiev, and a few chose Glinka

(4) Highlight?

- 'Everything! The conductor, the social events, the music, the soloist!'

(5) What could be done to make it even better?

- 'Nothing, really, for me. I really have enjoyed my 2 years in NYO. It's an absolutely fantastic experience, thank you!!'

A code of conduct

An important initiative to bring the youth orchestra into line with current requirements for young people was introduced in 2005. The first code of conduct contained a statement affirming the NZSO National Youth Orchestra's, 'commitment to the safety and well-being of the participants in the project. It provides an open, welcoming and safe environment for everyone participating in the course.'

The code established a standard of behaviour, which all participants on the NYO course – 'players, staff, volunteers, guest conductor, soloists and coaches' – were required to sign, and adhere to. Seventeen clauses cover almost every eventuality. As well as clauses dealing with insurance, health and safety, and unacceptable behaviour, participants were told:

1. Treat everyone with respect and honesty ...
2. Be on time ...
3. Bullying will not be tolerated ...
4. No tobacco, alcohol or drugs to be consumed on the premises ...
5. Sexual harassment will not be tolerated ...
6. To safeguard all parties always have another adult present or in sight, when conducting one-to-one coaching and instruction, etc.
7. At least one member of the NYO staff to be present at all official NYO activities ...

8. Persons over 18 ... are encouraged to make their own accommodation arrangements ...
9. The Youth Assistant will be dedicated to overseeing the players who are under 18 years of age ...

The team on tour

In line with regulations the NZSO National Youth Orchestra touring team now numbered six: a manager, youth assistant, stage manager, rehearsal stage manager, tour executive and instrument transporter. Three brought a wealth of orchestral experience and professionalism to the youth orchestra:[14] David Pawsey, the NZSO's respected former orchestra manager and tour executive (1982–2003), who on retiring after twenty-two years returned to his theatrical roots to manage productions at Wellington's St James Theatre as well as touring shows, including the annual youth orchestra tour; Grant Gilbert, from 1991 the NZSO's stage manager and more recently production manager; and Colin Isaac of Van Lines Freight, who has transported the NZSO's orchestral instruments and equipment for over thirty years. They had worked as a close team in the NZSO from the start, Grant says.[15] 'David and I both had theatre and stage experience, we were aware of stage presentation and professionalism. The attitude of the professional is "head not art", and we managed the NYO the same as the "big band" – the NZSO.'

'The NYO was just "part of the job"when I started', Grant recalls. 'Alwyn Palmer was the manager then, and after he left, there was a real problem; it could have collapsed. Professionally the NYO is no different from NZSO; it still needs the same amount of planning.'

2006

Wellington, Christchurch, Auckland, 28 August–September. Conductor: Simon Streatfeild. Beethoven – *Egmont* Overture; Claire Cowan – *Trains of Thinking*; Strauss – *Der Rosenkavalier* Suite; Shostakovich – Symphony no 10

Noted English conductor Simon Streatfeild was principal viola, London Symphony Orchestra, until 1959, when he helped to found the Academy of St Martin in the Fields with Sir Neville Marriner, Alex Lindsay, and others. Moving to Canada, he became principal viola, Vancouver Symphony, and its assistant conductor two years later. Streatfeild was music director and conductor of the Vancouver Bach Choir, 1969–81; the Regina Orchestra, 1981–84; and the Quebec Symphony, 1983–91; and music director of the

Conductor Simon Streatfeild and concertmaster Ben Morrison in rehearsal, Michael Fowler Centre. *MW2006*

Manitoba Chamber Orchestra, for eighteen years from 1982 to 2000. Now he often guest conducts major orchestras in Europe, and Canada, including the National Orchestra of Canada.

Streatfeild was the first conductor selected by Pascale. 'I'm rather proud of the line-up of conductors that I approached and managed to convince to come to New Zealand, using my Canadian and Montréal connections', Pascale says. 'I personally went to see Simon Streatfeild's agent, and I remember interest was particularly high, with a record number of applicants eager to accept the challenges of an especially demanding programme. The orchestra rose to new heights under Simon Streatfeild's expert guidance, as shown in both attendance figures and critical acclaim.'[16]

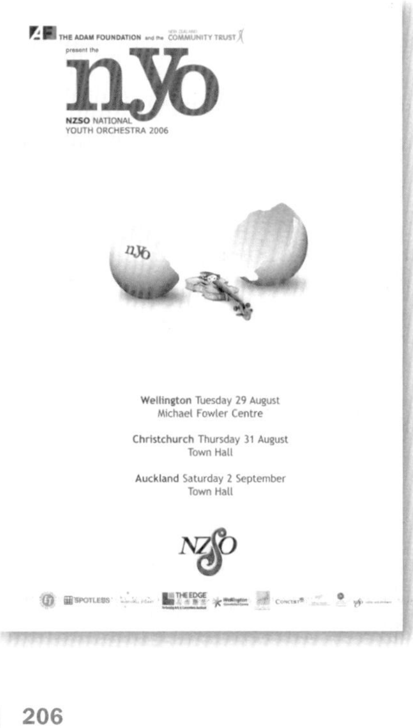

It was another world premiere, when the NYO performed *Trains of Thinking,* the work of its second composer-in-residence, 22-year-old Claire Cowan,[17] who also benefited from the opportunity to work with composer Ross Harris, as mentor.[18]

Among several other new achievements in this year, rehearsal days in the Michael Fowler Centre

Composers Claire Cowan, 2006 (left);
Karlo Margertić, 2007 (right)

were increased before the first concert, which had 'an extremely beneficial impact', Pascale recalls. 'There was also a proper glossy application form, and a new certificate was given to each player. Also, as a direct result of the new regional focus – three applicants from the Hawkes Bay region were successful – and the Napier centre was added on to the list of national auditions.'

2007

Wellington, Christchurch, Auckland, 30 August–3 September. Conductor: Yannick Nézet-Séguin. Ravel – *La Valse*; Bartók – Concerto for Orchestra; Karlo Margetić – *Belt Sander*; Debussy – *La Mer*

Pascale had never met Canadian conductor Yannick Nézet-Séguin, but discovered, 'by a lucky coincidence', that she knew the communication manager in his orchestra from the music camp at Orford. 'She remembered my name, and made sure that Yannick got my message.'[19]

Yannick Nézet-Séguin, aged thirty-one, had just been announced as music director of the Rotterdam Philharmonic, to replace Valery Gergiev, from the 2008/09 season, as the unanimous choice of that orchestra's musicians.[20] Making his European debut, the previous year, Nézet-Séguin had received re-invitations from every orchestra – including Dresden Staatskapelle, Orchestre National de France; London and Royal Stockholm Philharmonics; SWR Radio Orchestra, Baden Baden – and would make his debuts with National Symphony Orchestra, Washington, Philadelphia Orchestra, Tonhalle Orchestra, Zurich, and Deutsche Symphonieorchester Berlin. In between these prestigious engagements, Yannick Nézet-Séguin conducted the NZSO National Youth Orchestra, and the NZSO itself. John Button attended both concerts, and wrote of 'Thrilling moments from a dazzling star', and a young conductor who had 'burst on the music scene like a shooting star, dazzling musicians and audiences alike'. This was 'a large demanding programme, played by the National Youth Orchestra with finesse and fire, directed by Seguin with insight, superb technique – and boundless energy'.[21]

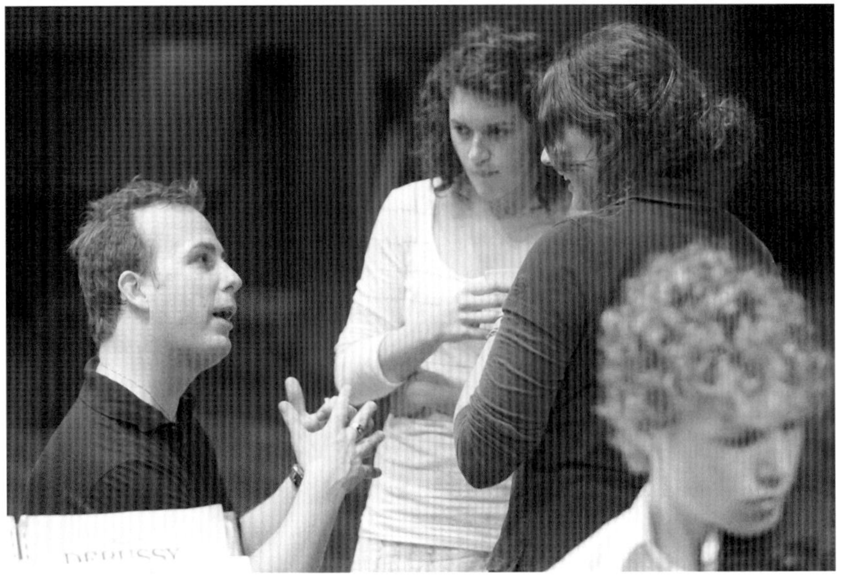

Conductor Yannick Nézet-Séguin talking to Annabella Leslie and Shandelle Horsford. © *Robert Catto, www.catto.co.nz, all rights reserved.*

'The quality of the conductor is central to the success of the NYO course', Pascale believes, 'and this has never been more evident than with the inspirational Yannick Nézet-Séguin not only guiding the young musicians through a programme of great difficulty but also establishing a rapport with them, that was apparent both on and off stage'.[22]

Following the 'tremendous impact' on the 2006 performances of rehearsing in the concert hall, Pascale again increased the number of rehearsal days in the Michael Fowler Centre from the usual three, to four days; considering that with 'French repertoire such as *La Valse* and *La Mer* that relies totally on colour and texture', this would be necessary.

2008

As a result of being able to extend the course to other centres, Pascale was 'determined to give financial assistance to as many NYO participants outside the Wellington region as possible'. Extra efforts were made to approach support organisations and find private donors, and in this season, a record number of National Youth Orchestra players (forty-six in total, or 48 percent) received some financial assistance, and the value of scholarships and awards made to players reached $20,190.

This was an extremely busy season, Pascale remembers. 'In addition to seeing through the current NYO in the 2008 season, I made a series of proposals to the NZSO, to celebrate the NYO 50th anniversary in 2009. An additional course to kick off the special season was approved, and that was the start of the NZSO NYO national music camp concept. It took over eighteen months to come to fruition.'

The sponsorship of 'orchestra chairs' had begun in 2003, with a few dedicated sponsors contributing each year, until 2008, when new sponsorship options were announced for 'Supporters of the NZSO NYO 50th Anniversary Celebrations'. These included a chair endowment scheme, to provide additional funding required for the extra activity associated with the national music camp and the 50th anniversary season. A new donation form was designed, and a successful campaign resulted in endowments for concertmaster ($7000), associate concertmaster ($3000), thirty-four player ambassadors ($1000) and ten green room endowments (up to $999).

An alumni database was prepared for the anniversary, and the NZSO Alumni Association, formed in 1998, became involved in setting up a similar association for former members of the National Youth Orchestra.[23] As a result, all alumni were invited to the 50th anniversary concert, alumni reunion, and associated activities.

The implementation of a health and safety component was a new and important requirement for the course. Free hearing tests were introduced for all youth orchestra participants, with a workshop held at which players received advice from a doctor, on how to protect their precious hearing.

The audition recording equipment system was updated, and the DAT technology, used for recording auditions over many years, was replaced as it was cumbersome and increasingly unreliable. 'The new equipment and associated technology is much lighter, more convenient and more reliable', Pascale explains. 'It has improved the actual mechanics of recording, and equally, direct-to-disc transcription has significantly reduced adjudication time. NZSO principals now receive auditions recorded on CDs, for their individual instruments.'

Principal sponsor Denis Adam, announcing NZSO NYO awards for 2007 at the Michael Fowler Centre. *Mabel Wong 2007*

From left: conductor Jacques Lacombe; composer Tabea Squire; soprano Madeleine Pierard

Wellington, Christchurch, Auckland, Napier, 26–31 August. Conductor: Jacques Lacombe. Ravel – *Albotada del Gracioso*; Roussel – *Bacchus et Ariane* 43 Suite no 2; Canteloube – *Chants D'Auvergne*; Tabea Squire – *Feverdream*; Stravinsky – *Firebird* Suite (1945)

Pascale, on one of her visits back home, admits to 'assisting' at a Montréal Symphony Orchestra rehearsal, with an ulterior aim of meeting conductor Jacques Lacombe.[24] 'We met backstage at "La Place des Arts", and I told him about my new role as manager of the NYO – and how fantastic it would be if he would accept an offer to come and conduct in New Zealand ... and he came and conducted four concerts in four cities in New Zealand in 2008.'

'The NYO does not have a soloist at each of its seasons', Pascale says. 'It is quite a special treat. I was aware of this, and that there had been less than a handful, in the last decade, mainly pianists, It had been ten years since a singer performed with the NYO, and only eight had sung with the NYO in over 49 years. So I was very keen to have a singer this year.' So when Madeleine Pierard, a lyric soprano, came to Wellington for a Naxos recording with the NZSO,[25] 'I took the opportunity to approach her personally. Madeleine Pierard[26] was winner of the Lexus Song Quest in 2005, and one of New Zealand's brightest young vocal talents. There was a real musical rapport between our soprano and our conductor, Jacques Lacombe, an artist so comfortable in this métier, and this was without doubt an artistic highlight for the orchestra and audience alike. This was central to the success of that year's course.'

The addition of Napier to the schedule had made it possible to present the programme in Madeleine's home town, and provided invaluable advance publicity for the upcoming 50th anniversary and reunion. The regional focus strategy had paid off as well, Pascale believes, leading to the highest number of applications received, since she became manager.

Rod Biss, as an 'invited observer' in August 2008 with the National Youth Orchestra in Wellington, was able to 'wander where I wished', as he later reported in the New Zealand *Listener*.[27] 'You the devoted audience are absolutely essential to a classical music concert, but what you're hearing down there in the auditorium is just a mere shadow of what the performers are experiencing on stage ... like watching a rugby match on TV, compared with actually getting mud on your boots and knees down there in the scrum.'

Biss followed the youth orchestra's week of 'hard work' – from first rehearsals in the Adam Concert room and School of Music practice rooms in Kelburn, to final rehearsals and first performance in the Michael Fowler Centre. He witnessed, 'the strange excitement, sense of involvement, struggle, achievement and the thrill of being as close to inside of a composer's mind as one can ever be', and listened to young composer Tabea Squire's 'intriguing score; a simple folk-like melody is haunted and chased by unwelcome harmonies, as though in a feverish nightmare'.

Jacques Lacombe, who conducted the Canadian Youth Orchestra for three years, talked to Biss about 'the special energy' a youth orchestra has. 'There is something very natural and direct about the way they make music, the way they take more chances than a professional orchestra ... you almost feel like a violin maker. My joy in doing this', Lacombe reveals, 'is to hear what they do in a week and to watch them realise what they have achieved, it's actually moving'.

Perceptively, Lacombe tells Biss, 'from what I've seen, you must have a high level of music education here, to have such a pool of young talent, is very impressive, you must at some point, have had the political will to build this kind of culture and support for art and music'.

Reviewer David Sell said that he, 'would have to give over this whole word-limited review to do justice to the new work by 19 year old Tabea Squire, just as she tried to cram her scrambled fever-distorted life into *Feverdream*. Not only are her musical ideas really interesting, but her technique in putting them together is quite brilliant ... what a wonderful opportunity for someone so young to hear her work so expertly played by a full orchestra.'[28]

William Dart was also impressed, calling *Feverdream* 'the strongest NZSO NYO commission I have heard ... her orchestral ingenuity was as astounding as her assurance in shifting between airy tunefulness and foreboding expression'.[29]

Members of the orchestra shared their impressions of NZSO National Youth Orchestra 2008.[30] 'Very French', wrote Shandelle Horsford, principal double bass, from Brisbane, one of four Australian players. 'A really great learning experience, and working with NYO players was Awesome! The touring was amazing! I loved seeing New Zealand, and made a bunch of great new friends, but the best memories will be made at the MFC. I gained contacts, and a wider orchestral understanding, and knowledge.'

'Exhausting, challenging', said Cameron Stuart, sub-principal cello, in his sixth year. 'My best memories are being recognised by the conductor at the end of the concert; the surge of applause when your section gets stood up individually; the socializing too.'

'A really fun year', recalls Hayley Roude, contrabassoon. 'Every year I get to do what I really want to do, play in an orchestra. It's a reminder of the reason I spend so much of the rest of my time alone in practice rooms. Even after five years I look forward to going to NYO and it has never disappointed me.'

'A fantastic learning environment, as always', said Luke Christiansen, principal trombone, 'fantastic concerts, insightful rehearsals, great programme for audience – fairly bland for trombone, awesome touring; great fun, great concerts, great people, great times!! Best memories? NYO, the whole experience, the magic of NYO, enthusiastic musicians having a great time, doing what they enjoy.'

'Top Notch!' said Ben Whitten, principal timpani, who gave his best memories of the youth orchestra as, '*La Mer* in 2007; Finale *Firebird* in 2008; talking to conductors post performance, especially Yannick after Auckland, and Jacques after Napier. What I've gained from NYO is a sense of pride and professionalism.'

'An amazing experience', said Bryony Gibson-Cornish, viola. 'Intense but enjoyable rehearsals, fantastic challenging repertoire we could get our teeth into, exciting performances. I gained insight into working as a professional musician, and it confirmed for me that this is what I would like to do.' 'Loved it!' said Alex Chan, principal bassoon. 'Very musically inspiring, and a very special opportunity; perfect repertoire; extremely valuable orchestral experience that will only make us get closer to becoming professional.'

Writing in the NZSO National Youth Orchestra's 2008 programme, Peter Walls announced 'a special 50th anniversary season that effectively, begins now'. A series of receptions for NZSO NYO alumni was already underway around the country, and these were part of the build-up towards the jubilee, he said. This would continue over twelve months, to encompass 'the NZSO NYO's first summer music camp in January and culminate in the Jubilee concert season, and the first Alumni Reunion in June–July 2009'.

Since 1959, the National Youth Orchestra has provided hundreds of talented young New Zealand musicians with the experience of 'playing under an excellent conductor in a quality full-size symphony orchestra. Many have gone on to make an enormous contribution to musical life in Aotearoa as members of the Southern Sinfonia, Christchurch Symphony Orchestra, Vector Wellington Orchestra, the APO' and – of course – the NZSO itself. Others have made their mark in orchestras overseas, or 'chosen careers outside music, but they look back with pleasure and satisfaction at their time in the NYO. The NYO, at 50 years, has built up a great family.'[31]

11 Celebrating 50 years, plus

2009–2010

> 'I well remember my first rehearsal as a cellist in the NYO, in 1961. We started with Rachmaninov's 2nd Piano Concerto. The sheer power of the orchestral sound was a thrilling experience ... Music continues to play a vital role in my life, both as a cellist, and as a listener.'
>
> – *Donald Best (NYO cello, 1961–66), Chairman NZSO Board, 2009–*

For fifty years the National Youth Orchestra had always met once a year in late winter or early spring, the one exception being a special summer concert tour to mark its 10th anniversary in 1969. Four decades later, NZSO National Youth Orchestra celebrated its 50th Jubilee with a national music camp, in Napier, from 8 to 18 January 2010 – at the height of summer.

Held at Napier Girls' High School, this residential camp provided a comprehensive programme over ten days for a course fee of $500, which covered all transport, tuition, accommodation, and meals. The entire planning of the national music camp had been done in consultation with Australian guest conductor Richard Gill,[1] artistic director of the Sydney Symphony's education programme, and music director of Victorian Opera; in collaboration with the NZSO concertmaster Vesa-Matti Leppänen,[2] and David Bremner, NZSO principal trombone (NYO 1995–97). The programme had been 'split into three main categories of solo, group ensembles and full orchestra', with care taken to ensure that 'all instrumental groups were equally busy and involved', and the right balance struck 'between workload and relaxation'.[3]

The camp provided inspiring leadership for seventy-eight young players, from Richard Gill, Israeli violinist Eyal Kless[4] – a dynamic and versatile musician who performs and teaches throughout the world – and thirteen highly experienced tutors: Vesa-Matti Leppänen, nine NZSO principals, and three pianists.

Players arriving on Thursday 8 January registered from 1 pm onwards, and then met for dinner in the wood-panelled school dining room. At 7 pm the first rehearsal was held: a read-through of Beethoven, Stravinsky, and Tchaikovsky symphonies, in the school hall where a large Rita Angus painting of the school hung above the stage. This was the start of ten days in which players experienced a full programme of tutorials, rehearsals, workshops, master classes, and chamber music coaching. In between these activities, players ate communal meals in the dining room – and enjoyed the school's excellent facilities.

The table tennis room was always a popular hive of activity, as was also the school swimming pool, very much appreciated in the heat of a Hawke's Bay summer. On evenings when there were no rehearsals or performances scheduled, in-house entertainment was provided on two occasions by Richard Gill. A friendly, relaxed figure in shorts and sandals, Gill was inspiring in any role, whether as conductor, teacher in master classes, or leading players with skill and good humour, in his popular 'Singing Together' sessions. Another evening, a panel discussion was held on entering the music profession.

Games in the swimming pool

Physiotherapist Greg Knight also was in attendance, his duties threefold: first, to educate orchestra players in injury prevention, how to minimise injury risk and prevent 'over-use' problems; secondly, to give one-to-one physiotherapy to any specific issues in twenty to thirty-minute consultations, with the chance to look at specific problems and identify technique issues around the instrument; and thirdly, to hold Pilates classes. These were held after breakfast each morning and attracted fifteen to twenty attendees. A game of Jail Break was a popular extra activity for all who played in the Saturday concert.[5]

National Music Camp Tutors' Recital

Hawke's Bay Opera House, Sunday 11 January, 3 pm. Poulenc – Sonata for French horn, trumpet and trombone; Rossini – Duo for cello and double bass; Debussy – Trio for violin, cello and piano; Rachmaninov – Valse and Romance; Gareth Farr – *Dua Lagu*; Mozart – Sonata in G minor for violin and piano; Ken Wilson – Quintet for flute, oboe, clarinet, bassoon, French horn; Poulenc – Sextet for piano, flute, oboe, clarinet, bassoon, French horn; David Bremner's arrangement of Ravel's *Bolero,* with all tutors

Left top–bottom: 1960, 1964 and 1965. Below: 1966

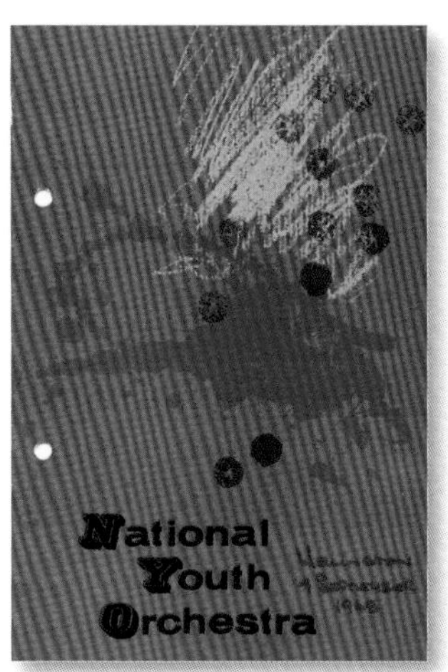

national youth orchestra '67
1967
Hastings 30 August
Lower Hutt 31 August
Wellington 2 September

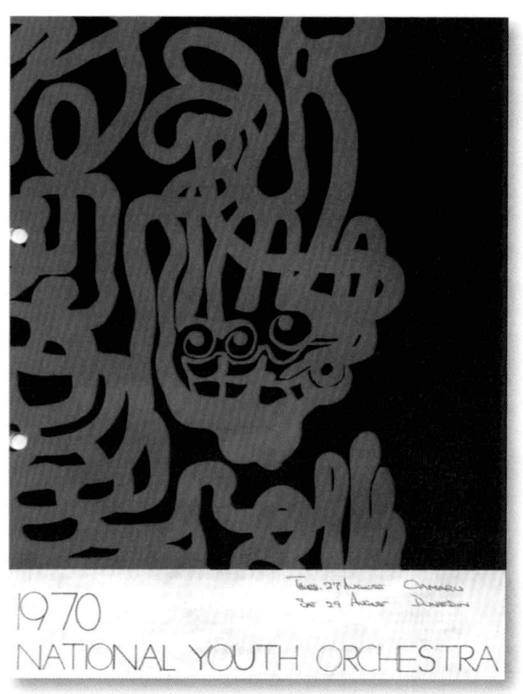
1970
NATIONAL YOUTH ORCHESTRA

1971
NATIONAL
YOUTH
ORCHESTRA
Auckland 26 August
Tauranga 27 August
Hamilton 28 August
1971

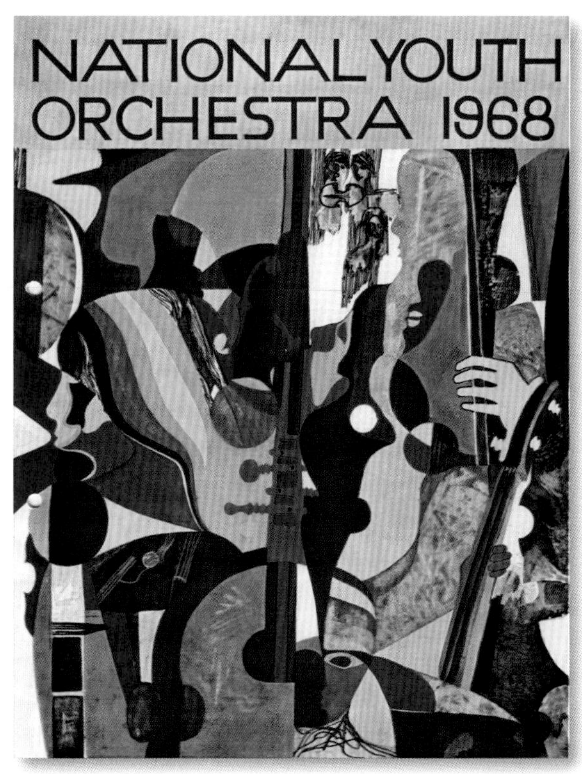
NATIONAL YOUTH
ORCHESTRA 1968

NATIONAL YOUTH ORCHESTRA
1969-70
WELLINGTON
31 AUGUST 1969

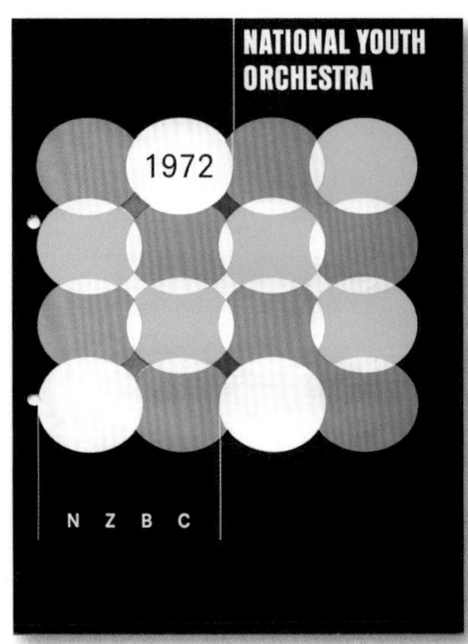
NATIONAL YOUTH
ORCHESTRA
1972
N Z B C

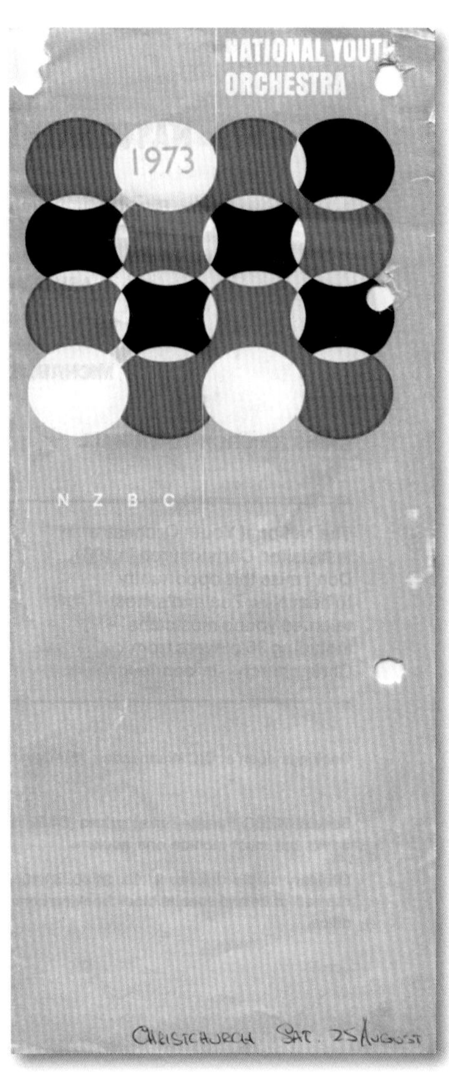
NATIONAL YOUTH
ORCHESTRA
1973
N Z B C
CHRISTCHURCH SAT. 25 AUGUST

The International Festival
of Youth Orchestras
and Performing Arts
Aberdeen: August 4-14
London: August 15-17
1975

1974 ▶

National
Youth
Orchestra
of
New
Zealand

THE PRESS AND JOURNAL TUESDAY AUGUST 5 1975

New Zealanders set the standard for others

Welcome Home

N the first of the formal oncerts in the Music Hall, Aberdeen, last night, the National Youth Orchestra of New Zealand set a racking standard for their ellow participants to emulate.

Indeed, I am prepared to ay that unless my memory s playing tricks, they are one of the best to appear in he festival since its Aberdeen inception in 1973.

The orchestra, as heard ast night, is not over-large, yet the corporate tone has real depth and resonance; ntonation does not appear o be a problem and in general the rhythmic ensemble deteriorates only at the sort of pitfall a professional orchestra would find troublesome.

The best items in the programme were those conducted by the orchestra's own conductor, Ashley Heenan. An overture by Douglas Lilburn entitled "Aotearoa" began proceedings. This proved to be a most attractive piece, richly, but not heavily, orchestrated and therefore one which immediately revealed the considerable technical strength of the orchestra.

It was a pity that there was no indication as to what the piece was about. Fortunately the other Antipodean export was self-explanatory —a sort of re-import, in fact. This was a suite of Scottish dances by Mr Heenan, which proved to be colourful and attractive realisations of music deriving from familiar materials and idioms.

In Elizabeth Turnbull, the principal violist, the orchestra have a confident and amply toned soloist, and the only regret is that Vaughn Williams, whose suite for viola and orchestra was played, could not provide something more substantial for this restricted repertoire.

In the first half Av Ostrowski directed a performance of Mozart's 39th Symphony which in the light of the rest of the programme was disappointing. The slow introduction was tense and tentative seemingly on account of the conductor's vague indications; the slow movement and the finale were too hurried, and overall there was a feeling of heaviness foreign to the generally accepted character of the music.

In fairness it must be said that the minuet was distinguished by pointed and buoyant rhythms.

The final item, Kodaly's "Dances of Galanta" outshone", all the rest in its power and assurance. Mr Heenan's interpretation was finely judged and he drew from his players a performance of authentic brilliance and mature splendour. It was truly magnificent. — G.E.A.

◀ 1975 'welcome home' programme cover

▼ 1985

NZSO
New Zealand Post
National Youth Orchestra
Lilburn
Sibelius
Tchaikovsky
Barber
Elgar
Isaiah Jackson
AND
Ashley Brown
New Zealand Post National Youth Orchestra Concerts 1995
Opera House Palmerston North
Wellington Town Hall
New Zealand Post

NYO
National Youth Orchestra
a division of NZSO
40th
Programme

The Adam Foundation
presents
NZSO
NYO
National Youth Orchestra
programme
AF

THE ADAM FOUNDATION PRESENTS
NZSO
NYO
National Youth Orchestra
PROGRAMME 2001
AF

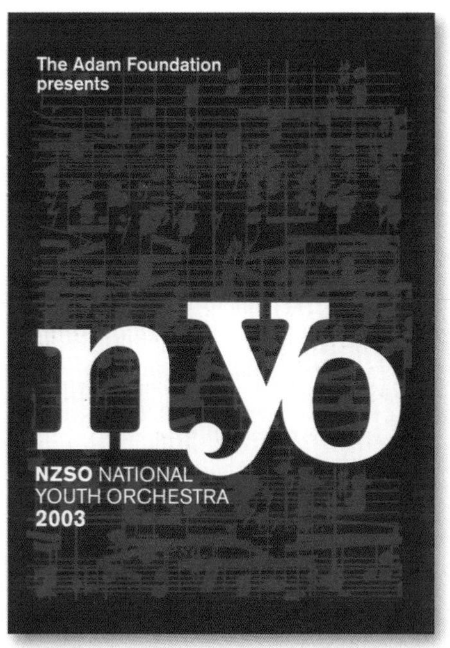
The Adam Foundation
presents
nyo
NZSO NATIONAL
YOUTH ORCHESTRA
2003

The Adam Foundation presents...
NZSO
National Youth
Orchestra
PROGRAMME

THE ADAM FOUNDATION and the NEW ZEALAND COMMUNITY TRUST
present the
nyo
NZSO NATIONAL
YOUTH ORCHESTRA 2005
Wellington | Christchurch | Auckland | 2005
www.nzso.co.nz

THE ADAM FOUNDATION and the NEW ZEALAND COMMUNITY TRUST
present the
nyo
NZSO NATIONAL
YOUTH ORCHESTRA 2004
the pick of the bunch

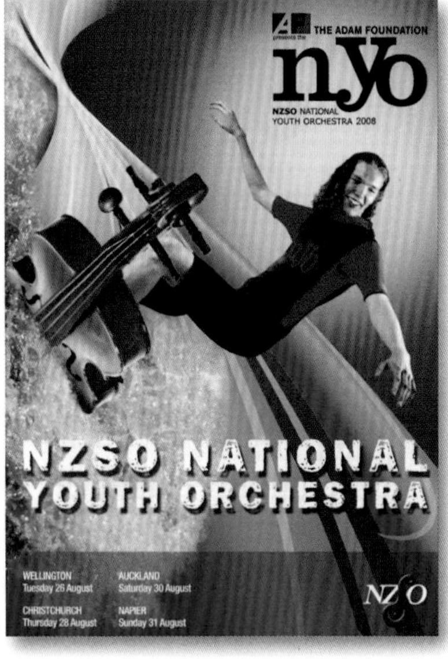

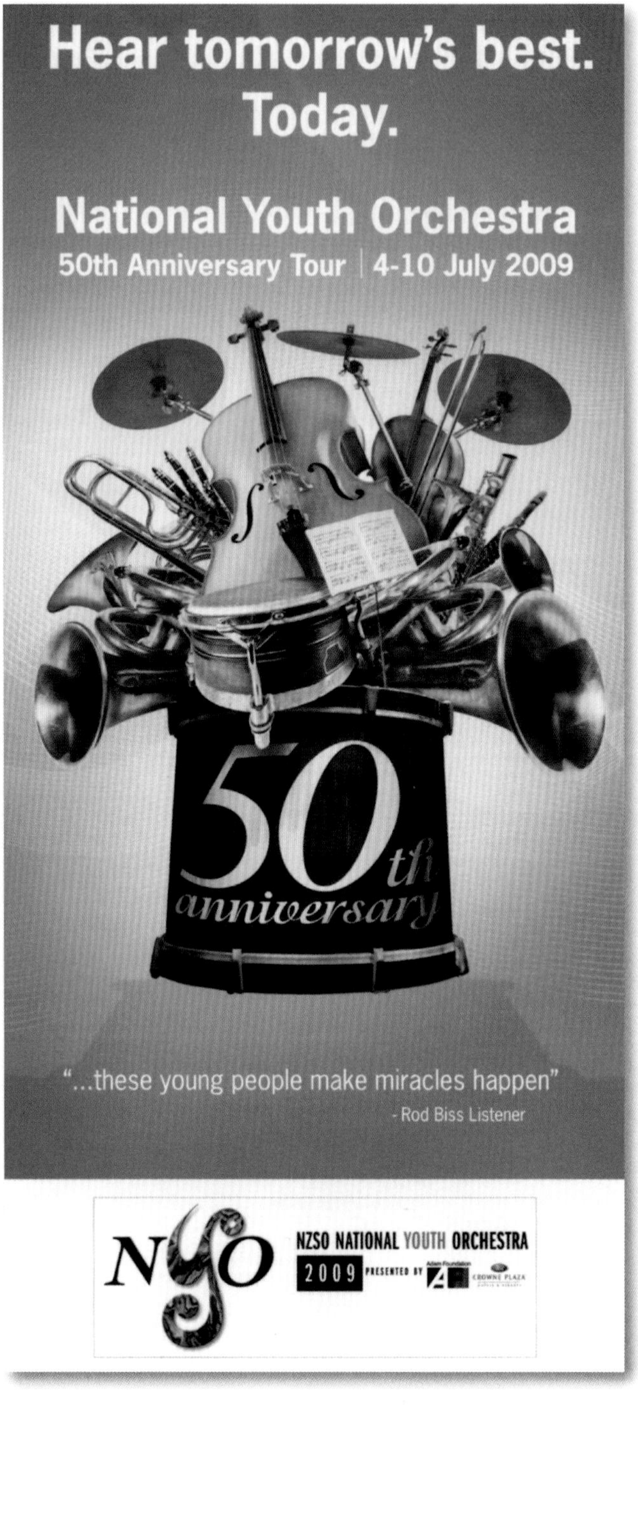

Hear tomorrow's best.
Today.

National Youth Orchestra
50th Anniversary Tour | 4-10 July 2009

50th
anniversary

"...these young people make miracles happen"
- Rod Biss Listener

Admittance was free to this first public concert showcasing fourteen music camp tutors, including Eyal Kless and Vesa-Matti Leppänen. Nine virtuoso works were performed by various combinations of instruments, offering a rare and stimulating opportunity for students to hear their tutors, performing repertoire that would be new to many of them.

Napier Girls' High School Hall Concert

Thursday 15 January. Conductor: Richard Gill. Works with reduced wind, brass and percussion; the brass band, cello and double bass sections, led by their respective coaches; and the Mendelssohn Octet, performed by Vesa, Eyal and string principals.

Ngatarawa Winery Outdoor Concerts

Friday 16 January 3 pm & 5 pm. Conductor Richard Gill. Works for reduced wind, brass and percussion (27 players). Brass ensemble: composers including Domenico Modugno; J S Bach; Jerome Kern; Monteverdi (arr. Peter Maunder); Elgar Howarth; Aurelio Bonelli; Richard Strauss; Copland; Byrd; Chris Hazell; Claude Gervis arr Peter Reeve; Dieterich Buxtehude. Combined items: Holst – Suite in E flat; Grainger – *Londonderry Air.* Wind items: Ligeti – *Sechs Bagatellen*; Arnold – *Three Shanties*; Ravel – *Sonatine* (Note: the strings were given 'the afternoon off')

Orchestra Concerts, Hawke's Bay Opera House, Hastings

Saturday 17 January, 7 pm. Conductor: Richard Gill. Soloists: Vesa-Matti Leppänen (violin) and Eyal Kless (viola). Copland – *Fanfare for the Common Man*; Byrd – *The Earl of Oxford's March;* Mozart – Sinfonia Concertante; Tchaikovsky – Symphony no 6, *Pathetique*

Sunday 18 January, 3 pm. Conductor: Richard Gill. Young – *Tribute* Fanfare; Strauss – *Vienna Brass* Fanfare; Stravinsky – Symphony in C; Beethoven – Symphony no 7

Peter Williams[6] reviewed both orchestral concerts, 'the result of 10 days of intense rehearsal for 77 extremely talented musicians, under the expert tuition of NZSO principals'. Stravinsky's Symphony in C, with its 'multiplicity of thematic material was a tough assignment for these players but it was accomplished with considerable skill and understanding ... Tchaikovsky's Symphony no 6 ... was an excellent choice by which to demonstrate [their] ability in the playing of the great Romantic symphony ... and Beethoven's Symphony no 7 made a magnificent end to the two concerts, a remarkably confident performance with a finale that surely captured all that Beethoven demanded in this masterpiece. There was absolutely no doubt about the contribution of Richard Gill to these performances. His direction capitalized on the special abilities of these fine musicians.'

Two official youth assistants (female and male), Megan Gyde[7] and Jochen Stossberg,[8] were part of the team at the camp. Megan, who has older children, had taken trips away with sports teams, but had no experience with an orchestra on tour until 2008, she says. 'The NZSO was on tour in China that year, so the usual "Ops" were not available. David Pawsey[9] had taken ill, and so Kurt Gibson from Vector Wellington Orchestra came. There were 21 under 18 year olds, that year. I could go home in Wellington, but in Christchurch I had to stay with the younger players in the YWCA, which had great accommodation and communal areas. In Auckland we stayed at the backpackers in Queen Street, next door to a nightclub – that didn't finish until 8 am! Some players stayed with family or billets, but I still felt responsible. Others would try and sneak out, they're just normal teenagers; they challenge authority and try it on.'

At the music camp, Megan was responsible for players aged under eighteen. 'The range in ages from 13 to 25 years makes it difficult, but the restrictions are for their own protection. We had minor injuries and one in the swimming pool, but no major problems, and there was never any problem in rehearsal. They are really dedicated, and practice, but I had to stop them at 10 pm, and they couldn't practice before 8 am. There was no back-up in Napier, so meal times were the only times off, and I was feeling exhausted, by the end. But overall, it's been an unbelievable experience, to see that talent, and to watch and hear them play.'

Valerie Rhodes, president of Wellington Friends of NZSO, and her husband Alan, also a member, were volunteers.[10] 'We prepared registration packs, assisted with orientation, ferried people to and from various venues, collected money at master-classes and did other small jobs as and when necessary', says Valerie, 'and Alan also took a lot of video footage, for a documentary record of the Camp. We parked our caravan in the courtyard, and expected to provide all our own meals, but two people did not turn up, and we were able to join everyone else for lunch and dinner.'

Wellington Friends' enthusiasm for the youth orchestra has been significant. The Friends have donated $43,470 to the NZSO National Youth Orchestra since 2001, and their support includes the barbecue lunch, underwriting the annual CD, an award for a player from the Greater Wellington area, two scholarships to assist players to attend NYO, and sponsorship of the concertmaster in 2009.

'Music camp 2009 will live in the memories of all who took part', Valerie says, 'and will be an inspiration to players who are planning a career in music. As a result of Pascale's work a wonderful precedent has been set, for any future music camp. If we could build on Richard Gill's thought of "elite musicians on a par with elite athletes", and put a case to the Minister of Arts for funding, the amount required (compared to that spent nurturing young athletes) – would be absolute peanuts!'[11]

Richard Gill's comprehensive conductor's report on the camp called it a 'landmark success on many levels', including camaraderie, professionalism, commitment and dedication of the tutors and the students, the extraordinarily high level of music-making and attention to all musical matters by the students, their willingness to try new ideas and question the old; and courage to sail into relatively unknown waters and to arrive in dry land enriched by the journey.[12]

Gill had been involved with music making for forty-five years, he said, and 'could say with honesty that this orchestra was one of the best youth groups I have ever worked with. I expected the standard to be high, but had no idea of the level of concentration, commitment and professionalism that these young people were capable of embracing.' This bore out all that he had heard about the orchestra, and demonstrated clearly why it has 'such a good work ethic, and such a well-deserved reputation'.

The singing was an aspect of the camp that Gill considered 'very important ... We had fun intermingling with some fairly serious aural training, reinforcing the notion that singing is fundamental to everything we do as musicians.' Among several thoughts for the future, Gill suggested that the national music camp meet in a different centre each year where there is a university, 'with the advantage that the camp atmosphere can build morale, cohesion and cooperation for all sorts of extra curricular activity, chamber music, in-house concerts, and the like ... Given that chamber music is the basis for all orchestra playing there may be a good reason to have a chamber music segment supervised by tutors which could include pianists.'

Gill also noted the importance of recreation and suggested that students had 'a recreational option under the heading Free Time that is free to choose what ever you wish to do. An organised series of recreation events would have its own rewards, such events including a bush dance – or the New Zealand equivalent.' Pilates was a 'wonderful adjunct'.

As a first-time participant in the National Youth Orchestra programme, violinist Amber Vickery[13] says the aspects which meant the most to her were

The National Music Camp Tutors' Recital at Hawke's Bay Opera House (l–r): David Bremner, trombone, Vesa-Matti Leppänen and Eyal Kless (violins), Euan Harvey (French horn)

'the master-classes and the opportunity to interact with professional musicians. I have recently been considering if I want to be a professional musician and this camp has played an important role in the process of this decision.

'I thoroughly enjoyed the opportunity to perform major symphonic works. The NYO was a major step up from my local orchestra: my awareness and my technical and musical skills were challenged and extended ... Richard Gill did an excellent job of making rehearsals both intellectually and musically stimulating. He used in-depth knowledge of the works, insightful questions and specific praise as tools to help us think about and understand what we were playing. However, we were all in agreement that his most striking accomplishment was learning everyone's name after only two days!

'On a practical level, the food was delicious, healthy and well balanced. Special treats like a cooked breakfast and pizza for supper (sponsored by Vesa-Matti Leppänen and Eyal Kless, on the day of our first concert), were lovely surprises.

'The varying bedtimes of the wide age range presented some problems in the non-soundproof dormitories, but as the camp wore on and people settled into routine, this became less of an issue. Our occasional free afternoons and evenings were enhanced by a ten per cent discount in a local bistro/bar; additionally, the freely available maps of the area were invaluable. I really appreciated the affordability of the camp, and the fact that all travel and meals were provided was a big selling point.'

Amber enjoyed the variety in rehearsals, from tutorials with individual sections, to sectionals, to full orchestra. What set this camp apart, she says, 'was the wide range of additional activities, including: Pilates sessions ... master-classes, which everyone had the opportunity to participate in; a tutor panel, which enabled us to ask questions about the practicalities of a career in music; the "singing together" sessions, ably led by Richard Gill; the tutors' concert ... the school hall concert, which gave opportunities for chamber and ensemble playing; an extra concert for the wind, brass and percussion at the winery ... and a large-scale game of "capture the flag", directed by Greg.

'These activities were well balanced with gaps in the schedule for practice and/or free time', Amber says. 'All of these aspects combined to make the NZSO NYO national music camp a holistic learning experience.'

Percussionist Tim Myhill (NYO 2008–10) says, 'I learnt lots from Bruce McKinnon,[14] the other tutors and of course Richard Gill. I really enjoyed my time on the camp, even the singing sessions, something I often dislike, but Richard kept it fun and lively. The accommodation was great as well as the rehearsal rooms, and I enjoyed the chamber music, which broke up the orchestral rehearsals – and the free time that us percussionists had. One great thing was that the orchestra bonded as such and created a tight-knit group, which will enhance the next tour, as there will not be a settling-in period of previous years. This will allow us to get straight into rehearsals. I would

In addition to music making, players enjoyed a range of other activities, including a table tennis tournament

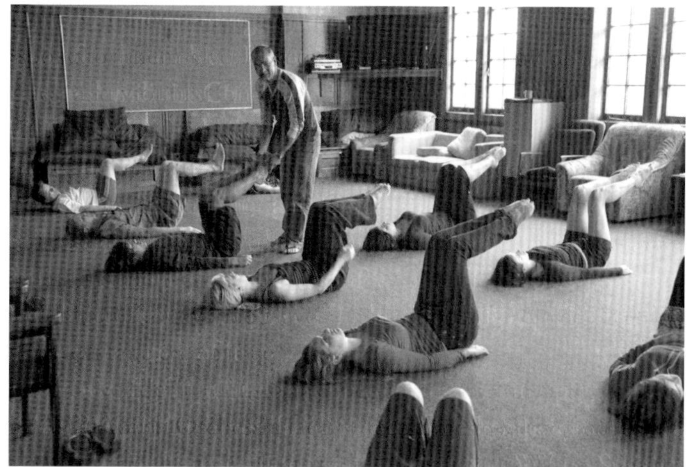

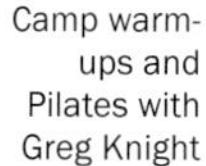
Camp warm-ups and Pilates with Greg Knight

definitely love to be part of a camp like this again, with NYO; it definitely could become an annual or biannual event.'[15]

A hope echoed by many participants of this very successful first NZSO National Youth Orchestra music camp.

The 50th anniversary concerts

Planning and preparations for the NZSO National Youth Orchestra's significant birthday had begun some considerable time earlier, but as the date drew nearer, anticipation was tempered with concern about two issues – the emergence of swine flu (the influenza A (H1N1) virus) with fears of a possible pandemic, and economic factors, that eventually led to the cancellation of the Dunedin concert from the anniversary tour – a considerable disappointment to audiences in the lower half of the South Island. This concert was replaced by two new activities: a conductor workshop, and a mock audition session. It also enabled a preliminary round of auditions and interviews for the new NZSO National Youth Orchestra Fellowship Programme.[16]

A major change to the timing of the youth orchestra was implemented in its anniversary year when, after always meeting in late August/early September since 1959 to fit in with the school holidays, it would now assemble in mid-July, to fit in with the 'university mid-term break with the five main New Zealand University semesters, and to coincide with school holidays'. However, as 'term-breaks for the universities do not coincide with each other ... we have quite a task in finding any period that does not encroach by one or two days on *any* university break ... [and the NZSO] liaises closely with each university to try and ensure the minimum impact on students' study'.[17]

Few changes were evident in the orchestra that assembled for the milestone 50th anniversary orchestra in 2009. As many also had attended the music camp in Napier, just six months earlier, almost everyone had worked together for at least a year, or more.

Two young reserve players from Dunedin did not have that advantage, but nevertheless were delighted when invited to replace players engaged in 2008, but now unavailable to play in 2009. Sarah Claman, a violinist in the Dunedin Sinfonia, recalls: 'On April Fool's Day I received a call asking me to take a place in the National Youth Orchestra. Naturally my initial reaction was disbelief! However this was quickly replaced by the excitement of being accepted into the orchestra, which is such a great stepping-stone towards a career as an orchestral musician; with the opportunity to learn and play with a talented set of young musicians.'[18]

Beth Goodwin also was contacted. After a relatively late start on the violin aged fifteen, in 2003, Beth switched to viola a year later, and says, 'I couldn't believe my luck to get a reserve place and then to be accepted for NYO in 2009!' She had played in the NZSO's Play with the NZSO sessions, which provided 'students and community musicians with the opportunity to rehearse a popular symphonic work with the NZSO'.[19] Beth found these sessions 'marvellous', but limited: 'they are occasional and only last a morning, and I looked forward to an intense week of rehearsals, and playing challenging music in a huge and talented viola section'.[20]

NZSO National Youth Orchestra concert and reviews

The NZSO National Youth Orchestra reassembled at Wellington High School on Saturday 27 June for the first of two days of tutorials with coaches. Each session ran from 10 am to 5.30 pm. One of the first actions was to provide full and comprehensive information to everyone involved about swine flu. A plan had been put in place in case of player, tutor, or staff illness; fortunately it was never required. On the second day, from 10 am to 5.30 pm, combined sectionals with NZSO coaches were held for strings, winds, and brass, and players met the conductor Paul Daniel before their first run through that evening. Wellington Friends hosted their usual welcome barbecue lunch.

Paul Daniel was musical director of the English National Opera, 1997–2005, debuting at the Metropolitan Opera in 2006; he received an Oliver Award for outstanding achievement in opera in 1998, and was awarded the CBE in 2000.[21] He has appeared as a guest conductor with major orchestras throughout the world; and in May 2009 took a position of principal conductor and artistic adviser of the West Australian Symphony Orchestra.

Pianist John Chen, making his second appearance with the NZSO National Youth Orchestra, after his performances in 2005, was now studying towards a doctorate in piano performance at the University of Southern California, Los Angeles. Chen, who is 'deeply committed' to New Zealand music, has given world premieres of works by Jenny McLeod, Ross Harris, and Claire Cowan.

Natalie Hunt was the fifth winner of the NZSO National Youth Orchestra Composer-in-Residence Award with her composition, *Only to the Highest Mountain.* 'Natalie's 's piece turned out to be ideal in the context of the 50th anniversary and the very demanding Mahler', said Ross Harris, the mentor to three of the five composers. 'Her overt references to New Zealand in the title and the chant like opening were the perfect start to the occasion.' The scheme is, 'clearly an excellent opportunity for budding composers ... It is hard to imagine a more exciting or rewarding opportunity for young New Zealand composers ... played by the best musicians in their age group in (up to four) halls round the country ... The NYO Composer in Residence Scheme is the perfect platform for launching the careers of young New Zealand composers ... it seems to me an important and indeed integral part of the NYO programme. Long may it continue.'[22]

NZSO National Youth Orchestra Concert Artists Programme

The cancellation of the NZSO National Youth Orchestra Christchurch Arts Centre series because of a lack of financial support was disappointing. The remaining lunchtime series in this anniversary season was an opportunity to showcase the combined talents of NYO concertmaster Ben Morrison, co-concertmaster Amalia Hall, and the NYO principals in two performances.

1. Master class

John Chen, Michael Fowler Centre, 7 pm, 30 June.

2. St Andrew's on The Terrace – Wednesday lunchtime concert (fifth year)

1 July, 12.15 pm. Vincent Persichetti – Serenade no 10, op. 79 (Lucy Anderson, flute, Ingrid Bauer, harp); Felix Mendelssohn – String Quartet no 4 in E minor, op 44 no 2 (Amalia Hall, violin I, Ben Morrison, violin II, Nicholas Hancox, viola, Edward King, cello); Maurice Ravel – *Introduction and Allegro* (Hannah Darroch, flute, Hayden Sinclair, clarinet, Amalia Hall, violin I, Ben Morrison, violin II, Nicholas Hancox, viola, Edward King, cello, Ingrid Bauer, harp).

This recital was recorded by Concert FM for later broadcast. The 50th anniversary had received very good coverage from Radio New Zealand, with a number of interviews broadcast on both networks over three months leading up to and including the NZSO National Youth 50th anniversary concert.[23]

The orchestra had moved to the Michael Fowler Centre on Monday 29 June, for five full days of rehearsals, the last three of which were full orchestra rehearsals. On Saturday 4 July, an open rehearsal was held for National Youth Orchestra alumni.

NZSO National Youth Orchestra alumni reunion

In parallel with the 50th anniversary Wellington performance, a youth orchestra alumni reunion was held to celebrate past and present together. A programme of activities was developed, following the model of the NZSO Alumni Association's successful reunions of 2001 and 2006.[24] A database was set up and efforts were made to contact the youth orchestra's former members, many of them now living overseas. Thanks to the extraordinary musicians' grapevine, the responses rolled in.

An eventful weekend began on Friday 3 July with registrations for a total of 222 alumni and friends. The major social event was the 50th Anniversary Gala Dinner Fundraiser at the Lambton Ballroom, Intercontinental Wellington, with 154 guests including New Zealand and international National Youth Orchestra alumni, distinguished guests and members of the NZSO board. The guest of honour was a beaming John Hopkins who, as founder of the National Youth Orchestra was clearly delighted to be present to see his offspring celebrate its 50th birthday, at a dinner at which almost $12,000 was raised for the orchestra.

The next morning, alumni met at the Michael Fowler Centre. They moved into the auditorium for an open dress rehearsal, to hear conductor Paul Daniel rehearse the orchestra in Mahler's massive seventh symphony for the anniversary concert that night. As former players crowded into one block of the venue, it was obvious that this was a very moving experience, bringing back memories of their own years playing in the orchestra – and for those who had not had the opportunity to hear the orchestra play in the interim, the standard of its current performance, clearly surpassed all expectations.

Following the rehearsal, awards were presented on stage to current players, by sponsors, including principal sponsor Denis Adam who spoke about the Adam Foundation involvement (Adam Foundation Scholarships); Angela Lindsay (Alex Lindsay Award), John Hopkins (John Chisholm Award),

Valerie Rhodes (Wellington Friends), and Alison Hansen (STANZA and Hawke's Bay Orchestras Scholarships).

An informal lunch followed in the Renouf Foyer, at which the speakers were the retiring NZSO chair Diana Fenwick, John Hopkins, and Angela Lindsay. Afterwards there was time to look at an exhibition of youth orchestra photos, posters and memorabilia on display on the first floor, at which an item of particular interest was Dog, the large *Footrot Flats* mascot that had accompanied youth orchestra members on the Brisbane tour in 1988.

2009 NZSO National Youth Orchestra 50th anniversary tour

Wellington, Christchurch, Auckland, 4–10 July. Conductor Paul Daniel.
Natalie Hunt – *Only to the Highest Mountain;* Ravel – *Piano Concerto for the Left Hand* (John Chen, soloist); Mahler – Symphony no 7

A full house at the Michael Fowler Centre included family members supporting their young players, NZSO subscribers, and NZSO National Youth Orchestra alumni, in a concert broadcast live to the nation on Radio New Zealand Concert. At 7 pm as the audience waited for the first young players to walk out, it was Wilma Smith, former NZSO concertmaster (and youth orchestra member), who took centre stage, with a very special guest to introduce – John Hopkins, the much loved and respected founder of the National Youth Orchestra, now in his eighties, who had travelled from his home in Melbourne for this special occasion. He received a prolonged and very warm round of applause from an audience clearly reluctant to let him go.

The programme was demanding for young players and, amongst alumni afterwards, one heard expressions of amazement at the standard of the orchestra now, playing works like Mahler 7 that would have seemed impossible to them, in their 'day'.

The reviews

John Button, writing in the *Dominion Post*,[25] noted the presence of John Hopkins and said that it was 'right to reflect on both his vision and skill, and where his efforts had taken music in this country. All we had to do was sit back and listen to some playing that would have been unthinkable, just a few short years ago, let alone when it all started. What we got was playing of astonishing quality that got better as the concert progressed and the music became more and more complex and demanding ... the final work, Mahler's least performed and most problematic symphony ... was given a performance of fantastic intensity ... a Mahlerian journey of tonal splendour, individual character and an understanding that belied the player's years.' Natalie Hunt's *Only to the Highest Mountain* was 'an atmospheric piece', Button said, and John Chen had played the Ravel Concerto 'superbly ... and the orchestra matched him all the way with weight and precision in ideal measure'.

'Young ones mark half a century with ascent of highest mountain' was the headline for William Dart's appreciative review of the Auckland concert. 'A high-spirited concert under the baton of Paul Daniel who has been unstinting in his praise of his young charges with their "huge amounts of energy"', commendations that Dart considered to be 'fully justified'. 'The NZSO NYO supports New Zealand composers, and Natalie Hunt's ... must be one of its finest commissions to date', Dart said. 'An evocation of our land and peoples, Hunt's piece stole upon us with mysterious incantations from off-stage oboe and cor anglais. Thematically the work was finely wrought especially in the inexorable build up to a massive chordal climax but many ears would have been drawn to Hunt's unexpected colours. And rare it is to have effects like rustling paper and exhaling breath sound as inevitable and right as a G major arpeggio.' The Mahler seventh symphony was 'an ambitious choice ... Problematic even to seasoned professionals ... it is an unpredictable and jagged journey. It was a thrill when this symphonic juggernaut took flight ... Without exception, the many solos demanded of the players were first rate, yet the impact of the full orchestra adroitly navigating the abrupt style shifts of Mahler's Finale was the undoubted highlight of an unforgettable Friday evening.'

'National Youth Orchestra Shines' John Daly-Peoples' review began. 'The concert showed that, not only are there a number of talented musicians there are some who proved to be impeccable soloists. Natalie Hunt put her stamp on the programme with a composition of great maturity; highlighting the strength of composition in our new and emerging composers ... The selection of Mahler's Symphony no 7 was a brave one. The work is nearly eighty minutes long with five movements and includes a huge range of instruments including two harps, a mandolin, guitar, and a bevy of percussion instruments. It is not one of his greatest symphonies ... but the orchestra, the various sections and soloists were able to engage with the music and provided a sumptuous interpretation ... This was an evening worthy of any major orchestra and is hopefully a reflection of the great musical talent which is being sustained in this country.'

In Wellington, after the concert, 150 guests of the NZSO and Adam Foundation, including alumni, sponsors, and other official guests, gathered for refreshments in the Lion Harbour View Lounge at the Michael Fowler Centre, where they heard speeches by the principal sponsor, Denis Adam; NZSO board member Richard Taylor; and sponsors Geoff Neumann (Intercontinental Hotels) and Andrew McDoaull (McDoaull Stuart).

On Sunday 5 July, from 10.30 am onwards, alumni enjoyed a relaxed farewell gathering in the function room at The Brewery Bar and Restaurant, overlooking the Wellington waterfront. Well-known NZSO viola player Norbert Heuser, a long-time member of the NZSO Alumni Association committee, had prepared a presentation of historic photographs and film featuring archival footage of the National Youth Orchestra and New Zealand Symphony Orchestra – including many who were former youth orchestra players. This gathering provided a last opportunity for alumni to spend quality time with John Hopkins, who was soon whisked away to attend his final activity of the weekend – the first conductor workshop, at the Adam Concert Room, New Zealand School of Music. Three young players participated: Ruth Kirkwood; Gemma New (NZSO NYO first violins, 2005–09); and Karlo Margetić (NZSO NYO clarinet and composer, 2009). All three conducted Beethoven's Symphony no 7, and Gemma[26] and Karlo also conducted Tchaikovsky's Symphony no 6.

'They all received coaching from Paul Daniel and John Hopkins', says Pascale Parenteau. 'I'm not sure what the conductors thought of their talent, but we got lots of feedback from the players themselves, who said how helpful and useful it was, to know that when a conductor does certain gestures it means "this or that".

'Plans have not been finalised yet', Pascale said, but, 'it is hoped to incorporate a composers workshop in some format or another, in the overall education programme – a conductor mentoring scheme would be fabulous – it is leaving some scope for a concept to be developed'. Another initiative for the anniversary year, the NZSO National Youth Orchestra Chair Endowment, had proved so successful that it too is likely to be continued.[27]

It had been a wonderful weekend for alumni, many of them meeting for the first time in decades. Among them, Marion Tulloch (Townend) (NYO viola, 1964–65),[28] who remembers 'the inspiring presence of John Hopkins, the exhilaration at being in that crowd of familiar and diversely interesting people, and the feeling of being part of a continuum of exuberant New Zealand youth music which is so strong today'.

For newcomers to the orchestra, this could not have been a more exciting first year. 'It was a great privilege to play in NYO for the 50th anniversary',

Beth Goodwin says, 'we got to talk to many older players who had followed musical careers, having decided after their first NYO experience that they would just *have to* continue playing music for the rest of their lives. My experience mirrored this; after having a fortnight completely saturated in beautiful music, one realises just how powerful and liberating music really can be. I was inspired by John Hopkins's talk on music, that it "must be played not for oneself but as a gift to others which simultaneously enriches one's own life" – and also to hear thoughts [on music] from our fantastic conductor and soloist. I came to the conclusion that music is more of a deep and beautiful mystery that I'd ever realised before.'[29] The presence of John Hopkins was a highlight for many alumni. An added bonus, was to see John's newly released first book, *The Point of the Baton*, to meet his American biographer William Cottam – and to hear that they would soon start work on a new collaboration.

For John Hopkins, himself, the anniversary and reunion was clearly a wonderful experience. 'I am so grateful to Pascale Parenteau for her months of careful planning and, of course, to Peter Walls who made this important milestone such a special occasion. It was heart-warming for me to see the National Youth Orchestra being nurtured in this way by the NZSO and the Adam Foundation as it moves into the next 50 years. So many wonderful memories flooded into my mind especially when I saw the large number of players from the first NYO at the 50th anniversary reunion. The playing of the 2009 orchestra was truly impressive and it was obvious that the young New Zealanders can bring special qualities to the most challenging works of the repertoire.'[30] Pascale Parenteau had managed the orchestra with flair and passion for six eventful years, in which time the operation became increasingly professional and many innovations were made, but things can still go wrong. It was six o'clock one concert evening, when Pascale discovered the flowers had not been ordered. A dash to the supermarket revealed just two bunches left, which she hastily put together – and then presented as a bouquet to the young composer, on stage. Afterwards, backstage, Pascale retrieved the flowers, and presented them to the soloist, after her performance – and then retrieved them again, to present for a third time – to the conductor. Later, Pascale explained what had happened to three confused artists – who by unanimous decision gave the flowers to the young composer!

A favourite moment that Pascale says she will miss, 'is waiting backstage at the end of the last concert, listening to them playing, hearing the applause, and peeping through the curtain to see them coming off stage. This was always very moving, for me, and makes all the work and effort seems worthwhile.'[31]

2010: The 50th season

Wellington, Auckland, 26–28 August. Conductor Rossen Milanov. Vaughan Williams – *Fantasia on a Theme by Thomas Tallis*; Stravinsky – Concerto for Piano and Wind Instruments; Adams – *The Chairman Dances*; Rachmaninov – Symphonic Dances

The new decade brought significant changes to NZSO National Youth Orchestra, following the previous year's excitement of the ground-breaking national music camp and 50th anniversary. Since then, Pascale Parenteau's designation and duties had changed from youth orchestra manager to NZSO education and community coordinator. Pascale brought considerable experience to this new role, working on the operational side of the education and community programmes with Claire Lewis,[32] from 2008 the NZSO's education and community programme manager, who is also the new manager of the youth orchestra.

Managing the orchestra 'was an honour and a challenge I could not wait to get my teeth into', Claire says. 'I was aware that with the engagement of new staff, there is the expectation that they will bring with them a fresh approach. I was however equally conscious that the orchestra is a well-established institution with a central objective at its core which should not be altered; the opportunity for the best young players from New Zealand to come together and play exciting and challenging repertoire under the baton of an exceptional conductor.'

In her first year, Claire says, 'I chose to keep the operation side of the orchestra simple, a comprehensive rehearsal period and tour with exceptionally executed concerts. The programme which I put together was experimental and demanding and through it I hoped that the musicians of the orchestra would have a truly unique training experience. By splitting the orchestra in the first half of the concert into groups of strings only and wind and brass (joined by the double basses, timpani, and solo piano) the players and conductor were able to work on subtle sonorities and colours in their playing, different to those of the full symphonic sound. This was an exercise which demanded a new approach to their understanding of playing as a section. The second half of the concert was technically demanding, requiring perfect rhythmical skills and endless counting. That the first half featured two works which looked back to older styles of music and a second half that was brought to life by two dances, and that the entire programme built from the hushed suspension of the Vaughan Williams to the exuberance of the Rachmaninov was an added bonus!'

The engagement of Rossen Milanov[33] was 'a wonderful coup', Claire says. 'His expertise for getting the best out of young players was evident from the first rehearsal. He has a patient and gentle approach but it is underpinned by an eagle-eye for detail and an unrelenting pursuit of excellence which brought the best out of all the players. He was the ideal Maestro for this young orchestra.'

Jason Jin-Hyung Bae, an eighteen-year-old pianist, born in South Korea, lives in New Zealand. He has been a pupil of Rae de Lisle for the past nine years, and is studying towards a Bachelor of Music degree at Auckland's School of Music.[34] Jason Bae was a delight to work with, and his engagement allowed the orchestra to promote an exceptional young New Zealand musician as a soloist,' Claire says.

Composer-in-residence programme

'The biggest change to the orchestra was through the composer-in-residence programme', Claire says. '2010 became a transition year during which I decided to advance the programme, based on feedback we invited from the young composers themselves, to enlarge what the residency offers them. In 2010/2011 we are giving Alexandra Hay,[35] a young Wellington-based composer, sonic artist and teacher, the chance to spend 12 months working with an established New Zealand composer, Gillian Whitehead, to create a new work, to be premiered in the 2011 programme. This work will be a maximum of fifteen minutes in duration, whereas five minutes was standard for previous years. This development will mean that the selected young composer will be able to create a more expansive work and develop a more meaningful relationship with an established composer.

'I come to the orchestra from a career organising community arts projects; predominantly choral projects for community choirs of up to 300 individuals. To have the opportunity to work with an elite group of young orchestral players and to witness their exponential capacity to develop and learn was a real treat and is something I relish revisiting next year.'[36]

Jessica Alloway was concertmaster of the orchestra in its 2010 season, and Olivia Francis, the associate concertmaster. There were eighty-five players and – surely a first – five sets of siblings. Four of them were from the Wellington area – including violinists Sophie Tarrant-Mathews (sixteen) and her sister Claudia (twelve), the youngest member of the NZSO National Youth Orchestra in 2010.

The inspiring NZSO National Youth Orchestra starts afresh each year with a new conductor, a soloist, a core of experienced players from previous years, and a set of newcomers eager to take the next big step on their musical journeys.

Peter Walls began his National Youth Orchestra journey in 1962, but this ended abruptly after four years, because of issues with its then conductor. Thirty or so years later, the New Zealand Symphony Orchestra faced a serious financial situation, and Peter Walls, by then professor of music at Victoria University and an NZSO board member (later deputy chair), stepped in. As acting artistic manager, he encouraged Brigid O'Meeghan to manage NZSO National Youth Orchestra, and the orchestra never looked back.

Now after twenty eventful years in a variety of roles, including the past nine as NZSO chief executive, Peter Walls has announced his retirement, with effect in December 2011. In his time, Peter has made an incalculable contribution, with both orchestras reaching unprecedented heights – NZSO National Youth Orchestra celebrating its first half century, in 2009, and the New Zealand Symphony Orchestra making its ground-breaking world tour in 2010.

'There has definitely been a really noticeable improvement in standards,' Peter Walls agrees, 'and generally the selection of the conductor each year has reflected a determination to regard NYO members as musicians with a professional future'. It is hard to make comparisons he says, because 'one can sometimes be surprised by listening to recordings of earlier years and realising that, actually, some quite remarkable standards have been achieved in the past too'. The big challenge for NZSO National Youth Orchestra, Walls believes, 'is how to spread more activity through the year, as the National Youth Orchestra of Great Britain, or even the Australian Youth Orchestra are able to do. This is more difficult in New Zealand simply because of limited resources.'

Walls is not worried about the future for the NZSO National Youth Orchestra, he says, 'at least certainly not from an institutional point of view. There is no difficulty in getting all stakeholders to realise the importance of the NYO as part of the country's musical infrastructure. Where I do have concerns is in the ability of New Zealand communities and schools to keep producing instrumentalists who have the musical grounding necessary to get into NYO. We are at a crossroads, but if the Sistema Aotearoa pilot programme that the Minister launched in Auckland (see page 239) takes off and spreads to other parts of the country (including rural communities), we would have nothing to worry about.'

Among the many remarkable achievements in Walls' tenure, he says, 'I regard the NYO as the pinnacle of the NZSO's important education programme. I don't think I should take any credit for what has been achieved in the last decade. In that period (and, actually, before with people like Lindy Tennant-Brown), the NYO has been sustained by idealistic and dedicated managers. I would like to acknowledge and thank them.'

Peter Nisbet, New Zealand Symphony Orchestra's first chief executive, once told the author that he was working to put NZSO 'into orbit'. After nine years in the same position, there can be no doubt that Peter Walls has achieved that goal, for both the NZSO and the NZSO National Youth Orchestra – and his 'retirement' is both well earned, and exceptionally well deserved.

NZSO National Youth Orchestra alumni in New Zealand and around the world, professional musicians or not, as these pages reveal, clearly still cherish memories of 'their' National Youth Orchestra years. Their sentiments, as first expressed by NYO world tour players in 1975, seem equally relevant today, given the uncertainty in New Zealand's art scene – 'Long live National Youth!'[37]

12 Future Proofing

Peter Walls

Programming involves dialogue. At least, it does these days. The starting point is generally an exchange of wish lists between the conductor and the artistic administrator (in this case, the National Youth Orchestra manager). There will, for example, be constraints that the conductor needs to be made aware of: we can't do such-and-such a work because it was programmed last year or is being done by another conductor this year (or next year, or by another orchestra ...) Our music director, Pietari Inkinen, is consulted at every point since he needs to ensure that the overall look of an NZSO season – including the National Youth Orchestra – is right and that there is a good fit between artists and the repertoire they have been assigned. At a certain point, this discussion is widened out so that those who will be involved in marketing the concerts or planning the logistics of the tour can think about it from their perspective.

The way we do this at the NZSO is through a bi-monthly meeting called the Artist Planning Forum (usually referred in house as APF). APF is a kind of clearing house for all NZSO programming decisions. Its monthly meetings are attended by key members of the management staff, our concertmaster, and members of the NZSO Players' Committee. The discussion is dominated by two standing agenda items: selection of artists for forward seasons (normally looking two to three years out), and repertoire for the next season.

In the past few years there has been surprisingly vigorous discussion about National Youth Orchestra repertoire at APF. Youth orchestra conductors, soloists, and programmes attract as much interest from the players attending these meetings as the repertoire that they will eventually be performing themselves in the NZSO. This in itself is indicates just how important the youth orchestra is to NZSO members. They realise (many of them thanks to having played in the youth orchestra) just what a valuable training opportunity it can provide aspiring professionals.

The debate always revolves around two possible views of what it is appropriate to put in front of young musicians. One school of thought prioritises manageability. Going down this path means that any work that is programmed must be one that these young musicians can perform credibly at the end of a week's intensive rehearsal. Anything that will expose weaknesses in the still-developing technique of student players should be avoided. As this discussion unfolds, it becomes clear that our NZSO principals, through their involvement in youth orchestra coaching and also through the teaching that they do at New Zealand's universities, are very aware of the range of young players who will be auditioning. Sometimes they will fret about a (hopefully always temporary) shortage of outstanding candidates for a particular instrument and want to avoid repertoire that will be too reliant on skill in that area.

In opposition to the 'safety first' lobby, there is another group who take the view that the way to really develop student players' abilities is to extend and challenge them. Leading the charge with this view has been the National Youth Orchestra manager, Pascale Parenteau. Pascale's predecessor, Brigid O'Meeghan, thought along similar lines. They always argued that putting big repertoire out in front of these players – repertoire that their university orchestras or their regional youth orchestras would not be able to tackle convincingly – would provide the kind of stimulation and excitement that makes the National Youth Orchestra experience so memorable and, ultimately, so worthwhile. Looking back through recent programmes, it is pretty clear that this view (always tempered by the realism of the more cautious participants in APF discussions) has won out: Mahler 7 with Paul Daniel in 2009, Stravinsky's *Firebird* with Jacques Lacombe in 2008, Debussy *La Mer* with Yannick Nézet-Séguin in 2007, Shostakovich Symphony no 10 with Simon Streatfeild in 2006 and so on. Richard Strauss did not make his debut with the National Youth Orchestra until the 21st century: Lutz Köhler conducted *Don Juan* in 2001 and Simon Streatfeild included the suite from *Der Rosenkavalier* in his 2006 offering. Sometimes it has seemed quite brave to be committing to these works – but the results have been spectacularly successful. Audiences have been inspired and, more importantly, the members of the National Youth Orchestra have had an experience that will not be matched until they successfully audition for a place in a major professional orchestra.

In 2010, Claire Lewis assumed overall responsibility for National Youth Orchestra programming as part of her NZSO education manager position. Claire, building on Pascale Parenteau's challenging repertoire choices, decided to create a programme that gave strings and wind players separate opportunity for intensive work with conductor Rossen Milanov. The strings studied Vaughan Williams' *Fantasia on a Theme of Thomas Tallis* while the wind players tackled Stravinsky's astringent-sounding but brilliant Concerto for Piano and Wind Instruments (with a young Korean New Zealander, Jason Bae, as soloist). In the second half of the concert, they came together for some big and colourful works: John Adams' *The Chairman Dances* and Rachmaninov's *Symphonic Dances.* All great music and a programme that, overall, acknowledged the importance of the National Youth Orchestra as a learning opportunity for its members.

I have no knowledge of what kind of discussion underpinned programming decisions for the youth orchestra before 2002 when I took up the position of NZSO chief executive. Looking through the programmes from 1959 forward, however, it seems that there has been an interesting evolution. To put this in its broadest terms, across the history of the National Youth Orchestra we see a progression from programmes that look as if they have been devised for young musicians, yet to reach their full technical and musical potential, towards programmes that would take large professional orchestras anywhere in the world to the edge of their capabilities.

Part of that evolution involves the context in which the National Youth Orchestra operates. When John Hopkins founded the orchestra in 1959 it was a bold move. There were very few precedents; the National Youth Orchestra of Great Britain had been founded in 1948, three years after the earliest (and longest lived) national youth orchestra – the National Youth Orchestra of Wales. The Australians beat us to it by two years, but most of the other well-known national youth orchestras are more recent foundations: The Canadian National Youth Orchestra was founded in 1960, the Simón Bolívar Symphony Orchestra (the outstanding Venezuelan youth orchestra) was founded in 1975 by a remarkable economist, congressman and musician, José Antonio Abreu. The European Community Youth Orchestra (now known as the European Union Youth Orchestra) was not formed until 1978 and its rival the Gustav Mahler Jugendorchester not until 1986.

Within New Zealand, too, there wasn't the infrastructure that now exists. The Auckland Junior Symphony Orchestra (now the Auckland Youth Orchestra) had been formed in 1948 by Dr Charles Nalden. (A former member recalls that 'The girls wore long white dresses, so we looked like milk bottles'.) The Christchurch School of Instrumental Music which nurtured the Christchurch Youth Orchestra was established in 1955, by Robert Perks (father of NZSO violinist Robin Perks). The Wellington Youth Orchestra was formed in 1959 – the same year as the National Youth Orchestra. All these orchestras were in their infancy. Moreover, the universities were only gradually edging their way into performance teaching. Auckland University first offered credit for an Executant Diploma of Music in 1956. By the early sixties they had a small but select faculty of instrumental lecturers – Marie Vanderwart (cello), Michael Wieck (violin), Winifred Stiles (viola), and Janetta McStay (piano). Canterbury University had ensembles in residence (first The Canterbury Trio, then the Alard String Quartet) from 1958, but was not formally teaching performance music for credit until 1965. Victoria University in Wellington began offering performance courses as part of the BMus degree (with Ruth Pearl as the violin lecturer). Otago did not offer performance for credit until 1971. In the late fifties and early sixties, none of these music schools were yet in a position to have an orchestra that could take a serious role in the development of professional musicians. The case for the establishment of the National Orchestra Trainees (later known as the Schola Musica) was still being formulated.

When John Hopkins met the first intake of National Youth Orchestra players in 1959, many of them had never played in an orchestra before – not even an inadequate one. Obviously, the kind of repertoire chosen in such circumstances would inevitably look very different from the 2009 programme. No Mahler 7 for these novices.

The most striking feature of the 1959 programme, apart from the fact that it is for an orchestra of modest proportions, is that there is a strong sense of period balance: Handel, Mozart, Beethoven (Symphony no 1), Mendelssohn, with a little Delius ('The Walk to the Paradise Garden' from *A Village Romeo and Juliet*) as a concession to the 20th century. This looks very like sensible programming for a training orchestra. None of the works present major technical difficulties for individual players, but the ensemble skills developed in playing Mozart and Beethoven on the one hand and Mendelssohn and Delius on the other are considerable. The Delius is the work with the largest orchestration in the 1959 list. It requires 2 flutes, 2 oboes (one doubling on cor anglais), 2 clarinets, 2 bassoons, 4 horns, 2 trumpets, 3 trombones, timpani, harp, and strings (so full string sections plus 19 other players). As a story of firsts and lasts (at least in so far as this book is concerned) it makes an interesting comparison with the Mahler Seventh Symphony performed in the 50th anniversary year. The Mahler requires 5 flutes, 4 oboes (or, rather, 3 oboes plus cor anglais), 5 clarinets (including the small e-flat instrument and a large bass clarinet), 4 bassoons (including contrabassoon), 4 horns, 3 trumpets, 3 trombones, 1 tuba and tenor horn, guitar, mandolin, timpani plus 5 percussionists, 2 harps, and strings (in other words, full string sections plus forty players). The growth is not just numerical; today's National Youth Orchestra members are confronting works of a complexity that would have seemed worse than foolhardy in 1959.

John Hopkins' programme for the second year began with Glinka's *Russlan and Ludmilla* Overture. A short National Film Unit documentary on the orchestra began with John tapping his music desk with his baton and then launching into the Glinka with a fizz and excitement that seemed to communicate youthful energy. This programme and those through to 1964 reflect his concern for stylistic balance and systematic building of ensemble skills.

Douglas Lilburn's *Aotearoa* Overture appeared on National Youth Orchestra players' stands in 1962. At that stage, it had only ever had two outings with the National Orchestra – the first a studio performance in Wellington in 1953 and then performances in Auckland and Wellington in 1960. Douglas was always vocal in his appreciation of John Hopkins for championing New Zealand music. The *Aotearoa* remains the youth orchestra's most performed New Zealand composition (having been featured in their programmes in five different years).

In terms of orchestral size, the stand out work in those first five years with John Hopkins was Kodály's *Háry Janós* Suite in 1963. This has an extraordinary line-up including 6 trumpets and 6 percussion in addition to timpani, but it is by turns exuberant and plaintive – a very extrovert piece which made a big impact on student players. This, as it happens, was my first year in the National Youth Orchestra and (apart from being *terrified* about the tricky upbeat sneeze that introduces the second-to-last movement (Intermezzo)) I remember being thrilled and enchanted by the extraordinary colours emerging from the woodwind and percussion sections behind me.

In 1965 Ashley Heenan began his long and unfortunate reign over the National Youth Orchestra. It had been wonderful to have the NZSO's music director devote himself to the youth orchestra's development in its first six years. Ashley Heenan, however, was an indifferent musician with an inadequate conducting technique and behavioural problems that should have made him ineligible for any sustained interaction with young people. He presided over the National Youth Orchestra for a decade and over the Schola Musica for even longer. (My own membership of the National Youth Orchestra ended after four years when, prompted by my violin teacher, Ruth Pearl, I phoned Ashley to ask for a couple of hours off during the rehearsal period to sit an exam; the call unleashed a torrent of abuse directed not just at me, but also at my fellow students at Victoria University. I had been looking forward to my first year in the first violin section – but there could be no going back after that phone call.)

He did, however, give the orchestra some challenging repertoire: The Shovetide Fair scene from Stravinsky's *Petrouchka* in 1965 and *The Firebird* Suite in 1970. His symphonic choices were interesting and appealing: Sibelius' Third Symphony (1965), the Schumann *Rhenish* Symphony (1967) and Dvořák's Sixth (1968).

In the National Youth Orchestra's first half century, the most frequently performed composer has been Tchaikovsky, who has featured seventeen times (with the Fifth Symphony in 1964 with Ashley Heenan, 1982 with Meredith Davies, 1998 with James Sedares). All the Beethoven symphonies have been performed except – surprisingly – no 6 (the *Pastoral*) and – even more surprisingly – given the occasional collaborations with the National Youth Choir – no 9 (the *Choral*). No 5 has been performed twice, first with Georg Tintner in 1979 and then with Kurt Sanderling in 1983. The Piano Concerto no 1 was performed in 1997 with Christopher Hinterhuber (a young Austrian pianist who was later to record two of the Ferdinand Ries piano concerti with the NZSO), but with that exception there has not been a major Beethoven work performed since 1989 – though Benjamin Zander opened his 1999 programme with the *Coriolan* Overture. This reflects the trend towards larger-orchestra works in the past two decades. Haydn has slipped completely off the list. John Hopkins included the Symphony no 104 in the 1963 programme and two more of the late London symphonies were performed in the seventies, but there has been nothing since then. Mozart has fared rather better with twelve appearances, though these have mostly been piano concerti (the favourite being K488 in A major which was performed by Ilse von Alpenheim (Austrian Mozarteum) in 1959 and Jacqueline Stone, Wanganui (Royal Academy, London) in 1972.

Stravinsky seems to be something of an exception to the idea that the National Youth Orchestra has tended to move from the classical building blocks like Beethoven to complex large-orchestra 20th and 21st century compositions. Stravinsky has, in fact, been well represented in youth orchestra programmes right through its history. *The Firebird* Suite and *Petrouchka* have featured four times. Doron Salomon tackled *The Rite of Spring* in 1985. Brahms, by contrast, did not appear at all in the eighties and nineties. Benjamin Zander conducted the Symphony no 4 in 2002 and Alasdair Neale the First Symphony in 2004.

The giants of modernism and 20th century music are all there somewhere in National Youth Orchestra programmes. Prokofiev, Bartók, Shostakovich have all appeared since 1990. One of the striking things about the orchestra's sampling of 20th century music in the early years was the quite strong representation of composers who wrote very accessible but ultimately rather trivial music – people such as Percy Grainger (1960 and 1972), Gordon Jacob (1975), Constant Lambert (1985). It is perhaps reassuring to realise that this is all a matter of fashion. The music of these composers was current in NZSO programmes in the sixties and seventies particularly – and the music of the *avant-garde* conspicuous by its absence. (The NZSO is yet to play a single piece by Boulez or Stockhausen in a public concert.)

The approach to New Zealand music was similarly conservative – a situation that has been well and truly remedied since the inauguration of the National Youth Orchestra Composer-in-Residence scheme in 2005 (the brainchild of Pascale Parenteau). Needless to say, Douglas Lilburn has been heard most often – but it has been the *Aotearoa* Overture (four times), the *Festival* Overture (twice), and the Suite for Orchestra (written originally for the Auckland Junior Symphony) once.

One remarkable thing about repertoire covered in the National Youth Orchestra is that – from the players' perspective – it makes an impact for life. I've compared notes with some of my contemporaries and we all seem to have similar reactions. I can't hear the Rachmaninov Second Piano Concerto without remembering the magic of hearing that from the middle of the orchestra. My favourite Sibelius symphony is still no 3. Like so many other alumni, the youth orchestra was my first experience of playing in a large and really proficient ensemble. Moreover, we were all excited by what we were doing – and I see that in today's players, too.

Where will the National Youth Orchestra be in another fifty years? Now that the orchestra is treated to a succession of top-rated conductors, the incentives for our best young players to want to be part of the action are huge. The orchestra's future should be assured and we ought to be able to expect each new generation of players to raise the bar in terms of quality.

But for that to happen, the National Youth Orchestra is going to continue to need the support of generous friends. There is a significant cost to sustaining quality orchestral training at this level. Even more, the youth orchestra (and, ultimately, the NZSO and the whole professional music sector in New Zealand) is going to need lots of talented instrumentalists to be coming through our school system.

This, unfortunately, is not guaranteed. There has been a real decline in the coverage of instrumental teaching in New Zealand. Comparatively few schools in the country participate in the itinerant music teaching scheme that receives (insufficient) funding through the Ministry of Education. Moreover, some of the networks that ensured equality of access to instrumental education have withered away. In my youth, it seemed that every second young player participating in local competitions was taught by nuns. Michael Houstoun's first piano lessons were at the convent in Timaru – and there are hundreds of examples like it throughout the country. (Dame Kiri Te Kanawa was nurtured by Sister Mary Leo at St Mary's Ponsonby – a school that still recognises that musical training helps with all learning.)

A few years ago, I asked the brass players in the NZSO how they had got started and the majority told me about the brass band movement, which is still strong, but not perhaps what it was in its heyday. (Remember at Christmas, there'd be at least *two* bands playing carols on your street corner? The Salvation Army and the local brass band would each be doing the rounds for several weeks before the stockings – well, pillow slips – got hung over the end of your bed.) In the 21st century, the brass band movement and – more particularly – the convents have withered away as a source of musical training for the underprivileged.

I am constantly reminded, every time the NZSO goes into a rural area to do education work, of the abundance of innate musical talent that exists throughout New Zealand society. The musical gifts of Māori children, in particular, are quite remarkable. Yet, we do very little about it. If I could be granted one wish for the future of music in New Zealand, it would be to have a revitalised itinerant music teaching scheme that would take affordable tuition on musical instruments into every town in New Zealand.

Every time I read any discussion of youth orchestras around the world these days, someone mentions the national youth orchestra of Venezuela. It was founded as The Youth Orchestra of Venezuela in 1975 by José Antonio Abreu, an economist, university professor, politician (Venezuelan Minister of Culture in 1983), and musician. The orchestra's success in 1977 at the very same festival in Aberdeen where our National Youth Orchestra had distinguished itself two years earlier convinced the Venezuelan government to fully finance the venture. Today, this orchestra (now known as the Simón Bolívar Orchestra) stands at the pinnacle of a whole network of youth orchestras which are themselves fed by a music teaching infrastructure known, simply, as 'The System' ('El Sistema'). Abreu described his vision as follows: 'For me, the most important priority was to give access to music to poor people. As a musician, I had the ambition to see a poor child play Mozart. Why not? Why concentrate in one class the privilege of playing Mozart and Beethoven? The high musical culture of the world has to be a common culture, part of the education of everyone.'[1]

If only the New Zealand Government had responded to the National Youth Orchestra's success in Aberdeen as the Venezuelan government was to do just two years later. But it is not too late. The Hon Christopher Finlayson, the current Minister for Arts, Culture and Heritage, has shown strong interest in developing an El Sistema style programme in New Zealand (Sistema Aotearoa), beginning with a pilot scheme in South Auckland but with the prospect of a national rollout in the not-too-distant future. What an amazing vision for New Zealand.

Acknowledgements

The NZSO National Youth Orchestra was written at the request of Peter Walls, chief executive, NZSO. I thank Peter for entrusting me with the responsibility of writing this first history, for his patience with my subsequent questions and for agreeing to write chapter 12, 'Future Proofing', on the orchestra's music performed in fifty seasons.

John Hopkins' interest in this book is greatly appreciated, and I thank him for his gracious Foreword. As 'father' of the orchestra, John continues to inspire generations of musicians; and a great bond exists between him, his pioneering players, and young players of today.

I acknowledge my sincere gratitude to the FAME Trust, for generous financial support during the research and writing of this book. The encouragement and understanding of Bob and Norma Hudson has been deeply appreciated throughout this long process.

My thanks to all who assisted my research – Peter Averi, for making available his extensive archive, memoir and NYO world tour diary entries, and providing prompt, generous answers to my enquiries; Alwyn and Gae Palmer, for interviews, subsequent follow-ups, photographs, and additional information, as requested; former NZSO and BCNZ management and staff – including Beverley Wakem, Beverley Malcolm, Wendy Allardice, and Joy Aberdein (also NYO manager in 1994); and for assistance by interview, reports, and answers to my subsequent requests: Lyndy Tennant-Brown, Brigid O'Meeghan, Pascale Parenteau, and Claire Lewis.

I thank three New Zealand conductors – Michael Vinten for his report on his years as assistant conductor, and conductor of the Australian tour; Michael Houstoun for his generous response and comments, as conductor, and also soloist on three occasions; and Gary Brain for his interview and subsequent information, recalled from his time conducting NYO in 1993.

Many NZSO musicians began playing in NZSO National Youth Orchestra, and memories, observations, opinions and photographs from those formative years were appreciated from Donald Armstrong, Peter Barber,

Bridget Douglas, Ursula Evans, Greg Hill, Bruce McKinnon, Simon Miller, and NZSO alumni Alison Bowcott, Jane Freed, Angela Lindsay, Robin Perks, Juliana Radaich, Linda Simmons, Wilma Smith, Glenda van Drimmelen, and Kenneth Young.

Significant assistance was provided by current NZSO management: Anne Phillips (Appendix of NYO Players and Artists); Hannah Anderson (NZSO NYO Alumni database and website) – together with Claire Lewis and Pascale Parenteau (NZSO NYO Appendix of Awards, and Appendix of Sponsors). I offer sincere thanks to them all; and for assistance given by Sarah Glasgow, Brian Morris, Rosemary Brown, Jennifer Jarden, and Grant Gilbert.

The book is enriched by illustrations ranging from high quality photographic and digital images from professional photographers, to informal black and white snapshots from alumni. I am especially indebted to Mabel Wong, NZSO Librarian and photographer, for her images, and for help and advice in processing and selecting others for the wider collection. My thanks to everyone who contributed; especially Kevin Currie for his 1975 World Tour collection, and Phillip Norman, for his photograph, suggestions and advice.

Permission to use images from the *Evening Post* Collection, and from Alexander Turnbull Library Wellington, is gratefully acknowledged; also assistance from Archives New Zealand, including Sara Knight, archivist Government Loans; and librarians from the microfiche section, Wellington City Library.

I acknowledge the patience of my publisher Fergus Barrowman, and his team at Victoria University Press; and offer sincere thanks to my editor John Huria, and designer Sarah-Jane McCosh, for brilliantly transforming my unwieldy manuscript into this elegant book.

Marion Townend's contribution over more than two years has been substantial – and includes editing, research, advice, and friendship. It has been a great pleasure to work with Marion, and I thank her most sincerely. I am grateful also for Philip Mann's advice, Julia Millen's encouragement, Vince Aspey's cheery phone-calls (to check the book's progress), for my husband Ralph's unconditional support, and the tolerance of my neglected family.

The patience of readers was also appreciated. NZSO National Youth Orchestra soon outgrew its tight timeframe, when eventually I realised that this is not the story of one orchestra, but fifty orchestras – each a unique little world, meeting (usually) for just one week, once a year, over fifty-two years.

It was inspiring to meet both ends of the spectrum at NZSO National Youth Orchestra Reunion 2009 – young players starting out, and youth orchestra alumni enthusiastically recalling 'their' days as if they happened yesterday. The NZSO's request for 'memories' drew responses for almost every year, in such numbers, that this too, impacted on the book's structure. It was not possible to publish every contribution, but each has been retained as an on-going NZSO NYO alumni collection, including some differing accounts of the same event. On occasions when this occurred, opinions were sought from other contemporaries, but although some spirited debates ensued, agreement did not always follow.

In a long association with NZSO, my involvement in the National Youth Orchestra was limited to Wellington concerts. It has been a particular pleasure to enter into its world, albeit briefly, as an observer, to meet dedicated young players, to hear them rehearse and perform, and to experience the exhilaration of NZSO NYO music camp in Napier, 2009.

NZSO National Youth Orchestra under various names has been the catalyst encouraging countless players towards musical careers, or lifetime amateur music-making and concert-going. It has enriched and inspired lives, created lifelong musical friendships, and enhanced the joy of music. It has been a privilege to tell its story.

Appendix A

* No concerts in 1977 and 1994

** Name in brackets indicates married name

MEMBERS OF THE NATIONAL YOUTH ORCHESTRA, NEW ZEALAND POST NATIONAL YOUTH ORCHESTRA, NEW ZEALAND YOUTH ORCHESTRA, NZSO NATIONAL YOUTH ORCHESTRA

VIOLIN

ABRAHAMSON, Charles 1996-99; **ADAMS**, Chris 1995; **ADAMS**, Miranda 1981; **ADAMS (Radaich)**, Juliana 1959-60; **AIKEN**, Megan 2006; **ALBERS**, Marike 1989; **ALEXANDER**, Brian 1961-64, 1967-69; **ALLEN**, Emily 1987; **ALLISON**, Iselta 1996-2000; **ALLISON**, Mary 1972-76; **ALLISON**, Megan 1996-2001; **ALLISON**, Susie 1996; **ALLOWAY**, Jessica 2007-08; **AMARASINGHAM**, Kemal 1989-90; **ANDERSON**, John 1974; **ANDERSON**, Gretchen 1992-93, 1996; **ANDERSON**, Tiffany 1996; **ANDREWES**, James 1997-98, 2000-03; **ANSELL**, Gillian 1974; **ANSELL** Simon 1979-1981, 1983; **ARMSTRONG**, Donald 1974-75; **ASPEY**, Vincent 1959; **AUSTIN**, Faith 1971-72; **BAIN**, Colleen 1963-68; **BAKER**, Margaret 1976, 1978; **BALLARA**, Carlo 1990-91; **BALLOG**, Catherine 1972; **BANKS**, Jennifer 1998, 2000-01, 2004; **BARRON**, Emma 1991, 1995; **BARRY**, Edward 1969-73; **BARTLETT**, Mark 1976; **BAYLISS**, Sharon 2003, 2005; **BAYNES**, Gillian 1964, 1966-67; **BEILBY**, Sarah 1996; **BENNETT**, Diedre 1995; **BENNETT**, Sonya 1987, 1989; **BENNITT**, Nikki 2006-08; **BERKELJON**, Manu 1992-93; **BIRCH**, Rodney 1965-66; **BIRD**, Sophie 2001, 2004, 2006; **BISLEY**, Brigid 1979-80; **BLOM**, Axel 1963; **BLOM**, Edward 1964; **BOUSFIELD**, Helen 1963, 1965-68; **BOUTEREY-ISHIDO**, Jun 2004-05; **BOWCOTT**, Alison 1970-72; **BOWDEN**, Sophie 1995-97; **BOYCE**, John 1961-62; **BRAND**, Rachael 1996-99; **BRASCH**, Nicola 1990; **BREWERTON**, Emma 1986-87, 1989; **BRIDGMAN COOPER**, Mahuia 1997; **BROADBENT**, Anna 1997, 1999-2000; **BROOM**, Julia 1998-2000, 2002; **BROOM**, Simeon 1996-1999, 2001-02; **BRUNSDEN**, Michel 1962-64; **BRUNTLETT**, Diana 1961; **BUI**, Huy-Nguyen 1990; **BUNT**, Belinda 1969-73; **BURFORD**, Peter 1962-68; **BUSH**, Allister 1982-86; **BUSSELL**, Graeme 1988-90; **CALDEN** Wendy 1978-80; **CALLANAN**, John 1959; **CAMPBELL**, Nicola 1976, 1979; **CANDY**, Kathleen 1982, 1985; **CAREY**, Richard 1962-63, 1965-67; **CARRIGAN**, Belinda 1993, 1995; **CARRYER**, Paula 1987, 1989-91; **CARTER**, Gwyneth 1968; **CARTER**, James 1995-96; **CASTLE**, Owen 1959; **CATANACH**, Rachel 1978, 1980-82; **CHAN**, Caron 1995-96; **CHANG**, Johnny 1995-99; **CHANG**, Joy 1996-97;

CHEN, Charles 2001; **CHEN**, Jenny 2004-08; **CHIANG**, Arthur 1999; **CHISHOLM**, John 1963-67, 1971; **CHOI**, Sol 2005-08; **CHONG**, Valerie 2004; **CHRISTIE (Vautier)**, Kerrin 1963-67; **CHRISTIE**, Lauren 2001-02; **CHURCH**, Hannah 2007; **CLARK**, Helen 1978; **CLARK**, Sandra 1980-85; **CLARKSON**, Charmian 1996-1999, 2001-02; **COBURN**, Mark 1983-85; **COCHRANE**, Diana 1985, 1988; **COCHRANE**, Fiona 2000-04; **COLEMAN**, Christine 1969; **COLLIGAN**, Emma 1998, 2001; **COLLINS**, Joyce 1960-64; **COLLINS**, Melanie 1992; **COLLIS**, John 1981, 1983; **CONNAL (Lindsay)**, Angela 1959-61; **CONNOR**, Corrina 2003, 2005; **COOKE**, Edwin 1965; **COOPER**, Christopher 1965-67; **CORBALLIS**, Michael 1991-93, 1995-96; **CORBY**, Jocelyn 1979; **CORLETT**, Bruce 1982; **CORMACK**, Justine 1986, 1989; **CORREA-HUNT**, Sabina 1982-83; **COSTA**, Adam 1995, 1997, 1999; **COUPER**, Sarah-Jane 1987; **COWDELL**, Alexander 1960-63; **CRAVEN**, Glenda 1974-75; **CRAWSHAW**, Sandra 1981-83; **CROWSEN**, Ruth 1981-82; **CRUTCHLEY**, Mary-Jo 1969; **CULLIFORD**, Lynley 1978-81; **CUNCANNON**, Anthony 1973-74; **DALRYMPHE**, Emily 2006-07; **DALY**, Peter 1969; **DALY** Sean 2007-08; **DAVIES**, Christine 1965-66; **DAWSON**, Penelope 1984-86; **DEBNAM**, Anna 1985-86; **DEIGHTON**, Timonthy 1986-87; **DEJONG**, Nathanael 2005; **DEWSON**, Caroline 1996; **DIBLEY**, Julia 1997-2002; **DOBREE**, Susan 1961; **DODDS**, Steffan 1976; **DODS**, Guy 1959-60; **DONALD**, Rhodes 1968; **DRAKE**, Jennifer 1967-68, 1971; **DRAKE**, Nicola 1999-2005; **DRAKE**, Sarah 2002-05, 2007-08; **DRIVER**, Gregory 1968-70; **DRIVER**, Phillip 1970; **DRUMMOND**, Annabel 2008; **DUNLOP**, Kirsty 1992; **EARLY**, Susan 1963-66; **EDWARDS**, Helen 1960-61; **EGEN**, Lisa 1983-88; **EINHORN**, Barbara 1960-62; **ELLINGHAM-HUNT**, Kate 2007-08; **ELLIOTT**, Emma 1999, 2001-03; **ELLIS**, Susan 1985; **ESLING**, Michael 1964; **EVANS**, Kathryn 1960-64; **EVANS**, Ruthchen 1974-76; **FAINITSKI**, Slava 1987-89; **FENNELL**, John 1986; **FERGUSON**, Gina 1999; **FERNANDES**, Marcel 2004; **FINCH**, Dominica 2008; **FITZGERALD**, Sharon 1961; **FLEWETT**, Samuel 1998-2001; **FLUHLER**, Trudi 1981-83; **FOGDEN**, Nicola 1982-84; **FOOTE**, Christine 1973-74, 1976; **FORDE**, Lucia 1969-70; **FORSYTH**, Janice 1963, 1965-68; **FRANCIS**, Olivia 2007-08; **FREED**, Jane 1959-60; **FUKUOKA**, Hiroo 2006; **FUNG**, Dickson 2003-06; **GARRITY**, Peter 1988-91; **GASH**, Diana 1969-71; **GASTON**, Jeanette 1965; **GEIRINGER**, Claudia 1983-84; **GILES**, Amelia 1999, 2001-02; **GILLING**, David 1978-80; **GILMORE**, Josephine 1959; **GITTINGS (Letcher)**, Beverley 1960-61, 1963; **GODFREY**, Belinda 1965; **GOH**, Yid-Ee 1989-90, 1992-93; **GOLDING**, Miles 1966-67; **GOLDSTEIN**, Jennie 1973, 1976; **McMILLAN (Goodbehere)**, Ann 1972-74; **GOODBEHERE**, Kate 2000-01; **GOPAL**, Malavika 1999-2005; **GORDAN**, Francis 1967; **GORE**, Geoffrey 1973; **GRAY**, Elspeth 1983-84, 1988; **GRAY**, Josephine 1976; **GREEN**, Sharyn 1966-71; **GREGORY**, Sarah 1993; **GREGORY**, Susan 1965-69; **GRENFELL**, Maria 1988-92; **GRIFFITHS**, Wendy 1973; **GUAN**, Judy 2003-04; **GUEST**, Stephen 1964-68, 1971; **GUMBLEY**, Freya 2000, 2002-03; **GUMBLEY**, Melody 1999-2002; **HAIGH**, Trevor 1961; **HALAPUA**, Peau 1995; **HALL**, Amalia 1999-2004, 2006-07; **HALL**, Elroy 2000, 2002-04; **HALL**, Lara 1992-1993, 1995, 1997, 1999-2000, 2002-03, **HAMILTON**, Suzanne 1990; **HANCOX**, Graham 1962; **HANCOX**, Nicholas 2003; **HANSEN (Kingston)**, Katherine 1990; **HARDEN**, Prudence 1966-67; **HARMER**, Reginald 1990;

HARRIS (Peak), Christine 1960, 1963-64; **HARRIS**, Irene 1959, 1962; **HARRIS**, Jeremy 1980-81, 1984; **HARRIS**, Katherine 1974-76; **HARRIS**, Lydia 2007; **HARRIS**, Mary 1969-72; **HARRIS**, Rosemary 1974; **HARROP**, Joe 1993, 1995-99; **HART**, Sarah 1969-74; **HAWKEY**, Bryce 1959; **HAYES**, Hilary 2008; **HAYSTON**, Nicola 1980-82; **HEINZ**, Douglas 1965-66; **HELYER**, Dorothy 1969-70; **HENDERSON**, Ana 1995; **HENDERSON**, Margaret 1971-72; **HENDL**, Jonathan 1996-97; **HENTSCHEL**, Martyn 1993; **HIGGS**, Susan-Jane 1976, 1979; **HILL**, Beatrice 1959-60; **HILL**, Caroline 1983-84; **HILLYER**, Giselle 1985-87, 1992; **HINDIN**, Jessica 1996-97; **HOGAN**, Seamus 1980-81, 1983-85; **HOLBOROW**, Shona 1992; **HOOKHAM**, Anna 1981; **HOOPER**, Sarah 2003-06; **HOPE**, Raymond 1961-62, 1966-67; **HOUTMAN**, Eleanor 1973-75; **HOWIE**, Lyn 1964-66; **HOY**, Kenneth 1960-63; **HSU**, Hsin Pai 1989-93, 1995-96; **HUNTER**, Vicki 1976; **HUNTER**, Terry 1959-60; **HUTTON**, Miranda 1996-2000; **INGLES**, Elaine 1959; **INNES**, Dawn 1959; **IRVINE**, Susan 1978-80; **JACKSON**, Christopher 1974; **JACKSON**, Rebecca 1979-81; **JANE**, Catherine 1976, 1980; **JANE**, Philip 1970, 1972-75; **JENNINGS**, Katrina 1992-93; **JIANG**, Ping 2003; **JIN**, James 2003-04; **JOEL**, Michael 1988, 1990; **JOHANSEN**, Emily 1998; **JOHNSTON**, Leah 2002; **JONES**, Geoffrey 1980-84; **JONES**, Helen 1970-71; **JONES**, Susan 1960; **JUDD**, Stephen 1985-87; **KALINOWSKI**, Angela 1964-65, 1967; **MOLLER (Kamlos)**, Maxine 1959; **KASZA**, Andrew 1973; **KASZA**, Susan 1970; **KEESTRA**, Sally 1988; **KEALL**, Marion 1960; **KEAY**, Charmian 2005-06, 2008; **KERR**, Hagen 1986; **KERR**, Heléna 2000; **KIERNAN**, Sarah 2006-08; **KIM**, Anne Seung Eun 2003-05; **KIM**, Hye-Won 1999-2000; **KIM**, Ji Hyun 2000; **KIM**, Young-Bin 2005; **KINGSLEY-SMITH**, Daphne 1961; **KIRIAEV**, Anna 2007-08; **KNIGHT**, Eric 1969-70; **KNIGHT**, Leslie 1968; **KNILL**, Roy 1976; **KNUFERMANN**, Kirsten 1983-85, 1989; **KOENIG**, Nicholas 1964-65; **KOKISCH**, Jan 1967; **KOMINIK**, Anna 1988, 1990; **KONISE**, Sam 1985-88; **KWOK**, Hai Won 1982; **KWON**, Donna 2008; **KWON**, In-Kyung 1995; **LACHMAN**, Stephan 1964; **LAMB**, Martin 1968-69, 1971-72, 1974-76; **LANGLEY**, Sally 1973; **LARDNER**, Anne 1986, 1991; **LARSEN**, Bernard 1976-79; **LARSEN**, Stephen 1988; **LAU**, Benjamin 1998; **LEE**, Hayley 2000-01; **LEE**, Jiwon 2004-07; **LEE**, Jung Wook 2004-07; **LEE**, Melissa 2007; **LEE**, Sherry 2007-08; **LEEN**, Patricia 1962-63; **LEIGHS**, Vanessa 1997; **LENART**, Anthony 1964; **LENNANE**, Richard 1960-62, 1964; **LEVIEN**, Richard 1990; **LEWIS**, Bethan 1997; **LEVY**, Michael 1967; **LIM**, Jennifer 2000-03; **LIN**, Christabel 2004-06; **LINH**, Dam Xuan 1963-64; **LIU**, Kuangda 2006; **LIU**, Li 1998; **LIVINGSTONE**, Donna 1981-82; **LOGAN**, Christabel 2006-07; **LORIER**, Keren-Peta 2001-02; **LOVIE**, Robert 1986-87, 1991; **LUDEMANN**, Helen 1968-71; **LUPI**, Tristan 1986-88, 1995-97; **MA**, Chris 2005, 2007; **McCALLUM**, Lois 1970-71; **McCARTHY**, Julia 2000-04; **McCLELLAND**, Sarah 1986-87, 1989-90; **McCRACKEN**, Sarah 1999-2003; **MacDONALD**, Katriona 1985-86; **MacFARLANE**, Claire 1998-99; **McGREGOR**, Valerie 1961; **MacHIRUS**, Gifford 1993; **McINTYRE**, Michael 1959-62; **MacKAY**, Richard 1967-69; **McKENZIE**, Sharon 1972-73; **MacLEAN**, Nigel 1980-84; **McLELLAN**, Simon 1985, 1987, 1989-91; **McMANUS**, Jennifer 1967-70; **McNAUGHTON**, Harry 1978-79; **McPHAIL**, Graham 1980; **McROBERTS (Hanna)**, Jacqueline 1978; **McRONALD**, Peter 1982; **MA**, Chris 2008; **MACKIE**, Malcolm 1959-60, 1963;

MAIN, Meryl 1982; **MAITRA**, Neepa 1991; **MAJOR**, Dean 1975; **MANAGH**, Stephen 1966-73; **MARRET**, Allen 1967; **MARTIN**, Kerry 1995-97; **MASON**, Ian 1959-60, 1962; **MAUD**, Rosalind 1976; **MAUNSELL**, David 1981, 1984; **MENZIES**, Mark 1981-82, 1984; **MILLER**, Simon 1973-75, 1977-79; **MOLLER**, Louise 1964; **MONAGHAN**, Michael 1968-70; **MONK**, Craig 1991-93; **MOON**, Chloe 1971; **MOREAU**, Jennifer 1978-82; **MORETTE**, Jennifer 2005-06; **MORRALL**, Nicole 1992-93; **MORRIS**, Kelda 2005-06, 2008; **MORRISON**, Ben 2006, 2008; **MOUNTFORT**, Catherine 1973-75; **MOUNTFORT**, Charles 1970-71; **MULLIGAN**, Andrea 1983; **MUNRO**, Bernice 1967-68; **MUNRO**, Neville 1973; **MURDOCH**, Geoffrey 1970-74; **MURRAY**, Ainsley 1988; **NALDEN**, Natalie 1991; **NALDEN**, Rosemary 1962-65; **NASH**, Carol 1972-74; **NEILSEN**, Susanne 1963-1967, 1969, 1971; **NEILSON**, Erica 1959; **NEILSON**, Meredith 1979-80; **NEW**, Gemma 2005-08; **NEWBAN**, Arwen 1984; **NEWBY**, John 1970-71; **NEWCOMB**, Raewyn 1978; **NEWHOOK**, Catherine 1970-72; **OETIKER**, Elizabeth 1973-74, 1976; **O'FLAHERTY**, Stephanie 1979-81, 1983, 1985; **OLIVER**, Louisa 1990-92; **OLLIVIER**, Katie 1993, 1996-98; **OOSTERHOFF**, Hedda 2001, 2003; **ORMEROD**, Andrew 1966-68; **OSWIN**, Kate 2008; **OWEN**, Mary Anne 1979, 1982-84; **PANCHA**, Aneela 1989-91; **PANCHA**, Sanjay 1992-93, 1995-97; **PANTING**, Richard 1965-66; **PARRY**, Nesta 1968-69; **PASCOE**, Jane 1968-70; **PASCOE**, Jenna 2004-08; **PATCHETT**, Elizabeth 1983, 1988; **PEAK**, Brian 1959-62; **PEARS**, Fiona 1988, 1991-92; **PERKS**, Robin 1959-66; **PETERSEN**, Tessa 1987; **PETHERAM**, Margaret 1959; **PIERARD**, Catherine 1972, 1974; **PIERARD**, Martin 1965; **PING**, Jiang 2002; **PITT**, Wendy 1959-60; **PLOWMAN**, Shona 1967-69; **POOLE**, Philip 1966; **POPLE**, Edward 1960-63, 1965-66, 1968; **POPLE**, George 1959-61; **POWELL**, Judith 1970; **PRESS**, Blythe 2002-04, 2007-08; **PRITCHETT**, Elizabeth 1982; **PRITCHETT**, Gerard 1980; **PROCTOR**, Helen 1984-85; **PUCHER**, David 1976, 1982; **PUGH**, Bronwen 1969-71; **RAE**, Allan 1959-60, 1962; **RAKENA**, Te Oti 1984; **RANFORD**, Arthur 1967-71; **REID**, Michael 1969; **RISELEY**, Martin 1985-87; **ROBERTS**, Sylvia 1959-60; **RODGERS**, Glenda 1978-80, 1982; **RODGERS**, Murray 1974-78; **ROGGEN**, Simone 1995-96, 1999; **ROSS**, Adam 1984-85, 1987; **ROSS**, Kevin 1995-96; **ROSS**, Matthew 1986, 1988-91, 1993; **ROSS**, Sarah 1989-91, 1993; **ROUGHTON**, Joanne 1991-93; **ROWE**, Katherine 1983-85; **RUBIE**, Edith 1961; **RUSHBROOK**, Rosemary 1963-65, 1967; **RYAN**, Eleanor 1995-2000; **RYMAN**, Marion 1965; **SALAMONSEN**, Anna 1974-76, 1978; **SALAS**, Margaret 1966; **SALINGER**, Peter 1961-62, 1964; **SANKARAN**, Shyam 2003-06; **SASAKI**, Chicako 2008; **SAUNDERS**, Christopher 1963; **SAUNDERS**, Helen 1996; **SAUNDERS**, Penelope 1959-60; **SCHAFER**, Madeline 1983-84, 1986; **SCHOLES (Van Leuven)**, Carolyn 1986-89; **SCOTT**, David 1966; **SCOTT**, Heléna 1998; **SEAGAR**, John 1976; **SECKER**, Anthea 1972-75; **SELBY**, Ian 1987; **SEWELL**, Andrew 1980-84; **SHATFORD**, Nigel 1985; **SHAW**, Arna 2007-08; **SHAW**, Nicola 1984; **SHEPHERD**, Howard 1965; **SHEPHERD**, Neil 1966-71; **SHORE**, David 1966; **SMITH**, Alana 2001; **SMITH**, Wilma 1973, 1975; **SNELLING**, David 1982; **SNEYD**, Elizabeth 1983-84, 1986; **SNEYD**, James 1978-79; **SONG**, Euna-Jenny 2005; **SONG**, Julianne 2005, 2007; **SOUTHGATE**, Brent 1959; **SPENCER**, Penelope 1986-88; **SQUIRE**, Tabea 2005-07; **STAPLETON**, Claire 1978, 1980;

STEEL, Penny 1987-88; **STEENSTRA**, Irena 1984; **STEPHENS**, Vivian 2005-07; **STEVENS**, Bevis 1987-90; **STRANGE**, Robyn 1979; **SUGANUMA**, Tomoko 2005, 2007; **DUMBLETON (Sutton)**, Marjorie 1959-61; **SUTTON**, Wayne 1968-70; **TAHATA**, Francis 1978-79; **TAM**, Boon Khiang 2006; **TAM**, Vanessa 2001-03; **TANG**, Joshua 2003-04; **TARRANT-MATTHEWS**, Sophia 2008; **TAYLOR**, Claire 1970; **TAYLOR (Hancox)** Jay, 1960; **TAYLOR**, Julie 1971-74; **TAYLOR**, Lilian 1960; **TAYLOR**, Penni 1990-93; **TEE**, Key Yong 1990; **THAURÉ**, David 2001; **THIN**, Nicholas 2003-04, 2006; **THOMAS**, Gail 1974-75; **THOMPSON**, Damon 1990-93, 1995; **THOMPSON (Farmer)**, Susan 1972-76; **THOMSON**, Andrew 1992-93, 1995; **THURLOW**, Serenity 2000-02; **TIMMINGS**, Philippa 1985-88; **TISO**, Emily 1981-83; **TITHER-SUTHERLAND**, Wilma 1959; **TOIME**, Lawrence 1995-96, 1998; **TONGS**, Sharon 1984, 1987; **TOOMER**, Pamela 1979-82; **TRENWITH (Bain)**` Colleen 1962; **TRUSSELL-CULLEN**, Marcel 1982-85, 1988; **TRUSSELL-CULLEN**, Rene 1987-91; **VAATSTRA**, Alexander 2004; **VAN AMERINGEN**, Marcus 1972-73; **VAN RIJ**, Inge 1993; **VEITCH**, Brenton 1982; **VERHOEVEN**, Piet 1961, 1963-64; **VERNER**, Antony 2002-04; **VERNER**, Asaph 2008; **VEYSEY**, Margaret 1962; **WALKER**, Judith 1984; **WALLS**, Helen 1998; **WALLS**, Peter 1963-66; **WALSH**, Diana 1985; **WALTON**, Antony 1970-75; **WANG**, Tammie 1999, 2001; **WANG**, Tracy 2005; **WARD**, Lynley 1987; **WARREN**, Allan 1988-92, 1995-97; **WATSON**, Bethany 1966; **WATSON**, Christine 1989; **WATSON**, Elisha 2006-08; **WATSON**, Helen 1983-86; **WATSON**, Marianne 1988; **WATSON**, Philippa 1990-91, 1995; **WESTBROOKE**, Alwyn 1995-96, 1998-2000, 2002, 2005; **WESTBROOKE**, Caitlyn 2003-05; **WHITAKER**, David 1995; **WHITE**, Bronwyn 1985; **WHITTAKER**, Christopher 1965-68; **WHITTON**, Gillian 1962; **WHITWELL**, Janice 1963-68; **WILDE**, Gillian 1961; **WILKINSON**, Kathryn 1970, 1972-74; **WILLIAMS**, Belinda 1988, 1991; **WILLIAMS**, Craig 1978-1983, 1985-86; **WILLIAMS**, David 1959; **WILLIAMS**, Janet 1978-82; **WILLIAMS**, Kathryn 1992, 1995, 1997-98; **WILLIAMSON**, Fiona 1981, 1985-87; **WILLIAMSON**, Georgiana 1993; **WILSON**, Alister 1988; **WILSON**, Amanda 1990-93; **WILSON**, Christopher 1978, 1980; **WILSON**, Katherine 1974, 1976; **WILSON**, Robin 1998; **WINN**, Graeme 1965-68; **WITHERS**, Helen 1960; **WITHERS**, Margaret 1960-62; **WITTON (Roberts)**, Gillian 1961; **WOLFF**, Thomas 1989, 1991; **WOOD**, Celia 1966; **WOOD**, Kerry 1985-89; **WOOD**, Kirsten 1989, 1991; **WRIGHT**, Jane 1983-86; **YANG**, Minsi 2002-03; **YFFER**, Moira 1970-72; **YOON**, Emma 2007-08; **YOON**, Miyo 2001, 2004, 2006; **YU**, Sujin 2006, 2008; **ZELINSKA**, Khrystyna 2002.

VIOLA

ACHESON, Sophia 2001-05; **ALBERS**, Marike 1990; **ANNALS**, Clare 1983-86; **ARCUS**, Cecil 1959; **ARCUS**, Douglas 1961-63; **ARMSTRONG**, Heather 1990; **ASPEY**, Edward 1964-65, 1968; **ATKINSON**, Katie 1990, 1996; **AUSTIN**, Faith 1973-74; **AYREY**, Craig 1973-74; **BARBER**, Peter 1974-75; **BARNES**, Marcelle 2004-05, 2008; **BARRATT**, Graham 2003; **BEALING**, Richard 1993; **BENNET**, Michelle 1986; **BEVIN**, Helen 2003, 2005-08;

BIGGS, Lisa 1985; **BIRD**, Justin 1999-2000; **BLANK**, Amy 1992-93, 1995; **BLINCOE**, Kate 2006; **BONIFANT**, John 1959-62; **BOWIE**, Christine 1987-88; **BOWCOTT**, Alison 1974; **BOYES**, Ngaire 1995-96; **BOYLE**, Deidre 1995-99; **BRAMLEY**, Margaret 1960-61; **BUCHANAN**, Raiha 2003-04; **BULMER**, Alice 1980-81; **BURGOYNE**, Janet 1976, 1980; **BUTLER**, Caughlin 2006-07; **BUXTON**, Sophie 1992-93; **CAMMELL**, Jennifer 1965-66; **CAMPBELL**, Mary 1993; **CARPENTER**, Sam 1995; **CARTER**, William 1969; **CAUGHEY**, Helen 1967, 1969; **CHAN**, Hang 1989-90; **CHOI**, Kiros 2002; **CLAYTON**, Megan 1995-97; **CLEMENTS**, Elizabeth 1973; **COCHRANE**, Joanna 1999-2001; **COCKS**, Stephanie 1981-85; **COWAN**, Amanda 1996-2002; **COX**, Stephanie 2004, 2006; **CROCKETT**, Anne 1999-2003; **CUNCANNON**, Michael 1974-76; **DANSON**, Anna 2005; **DAVIES**, Kathryn 1967; **DAWSON**, Anna 2006-08; **DEAN**, Bronya 1993, 1995; **DEBNAM**, Anna 1988-89; **DEPLEDGE**, Stephen 1987-90; **DEWSON**, Caroline 1997-98; **DING**, Li 2007; **DOBSON**, Andrea 1993; **DRAFFIN**, Anne 1974, 1976, 1978; **DRIVER**, Philip 1972; **DUNFORD**, Heather 1979-80, 1982; **EDGAR**, Mei Fong 1996; **ELLERM**, Jessica 2006; **EMSLIE (Palmer)**, Sharyn 1966; **ESTALL**, Stephen 1963-64; **FERWERDA**, Irene 1962-63; **FETHERSTON**, Charlotte 2005-08; **FETHERSTON**, Emma 2002-05, 2008; **FULLERTON-SMITH**, Susan 1991-92; **GARBUTT**, Russell 1963; **GARDINER**, Wendy 1986-88; **GARVIN**, Jocelyn 1959-60; **GEARD**, Linda 1968; **GIBSON-CORNISH**, Bryony 2007-08; **GLASGOW**, Susan 1967-68, 1970; **GODFREY**, Belinda 1966-67; **GOOD**, Hugh 1997-98; **GUDE**, Anita 1983-84, 1986-88; **HALIBURTON**, Nancy 1997; **HALL**, Elroy 1997-99, 2001; **HAMILTON**, Rachel 1980; **HANCOX**, Nicholas 2004-07; **HARDING (Abrahams)**, Suzanne 1961-62; **HAUGHEY (Robinson)** Frances 1964-65; **HEENAN**, Alison 1974-75; **HO**, Melissa 1999-2002; **HODGKINSON (Grindley)**, Anna 1997-2002; **HOOPER**, Sarah 2002; **HOWARTH**, Richard 1969-74; **HOY**, Kenneth 1965-66; **HUNT**, Francesca 2004-05; **HUNT**, Margaret 1967-71; **IBELL**, Catherine 1982-84; **JECKS**, Patricia 1970-71; **JEE**, Yoon Joo 2005; **JACKSON**, Christopher 1974;**JEMMETT**, Belinda 1995; **JOEL**, Michael 1992; **KILLOH**, Evelyn 1962-63; **KING**, Pauline 1959; **KOKICH**, Jan 1968; **LAWRENCE**, Amanda 1990; **LEGGE**, Katherine 1990-92; **LETCHER**, Rosiland 1997-2000; **LEWIS**, Bethan 1998, 2000; **LOGAN**, Christopher 1982-85; **LYNCH**, Lisa 1995; **LYTTLE**, Denise 1963-66; **McDONALD**, Craig 1981; **McDOUGALL**, Jane 1989; **McIVOR**, Alice 2007-08; **McKEAN**, Steve 1998; **McLAY**, Lindsay 2007-08; **McMILLAN**, Mary 1978-80; **McNEILL**, Robin 1980; **MARK**, Greta 1990-93; **MARTIN**, Lisa 1993; **MAURICE**, Donald 1970-73; **MAWHINNEY**, Malcolm 1996-2000; **MILLER**, Bhaady 1978; **MILLS**, Pippa 1982-84; **MITCHELL**, Judith 1959-63; **MOUNTFORT**, Charles 1972-74; **MOUNTFORT**, Lindsay 1978-79, 1982; **MOUNTIER**, Vivienne 1973-75; **MURDOCH (Polglase)**, Christine 1960-62; **NASH**, Leslie 1972-73; **NESBIT**, Kylie 2006; **NEWMAN (Taber)**, Helen 1959-64; **NICOL**, Heather 1986-88; **O'HANLON**, Anne 2004; **OETIKER**, Elizabeth 1974; **OLIVER**, Karen 1965-68; **O'NEIL**, Donald 1968-71; **OSWIN**, Kate 2007; **PARSONAGE**, Vincent 1984-86; **PAUSLER**, Sandra 1983-86; **PEEK**, Ingrid 1990-91; **PETOE**, Catherine 1996-97, 1999; **PIERARD**, Catherine 1974; **PIERARD**, Janet 1967-69; **PINKNEY**, Benjamin 2008; **POKLOWSKI**, Charles 2001; **POLGLASE**, Christine 1964;

PRENTICE, Belinda 1976, 1978-79, 1982; **RADFORD**, Amelia 2004; **RAINY**, Peter 1976-80; **RICHARDSON**, Sandra 1982-85; **RICHES**, Sheila 1960-61; **ROBERTS (Simmons)**, Linda 1964-67; **ROBB**, Tim 1992-93; **ROBINSON**, Berys 1976; **ROGERS**, John 1978-83; **ROXBURGH**, John 2005-08; **SALMONS**, Alison 1993, 1995; **SANDS**, Alastair 1976; **SECKER**, Anthea 1972; **SHALLCRASS**, Karen 1966-68; **SHARMAN**, Peter 1978; **SHILLITO**, Brian 1965-68; **SMITH**, Alisa 2001-06; **SMITH (Love)**, Patricia 1959; **SNEYD**, Mary-Jane; **STRONACH**, Marian 1961-63; **SWEDLUND**, Sally 1980-81; **THURLOW**, Serenity 2005; **THOMAS**, Rebecca 1998, 2001, 2003; **THOMPSON**, Rachel 1978-79; **TONGS**, Sharon 1985; **TOWNEND**, Andrew 2000; **TOWNEND**, Hugh 1964-67; **TULLOCH (Townend)**, Marion 1965; **TULLOCH**, Stephanie 1985, 1987-88, 1991; **TURNBULL**, Elizabeth 1966-72; **UTTING**, Craig 1987-89; **VAN AMERINGEN**, Samuel 1972-74; **VAN BUREN**, Anthony 1982-87; **VAN DER ZEE**, Christiaan 2000-01; **VAN DYK**, Stephanie 1987; **VAN LEUVEN**, Stephanie 1986-87; **VAUGHAN**, Catherine 1964-68; **VERNER**, Amanda 2002-04; **WALKER**, Diana 1981-82; **WALKER**, Karen 1989-90; **WALTON**, Thomas 2008; **WARD**, Diane 1961; **WATSON**, Margaret 1965-69; **WATTERS**, Cushla 1970-71; **WEDDE**, Susan 1976, 1979-81, 1983-84; **WELLWOOD**, Michael 1989-90; **WESTRUPP**, Jeannine 1971; **WHITE**, Bronwyn 1989; **WHITE (McNeill)** Marise 1978-79; **WIGGINS**, Warren 1972-76; **WILLIAMS**, Belinda 1992; **WILLIAMS**, Rebecca 1981; **WITTCHOW**, Leoni 2006-08; **WONG**, Amelia 1995-96; **WOODLEY**, Deborah 1985-90; **WOODWARD**, Lucy 2000-01; **YEOMAN**, Trevor 1959-60; **YOUN**G, Timothy 1982-86.

CELLO

ADAMS, Martin 1993; **ALEXANDER**, Susan 1966, 1968; **ANDREWS**, Ivan 1967-69; **BAILLIE**, Heidi 1997; **BARKER**, Miriam 1991-93; **BARRETT**, Simon 1981-82;

BEECH, Soren 1991-92; **BELCHER**, Richard 1995-96; **BEST**, Donald 1961-66; **BISLEY**, Sarah 1978-79; **BLACK**, Peter 1983-85, 1988; **BLACKMORE**, Caroline 2003, 2005; **BOLLARD**, Bryce 1976; **BRAMLEY**, Mary 1959-60; **BROMBERG**, Brian 2006; **BROOKER**, Edgar 1978; **BROOKS**, Charles 1998-99; **BROWN**, Ashley 1989-92; **BROWN**, Gregor 1968-71; **BROWN**, Roger 1972-75; **BROWN**, Sally-Anne 1980; **BRUSE**, Art 1964; **BUCKLEY**, Veronica 1974; **BULL**, Anna 1995, 1997-99; **BUNT**, Angela 1972-74; **BURNS**, Colin 1973; **BURNSTEIN**, Donald 1963, 1965-66; **BUSH**, James 1987-90; **CAVE**, Caroline 1983-85; **CHEN**, Sherry 1996-98; **CHEN**, Thomas 1995; **CHESTER**, Robyn 1970; **CHIANG**, Sabrina 2003-04; **CHISHOLM**, Allan 1963-67; **CHOUNG**, So-Young 1999, 2001; **CLARK**, Anne 1978; **COOKE**, Margaret 1978; **COOPER**, Georgina 1998-2001; **COOPER**, Jane 1993; **CORMACK**, Robyn 1985-89; **COWIE**, Lissa 1993; **COXHEAD**, Gloria 1966-68; **CRANEFIELD**, Jocelyn 1983-84; **CULLIFORD**, Dale 1978-80; **DAVIES**, R 1962; **DAVIS**, Robert 1963-64; **DEARLOVE**, Sharon 1986; **DIPROSE**, Margaret 1962; **DOBBS**, Sarah 2005-06; **DUFFILL**, Emily 1996-97; **ELMSLY**, Anthony 1976; **FAN**, Lydia 2002; **FLEISCHEL**, Peter 1973-74, 1976;

FRASER, Raymond 1959; **FRENCH**, Karen 2003-06; **FULLER**, Rachel 1993; **GADSBEY**, Alison 1978; **GIBSON-LANE**, Mok-Hyun 1995-96, 1998-2000; **GODFREY**, Patricia 1972-74; **GRIFFITHS**, Martin 1990; **GŸSBERS**, Lucy 2007-08; **HADCROFT**, Gaye 1974; **HADCROFT (Davey)**, Jennifer 1976; **HALE**, Bradley 1998; **HALL**, Callum 2000.2003-07; **McKENZIE (Hansen)**, Alison 1960-66; **HARDING**, Phillippa 1959; **HARRIS**, Blair 2000-01; **HARRIS**, Gillian 1972-74; **HARTLEY**, Greg 1974; **HARRIS (Constantino)**, Josephine 1973-76; **HARVEY**, Elaine 1991; **HAYES**, Charlotte 1978-80; **HAYSTON**, Phillip 1981-83; **HEATH**, Geoffrey 1995-98; **HEBLEY**, Katherine 1986-90; **HELYER**, Kathleen 1965-70; **HELYER**, Susan 1970; **HENDL**, Rebecca 1993; **HILL**, Mark 1987; **HILL**, Rosalind 2003, 2005; **HOFFMAN**, Johanna 1982; **HOGAN**, Timothy 1980; **HOLBOROW**, Janet 1988, 1991-92; **HOLDING**, Fiona 1998-99; **HOPKINS**, Virginia 1967-69; **HORRILL**, Judith 1984; **HOSTED**, Tom 2000-02, 2004; **HUNT**, Ann 1972-76; **HUTCHINSON**, Kathleen 1971; **IBELL**, Robert 1981-83; **JACKSON**, Mark 1965-67; **JENKINS**, David 1972; **JOHANSEN**, Lars 1959-61; **JOHNSTONE**, Rachel 1996; **JOLLY**, Kathleen 1979, 1982; **JONES**, Victoria 1976; **KANE**, Christopher 1980; **KERR**, Felicity 1962-64, 1966; **KILROY**, Pauline 1970; **KIM**, Jisun 2006-07; **KING**, Edward 2007-08; **KNAGGS**, Graeme 1969; **KNIGHT**, Sarah 1988; **KREYMBORG**, Tamsin 2008; **LAWRENCE**, Anthony 1978; **LEE**, Jahun 2007-08; **LEE**, Sunny 2006; **LEWIS**, Heather 2007-08; **LIVINGSTONE**, Gael 1967; **LUCAS**, Sarah 1959-60; **LYONS**, Ian 1990; **MacKENZIE (Sachtleben)**, Annette 1963-66; **MacLENNAN-COWIE**, Lissa 1995; **McCAFFREY**, Clare 1983; **McCURDY**, Stephen 1965-67; **MAIOHA**, Quentin 1985; **MANN**, Helen 1983-84; **MAWSON**, Catherine 1968; **MEIJERS**, Annemarie 1979-80; **METCALF**, Ruth 1965-68; **MITCHELL**, Paul 1983-86; **MONAGHAN**, Dominic 1997; **MORGAN**, Richard 1980-81; **MOSLEY**, Eleanor 1986-90; **MOUNTFORT**, Helen 1979-81; **MUNDY**, Andrea 1999, 2001-03; **MURDOCH**, Euan 1976-79; **MURRAY**, David 2000; **NATION**, Benjamin 2001-02; **NEAS**, Victoria 2000-02, 2004; **NOBLE**, Donna 1971; **NORTON**, Blanche 1966-69; **OGILVIE**, Graeme 1962-65; **OLIVER**, Gerald 1969-73; **O'MEEGHAN**, Brigid 1972-74; **O'REGAN**, Michael 1969-71, 1973; **OREMLAND**, Claire 1979-80; **OWEN**, Kathryn 1991-93; **PANG**, Francis 1999; **PARK**, Grace 2005; **PARK**, Chris 2008; **PARTRIDGE**, Alexandra 2006-08; **PATERSON**, Douglas 1973; **PEAK**, Alan 1961; **PERKS**, Wendy 1965-66; **PETERSEN**, Anna 1982; **PETERSON**, Alice 1990; **PLATT**, Julie 1991-92; **POLGLASE**, Helen 1986,1988-90; **POPLE**, Ross 1959-61; **PRIOR**, Rowan 1980-82; **RAH**, Paul 1999; **ROBERTS**, Charlotte 2003; **ROBSON**, Bridget 1978; **ROGERS**, Simon 1987, 1990-92; **SALMON**, Christopher 1961-63; **SANDLE**, Brian 1961-64, 1966; **SAYERS**, David 1983; **SCOTT**, Gregory 1981-82; **SHARMAN**, Katherine 1978, 1981-82; **SHARP**, David 1986-87, 1989; **SHEARER**, Jane 1982; **SHEATH**, Stephen 1971; **SHEPPARD**, Mark 1985-89; **SHUM**, Davina 2006, 2008; **SHWER**, Ruth 1997; **SIM**, Janet 1983-87; **SIMONSEN**, Victoria 1999-2002; **SKIPP**, Roderick 2000, 2002; **SMITH**, Susan 1961-62, 1964-65; **SMIT**, Hugo 2000-04; **SNELLING**, Rachel 1981; **SOUSTER**, Graeme 1960-64; **SPITTLE**, Evelyn 1997; **SQUIRE**, Jonathan 2005-08; **STAMP**, Lisa 1985-87; **STICHBURY**, Rebecca 1984; **STUART**, Cameron 2004-08; **STUBBS**, Siobahn 2000-02; **SUSSEX**, Mary-Grace 1967; **SUZANNE**, Gadsbey 1983; **SWEDLUND**, Ian 1979;

SZABO, Claire 1997-98; **TATE**, Melanie 1988; **THEOBALD**, Natarani 1990; **THOMAS**, Rhiannon 1992, 1995-96; **THOMAS (Chisholm)**, Vivien 1968-71; **THOMPSON**, Christina 2002-03; **THOMPSON**, Louise 1985-86; **THOMSON**, Louise 1984; **TOLSMA**, Femke 1982, 1984; **TRINGHAM**, Kate 1995-96; **TURNER**, Rebecca 1996-99; **VAN DER VISS**, Willem 1971; **VAN HOUTTE**, Paul 2004-05, 2007; **VAUGHAN**, Dennis 1971; **VEITCH**, Brenton 1984; **VERNER**, Aleisha 2004; **VINCE**, Judith 1959, 1962; **WALLACE**, Joan 1959-61; **WATSON**, Paula 1992; **WATT**, Emily 1995-97; **WERRY**, Anne 1987, 1989, 1991; **WHITE**, Julie 1967-74; **WILKINSON**, Barbara 1975; **WILKINSON (Radford)** Jane, 1974; **WILLIAMS**, Judith 1973-75; **WILLIAMS**, Mary 1960-63; **WILLIAMSON**, Edwina 1993, 1995-96; **WILSON**, Miranda 1995-97, 1999; **WOODCOCK (Lever)**, Rhona 1965-68; **WOODLEY**, Jocelyn 1981-85; **YOUNG**, Jane 1986-89; **ZANKER**, Hugo 2003-05.

BASS

ABERDEEN, Valerie 1959; **ABRAHALL**, Steven 1982-85; **ANDERSON**, Dean 1981-82; **ANDZAKOVIC**, Darija 2005-07; **ATKINSON**, Denise 1961; **BEUZENBERG**, Evelyn 1971-72; **BLACK**, Pierce 2003; **BOND**, Rupert 1974; **BOTICA**, Peter 1996-98; **BURNS**, Malcolm 1976-78; **CARGO**, Keren 1968-69; **CARR**, Miriam 1959; **CATER**, William 1960-68; **CAVE**, Matthew 1995-97, 2000, 2003; **CHIH**, Wendy 2000; **CHIH**, Yu San 2001; **CHOW**, Kent 2000-01; **COATSWORTH**, Jeanette 1970; **CONRAD**, Laura 1996-97; **CULLEN**, Susan 1979; **DREW**, Philippa 1991; **EASTWOOD**, Simon 2004-08; **ELLIS**, Robbie 2004; **ENGEL**, Thorsten 1986-89; **EVANS (Squires)**, Gwyneth 1960; **FIELDES**, Matthew 1990-93; **FINN**, Philippa 1997, 2000; **FINNIE**, Graeme 2008; **GIBBS**, Terrence 1979-81, 1983; **GRACE**, Tagan 2005; **GRAINGER**, Nicola 1971; **GUNCHENKO**, Alexander 2001-02; **HAINSTOCK**, Stephen 1990-91; **HAMBLY**, Katherine 1987-89, 1992-93; **HARDIE**, Richard 1985, 1987-90; **HARRE**, Anna 2008; **HARRIS**, Barbara 1966-68; **HODGSON**, Toni 1983-85; **HORSFORD**, Shandelle 2006-08; **HUNTER**, Allan 1967; **HYLAND**, Judith 1960; **ISLIP**, Karen 1982; **JARMAN**, Glennys 1964; **JARY**, Andrew 1989; **JENSEN**, Gail 1959; **JOHNSON**, Fiona 1976; **JOHNSTONE**, Barry 1969-70; **JOHNSTONE**, Nathaniel 1995-99; **JOWSEY**, Neil 1962; **KAYES**, Gareth 1995-97; **KIKUCHI**, Yumiko 2008; **KINCAID**, Andrew 1981-83; **KIRK**, Vivien 1984; **LAU**, Elizabeth 1998-2001; **LEAHY**, David 1990-92; **LEES-JEFFRIES**, Susannah 1991-93, 1995-97; **LESLIE**, Annabella 2003-07; **LEVER**, Penelope 1995-97, 1999; **LIPSKI**, Mark 2002-08; **LISTER**, Annabel 1976, 1978-80 **McCOY**, Adam 2007-08; **McDOWELL**, Claire 1996; **McGREGOR**, Andrew 1987-93; **McKENZIE**, Judith 1973-76; **McKEOGH**, John 1984-85; ; **MACE**, Ken 1999-2001; **MAJOR**, Louise 1988-93; **MELTZER**, Miriam 1962; **MENZIES**, Andrew 1998-2000; **MIDDLETON**, John 1978-80; **MORRISS**, Wayne 1984-86; **NEWSON**, Gerald 1961-66; **NICHOL**, Kelly 2002-06; **PARKER**, Graham 1982, 1985; **PEARSON**, Anna 1978, 1980-81, 1983; **PERKINS**, Brian 1962; **PETERSON**, Frank 1965; **POTTER (Lovell)**, Kathryn 1963-66; **PROWSE**, Daryl 1985-87; **RADFORD**, Lachlan 2002-07; **RADFORD**, Ross 1974-75; **RAE**, Simon 1998; **RIVE**, Anthony 1968-71; **ROBERTS**, Nicholas 1982; **RUSH**, William 1999-2001;

SANDLE, Nicholas 1969-74; **SATHERLEY**, Dawn 1966-68; **SAUNDERS**, Zane 1992-93, 1995; **SECOR**, Kirstin 1984; **SHIN**, Kiyoung 2004; **SIMPSON**, Barbara 1971; **SINGLE**, Michael 1972-73; **SLATER**, Richard 2001-05, 2007; **SMITH**, Desmond 1961-63; **SMITH**, Stephanie 1991, 1993, 1995; **SMYTH (Blackstein)**, Sonya 1959-62; **SNEYD**, Catherine 1983-84; **SOMERVILLE**, Mandy 1988-90; **STEER**, Michael 1979-83, 1986; **STENTIFORD**, Murray 1964; **STEVENSON**, Helen 1968-74; **STEWART**, Joanne 1986; **STRUTHERS**, Malcolm 1985-87; **TAYLOR**, Adrienne 1972-74, 1976; **TAYLOR**, Steve 1998-99, 2001-02; **THOMPSON**, Jane 1972-76; **TIPPING**, Simon 1965-68; **TURNBULL (Isaac)**, Joan 1959, 1961; **UTTING**, Steven 1990; **VAUGHAN**, Dennis 1967-68, 1970; **WALSH**, David 1959-67; **WARNER**, Leigh 1962-63; **WHITLOCK**, Rosemary 1982.

FLUTE/PICCOLO

ADLAM, Julia 1987; **ANDERSON**, Lucy 2007-08; **ANDERSON**, Robert 1959-63; **AVERILL**, Joanne 1984-86, 1989; **BAIGENT**, Jennifer 1959-62; **BAKER**, Lal 1990, 1992-93; **BARTLETT**, Ann 1978-79; **BATTEN**, Karen 1990-91; **BOWIE**, Catherine 1985-86; **BRADY**, Katherine 1987-88; **BUSH**, Helen 1990; **CATANACH**, Alison 1979-83, 1985; **CHANG**, Christine 2006; **CLARK**, Felicity 1962-63; **CIHELKA**, Oldriska 2000-03; **COLTHART**, Helen 1963-64; **CRUMP**, Barry 1965, 1967-69; **CULLIFORD**, Ingrid 1968-71; **CURZON-HOBSON**, Andrea 1996; **DARROCH**, Hannah 2007-08; **DAVIES**, Bronwyn 1965-66; **DAWSON**, Jane 1982; **BELTON (De Lucenay)**, Loïs 1960-67; **DONNETHORNE**, Sally 1969; **DOUGLAS**, Bridget 1991-93; **EADE**, Kirstin 1996; **ELL**, Christiana 2005; **FARRELL**, Elizabeth 1999, 2002; **FERNER**, Anthony 1969-73; **FRANK**, Evelyn 1959-61; **GILL**, Susan 2003; **GOLTHART**, Helen 1962; **GRENFELL**, Julia 1992-93, 1995; **GUNZ**, Phillipa 1966-67; **HAINSWORTH**, Rosalyn 1976; **HALL**, Tim 1988; **HAMILTON**, Paula 1991; **HAY**, John 1965-69; **HILL**, Barbara 1968-69; **HIRST**, Elizabeth 1989-90; **HOLLINS**, Amanda 1974; **JOHNSTONE**, Katherine 1984-86; **JOHNSTONE**, Kirsten 1998-2001; **KEIGHTLEY**, Pamela 1978-79, 1981; **KING**, Phillipa 1966; **LIDDELL**, Michael 1982; **LOVE**, Joanna 1976; **MADDEN-GREY**, Simone 1995; **MALLETT**, Liam 2002-04; **MARTIN**, Mary 1972-75; **McEWEN**, Mitchell 2004; **McFARLANE**, Katie 1997-98; **McLEOD**, Heather 1976; **MOUNTFORD**, Clare 1964; **NEWTON**, Nicky 1981; **LAMB (Oswin)**, Karin 1970-72; **PARKHILL**, Dana 1996-97; **PEAK**, Roger 1959-60; **SEDDON**, Jennifer 1980; **SEWELL**, Jacqueline 1980; **SINDEN**, Amie 1997-99; **SLATER**, Amanda 2008; **SPENCE**, Rosene 1983; **SKINNER**, Rachel 1973-74; **SOMERVILLE (Cooke)**, Juliet 1964-65; **STAPLES**, Jocelyn 1964-66; **STAPLETON**, Alan 1974-75; **STEVENS**, Andrew 1970; **STILL**, Alexandra 1979-80; **TAMASHIRO**, Yuri 2006; **TEASDALE**, Roslyn 1973; **THOMSON**, Mary-Kate 1983-85, 1987-88; **TOMLINSON**, Sophie 1978, 1980; **TOWERS**, Briar 1995; **TSAO**, Catherine 2003-05; **VAN BOHEEMEN**, Ingrid 2005-06; **VAUGHAN**, Jennifer 2007; **VERHURG**, Monica 1983; **WEST**, Nicola 2001; **WILLIAMS**, Bridget 1965-67; **WILLIS**, Alisa 2000; **WILSON**, Patricia 1992; **WOOD**, Kathleen 1972-73.

OBOE/COR ANGLAIS

ANDERSON, Helen 1962-64; **BEECH**, Lukas 1998-99; **BENTON**, Cherry 1963; **BIGGS**, Catherine 1985; **BISSETT**, Helen 1973-74; **BUTLER**, Olivia 2001; **CASHMORE**, Rachel 2006-07; **CHENG**, Doris 2003; **CHRISTENSEN**, Stephen 1985; **COFFEY**, Georgina 1995-98; **COOKE**, Merran 1989-92; **COX**, Louise 2001-02; **DAVIES**, Lucy 1983; **DIXON**, Stacey 1993, 1996-2000; **DONELLY**, Kate 2002-04; **EAGER**, Naomi 2000; **FALLOON**, Ian 1972-75; **FIELD**, Nicolas 1981, 1983-84; **GIBBONS**, Rainer 1993, 1995-97; **GIBSON**, Catherine 1976-79; **GLAZEBROOK**, Susan 1973; **GLEN**, Mary 1979; **GODFREY (Tipping)**, Rachel 1967-68; **HADDOCK**, Tanya 1986; **HARVEY**, Simon 1969-70; **HUTTON**, Paula 1966-67; **JACKSON**, Stanley 1966-67; **JACKSON**, Wilfred 1965; **JOHNSON**, Jenny 2007-08; **JUNG**, Da Hye 2001; **JUST**, Wolfgang 1964-66; **LITHGOW**, Stuart 1968-72; **LIU**, Joy 2003-06; **MacKENZIE**, Kenneth 1959, 1965; **McCAHON**, Brian 1960-63; **McLAREN**, Sinclair 1978-81; **McMILLAN**, Fiona 1980; **MALCOLM**, Andrew 1982-83, 1985; **MORISON**, Ian 1980-82; **NEAL**, Margaret 1959-61; **O'MEEGHAN**, Rosemary 1970-74; **ORR**, Robert 1989-92; **OWENS**, Samantha 1987; **PARRY**, Gareth 1963-67; **PARSLOE**, Virginia 1976; **PATISOLO**, Ina 2000; **PEARCE**, Geoffrey 1976; **PENTECOST**, Suzanne 1990, 1993; **PHARO**, Greg 2005-06, 2008; **PHILIPSON**, Vicki 1974-75; **RACKHAM**, Madeline 1990-92; **ROBERTSON**, Wendy 1984; **SAYERS**, Keith 1960-63; **SCHARNKE**, Gudrun 1984-88; **SCOTT**, Calvin 1986, 1988; **SIMPSON**, Heather 1968-72; **SIMPSON**, Warwick 1999, 2003; **STILL**, Victoria 1985, 1987-88; **THORPE**, Ian 1966; **TODD**, Glenys 1978; **VINCENT**, Alexandra 2007-08; **WEBB**, Ronald 1959; **WHITTLE**, Caroline 1983; **WILTON**, Peter 1967-70; **WITHY**, Alan 1960-61.

CLARINET/BASS CLARINET

ADAMS, Jennifer 1964-65; **ADAMS**, Peter 1979-81; **ADLAM**, David 1976; **BAKER**, Mathew 2005; **BRUNT**, Johanna 2000-02; **BURTON**, Catherine 1995-98; **BYNG**, June 1966-69; **CAREW**, Robert 1965-66, 1968; **CARTER**, Melissa 2006-07; **CHARLTON**, Shona 1985, 1987; **CHILDS**, Terence 1972; **COOKSON**, Mark 1995-97; **CORMACK**, Erin 1983; **CRANEFIELD**, Stephen 1983, 1985; **DAVIES**, Teresa 1998-90; **DEKKER**, Naomi 2004; **DEVERALL**, Ellen 2003-06; **DILL**, Robert 2006; **DRAIN**, Pauline 1961-66; **DURRANT**, Andrew 2008; **EADY**, John 1986, 1990; **EAST**, Andrew 1990-93; **FINDLEY (Streat)**, Gloria 1959-61; **FOREMAN**, Richard 1983, 1985; **GILBERT**, Sophie 2001-02; **HANSSON**, Deborah 1974, 1976; **HARRIS**, Simon 1982, 1984-86; **HAVELOCK**, Kirk 2003; **HILLIER**, Carol 1960-61; **HOPKINS**, Ashley 1984; **HOUGHTON**, Bruce 1985; **HUGGETT**, Euan 1963-64; **HURST**, Moira 1988; **KHOURI**, Murray 1959; **KINGDON**, Dale 1959-62; **KINGDON**, Nora 1963; **KNIGHT**, Fiona 1967-69; **KRAUS**, Carol 1974; **LIM**, Cyril 1997, 1999; **LOGAN**, Emily 1998-2000; **McCAMMON**, Catherine 1974; **McGREGOR**, Anna 2008; **MacKAY**, James 1966-69; **MASTERS**, Sarah 2001; **MAY**, Nicola 1987; **MAYSON**, Greg 1967; **MILES**, Bridget 1993; **MONK**, Stella 1970, 1972; **MORI**, Don 1962; **NICHOLLS**, Donald 1989, 1991-92; **NICHOLSON**, Rachel 1978-81;

OGILVIE, Simon 1990-91; **PALMER**, Juliet 1987-90; **PAULO**, Janina 2004; **RAWSON**, Deborah 1970-73; **REEVE**, Anthony 1963-66, 1968-69; **ROBINSON**, John 1981-84; **ROBINSON**, Warwick 2000-01, 2003; **RUDDY**, Anne 1971-72; **SCHOLES**, Peter 1978; **SCOTT**, Mary 1979-80; **SHIEFF**, Sarah 1980; **SINCLAIR**, Hayden 2007-08; **SPRAGG**, Keith 1969-75; **SPURDLE**, Andrea 1996; **SUSSEX**, Roland 1960-62, 1964; **THIRTLE**, Jenny 1979; **TOAN**, Robin 2002-03; **UREN**, Andrew 1992-93; **WALTON**, Mark 1972-75; **WALTON**, Nicola 2005-07; **WINSTANLEY**, Philip 1976, 1978; **WORKMAN**, Tim 1988; **WYATT**, Margaret 1959.

SAXOPHONE

EAST, Andrew 1990; **STENTIFORD**, Murray 1962-63; **WALKER**, Christopher 1972-73

BASSOON/CONTRABASSOON

ALBERS, Milja 1985-86; **ANGUS**, David 1972-74; **BARKLE (Orwin)**, Selena 1989-91; **BESTLEY**, Christopher 1963-68; **BLASCHKE**, Paul 1976; **BRADFIELD**, Craig 1978, 1980; **BRAITHWAITE**, Irene 1987-88; **BRINKMAN**, Ruth 1980; **BRYANT**, Michelle 1982; **BURNS**, Michael 1981, 1983-86; **CAMMELL**, Terence 1960-64, 1966; **CAMPBELL**, Meredith 1987; **CHAN**, Alexandra 2005-08; **CHANDLER**, Richard 1981, 1986; **CHUA**, Melanie 2001-04; **COLEMAN**, Bruce 1966-67; **DODD**, Timothy 1982; **DONNELLY**, Joseph 2007-08; **EDWARDS**, John 1962; **FIFIELD**, Ruth 1996; **FORBES-ABRAMS**, Colin 1999, 2001; **FORSYTHE**, Neville 1970-73; **GARDNER**, Martin 1985-88, 1990; **GARVITCH**, Michele 1968-71; **GELLER**, Timothy 1976; **GILL**, Liam 1972; **GOLDSTONE**, Kate 1993, 1995-96; **GRANWAL**, Ronald 1959-63; **HARRIS**, Fleur 1992; **HARTLEY**, Susan 1974; **HEMMINGSEN**, Colin 1964, 1966-67; **HICKTON**, Ruth 1997-2000; **HOADLEY**, Ben 1992-93; **HOCKEN**, Susan 1969; **KIRCHER**, Jane 1998-2000; **KLOOGH**, Noeline 1959-62; **LAVËN**, Oscar 2007; **LEE**, Teri 2003-04, 2006; **LIGHTBAND**, Paul 1969; **LYND**, Bridget 2004-05; **MACKIE**, Melbon 1963-66; **MANDER**, Carolyn 1995; **McEWEN**, Mark 1978; **McFARLANE**, Leonie 1968-71; **McKEICH**, Hamish 1983-85; **McLENNAN**, Susan 1990; **McNEILL**, Jeffrey 1979; **MEGGET**, Anne 1978-79; **MEIJERS**, Leida 1983; **MILES**, Penelope 1995, 1997; **OLIVER**, Emily 1989, 1991-92; **PURDY**, Nigel 1983-85; **ROBINSON**, David 1960-61; **ROBINSON**, Lynn 1990-91, 1993; **ROUD**, Hayley 2003-04, 2006-08; **SPRAGG**, Christopher 1965; **TAYLOR**, Juliet 1997-98; 2002; **THOMSON**, Jeremy 1974-76; **WEBSTER**, Edwin 1970; **WHITE**, Shannon 2001-02; **WIGLEY**, Richard 1979-80; **YOUNG**, Jennifer 1972-75.

HORN

ALLEN, Bruce 1970; **AVERILL**, Nicola 1983-86, 1989; **BACON**, Mark 1980-82; **BARTLEY**, Bryce 1959-63; **BAYLIS**, Graeme 1968; **BAYLISS**, Norman 1967; **BISLEY**, Charles 1974;

BOWEN, Christopher 1992; **BROWNE**, Kevin 1983; **BURTON**, Ilana 1998; **BYARS**, Angus 1983-85, 1987-88; **CHALLIS**, Erica 1982, 1984-87; **CHIRNSIDE**, Graham 1962; **CLARK**, Heather 1970-71; **COX**, David 1976-80; **COX**, Stephen 1978; **CUDBY**, Neville 1959; **CURRIE**, Kevin 1973-75; **DAY**, Rachel 1989-90; **DEANS**, Paul 1969; **DOE**, Henry 1996; **DUNFORD**, Heather 1985; **EDLIN**, Abbey 2006-07; **EDWARDS**, Jennifer 1985; **ELLIS**, Howard 1961-65; **EVANS**, Jenny-Marie 2002-04; **FERRABEE**, Jillian 1980-82; **FOSTER**, Philip 1990-92; **GREGORY**, Judith 1966-69; **GROOM**, Dominic 1993, 1995-97; **HARRIS**, Mary 1974; **HARRIS**, Melanie 1976; **HARRIS**, Ross 1966; **HARVEY**, Euan 1995-97; **HILL**, Douglas 1964-65; **HILL**, Gregory 1972-75; **HOSKEN**, Philippa 1995; **HSU**, Jennifer 2001-03, 2005; **HUGHES**, Michael 1961; **IMAGE**, Elizabeth 2000-02; **INSALL**, Rodney 1973-74; **JONES**, Michael 1963-64, 1966-67; **KAY**, David 2002-04; **KEAY**, Janice 1964-66; **KENNEDY**, Phillip 1966-67; **KOPITTKE**, Andrew 2006; **LE HEUX**, Benjamin 2001, 2003; **LEWIS**, Anna 2006; **LIGHTFOOT**, Eleanor 1967; **LIU**, Cindy 1996-97; **LOVE**, Thomas 1990, 1992-93; **LYTTLE**, Nicholas 1974, 1976; **MADDREN**, Charlotte 1991-93; **MANN**, Bernard 1986; **MAYHEW**, Dillon 1993, 1995-97, 2007; **McGLASHAN**, Donald 1979; **McGUIRE**, Jeffrey 1987-88, 1990; **McKEICH**, Andrew 1978; **MORTON**, Alexander 2007-08; **MÜLLER-CAJAR**, David 2005, 2007-08; **MUNDEN**, Caryl 1981-83; **MUTTON**, Gary 1969; **PEARCE**, Wendy 1991-93; **PLUCKER**, John 2003; **POTTER**, Janet-Alys 1979; **POTTER**, Megan 2005; **POWELL**, Jenny 1978-79; **PURVES**, Robert 1964-68; **REID**, Vivien 1989-90; **RICHARDS**, Emma 2003-06; **RIMMER**, John 1960, 1963; **ROBB**, Hamish 1995, 1998-99; **ROSE**, Meredith 1998; **ROUSE**, Jerome 2007-08; **ROWDEN**, Lydia 1999; **RYAN**, William 1967-70; **SCHACHERER**, Nathan 1999-2002; **SCHWABE**, John 1959; **SCOTT**, Malcolm 1968-70; **MANN**, Bernard 1990-91; **SHARMAN**, Peter 1980-81; **SMALE**, David 1959-60; **SNEYD-MARSHALL**, Anna 2000-01; **SOUTHGATE**, William 1960-62; **SPARKE**, Alyson 1997-2000; **STENTIFORD**, Graeme 1960-63, 1965; **THOMAS**, Mark 1971-75; **THOMPSON**, Sarah 1984-87; **TREVETHICK**, Simon 1972-73; **TULLOCH**, Tracy 1985-89, 1991; **UNNO**, Yuki 2003-04; **URE**, John 1968-69, 1971-76; **VAN WYK**, Shadley 2004-06; 2008 **VEALE**, Samuel 1981-86; **WEIR**, Julian 1993; **WRIGHT**, Miriam 1998-2000; **WRIGHT**, Tessa 2003; **WYLIE**, Kevin 1970; **YOUNG**, William 1985.

TRUMPET

ABRAHAMS, Bruce 1959, 1963; **ARMSTRONG**, David 1978, 1981-83; **ASHBY**, Nigel 1969, 1971; **BAREHAM**, Nigel 1996; **BARKER**, Laurence 1991, 1993; **BARSBY**, Helen 1990-91; **BEMELMAN**, Stephen 1991; **BOOTH**, Michael 1973-74; **BRADY**, Malvin 1985-87; **BRAITHWAITE**, Eric 1985-88; **BREMNER**, Mark 1996-99; **BROSNAHAN**, Anthony 1974; **BROWN**, Alan 1964-67; **CHAPMAN**, Stephen 2001; **CHRISTIE**, Owen 1981, 1984-85; **CLARK**, Chris 2005-06; **COLEMAN**, Trevor 1978-79; **CONSTABLE**, Mathew 1992-93, 1995, 1997; **COOKE**, Jennifer 1981; **COOPER**, Benjamin 1992-93, 1996; **COOPER**, Grant 1971-75; **CRAVEN**, Michael 1976; **CUNLIFFE**, Mark 1999-2000, 2002; **DAVIES**, Lindsey 1973-74, 1976, 1980; **DYER**, Christopher 1976; **EVANS**, Gareth 1985; **EVES**, Thomas 2008;

FALLOON, Trevor 1979-80; **FERGUSON**, Donald 1962; **FOX**, Louis 1962; **FURNEAUX**, Oliver 2003; **GEARD**, Malcolm 1966-68; **GILLIES**, Robert 1960; **GORRIE**, Jon 2001; **GRAY**, John 1978; **GRESSON**, Stephen 1972; **HAGEN**, John 1972; **HENDERSON**, Toby 1995; **HOCKING**, Barrett 2004-07; **HOCKING**, Slade 2007-08; **HOPPER**, Derek 1985-86; **HORNIBROOK**, Mark 1969; **HOWIE**, Martin 1988-90; **HUGHES**, David 1963-69; **HUNTER**, Ivan 1971; **HUNTER**, Keith 1961-63; **KEMPTON**, David 2003-04, 2006-08; **KIRGAN**, Danny 2006-08; **LAURENCE**, Chris 1998; **LAW**, Gavin 1972; **MARTIN**, Kenneth 1961; **MARTIN**, Nicholas 1987; **MATSON**, William 1959-61; **McFARLANE**, Norman 1973-75; **McGOWAN**, Michael 1998-2000; **McKINLEY**, Amanda 2000-04; **McLEOD**, Craig 1963; **McMILLAN**, John 1967-69; **MEAR**, Andrew 1995, 1997; **NEILSON**, Chris 1969-70; **O'DELL**, Alan 1979-80; **OGLE**, Peter 1990; **PAGE**, John 1992-93; **PRYCE**, Rhoderick 1962-66; **QUINN**, Mary 1995-97; **REID**, Maurice 1984, 1988; **ROBERTSON**, Garry 1964-67; **RUSSELL**, Andrew 1981-86; **SMYTH**, Gerald 1969-70; **SMYTH**, Vere 1972; **SNELGROVE**, John 1959; **STENBO**, Mathew 2004; **STONEHAM**, William 2005; **SUTTON**, Susan 1963; **SWAIN**, Evan 1961-63; **SYMES**, Robert 1960; **THORNE**, Edwina 1976; **VERRILL**, Matthew 1999-2000; **WEIR**, Andrew 1992-93; **WILKINSON**, Kim 1987-89; **WILLIAMS**, Bede 2001, 2003; **WOOLF**, Vance 1990-91; **WOOLLEY**, Christopher 2007; **YORK**, Graeme 1973; **YOUNG**, John 1982-83.

TROMBONE/BASS TROMBONE/B flat BARITONE

ADAMS, Christopher 1960; **ADAMS**, Ronald 1963; **AHN**, Yohan 2001; **ALLISON**, Matthew 1999-2000; **BARTON**, Kali 1992-93; **BRACEGIRDLE**, Anthony 2005-08; **BREMNER**, David 1995-97; **CAUDWELL**, Christopher 1962; **CHRISTIANSEN**, Luke 2005-08; **CLAMAN**, Paul 1978-79; **CLARKE**, Owen 1990-93, 1995; **CLOSE**, Mark 1990; **CROSS**, Douglas 1993; **DAVEY**, Mark 2006, 2008; **DEAN**, Hamish 1996-99; **DONALDSON**, Paulette 1978, 1982; **DUNCAN**, Douglas 1960-61; **FOX**, Roger 1969-70; **FREEMAN**, Dennis 1974, 1976; **GIBSON**, Kurt 2001; **HAMID**, Barnaby 1966-68; **HANSSON**, Glen 1976; **HARKER**, Jonathan 1996-98, 2000; **HENRY**, Alison 1984; **HICKMAN**, Roberta 1997-98; **HUNTER**, Clive 1960-61; **HUNTER**, Iain 1987-88; **HUNTER**, Leslie 1959, 1962; **INSALL**, Howard 1973-74; **JAMESON**, Graham 1963-66; **JELLYMAN**, Brian 1971-72; **JOHNSTONE**, Barry 1966-70; **KEMP**, Malcolm 1970, 1972 **KEYS**, Kevin 1999; **LAW**, Ross 1978-79, 1981; **McKENZIE**, Alan 1968-73, 1975; **MENDEL**, Philip 1963-69; **MORRIS**, Paul 1972-75; **NAYLOR**, David 1966; **PALMER**, Richard 1984; **PAYNE**, Kelvin 2002; **PRANKERD**, Richard 1969; **PRICE**, Kevin 1983-87; **RIGDEN**, Earl 1964-67; **SCUDDER**, Michael 2003-04; **SHEA**, David 1991-93; **SINCLAIR**, Blair 2000-04; **SINCLAIR**, Grant 2002-05; **SPURDLE**, Karen 1980; **SUTTON**, Timothy 1988, 1991; **THORNER**, Gerald 1970-71; **VAN DYK**, Nick 1984; **VAN GINKEL**, Margaret 1985-87; **VAN LIESHOUT**, Stephanus 1990; **WALSH**, Timothy 2006-08; **WATT**, Peter 1973-76; **WILLIAMS**, Craig 1980-86; **WOODBRIDGE**, David 1979-83; **WRIGHT**, Grace 1995; **WRIGHTSON**, Robert 1959, 1961-62.

EUPHONIUM

GILLIES, Graham 1972.

TUBA

ALLELY, Thomas 1997-2001, 2004; **BAKER**, Jonathan 1990-92; **BENGE**, Kerry 1996; **COLLINGS**, Christopher 1993, 1995; **HAMID**, Barnaby 1965; **HARRIS**, Ross 1964; **HENDY**, Christie 1966; **LAIRD**, Wayne 1970-72; **MANDER**, Donald 1968-69; **McFARLANE**, Allan 1979; **PEARCE**, David 1981-82, 1984-87; **PENI**, Ryan 2002-03, 2007; **RYAN**, Michael 1972; **SHACKLOCK**, Tony 1980; **SLINN**, Errol 1959-63; **SLINN**, Warwick 1962-64; **SUGGER**, Matthew 2005; **SUTHERLAND**, James 2008; **THOMAS**, Peter 1988; **WALSH**, Amy 2006; **WELLS**, Peter 1967; **YOUNG**, Kenneth 1974, 1976, 1986.

TIMPANI/PERCUSSION

ANDERSON, John 1972; **BARR**, Barry 1965-66; **BARTLETT**, Gregory 1969-71; **BATSON**, Joel 2000-02, 2005; **BRAIN**, Gary 1963, 1965-66; **BREMNER**, Fraser 1999, 2007; **BREMNER**, Stephen 1997, 1999; **BURGE**, Ross 1972; **CASTLE**, Sarah 1980; **CATANACH**, Duncan 1982-86; **CHAMBERLAIN**, Andrew 1998; **CHILDS**, Terence 1972; **CLARK**, Linden 1980, 1982-85; **CLAYTON**, Matthew 1984-87, 1989; **COOPER**, Roanna 1996, 1998-99, 2001-03; **CRAIGIE**, Robert 1998-2000, 2003; **CURREY**, Shane 1992-93, 1995; **CUTTS**, Peter 1966; **DEAN**, Trevor 1960-64; **EAST**, William 1972; **FARMER**, Georgia 2004-06; **GARTHWAITE (Farr)**, Sian 1976, 1979-80; **FITZSIMMONS**, Jeremy 1992-93, 1995; **GABITES**, Janet 1972; **GADD**, Paul 1972-73; **GADD**, Sharon 1970-75; **GILCHRIST**, David 1967; **GIVEN**, Craig 1997-98; **GORDON**, Joel 2007-08; **GREGORY**, Paul 1990-91; **GRIFFITHS**, David 1973; **GRIFFITHS**, Kerry 1974, 1977; **HALL**, John 1964-65; **HARKER**, Stephen 1993, 1995, 1998; **HARROP**, Catherine 1962-64; **HAYWARD**, George 1959-60; **HEENAN**, Alison 1972; **HEMMING**, Rebecca 1990, 1992; **HENDRICKSEN**, Sylvia 1965-68; **HICKMAN**, Murray 1991-93; **HOADLEY**, Jennie 1990-92; **HORNE**, Richard 1985-87; **HUNT**, Ben 2006-08; **JEFFRIES**, Rachel 2001; **JELLYMAN**, Dayle 2004, 2006; **JOHNS**, Graham 1972-75; **JONES**, Frederick 1963-65; **KELLY**, Lindy 1972-73; **LA ROCHE**, Mark 1990-91; **LAING**, Lindsay 1959, 1961, 1965; **McDONALD**, Kerry 1968; **McFARLANE**, Laurence 2008; **McGREGOR**, Nigel 1988-90; **McKINNON**, Bruce 1971-72; **MARLES**, Ashley 1982; **MEGGET**, Anne 1981; **MISKELLY**, Murray 1988; **MONTGOMERY**, Garry; **MOON**, Clive 1966; **MORGAN**, David 1967-69; **MOTOKAWA**, Takumi 2003-07; **MYHILL**, Tim 2008; **NEILL**, John 1969-70; **OXFORD**, Kenneth 1967; **PAINTER**, Brett 1987-88, 1990; **PALLISTER**, Stefan 1959-62; **PHILIP**, Lance 1985-87; **POPE**, Sarah 1972; **PRICE**, Vicki 2002; **QUINN**, Philip 1996-97; **WILKINSON (Radford)**, Jane 1972; **RAE**, Duncan 1993, 1995, 1997; **RAINS**, Andrew 1982-84; **RANCE**, Jonathan 1996;

REA, Bruce 1970, 1972; **ROBERTSON**, Paul 2008; **ROGERS**, Murray 1972; **SAMPSON**, David 1978; **SARCICH**, Paul, 1971 **SHIRLEY**, Jane 1976; **SITTER**, Greg 1973; **SITTIER**, Gregory 1972; **SOMERVILLE**, Jane 1990; **STEEL**, Anthony 1967-70; **STEWART**, Brent 2005-07; **STRÖM**, Svenda 2007; **THIN**, Jeremy 1998-99, 2001-03; **THORNE**, Craig 2001; **TRENWITH**, Sarah 2003-04; **TSURUTA**, Yoshiko 2008; **TUNE**, Stephen 1969-70; **WAIN**, Gary 1979-81; **WARNER**, Suzanne 1983; **WEIR**, Stephen 1991; **WESTON**, Peter 1964-66; **WHITE (McNeill)**, Marise 1974-77; **WHITTA**, Tim 1998, 2000; **WHITTON**, Ben 2006-08; **WILKINSON**, Mary 1972; **WILSON**, Graham 1968; **WILTSHIRE**, Alex 1972; **YOUNG**, Kenneth 1975.

HARP

ANDERSON, Mary 1965-66; **BAUER**, Ingrid 2000-03, 2006-08; **CHRISTENSEN**, Anna 1980-81; **CONDON**, Beth 1990; **DUNWOODIE**, Anna 1993; **HARRIS**, Rebecca 1960, 1961-62; **HASSALL**, Barbara 1973-74; **HOPE**, Rebecca 1997; **MANN**, Natalia 1992-93; **McDONNELL**, Kerry 1968-70; **MILLS-WILLIAMS**, Carolyn 1990; **NEWTH**, Jennifer 2008; **PEEMOELLER**, Tegan 2007; **SOUTER**, Vanessa 1982, 1986-87; **SU**, Yi 2001-02; **WARD**, Robin 1999-2000; **WEBBY**, Helen 1985-86, 1988; **WILSON**, Katherine 1976; **WINCHESTER**, Barbara 1960.

KEYBOARD/ORGAN/HARPSICHORD

ANDERSON, Dale 1980; **BARKLE (Orwin)**, Selena 1987-88; **BERGIN**, Susan 1976; **BIRD**, Justin 1999; **BURRY**, Josephine 1965; **CAMERON**, Amy 1998; **CRAWSHAW**, Sandra 1983; **DURHAM**, Ad 1993; **GLUBB**, Nanette 1963; **INGRAM**, Laura 1980; **KING**, Evelyn 1972; **LAI**, Ju-Yin 1998; **LAMB**, Martin 1969; **LOCKE**, Kirsten 1998; **McCABE**, Fiona 1990; **McTAGGART**, Peter 1970; **MARTIN**, Catherine 1973; **NARRAWAY**, Guinevere 1993; **NICOLSON**, Donald 2001-02; **OLDCORN**, Jocelyn 1992; **PACZIAN**, Rita 1993; **PORATH**, Sandra 1963; **RAINEY**, Amber 2006, 2008; **REDSHAW**, Michael 1966; **WALLIS**, Ann 1979; **WHEELER**, Nicholas 1985; **WILLIAMS (Kingsbury)**, Janet 1982.

Appendix B

LEADERS/CONCERTMASTERS/CO-CONCERTMASTERS 1959–2009

ANDREWES, James 2001; **ANSELL,** Simon 1983; **ASPEY,** Vincent 1959; **CHISHOLM,** John 1967, 1971; **CORMACK,** Justine 1989; **DEBNAM**, Anna 1986; **EGEN,** Lisa 1987–88; **GOH,** Yid-Ee 1993; **HALL,** Amalia 2009; **HALL,** Lara 2002–03; **HARROP,** Joe 1999; **HOY,** Kenneth 1963; **HILLYER,** Giselle 1992; **JONES,** Geoffrey 1984; **LIU,** Li 1998; **McCARTHY,** Julia 2004; **McCLELLAND,** Sarah 1990; **McINTYRE,** Michael 1960–62; **MANAGH,** Stephan 1972–73; **MILLER,** Simon 1978–79; **MONAGHAN,** Michael 1969–70; **MOREAU,** Jennifer 1981–82; **MORRISON,** Ben 2006, 2008–09 **NALDEN,** Natalie 1991; **PERKS,** Robin 1964–66; **PETERSEN**, Tessa 1987; **PRESS,** Blythe 2007; **POPLE,** Edward 1968; **SECKER,** Anthea 1975; **STAPLETON,** Claire 1980; **TAYLOR,** Julie 1974; **THOMPSON,** Susan 1976; **WARREN,** Allan 1995–97; **WESTBROOKE,** Alwyn 2005; **WRIGHT,** Jane 1985–86

DEPUTY LEADERS, ASSOCIATE CONCERTMASTERS

ALEXANDER, Brian 1968–70; **ANDREWES**, James 2000, 2003; **ANSELL,** Simon 1981; **CAREY,** Richard 1965–66, 1969; **CASTLE,** Olwen 1959; **CHANG,** Johnny 1997; **COLLINS,** Joyce 1964; **DEBNAM,** Anna 1986; **DIBLEY,** Julia 2001; **GOH,** Yid-Ee 1992; **GOPAL,** Malavika 2004–05; **HALL,** Amalia 2006; **HALL,** Lara 1999; **HSU,** Hsin 1996; **KNUFERMANN,** Kirsten 1989; **MANAGH,** Stephen 1970; **MOREAU,** Jennifer 1980; **NIELSEN,** Susanne 1969–71; **O'FLAHERTY,** Stephanie 1985; **OWEN,** Mary Anne 1983–84; **PETERSEN,** Tessa 1987; **POPLE,** Edward 1960, 1963; **PRESS,** Blythe 2007–08; **PUCHER,** David 1982; **RODGERS,** Glenda 1979; **ROSS,** Matthew 1990–91, 1993; **SALAMONSEN,** Anna 1978; **SECKER,** Anthea 1974–75; **TAYLOR,** Julie 1972–73; **THOMSON,** Andrew 1995; **THOMPSON,** Susan 1975; **WESTBROOKE,** Alwyn 2002; **WILSON,** Katherine 1976; **WILSON,** Robin 1998

Appendix C

CONDUCTORS 1959–2009

BRAIN, Gary 1993; **BRAITHWAITE,** Nicholas 1992; **CHURCHILL**, Mark 2000; **DANIEL**, Paul 2009; **DAVIES**, Meredith 1982; **DECKER,** Franz-Paul 1984; **GAMBA,** Piero 1987; **GRYLLS,** Karen 1990; **HEENAN,** Ashley 1965–70, 1972–75; **HOPKINS,** John 1959–64, 1971, 1978, 1990; **HOUSTOUN,** Michael 1991; **JACKSON,** Isaiah 1995; **KÖHLER,** Lutz 2001, 2003; **LACOMBE,** Jacques 2008; **LOUGHRAN,** James 1989; **NEALE,** Alasdair 2004; **NÉZET-SÉGUIN,** Yannick 2007; **OSTROWSKI,** Avi 1975; **OUTWATER,** Edwin 2005; **ROBERTSON,** James 1976; **SALOMON,** Doron 1985; **SANDERLING,** Thomas 1983, 1986; **SEAMAN,** Christopher 1981; **SEDARES,** James 1996–98; **SEGAL,** Uri 1980; **STREATFEILD,** Simon 2006; **TINTNER,** Georg 1979; **VINTEN,** Michael 1988; **WATTS,** Peter 1998; **ZANDER,** Benjamin 1999, 2002

* 1977 and 1994 concerts cancelled

Appendix D

SOLOISTS AND GROUPS 1959–2009

PIANO

ALBULESCU, Eugene 1989; **AUSTIN,** Katherine 1984; **BIRD,** Justin 2001; **BOLLARD,** David 1963; **BURRY,** Josephine 1965; **CHANDLER,** Richard 1985; **CHEN,** John 2005, 2009; **CUMING,** Christine 1967; **GALBRAITH,** David 1968; **HINTERHUBER,** Christopher 1997; **HOUSTOUN,** Michael 1973, 1983, 1988, 1991; **JAMES,** David 1969/70; **LION,** Margaret 1974; **McSTAY,** Janetta 1960; **MATHERS,** Rosemary 1971; **STONE,** Jacqueline 1972; **TILL,** Maurice 1964; **VON ALPENHEIM,** Ilse 1959

VIOLIN

ANTHONY, Adele 1986; **ITO,** Kanako 1992; **MENZIES,** Mark 1987; **OZIM,** Igor 1959; **POPLE**, Edward 1970; **SCHAFFER,** Peter 1978

VIOLA

TURNBULL, Elizabeth 1975

CELLO

ANDREWS, Ivan 1970; **BROWN,** Ashley 1995, 2000; **POPLE,** Ross 1966

FLUTE

EADE, Kirsten 1998

CLARINET

SPRAGG, Keith 1975; **WALTON,** Mark 1975, 1982

TRUMPET

COOPER, Grant 1980

TUBA

HENDY, Christie 1969–70

SINGERS

ALEXANDER, Shelley 1985; **ANDREW,** Milla 1976; **COKER**, Geoffrey 1998; **GRIFFITHS**, David 1998; **HEATHCOTE**, Karen 1998; **LOADER,** Linden 1981; **PIERARD,** Madeleine 2008, **SMITH**, Malcolm 1979

NARRATOR

POLLOCK, Craig 1970

TAONGA PŪORO – TRADITIONAL MĀORI INSTRUMENTS

HOHAIA, Mark Te Tane 1988

GROUPS

NZ NATIONAL YOUTH CHOIR 1998; NATIONAL YOUTH BRASS BAND 1990; NATIONAL YOUTH CHOIR 1990; TE RANGATAHI MAORI CULTURAL GROUP 1988

Appendix E

NZSO NATIONAL YOUTH ORCHESTRA SPONSORS

2000

Principal Sponsor Adam Foundation

Support Organisations School of Music, Victoria University; New Zealand Symphony Orchestra Foundation Trust Board

2001

Principal Sponsor Adam Foundation

Supporting Sponsors Forsyth Barr, Ltd; Forsyth Barr Frater Williams, Ltd

Sponsors Spotless Services; The Edge® Community Arts Programme; School of Music, Victoria University; Wellington Convention Centre; Concert FM, New Zealand Symphony Orchestra Foundation

2002

Principal Sponsor Adam Foundation

Supporting Sponsors Forsyth Barr, Ltd, Forsyth Barr Frater Williams, Ltd

Sponsors Spotless Services; The Edge® Community Arts Programme; School of Music, Victoria University; Concert FM, New Zealand Symphony Orchestra Foundation

2003

Principal Sponsor Adam Foundation

Sponsors Spotless Services; McDouall Stuart; Wellington Convention Centre; The Edge® Community Arts; School of Music, Victoria University; Concert FM; Wellington Friends of the NZ Symphony Orchestra; New Zealand Symphony Orchestra Foundation; Garth Williams

Chair Sponsors Victoria Jones – Lachlan Radford (double bass); Leslie Austin – Vanessa Tam (violin)

2004

Principal Sponsors Adam Foundation; New Zealand Community Trust

Sponsors Spotless Services (NZ) Ltd; McDouall Stuart Group Ltd; Garth & Sue Williams; The Edge® Community Arts Programme; Wellington Convention Centre; School of Music, Victoria University; Concert FM; New Zealand Symphony Orchestra Foundation; Auckland Friends of the NZSO; Wellington Friends of the NZSO; Sibelius Software (UK) Ltd & MusiTech (NZ) Ltd; APRA/AMCOS; Garth Williams

Chair Sponsors Leslie Austin – Naomi Dekker (clarinet); Maribeth Coleman – Barrett Hocking (trumpet)

2005

Principal Sponsors Adam Foundation; New Zealand Community Trust

Sponsors Spotless Services (NZ) Ltd; McDouall Stuart; The Edge® Community Arts Programme; Wellington Convention Centre; School of Music, Victoria University; Concert FM; New Zealand Symphony Orchestra, New Zealand Symphony Orchestra Foundation; Wellington Friends of the NZSO; Auckland Friends of the NZSO

Chair Sponsors Leslie Austin – Nicola Walton (clarinet); Maribeth Coleman – Barrett Hocking (trumpet)

2006

Principal Sponsors Adam Foundation; New Zealand Community Trust

Sponsors Eureka Trust; Spotless Services (NZ) Ltd; McDouall Stuart; Wellington Convention Centre; Te Koki New Zealand School of Music; The Edge® Community Arts Programme; Concert FM; New Zealand Symphony Orchestra Foundation; Wellington Friends of the NZSO; Auckland Friends of the NZSO; Friends of Concert FM; Sibelius Software (UK) Ltd & MusiTech (NZ) Ltd; APRA/AMCOS; Composers Association of NZ (CANZ)

Chair Sponsors Leslie Austin – Jonathan Squire (cello); Maribeth Coleman – Ben Whitton (assnt timpani/percussion); Michael Moodabe – Cameron Stuart (cello)

2007

Principal Sponsors Adam Foundation; New Zealand Community Trust;

Sponsors Eureka Trust; Spotless Services (NZ) Ltd; McDouall Stuart; Wellington Convention Centre; Te Koki New Zealand School of Music; The Edge® Radio New Zealand Concert; New Zealand Symphony Orchestra Foundation; Wellington Friends of the NZSO; Auckland Friends of the NZSO; Friends of Radio New Zealand Concert; Sibelius Software (UK) Ltd & MusiTech (NZ) Ltd; APRA/AMCOS; Composers Association of NZ (CANZ)

Chair Sponsors Leslie Austin – Jung Wook Lee (violin); Maribeth Coleman – Slade Hocking (trumpet)

2008

Principal Sponsor Adam Foundation

Sponsors Infinity Foundation; Eureka Trust; McDouall Stuart; Spotless Services (NZ) Ltd; Wellington Convention Centre; Te Koki New Zealand School of Music; McDouall Stuart; The Edge® New Zealand Symphony Orchestra Foundation; Radio New Zealand Concert; Wellington Friends of the NZSO; Auckland Friends of the NZSO; Christchurch Friends of the NZSO; Sibelius Software (UK) Ltd & MusiTech (NZ) Ltd; APRA/AMCOS; Composers Association of NZ (CANZ)

2009

Principal Sponsors Adam Foundation; Crowne Plaza

Supporting Sponsors: McDouall Stuart; FAME Trust; New Zealand Symphony Orchestra Foundation; Wellington Friends of NZSO; Eureka Trust

Sponsors Radio NZ Concert FM; Sibelius Software (UK) Ltd & MusiTech (NZ) Ltd ; APRA/AMCOS; Wellington Convention Centre; Friends of Radio NZ Concert; The Edge; Auckland Friends of NZSO; STANZA; Hawkes Bay Orchestras; Christchurch Friends of NZSO; Composers Association of NZ (CANZ)

2010

Principal Sponsors Adam Foundation; Crowne Plaza

Supporting Sponsors NZSO Foundation; Wellington Friends of NZSO; The Edge

Sponsors Radio New Zealand Concert; APRA/AMCOS; Wellington Convention Centre; Friends of Radio New Zealand Concert, Auckland Friends of NZSO; New Zealand School of Music; CANZ; SOUNZ

CHAIR, SECTION, AND GREEN ROOM ENDOWMENTS

From 2008 significant support for the NZSO National Youth Orchestra has been received annually from alumni, including NZSO players, and other individuals, through an endowment programme.

2008

Concertmaster Endowment Wellington Friends of NZSO – Ben Morrison

Associate Concertmaster Endowment Peter and Juliet Rowe – Amalia Hall

Player Endowments 34 players endowed by individuals

Green Room Endowments 10 donors

2009

Concertmaster Endowment Wellington Friends of NZSO – Ben Morrison

Co-Concertmaster Endowment Peter and Juliet Rowe – Amalia Hall

Section Endowment Michael E McIntyre – 1st violins

Player Endowments 44 players endowed by individuals

Green Room Endowments 20 donors

2010

Section Endowment Michael E McIntyre – 1st Violins; Dale Hunter – clarinets

Player Endowments 47 players chairs endowed

2009 NZSO NATIONAL YOUTH ORCHESTRA 50TH ANNIVERSARY NATIONAL MUSIC CAMP SPONSORS AND SUPPORTERS

Principal Sponsor Adam Foundation

Sponsors and Supporters McDouall Stuart; New Zealand Symphony Orchestra Foundation through the Mary Fitzwilliam Award, Reeves Harris Orchestra Fund and Jack and Emma Griffin Trust; Hawkes Bay Opera House; Queenstown Violin Summer School; Napier Girls' High School; Wellington Friends of the NZSO.

Appendix F

AWARDS AND SCHOLARSHIPS

SHELL YOUTH SCHOLARSHIP

1982 Nigel MacLean (violin) – for 1983

1983 Caroline Cave (cello) – for 1984

1984 Tim Young (viola) – for 1985

NEW ZEALAND POST

NZSO Post Office Awards for Excellence

1985 Jocelyn Woodley (cello); Stephanie O'Flaherty (violin); Andrew Malcolm (oboe); Stephanie O'Flaherty (violin); Andrew Malcolm (oboe); Hamish McKeich (bassoon); Duncan Catanach (timpani); Lisa Egen (violin); Timothy Young (viola)

1986 Paul Mitchell (cello); Craig Williams (trombone); Joanne Averill (flute); Nicola Averill (horn); Nicola Michael Burns (bassoon); Tim Young (viola); Duncan Catanach (timpani); Jane Wright (violin/leader)

New Zealand Post Music Study Awards

1987 Gudrun Scharnke (oboe); Kevin Price (trombone); Malcolm Struthers (double bass); Tessa Peterson (violin); Anthony Van Buren (viola); Lisa Egen (violin); Martin Risely (violin)

1988 Not awarded (Brisbane tour)

1989 Kim Wilkinson (trumpet); Robyn Cormack, James Bush and Katherine Hebley (cellos); Anna Debnam (viola); Elizabeth Hirst (flute); Matthew Ross (violin)

1990 Mark Close (trombone); Helen Polglase (cello); Robert Orr (oboe); Jonathan Baker (tuba); Richard Hardie (double bass); Deborah Woodley (viola); and Sarah McClelland (violin)

1991 Katie Atkinson (violin); Jonathan Baker (tuba); Selina Barkle (bassoon); Helen Barsby (trumpet); Tim Sutton (trombone); Anne Werry (cello); Vance Woolf (trumpet)

New Zealand Post Awards

1992 Merran Cooke, Robert Orr (oboes); Sanjay Pancha, Manu Berkeljon and Giselle Hillyer (violins); Andrew East (clarinet) and Philip Foster (horn).

1993 Manu Berkeljon (violin); Bridget Douglas (flute); Mathew Fieldes (double bass); Murray Hickman (percussion); Bridget Miles (clarinet).

1994 Not awarded (NYO cancelled)

JOHN CHISHOLM CONCERTMASTER PRIZE

John Chisholm (1947-84) was a member of the National Youth Orchestra from 1963 to 1966 and National Youth Orchestra concertmaster in 1967 and 1971. In his memory, the John Chisholm Prize is awarded annually to the Concertmaster of the NZSO National Youth Orchestra.

1988 Lisa Egan

1989 Justine Cormack

1990 Sarah McClelland

1991 Natalie Nalden

1992 Giselle Hillyer

1993 Yid-Ee Goh

1994 Not awarded (NYO cancelled)

1995 Allan Warren

1996 Allan Warren

1997 Allan Warren

1998 Li Liu

1999 Joe Harrop

2000 Lara Hall

2001 James Andrewes

2002 Lara Hall

2003 Lara Hall

2004 Julia McCarthy

2005 Alwyn Westbrooke and Malavika Gopal (co-concertmasters)

2006 Ben Morrison

2007 Blythe Press and Amalia Hall (co-concertmasters)

2008 Ben Morrison

2009 Ben Morrison

2010 Jessica Alloway

ALEX LINDSAY MEMORIAL AWARD SPECIAL PRIZE

Founded in memory of Alex Lindsay (1919-74), former NZSO Concertmaster. This prize is awarded annually to an outstanding member of the NZSO National Youth Orchestra.

2000 Stacey Dixon, oboe

2001 Christiaan van der Zee, principal viola

2002 Joel Batson, percussion

2003 James Andrewes, associate concertmaster

2004 Blair Sinclair, principal trombone

2005 Joy Liu, principal oboe

2006 Annabella Leslie, principal bass

2007 Barrett Hocking, principal trumpet

2008 Amber Rainey, keyboard

2009 Amalia Hall, co-concertmaster

2010 Mark Davey, principal trombone

ADAM FOUNDATION SCHOLARSHIPS

Awarded to NZSO National Youth Orchestra players in recognition of their performance excellence.

2006 Miyo Yoon (violin); Ingrid van Boheemen (flute); Joy Liu (oboe); Ellen Deverall (clarinet); Teri Lee (bassoon); Emma Richards (horn); Barrett Hocking (trumpet); Luke Christiansen (trombone); Brent Stewart (timpani); Georgia Farmer (percussion).

2007 Sarah Drake (violin), Emma Yoon (violin); Nicholas Hancox, (viola); Shandelle Horsford (double bass); Jennifer Vaughan (flute); Melissa Carter (clarinet); Alexandra Chan (bassoon); Abbey Edlin (French horn); Luke Christiansen (trombone); Takumi Motokawa (timpani); Ben Whitton (percussion).

2008 Jessica Alloway (violin); Helen Bevin (viola); Edward King (cello); Lucy Anderson (flute), Hannah Darroch (flute); Hayden Sinclair (clarinet); Shadley van Wyk (French horn); David Kempton (trumpet); Luke Christiansen (trombone); Ben Whitton (timpani); Yoshiko Tsuruta (percussion).

2009 Nicholas Hancox (viola); Edward King (cello); Shandelle Horsford (double bass); Lucy Anderson (flute), Hannah Darroch (flute); Jenny Johnson (oboe); Hayden Sinclair (clarinet); David Müller Cajar (French horn); David Kempton (trumpet); Luke Christiansen (trombone), Mark Davey (trombone); Ingrid Bauer (harp).

2010 Jonathan Tanner (violin); Emma Fetherston (viola); Karen French (cello); Alanna Jones (double bass); Hugh Roberts (flute); Thomas Hutchinson (oboe); Natalie Harris (clarinet); Kylie Nesbit (bassoon); Danny Kirgan (trumpet); Jessica Rodda (tuba).

NZSO FOUNDATION

NZSO Foundation financial support for young 'conductor observers'

2002 Joanna Drimatis and Andrew Crooks

NZSO Foundation Reeves Harris Trust Awards

Awarded to section principals, 'in recognition of their achievements as leaders of their section' – or towards the payment of players' tuition or travel fees.

2000 15 section principal awards

2001 16 section principal awards

2002 16 section principal awards

2004 Jennifer Banks, Marcel Fernandes, Joshua Tang, Alexander Vaatstra (violins); Victoria Neas, Hugo Smit (cellos); Kiyoung Shin (double bass)

2005 Sol Choi, Charmian Keay (violins); John Roxburgh, Alisa Smith (violas); Jonathan Squire (cello); Tagan Grace (bass); Darija Andzakovic (double bass); Christina Ell (flute); Bridget Lynd (bassoon); Brent Stewart (percussion)

2006 Jenny Chen, Nicholas Thin, Megan Aiken, Boon Khiang Tan (violins); Charlotte Featherston (viola); Jisun Kim, Brian Bromberg (cellos); Shandelle Horsford (bass); Christine Chang (flute); Alexandra Chan (bassoon).

NZSO Foundation Jack & Emma Griffin Trust Scholarships

2001 Justin Bird (piano soloist)

2004 Serenity Thurlow (viola); Kelly Nichol (double bass)

Scholarships awarded to players who attended the Australian Youth Orchestra's national music camp, in January.

2005 *Melbourne*: Jun Bouterey-Ishido (violin); Paul Van Houtte (cello); Sophia Acheson (viola); Richard Slater (bass)

2006 *Canberra*: Nicholas Hancox (viola); Annabella Leslie (bass); Ingrid Bauer (harp)

2007 *Adelaide*: Alisa Smith (viola); Callum Hall (cello); Simon Eastwood (double bass)

2008 *Canberra*: Helen Bevin (viola)

NZSO Foundation Mary Fitzwilliam Awards

2007 *Awarded to players to assist with travel expenses.* Jenny Chen, Arna Shaw, Julianne Song, Sol Choi, Kate Ellingham-Hunt (violins); Charlotte Featherston, John Roxburgh (violas); Callum Hall, Jonathan Squire, Edward King (cellos), Darija Andzakovic (double bass); Jenny Johnson, (oboe); Alexandra Vincent (cor anglais); Nicola Walton (clarinet); Hayley Roud (contrabassoon); David Müller-Cajar (French horn)

2008 *Awarded to players who attended the Australian Youth Orchestra's national music camp in Canberra.* Cameron Stuart (cello); Lachlan Radford (double bass)

2009 *Awarded to players to assist with travel expenses (NZ).* Jenny Chen, Gemma New (violins); Bryony Gibson-Cornish (viola); Cameron Stuart, Jonathan Squire (cellos); Victoria Churchill (oboe); Alexandra Vincent (cor anglais); Hayley Roud (contrabassoon); Jerome Rouse (French horn)

NZSO Foundation Section Leader Awards

Awarded for performance excellence.

2005 Serenity Thurlow (viola); Paul Van Houtte (cello); Kelly Nichol (bass); Catherine Tsao (flute); Ellen Deverall (clarinet); Alexandra Chan (bassoon); Jennifer Hsu, Emma Richards (horns); William Stoneham (trumpet); Joel Batson (timpani); Georgia Farmer (percussion)

NZSO Foundation Trust Awards

Awarded to South Island players to assist with travel expenses.

2007 Jiwon Lee (Christchurch); Li Ding (Dunedin, viola)

CAFAmerica Travel Scholarship

Administered through the NZSO Foundation and awarded to a player based overseas to assist with travel expenses.

2008 Blythe Press (assistant concertmaster)

The NZSO Foundation also funded the John Chisholm Concertmaster Prize in 2010.

FORSYTH BARR LTD, FORSYTH BARR FRATER WILLIAMS LTD SCHOLARSHIPS

Awarded to assist towards travel expenses and orchestra fees.

2001 Blair Harris (cello); Alisa Hunt (Smith) (viola); Alexander Gunchenko (double bass); Johanna Brunt (clarinet); Yi Su (harp)

2002 Kate Donnelly (oboe); Emma Fetherston (viola); Kelly Nichol (double bass); Antony Verner (violin)

THE GARTH WILLIAMS SCHOLARSHIPS

Awarded for performance excellence.

2003 Julia McCarthy, Fiona Cochrane (violins); Serenity Thurlow (viola); Hugo Smit (cello); Kelly Nichol (double bass); Kate Donnelly (oboe); Bede Williams (trumpet); Blair Sinclair (trombone); Ryan Peni (tuba); Roanna Cooper (percussion)

2004 Amanda Verner (viola); Kelly Nichol, Richard Slater (double bass); Liam Mallett, Catherine Tsao (flute); Kate Donnelly (oboe); Janina Paulo (clarinet); Teri Lee (bassoon); David Kay (horn); Amanda McKinley, Mathew Stenbo (trumpet); Sarah Trenwith (timpani); Takumi Motokawa (percussion)

FRIENDS CONCERT FM* / RADIO NEW ZEALAND CONCERT SCHOLARSHIPS

Awarded to instrumentalists, to assist with travel and course fees.

2006 Ingrid Bauer (harp); Robert Dil (bass clarinet); Hayley Roud (contrabassoon); Amy Walsh (tuba)

2007 Joseph Donnelly (bassoon); Jerome Rouse (French horn); Timothy Walsh (bass trombone); Ingrid Bauer (harp).

2008 Shandelle Horsford (double bass); Hayley Roud (bassoon/contrabassoon); David Müller-Cajar (French horn); Ingrid Bauer (harp)

2009 Emma Fetherston (viola); Davina Shum (cello); Alexandra Chan (bassoon); Ben Whitton (timpani)

2010 Olivia Francis (violin); Sebastian Lowe (viola); Umar Zakaria (double bass); Jehanne Bastoni (cello); Justin Standring (flute/piccolo); Lilla Dittrich (French horn); Reuben Chin (saxophone); Harry Peirse (piano)

McDOUALL STUART (Securities Ltd)

Awarded to first-time players to assist them with this opportunity.

2007 Alice McIvor (viola); Jahun Lee (cello)

WELLINGTON FRIENDS OF THE NZSO SCHOLARSHIPS

Awarded to players from the greater Wellington region, for excellence and potential.

2003 Sarah Drake (violin); Oldriska Cihelka (flute)

2004 Malavika Gopal (violin)

2005 Sarah Drake (principal 2nd violin)

2006 Nicholas Hancox (principal viola)

2007 Rachel Cashmore (principal oboe)

2008 Greg Pharo (principal oboe)

2009 Joel Gordon (percussion)

2010 Slade Hocking (trumpet)

Awarded to players to assist with course fees.

2003 Antony Verner, Amanda Verner (violins)

2004 Nicola Drake (violin); Aleisha Verner (cello)

2005 Grant Sinclair (bass trombone); Megan Potter (horn)

2006 Jung Wook Lee (violin); Mark Lipski (bass)

2007 Jung Wook Lee, Tomoko Suganuma (violins); Leoni Wittchow (viola)

2008 Emma Fetherston (viola); Jerome Rouse (French horn)

2009 Julianne Song (violin); Adam McCoy (bass); Sung-Soo Hong (French horn)

2010 Steve Park (violin); Fiona Cairns (bass); Hayley Road (bassoon)

AUCKLAND FRIENDS OF THE NZSO SCHOLARSHIPS

Awarded to a player from the Greater Auckland Region, for excellence and potential.

2005 Luke Christiansen (principal trombone)

2006 Callum Hall (principal cello)

2007 Paul Van Houtte (principal cello)

2008 Alexandra Chan (principal bassoon)

2009 Jessica Alloway (principal 2nd violin)

2010 Sung-Soo Hong (French horn)

The Auckland Friends of the NZSO also funded the John Chisholm Concertmaster Prize 2008/09.

CHRISTCHURCH FRIENDS OF THE NZSO

Awarded to a player from the greater Christchurch region, for excellence and potential.

2008 Thomas Eves (trumpet)

2009 Christopher Woolley (trumpet)

STANZA SCHOLARSHIPS

Awarded to players to assist with travel expenses.

2009 Sarah Claman (violin, Otago); Sol Choi (violin, Christchurch); Alice Gott (cello, Wellington); Alice McIvor (viola, Hawkes Bay); Alanna Jones (double bass, Auckland)

HAWKES BAY ORCHESTRAS SCHOLARSHIPS

Awarded to players from the Hawke's Bay region, for excellence and potential.

2009 Alice McIvor, Leoni Wittchow (violas); Ben Hunt (percussion)

GIFTED AND LOANED INSTRUMENTS

Erika Schorss (violin, National Orchestra/NZBCSO 1947-73)
Bequeathed a violin to be used by a promising NZSO National Youth Orchestra player.

2010 Olivia Francis

Richard Panting (violin, NYO 1965-66, NZBCSO 1967-69, NZSO 1986–89)
Loaned a violin to be used by a promising NZSO National Youth Orchestra player.

2010 Asaph Verner

COMPOSER IN RESIDENCE, AND COMPOSER MENTOR

2005 Robin Toan, Auckland – John Psathas ONZM

2006 Claire Cowan – John Psathas ONZM

2007 Karlo Margetić– Ross Harris

2008 Tabea Squire – Ross Harris

2009 Natalie Hunt – Ross Harris

2010 Alexandra Hay – Gillian Whitehead

Notes

Chapter 1: Prelude

1. Angela (Connal) Lindsay, violin, foundation player NYO 1959–61 and NZBC orchestra trainees, 1961; National Orchestra/NZBC/NZSO 1961–84 1st violins. Widow of Alex Lindsay (NZBCSO concertmaster). Commitment to NZSO and NYO continues through the Alex Lindsay Prize for an NYO player with potential, and the Alex Lindsay Memorial Award (ALMA), administered by NZSO, whose winners include NYO members; chair of Auckland Friends of NZSO. Emails to author, 16–17 February 2009.
2. Juliana Radaich, Jane Freed, and Robin Perks, NZSO violins, interviewed by author, 22 March 2009.
3. Jane Freed, foundation player, NYO 1959–62; foundation orchestra trainee 1961–62; overseas (11 years): Bournemouth Symphony (3 years); Royal Opera House Orchestra (1 year); Hamburg Sinfonika; freelanced (3 years) in Royal Philharmonic, London Philharmonic, Welsh Opera, Royal Ballet, and all BBC orchestras. Session work in Britain, Australia, New Zealand. NZSO 2nd violins 1983–2010.
4. Juliana Radaich, foundation player NYO 1959. Completed a business course and trained as a secretary, began professional career in Auckland String Players, played in the *Porgy and Bess* touring production featuring bass-baritone Inia Te Wiata in Christchurch in 1965; joined NZSO 1975, and retired in 2010, having played in the 1st violins for almost 35 years.
5. Robin Perks, foundation player NYO, 1959–63, leader 1964–66. Orchestra trainee 1964–65; NZBCSO 1965–67; QE2 scholarship 1965; studied in West Berlin and played in Deutsche Oper, Berlin, Konstanze Sinfonie Orchestre (3 years), Bodersee Sinfonia (3 years); England (2 years); played in the Royal Ballet Orchestra and BBC Orchestra in Bristol (2 years); rejoined NZSO 2nd violins 1975–2011.
6. Vincent Aspey OBE, 1909–87. Studied at New South Wales Conservatorium, and led Australian Broadcasting Commission orchestras 2XC and 2BL, before returning to New Zealand in 1931. Leader of the Auckland 1YA Studio Orchestra; leader of NBS String Orchestra, from 1939; sub-leader of the Centennial Orchestra,1940. Founding leader of the National Orchestra/NZBCSO, 1946–67.
7. Maurice Clare, in JM Thomson, *Oxford History of New Zealand Music*, Oxford University Press, 1991, p 174.
8. John Hopkins was appointed principal conductor of the New Zealand National Orchestra in 1958.
9. *New Zealand Listener*, 29 May 1959.
10. Vincent John Aspey, first leader of the NYO. 1959. National Orchestra/NZBCSO 1958–60, 1963–65, 1969–74, Royal Liverpool Philharmonic, and Covent Garden Orchestra. Interview with author, Tawa, 27 December 2008.
11. *New Zealand Listener*, 29 May 1959.
12. Ibid.
13. Ibid.
14. Robin Perks, interview with author, 2 March 2009.
15. Charles Nalden, 1908–2002. Established the Conservatorium of Music at the University of Auckland in 1955, initiated the Executant Diploma course, and conducted New Zealand's first youth orchestra, the Auckland Junior Symphony Orchestra, from 1950 until the early 1970s (Thomson, *Oxford History of New Zealand Music*, p 277).
16. William Walden-Mills, English bandmaster, conductor and music organiser, began the New Zealand national secondary schools orchestral (1953) and choral (1966) courses (Thomson, *Oxford History of New Zealand Music*, pp 271–72).
17. Beatrice Hill was eighteen when she played in the first NYO. After graduating MSc from Canterbury University she went to the United States to begin her life's work studying the origins and evolution

of galaxies and the universe, eventually becoming professor of astronomy at Yale. She died aged forty. (Christine Cole Catley, *Bright Star: Beatrice Hill Tinsley – Astronomer*, Cole Catley, 2006, and later adapted for broadcast on Radio New Zealand National, 2009.)

18. *Evening Post*, 11 May 1959.
19. *The New Zealand Free Lance*, 20 May 1959.
20. Ross Pople, cello, NYO 1959–61. Studied at the Royal College of Music in London, and the Paris Conservatoire. Solo principal cellist for the Menuhin Festival Orchestra and the BBC Symphony Orchestra, founder and conductor of the London Festival Orchestra.
21. Edward (Ted) Pople, violin, NYO 1959–63, 1965–66 (leader 1968); NZSO violinist, 1964–75 and administrator, 1975–78; BMus Victoria University. Formerly, Secretary School of Music, Victoria College of the Arts, is currently general manager Australian Music Examination Board. A violin performer and teacher, he also conducts, and gives master classes and workshops in Malaysia and Indonesia; and adjudicates there, and in Thailand and New Zealand.
22. Marie's Folksong Centre, 1958–70. Its proprietor was the granddaughter of former Prime Minister Richard Seddon.
23. *New Zealand Listener*, 29 May 1959.
24. John Hopkins, interview with author, 1983.
25. NZBS National Orchestra file 21/12/1, May 1959, Archives New Zealand.
26. Ibid., 24 June 1959.
27. Ibid., minutes working party meeting, 5 March 1959.
28. John Hopkins, interview with author, 1983
29. Michael McIntyre NYO 1959–62 (leader 1960–62). Chose a career in academia as a scientist. Emeritus professor, Centre for Atmospheric Science at the Department of Applied Mathematics and Theoretical Physics, Cambridge University, United Kingdom. Email to author, 24 February 2009.

Chapter 2: Realising the Dream

1. Thomson, *Oxford History of New Zealand Music*, p 115.
2. Ibid.
3. Alfred Hill (1870–1960) was born in Australia and immigrated to New Zealand in 1872. He studied violin and composition at the Leipzig Conservatorium, and played in the Gewandhaus Orchestra, before returning to New Zealand in 1892. Hill conducted and wrote mainly light romantic operas, and had a deep interest in Māori music. He became professor of harmony and composition at the New South Wales Conservatorium of Music 1916–34 (J M Thomson, 'Alfred Hill', *Dictionary of New Zealand Biography*).
4. The orchestra at that time was hailed as 'the best in the colony' by the *Triad*, a monthly magazine of music, science, and art, established in 1893 by Charles Baeyertz, its editor for 32 years.
5. Leela Bloy (later McLean). Member of the NBS String Orchestra, Centennial Orchestra, and National Orchestra, 1946–50 (Tonks, *New Zealand Symphony Orchestra*, Reed Methuen, Auckland, 1986, pp 1, 274).
6. Violinist Leon de Mauny immigrated to New Zealand from England in 1923; founded Wellington Symphony Orchestra 1928, and was assistant conductor and music editor of the National Orchestra in 1946–47, and 1950. Tonks, *New Zealand Symphony Orchestra*, pp 2, 4, 9, 53.
7. Tonks, *New Zealand Symphony Orchestra*, p 4.
8. Professor John Bishop, director from 1948 of the Elder Conservatorium, University of Adelaide, and founder of the Adelaide Festival, 1960. Conducted the New Zealand National Orchestra in the 1957 Proms.
9. Thomson, *Oxford History of New Zealand Music*, p 118.
10. Angela Lindsay, interview with author, February 2009.

11. Thomson, *Oxford History of New Zealand Music*, pp 118–19.
12. *Triad*, May 1907.
13. Baritone John Prouse, 1856–1930. Thomson, *Oxford History of New Zealand Music*, pp 118–83.
14. Ibid, pp 154–57.
15. Maurice Hurst, *Music and the Stage in New Zealand*, Charles Begg & Co, p 194.
16. Thomson, *Oxford History of New Zealand Music*, p 155.
17. *Press* editorial, 3 February 1920, quoted in Thomson, *Oxford History of New Zealand Music*, pp 155–56.
18. Ibid.
19. JM Thomson, *A Distant Music: The Life and Times of Alfred Hill, 1870–1960,* Oxford University Press, 1980, pp 188–89.
20. Joseph Gordon Coates was chosen as prime minister by caucus, on the death in 1925 of Rt Hon William Ferguson Massey.
21. The Radio Broadcasting Company chairman was William Goodfellow, and its general manager, Ambrose Reeves Harris.
22. Patrick Day, *The Radio Years: A History of Broadcasting in New Zealand*, Auckland University Press, 1994, p 66.
23. Peter Downes and Peter Harcourt, *Voices in the Air: Radio Broadcasting in New Zealand – A Documentary*, Methuen/Radio New Zealand, 1976, p 38.
24. Day, *Radio Years*, p 89.
25. Ibid.
26. Thomson, *The Oxford History of New Zealand Music,* p 142.
27. Announcement made by James Shelley, on opening the Titahi Bay transmitter, 25 January 1937, *Radio Record*, 20 August 1937.
28. Letter: Messrs Moston, Caldew and Buick, led by AR Wright. NBS file, now Archives New Zealand.
29. Later Sir Joseph Heenan (1888–1951), undersecretary of Department of Internal Affairs.
30. Centennial Music Festival Committee: Tonks, *New Zealand Symphony Orchestra*, pp 10–14.
31. Maurice Clare, a highly regarded violinist from London, entered military service in 1941 and left New Zealand.
32. Isobel Baillie, *Never Sing Louder than Lovely*, Hutchinson, 1982, pp 124–128.
33. NZBS file, now Archives New Zealand.
34. Owen Jensen, *The NZBC Symphony Orchestra*, AH & AW Reed, 1966, p 23.
35. Peter Glen (principal horn, 1946–82), interview with author, May 1982.
36. Tonks, *New Zealand Symphony Orchestra*, p 20.
37. The speakers were Walter Nash, Deputy Prime Minister, later Prime Minister, 1957–60; Professor Shelley; Jim Collins, secretary, New Zealand Musicians Union; and George Poore, principal flute, National Orchestra.
38. Alex Lindsay 1919–74. Studied at Royal College of Music and served in Royal and New Zealand navies, before returning as founding sub-leader of the National Orchestra, 1946–47. He established the Alex Lindsay String Orchestra – New Zealand's second professional orchestra (1948–73). Awarded an Arts Advisory Council grant in 1963 Lindsay studied at the Salzburg Mozarteum, and later freelanced in leading London orchestras, becoming principal of the 2nd violins in both the London Philharmonic and the London Symphony. In 1969 he rejoined NZBCSO and was its first concertmaster, until his death in 1974.
39. Tonks, *New Zealand Symphony Orchestra*, pp 43–44.
40. Thomson, *Oxford History of New Zealand Music*, p 125.
41. John Hopkins, interview with author, 1983.
42. Ibid.

43. John Hopkins, interview with author, 1983
44. Sir Charles Groves (1915–92) English conductor. Conducted NZSO in 1976, 1980, 1982, 1984, and 1987.
45. Tonks, *New Zealand Symphony Orchestra*, p. 88.
46. John Hopkins, interview with author, 1983.
47. James Hartstonge, interview with author, 13 May 1983.
48. John Hopkins, interview with author, 1983.
49. National Orchestra of New Zealand, Appointment of Conductor 1956–1959, NZBS 21/2/1 part 4.
50. Tonks, *New Zealand Symphony Orchestra*, p 115. NZBS 21/2/1 part 4.

Chapter 3: Into Orbit

1. *Christchurch Star Sun*, 1 February 1958.
2. *Auckland Star*, 6 March 1958.
3. *Christchurch Star Sun*, 12 April 1958.
4. James Robertson, interview with author, 1981.
5. T Telford, letter, *Otago Daily Times*, undated clipping, circa 1958.
6. NZBS, letter, *Otago Daily Times*, undated clipping, circa 1958.
7. John Hopkins, interview with author, 1983.
8. Ibid.
9. Angela Lindsay, interview with author, February 2009.
10. Coralie Leyland, violin, NZBC Concert Orchestra and National Orchestra, 1962–64.
11. Thomson, *Oxford History of New Zealand Music*, p 277.
12. John Hopkins, interview with author, 1983.
13. Thomson, *Oxford History of New Zealand Music*, p 125.
14. NZBCSO National Youth Orchestra File, 21/12/1, Archives New Zealand.
15. Tonks, *New Zealand Symphony Orchestra*, p 116.
16. NZBCSO National Youth Orchestra File, 21/12/1, Archives New Zealand.
17. Walter Harris to Dr Bernard Beeby, Director of Education, 23 May 1958.
18. NZBS NYO file, 21/12/-, Archives New Zealand.
19. James Hartstonge, concert manager 1951–59; first Director-General, Radio New Zealand, 1975–77.
20. Tonks, *New Zealand Symphony Orchestra*, p 116.
21. NZBS file, 8 October 1958, Archives New Zealand.
22. Ibid.
23. Ashley Heenan 1925–2004, the son of Sir Joseph Heenan. BMus, Victoria University. Awarded a government bursary 1948, studied Royal College of Music (London) 1948–50. Service in NZBS/BCNZ and NZSO 1943–47, 1951–84, as music librarian; concert section touring representative; musical assistant to resident conductors, 1954–67; music organiser 1964–67; conductor and musical director NYO 1965–75 and Schola Musica 1961–84. Musical co-ordinator QE2 Arts Council, 1964–65; musical director NZ Ballet Co, 1966–68, New Zealand consultant (and from 1956) New Zealand writer-director APRA; chairman APRA Music Committee in New Zealand, 1966–81; chairman New Zealand Composers Foundation from inception 1981 until 1992, when it was discontinued. Author and writer of many articles, and publications on musical subjects; UNESCO Fellowship 1962–63. Composer of 21 compositions listed in Philip Norman (ed.), *Bibliography of New Zealand Compositions*, Nota Bene Music, 1991.
24. Peter Averi, ONZM, organist, arts administrator, and broadcaster. NZBS programmes division 1951–1973, NZSO concert manager/assistant general manager 1974–87; Wellington City Opera controller of productions, 1988–90; artistic administrator, 1991–96; musical director of *Praise Be* (TVNZ) from 1999.

25. Geoffrey Newson, foundation double bass player, National Orchestra 1946–48; NZBS; Radio New Zealand 1978, first manager of National and Concert Networks; NZSO music administrator 1975–78; manager, Alex Lindsay String Orchestra, 1948–73.
26. Peter Averi, interview with author, 1984.
27. David Smale has played in amateur and semi-professional orchestras since his NYO years, in conjunction with his professional life as a geologist. Email to author, 15 September 2009.
28. *Dominion*, 18 April 1959.
29. *Christchurch Star*, 15 May 1959.
30. Brent Southgate, violin, did not reapply for the NYO; later first director of schools broadcasts. Brent's brother, Sir William Southgate (NYO French horn, 1960–62), is an international conductor, and composer.
31. *Evening Post*, 5 September 1959.
32. Michael McIntyre, email to author, 24 February 2009.
33. National Youth Orchestra brochure and programmes, September 1959.
34. *Evening Post*, 5 September 1959.
35. Ibid., 11 September 1959.
36. Ibid., 12 September 1959.
37. *Dominion*, 11 September 1959.
38. *Dominion*, 12 September 1959.
39. Radio broadcaster 'Aunt Daisy' Basham was known nationally for her daily *Morning Session*, which was broadcast on all stations of the Commercial Broadcasting Service, 1936–63.
40. Juliana Radaich, interview with author, 22 March 2009.

Chapter 4: 'A Harvest Rich Beyond our Knowing'

1. NZBS file 21/12/1, 8 December 1959.
2. *Taranaki Herald*, 4 May 1959; *Hawkes Bay Tribunal*, 23 May 1959.
3. Report, 23 June 1959, NZBC NYO file B5 21/12/1
4. Michael McIntyre, email to author, 22 February 2009.
5. Tonks, *New Zealand Symphony Orchestra*, p 120.
6. Ibid.
7. Janetta McStay, pianist, teacher, accompanist, and chamber musician. A New Zealand Scholarship winner and gold medalist at the Royal Academy of Music, she toured Britain under the auspices of the Arts Council and broadcast on all services of the BBC. On her return in 1954, she performed with: the National Orchestra/NZBCSO/NZSO between 1964 and 1969, and 1974 and 1976; the Alex Lindsay Orchestra; the Chamber Music Federation New Zealand, and accompanied many international artists. She became professor of music at the University of Auckland in 1963.
8. NZBC memo, 4 September 1960.
9. Letter, *Evening Post*, 1 September 1961.
10. Lois Belton de Lucenay abandoned her work towards a doctorate in French literature at the university in Aix-en-Provence when, after a year of flute lessons in Zurich with André Jaunet, she became drawn to recorder and one-keyed baroque flute. Intense studies, including solfège, followed, and Lois qualified in the French conservatorium system. Now a teacher and performer, she lives in Charolles in Burgundy, and heads a team which aims to build an organ for the local church, suitable for 17th-century European (especially French) music.
11. Alex Cowdell, violinist, teacher, and composer. Orchestra trainee 1961–63. Born in Scotland, and educated at Waihi College where his music teacher was Christopher Small. Studied at Elder

Conservatorium. Played in the South Australian Symphony Orchestra, then was for many years 1st violinist in the English National Opera Orchestra. Returned to New Zealand in 2005. Freelance player in Auckland.

12. Russell Bond, *Dominion*, 1 September 1961.
13. Gerald Newson, NZBCSO 1965–67; freelancing London (one year); London Symphony Orchestra bass section 1969–2009 (40 years). Now retired, he maintains his keen interest in the welfare of musicians, through involvement at the highest level in the Musicians Union and the Performer Board of Phonographic Performance Ltd.
14. Gillian Witton (Roberts) became a primary school teacher because her father thought that the 'life of a professional musician was too precarious'. First director of Howick School of Music; first leader of Howick Orchestra; has had a 30-year association with Wellington Chamber Orchestra – as player, immediate past president, and life member.
15. NZBC memo, Archives New Zealand.
16. Gail Jensen, NZBCSO 1961–66; 1974; daughter of well-known musician and music writer, Owen Jensen.
17. Concert manager 1959–66.
18. Tonks, *New Zealand Symphony Orchestra*, p 122.
19. Turnovsky to Schroder, 11 November 1959.
20. Tonks, *New Zealand Symphony Orchestra*, pp 123–24.
21. Ibid.
22. Sir Joseph Heenan was the first public servant to be knighted in New Zealand. As Internal Affairs undersecretary and clerk of the writs, 1935–49, he played a central role in New Zealand's musical emergence. He also co-founded the Olympic movement in New Zealand, and was manager and coach of the New Zealand boxing team for the 1932 Olympics.
23. JW Heenan to Prime Minister and Minister of Internal Affairs, 12 February 1948. NZBS file, 'Overseas Artists Employed by NZBC, Policy File'.
24. Ashley Heenan, interview with author, September 1984.
25. Ashley Heenan, *NZBC Schola Musicum: A Commentary & some Personal Reminiscences on the NZBC Orchestral Trainee Scheme*, 1974, p 6.
26. Now Toi Whakaari, home to New Zealand Drama School, and New Zealand School of Dance, Newtown.
27. NZBC Concert Orchestra, formed 1962–64, accompanied the New Zealand Opera company and New Zealand Ballet company. It also performed concerts in its own right. James Robertson was resident conductor.
28. Gary Brain, orchestra trainee 1964–65; NZBCSO Study Training Bursary (Berlin Staathche Hochscule (5 months)); played 3rd timpani, Berlin Philharmonic under Karajan; Indiana University (summer semester); extra BBC Welsh Orchestra; Royal Philharmonic and BBC Training Orchestra 1967–68. NZBCSO/NZSO 1965–89.
29. Heenan, *NZBC Schola Musicum*, pp 13–14.
30. Ibid, p. 6; 1962 NYO Programme.
31. Bela Siki performed with the National Orchestra/NZBCSO/NZSO in 1954, 1960, 1962 and 1984.
32. 1962 NYO Programme.
33. CFB [Charles Foster Browne], *Press*, 31 August 1962.
34. Ron Adams, a former member of the John Ritchie String Orchestra and Christchurch Civic Orchestra, has played in major choral, opera, ballet and symphonic works, under conductors including Hopkins, Matteucci and Dobbs: 'Enjoyable though these years were, they were only possible through the experience and grounding received as a member of the NYO, for which I will always be grateful.'
35. Warwick Slinn, tuba 1959–63. Professor of English, head of the School of English and Media Studies at Massey University (2002–07) and deputy pro-vice chancellor for the College of Humanities and Social

Sciences (2007). Now professor emeritus of Massey University. Warwick Slinn, email to author, 1 March 2009.

36. *New Zealand Herald*, 6 September 1963.

37. Linda Roberts (later Geard, now Simmons). Orchestra trainee 1967–68; NZBCSO/NZSO 1968–69; 1972–90; Vector Wellington Orchestra, viola, from 2003. Linda retired because of over-use syndrome, in 1990. She was a self-employed landscape designer for 13 years. After returning to playing in 2003, she says: 'My soul has finally been returned.'

38. Linda Simmons, email to author, February 2009.

39. Peter Walls, chief executive NZSO from 2002, Previously deputy chairman NZSO Board 1996–2002; BMus, MA (Hons) (Victoria University), DPhil (Oxford), LRSM, LTCL, professor of music, Victoria University, 1993–2002, emeritus professor of music 2006; music director of The Tudor Consort, 1990–99; conductor (orchestral, choral, and opera); early music specialist; author of the award-winning *Music in the English Courtly Masque* (Oxford 1996) and *History, Imagination and the Performance of Music* (Suffolk UK, Rochester NY, 2003); trustee of New Zealand String Quartet; member, Music Advisory Committee of the Lilburn Trust; chair, Creative and Performing Arts Panel for the New Zealand Tertiary Education Commission – and a member of the equivalent panel in Britain; music director of Opus Orchestra, Hamilton.

40. *Wanganui Chronicle*, 7 September 1963.

41. Programme, NYO, 1963.

42. Keith Hunter played trumpet in the Auckland Symphonia (now Auckland Philharmonia) before beginning a career as a broadcaster, and later as a freelance film maker, writer and director.

43. Charles Buttrose, *Playing for Australia: A Story about ABC Orchestras and Music in Australia*, Australian Broadcasting Commission, 1982, p 71.

44. John Hopkins, *Auckland Star*, 3 October 1963.

45. *New Zealand Herald*, 2 October 1963.

46. Juan Matteucci OBE studied conducting at the Verdi Conservatorium in Milan, both cellist and conductor he held positions with leading Chilean orchestras, and was principal conductor, Philharmonic Orchestra of Chile (8 years); principal conductor, NZBCSO, 1964– 69; resident conductor, Auckland Regional Orchestra 1969–80; musical director for National Opera and Mercury [Auckland] Opera, and guest conducted internationally. Died Auckland 1990, aged 70.

47. László Heltay attended the State Conservatoire and Franz Liszt Academy in Budapest, where he studied with Zoltán Kodály and Matyás Seiber, and at Merton College, in Oxford where he formed the Kodály Choir and Orchestra. He returned to England in 1966.

48. In a distinguished career from 1927 to 2011, Maurice Till has accompanied many leading artists, including Berl Senofsky, Elisabeth Schwarzkopf, Uto Ughi, Victoria de los Angeles, Kiri Te Kanawa, and Pierre Fournier. He has taught major New Zealand pianists (including Richard Mapp, Michael Houstoun, Sharon Joy Vogan, Terrence Dennis, and Sarah Watson) at the universities of Otago and Christchurch; the latter institution awarding him the honorary degree of Doctor of Music, in 2000.

49. Stephen Guest, NYO violin 1964–68, 1971. Studied philosophy and law, and is Professor of Legal Philosophy at University College London.

50. NYO Programme, 1965.

51. *New Zealand Listener*, 7 September 1965.

52. Neil Shepherd settled down to a banking career, and then became an analyst programmer. He retired in 2007 after 43 years. Now, he says, 'Violin and viola playing on a non-professional basis have taken me around the world, to Germany: Bach 250th anniversary; to Tonga with a Tongan Methodist Choir, in 2003; Iceland, with the Viola Society, 2005; and China, with the Auckland Symphony Orchestra, a large community orchestra, in 2007.' Shepherd to author, undated.

53. Glynne Adams, principal viola, National Orchestra/NZBCSO (violin and viola, 1950–51, 1955–66); first recipient NZBC Orchestra Bursary.

54. Vyvyan Yendoll. Principal viola NZSO 1966–2009, principal emeritus, 2009. Linda Simmons email to author, 8 August, 2009.

55. Hugh Townend, NYO 1964–67. Through his student years he played in the Dunedin Civic and Symphonia of Auckland. He has practised medicine in Rotorua, the United Kingdom, and Wellington, and has enjoyed playing viola in amateur orchestras and chamber music groups whenever possible.
56. Hugh Townend to author, 20 September 2009
57. Donna Awatere (later Awatere-Huata) then a promising young opera singer and contralto profundo recitalist, won the *New Zealand Herald* Aria Competition, 1969. A member of the Māori protest group Ngā Tamatoa in the early 1970s, Awatere was a prominent figure in opposition to the 1981 Springbok Tour, and was author of *Maori Sovereignty* (1984) and other publications. The holder of many prominent appointments, she became an Act Party list MP in 1996.
58. Linda Simmons to author, February 2009 (see note 38 in this chapter).
59. Wellington Polytech School of Design.
60. Department of Industry and Commerce.
61. Peter Wilton, orchestra trainee 1968–69; NZBCSO 1970–71; co-principal oboe, Berlin Symphony Orchestra 1976–1988.
62. Fiona Knight to author, 18 February 2009.
63. Thomson, *Oxford History of New Zealand Music*, p 191.
64. Fiona Knight to author, 18 February 2009.
65. Belinda Blunt, aged 10, was the youngest player. She was placed second in the Concerto Competition aged 12, and later studied in London with judge Alfredo Campoli. Joined London Philharmonic aged 19.
66. Craig Pollock became the NZSO's marketing manager, in the 1990s.
67. Fiona Knight to author, 18 February 2009.
68. Peter Nisbet, then NZBC head of music.
69. Nicholas Sandle, orchestra trainee, 1970–73; NZSO 1973–.
70. Alwyn Palmer, interview with author, 3 December 2008.
71. John Chisholm, assistant concertmaster and acting concertmaster NZSO, 1970–84, died in 1984, aged 37. His name is commemorated in the John Chisholm Concertmaster Prize, awarded annually to NYO concertmasters.
72. Bruce McKinnon's career began aged 10, in the Mt Roskill Brass Band; he was the first New Zealand percussion student at Victoria University of Wellington, graduating 1974; he has toured with many international acts and musicals; presented a series on National Radio, *Lightly Percussive* 1976–85; was an arranger and conductor for TVNZ; a founding member of CadeNZa; an occasional player with Stroma. Principal percussion, Auckland Philharmonia, 1980–88; principal percussion, NZSO, 1989–2007; section principal emeritus 2007–. Bruce has taught at Cambridge Music School, Auckland University; and currently teaches percussion at the New Zealand School of Music.
73. Bruce McKinnon, emails to author, April–May 2009.
74. Michael Houstoun, a pupil of Maurice Till, first performed with NZBCSO aged twenty, in 1971. He was placed third in the Van Cliburn International piano competition, in Texas, in 1973; fourth in the Leeds Competition, in 1975; and sixth in the Tchaikovsky Competition in Moscow, in 1982.
75. John Hopkins had conducted the adagietto from Symphony no 5 in 1960.
76. Programme note.
77. Alwyn Palmer, interview and emails to author, February–June 2009.
78. Ibid.

Chapter 5: The Grand Tour

The primary source in this chapter is Peter Averi (RNZ transcripts; Averi interviewed by author: 1984–85, 2008–09; 'A Musical Journey', vols 1 & 2, unpublished memoir; Averi, emails to author, 2008–10).

1. David Bollard, New Zealand born, and a long-time resident of Australia; eminent chamber music and recital pianist and teacher.
2. Peter Averi, email to author, 14 March 2009.
3. Phillip Sametz, in *Play On! 60 years of Music-making with the Sydney Symphony Orchestra*, Australian Broadcasting Corporation, 1992, p 290.
4. Peter Averi, email to author, 14 March 2009.
5. Ibid.
6. *The Australian*, 22 October 1974. The comment acknowledges the orchestra's heavy workload on this tour.
7. *Mirror*, 16 October 1974.
8. Peter Averi, cable to NZBC, 21 October 1974.
9. A memorial concert was held for Alex Lindsay MBE on 23 March 1975, at which the establishment of the Alex Lindsay Memorial Award was announced, to assist young instrumentalists to further their musical studies.
10. *Sydney Morning Herald*, 16 October 1974.
11. *Sunday Telegraph*, 16 October 1974.
12. International Festival of Youth Orchestras, Aberdeen, Brochure, 1975.
13. The Long Island Youth Orchestra had visited New Zealand, and invited NYO to perform in Long Island.
14. Alwyn Palmer, internal report,NZSO National Youth Orchestra World Tour, 1975, BCNZ 21/12/4 Archives New Zealand.
15. Peter Nisbet, later appointed NZSO's first general manager and artistic director, April 1977.
16. Grant Cooper, personal communication, March 2009. Virginia Symphony Orchestra, Charleston, West Virginia, United States; was previously resident conductor, Syracuse Symphony Orchestra, 1997–2007, after studies with principal trumpets of Cleveland and New York Philharmonic orchestras; principal trumpet Tulsa Philharmonic ('for a couple of years') then Professor of Trumpet, State University of New York (11 years), where he gradually transitioned into conducting. Grant continues to compose music, much of it specifically designed to introduce young audiences to the symphony orchestra.
17. Juan Matteucci was then conductor of the Symphonia of Auckland.
18. Grant Cooper, email to author, March 2009.
19. Averi, 'A Musical Journey', p 838.
20. Ibid, p 840.
21. Peter Averi, personal communication, January 2009.
22. *National Youth Orchestra of New Zealand Overseas Tour'75*, booklet,1975.
23. Rex Collins organised this world tour and would have accompanied it, but had to withdraw for health reasons. He became NZSO travel manager, 1989–92. In 2002 he joined the subcommittee, NZSO Alumni Association, and chaired reunions in 2002 and 2006; by then he had been elected chairman.
24. Donald Armstrong, violin, orchestra trainee 1974–76; leader NYO 1974–75; NZSO 1977–78, Arts Council Bursary, ALMA Scholarship; post-graduate diploma, Mannes College, New York; masters degree, New England Conservatory; principal 2nd violin, Tivoli Sinfoniorkester Denmark; concertmaster, Orchestre Philharmonique de Nice; associate concertmaster, NZSO 1987– (acting concertmaster 1992–93); leader and musical director, New Zealand Chamber Orchestra, 1987–2004. Donald also performs with his own chamber group, the Amici Ensemble, conducts other New Zealand orchestras, and is an artist teacher, New Zealand School of Music.

25. RNZ broadcast report, prepared and presented by Peter Averi. A series of live radio reports were broadcast twice weekly on the National Programme of Radio New Zealand throughout this tour – a feature especially appreciated not only by the families and friends of NYO players, but also of interest to the wider music community in New Zealand.
26. *Press and Journal*, 5 August 1975.
27. August, undated clipping.
28. Also known as the 'Bavarian Brass Beer Band'.
29. Alan McKenzie and Paul Morris are both since deceased.
30. Kenneth Young, tuba, NYO 1974–76, 1986; principal tuba NZSO, 1976–2003; NZSO conductor-in-residence 1993–1996 and composer.
31. Ken Young, emails to author, May 2010.
32. Warwick Braithwaite, guest conductor National Orchestra 1947; resident conductor 1953–54.
33. Peter Averi, quoting his letter to Lilburn in an interview with author, January 2009.
34. *Press and Journal*, 15 August 1975.
35. Simon Miller, NYO violin, 1973–77, leader 1978–79; orchestra trainee, 1974; gained degrees in history and music from Otago and Victoria universities; post-graduate studies for Dip Mus in Brisbane and Hobart; played in Queensland Symphony and Theatre orchestras; joined Tasmanian Symphony (3 years); NZSO 2nd violins, 1986–. Email to author, 20 April 2009.
36. Ursula Evans, NYO violin, 1974–76. Awarded DAAD Post Graduate Scholarship musikhochschule, Cologne; member Philharmonic Essen 1987–91; NZSO first violins 1991–.
37. Wilma Smith, NZSO 1977–78. Studied performance New England Conservatory, in Boston; 1st violin, Lydian String Quartet, Brandeis University, Massachusetts; established and led New Zealand String Quartet 1981–; NZSO concertmaster, 1993–2002; associate concertmaster, Melbourne Symphony Orchestra, 2003–.
38. Wilma Smith, emails to author, January 2009.
39. Averi, RNZ broadcast transcript.
40. Ibid. Roger Brown studied with Jacqueline du Pré and Antonio Janigro. He returned to New Zealand after 23 years in London and joined the NZSO in 1999.
41. Abbado was simultaneously director of the Vienna Philharmonic Orchestra.
42. Grant Cooper, emails to author, March 2009.
43. Averi, 'A Musical Journey', p 855; Averi, interviewed by author, January 2009.
44. Averi, RNZ broadcast transcript.
45. James Robertson (1912–91). Conductor of National Orchestra (1954–57) and NZ Opera (1962–63, 1978–81).
46. John Matheson (1928–2009). Conductor, studied at the Royal College of Music, and had a distinguished international career based in the United Kingdom, particularly in positions at Sadlers Wells and Covent Garden.
47. Marise White (now McNeill). After NYO, studied in Brussels; taught percussion and violin at British School of Brussels. Trained at Christchurch Teachers' College; taught Hutt Valley High School (4 years), now has a private music studio in Palmerston North teaching young children violin and viola.
48. Rupert Bond lives in Kingsbridge, United Kingdom. He is a conductor, composer, and educator, and was made an associate of the Royal Academy of Music for his services to music, in 1999. Returned to New Zealand 2006–2007, performed with Auckland Philharmonia and Christchurch Symphony Orchestra, and was principal conductor Camerata Strings.
49. Averi, 'A Musical Journey', p 862.
50. *Evening Post*, September 1975.
51. Averi, 'A Musical Journey', pp 866–67.
52. Ibid.
53. Ibid., p 868.

54. In return for this visit by New Zealand's National Youth Orchestra, the Shanghai Philharmonica made its first visit to New Zealand, in November 1975, giving performances in Hamilton, Auckland, Christchurch, and Wellington.
55. Keith Spragg, NYO clarinet 1969, 1970–75 (principal). Christchurch Symphony Orchestra, performed regularly from 1970 (10 years); Tasmanian Symphony, from 1980, full-time (one year) part-time (4 years). Keith is now business manager, Middleton Grange School, Christchurch, but 'still plays in the CSO, from time to time'. Email to author, 10 February 2009.
56. One of the infamous Gang of Four, deposed fourteen months later, in October 1976.
57. Greg Hill, French horn, NYO 1972–75; Elizabethan Orchestra, Sydney (18 months); Melbourne Symphony (12 months), Tasmanian Symphony, and concurrently lecturer in horn at the Conservatoire of Music, Tasmania (6 years), NZSO, 1987– now principal horn. Interview with author, 11 February 2009; email to author, May 2010.
58. Ken Young interview and emails to author, 21–23 May 2010.
59. Averi previously had been given a leather wallet and signed card, and he later joined orchestra members 'for a few drinks and a sing-along'until 3 am.
60. Glenda Craven (now van Drimmelen) violin, NYO 1974–75; orchestra trainee 1974–76; NZSO 1977–93. An excerpt from Glenda's talk on the tour, given to pupils at Samuel Marsden Collegiate, her former school.
61. *Press*, 22 September 1975.
62. Advertising flyer, 1975.
63. Soloists alternated on tour, but due to some unscheduled changes in programmes, some listings may not be accurate.

Chapter 6: In the Aftermath

1. John Hopkins with William Cottam, *The Point of the Baton*, Lyrebird, 2009, p 69.
2. Peter Averi, 'A Musical Journey', p 848.
3. Undated letter to Averi from the Festival of Youth Orchestras and Performing Arts, Signed by Joy Bryer.
4. Averi, 'A Musical Journey', p 843.
5. Ibid., p 851.
6. This letter was typed on the letterhead of the hotel in Tokyo, so it was not compiled or signed until the end of the tour. It is not known if any orchestra trainees were aware of this letter, or invited to sign it.
7. Averi, email to author, 15 June 2010.
8. 'Some senior players who felt demoralised by Heenan's attitude approached me in Aberdeen', Averi says. 'I suggested they put their concerns in writing, and I would pass them on to the Director General. Bev Malcolm and I then had a meeting with Ashley Heenan, and I told him he was "ruining the tour." He sulked for a day or two after this and then refused to go to the Lord Provost Dinner, when his hatred of the "Bryer Mob" reached a climax.' Averi, email to author, 15 June 2010.
9. Averi to director general BCNZ, 29 September 1975.
10. Averi to author, 6 January 2009.
11. According to Donald Armstrong, 'the dissident group was pretty much everyone outside the trainees by the end of the tour'. Email to author, 10 October 2009.
12. Heenan, 24 November 1975.
13. Averi to Heenan, 5 January 1976.
14. 30 December 1975.
15. The 'doubt' refers to Ashley Heenan's unsuccessful attempts to discover the ownership of the typewriter on which the player's letter was written. Director General's file, 1975 World Tour.
16. Heenan insisted that there was 'a dissident group' on the tour, and Averi remains adamant that there was not.

17. The author is not aware of any other correspondence or disciplinary action taken subsequently, after Hartstonge retired.
18. Ashley Heenan, 'Annual Assessments', BCNZ and RNZ, personal file.
19. Edward Pople, interview with author and emails, February–May 2009.
20. As confirmed by Beverley Wakem. Personal communication, 5 October 2009.
21. Geoffrey Whitehead, BBC 1967–74; assistant director general Radio New Zealand 1974–76, director general 1976–84; manager director Australian Broadcasting Corporation 1984–86; director New Zealand Historic Places Trust 1989–97.
22. Beverley Wakem CBE (1990), chief ombudsman of New Zealand in 2008, was one of the first New Zealand women to break through the so-called 'glass ceiling' with her appointment as director general of Radio New Zealand, 1984–88. She has also held positions as chief executive officer of Radio New Zealand, 1988–91, and general manager, Wrightson Ltd, 1991–96; and has served on the Remuneration Authority, 1997–2005.
23. Heenan's behaviour was said to include sarcasm, aggression, and the bullying of players, colleagues, and outsiders alike.
24. Julia White, now McNeill, NYO percussion 1974–79. Emails to author January–April 2009.
25. Wilma Smith, emails to author, January–April 2008.
26. Elena (Eleanor Houtman), of Ngāti Kahungunu and Rongomaiwahine descent, orchestra trainee and NYO violin, 1973–75, well-known and flamboyant violinist. Elena plays in the Vector Wellington Orchestra, and also enjoys the versatility of freelancing. Elena's Cultural Symphony premiered at Michael Fowler Centre, Wellington, in 2004, and in 2006 she performed this at the Shanghai International Arts Festival, in China, where she was praised for 'mixing Maori music into classical music in an extraordinary way'. Elena led a cultural delegation to Xiamen, Wellington's sister city, in 2008, and returned to Shanghai in 2010 to perform in the opening ceremony of the World Expo. She is the subject of two documentaries, *Pushing the Boundaries* (on her life), and *Breaking the Boundaries* (on her journey to China).
27. Alison Heenan, NYO viola 1975–1977, now Western Australia Symphony Orchestra.
28. Donald Armstrong also notes: 'I suspect Heenan was worried that most of the trainees would not pass audition, and I think this could have been the case.' Email to author, October 2009.
29. Wilfred Simenauer, co-principal cello, NZSO 1965–93
30. Peter Averi, 'A Musical Journey'; Averi, personal communication, 16 April 2010.
31. The *Turandot* performances were on 19 and 21 August 1976.
32. The NZBC Concert Orchestra, formed in 1962 to accompany the National Opera and New Zealand Ballet companies, also performed its own concerts. It was dissolved in 1964, and many of its players joined an expanded NZBC Symphony Orchestra.
33. James Robertson was musical and artistic director of the National Opera, and first director of the London Opera Company.
34. Milla Andrew was born in Canada of Russian parents, and made her operatic debut in Canada. Subsequently she sang leading roles with Sadlers Wells, Glyndebourne, Covent Garden, and in the United States and Europe.
35. J L Hartstonge, *An Introduction to 1976*, printed programme.
36. Averi, 'A Musical Journey'; emails to author, June 2010.
37. The name was changed in 1977, on advice from an academic at Victoria University, that 'Musicum' was inaccurate because of the confusion of Greek and Latin texts, and the correct title should be "Schola Musica." The change was made 'immediately', Averi says.
38. Kenneth Young to Peter Nisbet, 22 May 1977.
39. Various letters, BCNZ and NZSO files, May–June 1977
40. March 1976, exact date unknown.
41. *Sunday News,* 29 August 1977.

42. Refer chapter seven.
43. Pat Downey, chairman, Radio New Zealand 1975–76; board member NZBC 1973–78; OBE, 1991.
44. The Orchestra Advisory Committee was set up by Pat Downey.
45. Heenan was on sick leave for 82 days, from 31 October 1977 to 20 January 1978.
46. Ted Pople held this position while maintaining his career as a performing artist and music educationalist.
47. *Heenan v Broadcasting*, Supreme Court of New Zealand, 24 April 1979.
48. Judgment of Vautier J, 24 April 1979.
49. Letter dated 12 May 1980.
50. Awarded by Composers Association of New Zealand, for 'Outstanding Services to New Zealand Music, as Musical Director of Schola Musica'.
51. *Concert Pitch* 17, January 1985.
52. Glenda van Drimmelen, interview with author, 16 March 2010.
53. Alison Bowcott-Gibbs, NYO viola, 1974; orchestra trainee 1971–74; NZSO 1974–94, Dunedin Sinfonia, June 1994–; BA in philosophy, Dip Grad in bioethics, Otago University; accepted into 2nd year law but decided not to continue, as she can only do one paper per year, and would be '104 when I graduate!'
54. Reginald Sutton, foundation player, violin, National Orchestra/NZBCSO, 1946–70.
55. *Concert Pitch* 17, January 1985, pp 10–12.

Chapter 7: Guest Conductors and an Australian Tour

1. American Peter Schaffer was concertmaster, San Francisco Opera Orchestra, before becoming the NZSO's first non-NZ concertmaster, 1976–1984.
2. German-born US based conductor André Previn was then conductor of the London Symphony Orchestra.
3. NYO printed programme, 1978.
4. Glenda Rodgers, violin NYO 1978–80, 82, orchestra trainee 1981–82, has lived and and worked in London for 24 years, and played in orchestras including English Concert Orchestra; Kings College, Cambridge; London Soloists Chamber Orchestra, City of London Sinfonia. In collaboration with a designer, Glenda also works on books and material for teaching string instruments; and art works. Glenda Rodgers, emails to author, January 2009.
5. Georg Tintner, 1917–99, was resident conductor of the Australian Opera, 1968–71, and also conducted the youth orchestras of both Australia and Canada.
6. Formerly Mary-Anne Owen, violin, orchestra trainee 1980–83, leader Schola Musica. Married to conductor Andrew Sewell, lives in the United States.
7. Terry Gibbs, son of Michael (Mike) Gibbs, legendary NZSO (1953–1994) and jazz trumpeter, lives in London, and works in UK Immigration. Terry says he is a keen concert-goer, and also plays in many and varied amateur music groups in West London. Terry Gibbs email to author, 5 March 2009.
8. Jeff McNeill is senior lecturer in environmental planning, Massey University, Palmerston North. Email to author, 15 February 2009.
9. Uri Segal conducted six NZSO tours over 16 years (1971–86), and an acclaimed EMI recording of Mahler's Fourth Symphony, with soprano Malvina Major, in 1976.
10. Grant Cooper was a fellow in trumpet at Tanglewood 1978, assistant director of bands at Yale University 1977–79, and in 1980 was principal trumpet in the Tulsa (Oklahoma) Philharmonic. He became music director, West Virginia Symphony Orchestra, in 2001.
11. Richard Wigley became a member of the bassoon section of the Halle Orchestra in Manchester, and is presently general manager, BBC Philharmonic. Richard Wigley, email to author, 16 February 2009.

12. Philip Jane (MusB, Dip Lib, PhD) NZSO 2nd violins, 1976–89, was a librarian, University of Canterbury and is now a private researcher in music history. Email to author, 3 May 2011.
13. *Concert Pitch* 3, July 1980.
14. Sandra Crawshaw (violin and keyboard, 1981–83). Played casually in Auckland Philharmonia Orchestra while studying piano with Brian Sayer at the University of Auckland, and became principal 2nd violin, Southern Sinfonia (Dunedin).
15. *Concert Pitch* 9, March 1982.
16. Ibid.
17. Ibid.
18. *Concert Pitch* 10, July 1982.
19. Mark Walton later served on the Royal Overseas League's panel of adjudicators; he is currently head of the Christchurch School of Instrumental Music.
20. Now known as Marya Martin.
21. Beverley (Bev) Malcolm, interview with author, *Concert Pitch* 10, July 1982, p 22.
22. Schola Musica, *Canzona Music for Strings and Voices* by Douglas Lilburn. They recorded a fifth, *Music for Strings*, featuring John Ritchie's *Aquarius* Suite, and works by Anthony Ritchie and others.
23. *Concert Pitch* 11, November 1982.
24. Houstoun's career by now included significant placings in 3 major international piano concerto competitions: Van Cliburn 1972, placed 3rd (aged 20); Leeds 1975, 4th (aged 23), and Tchaikovsky in Moscow, 1982, 6th. His first appearance as an NZSO soloist was in 1972, and he performed with the orchestra on tour to Australia, 1974, and Hong Kong, 1980, in the same year that he made his debut at Carnegie Hall in New York.
25. Palmer, personal communication, 13 June 2009.
26. Derek Hopper, trumpeter (1984–85), is now a high school music and chemistry teacher, 'still playing a lot'. Derek Hopper, email to author, 11 February 2009.
27. *Concert Pitch* 16, August 1984.
28. Dr Franz-Paul Decker, NZSO principal guest conductor, 1984–88; chief conductor 1990–94; conductor laureate from 1995.
29. Katherine Austin is lecturer in piano at the School of Music, University of Waikato.
30. Palmer, personal communication, 13 June 2009.
31. Mary Sewell, email to author, 13 February 2009.
32. Peter Shaw, writer and presenter of *The Decker Years*, a four-part series of music, and commentary on Franz-Paul Decker's years conducting the NZSO, produced by Radio New Zealand Concert, first broadcast October 2009.
33. Peter Shaw, email to author, 20 March 2009.
34. Principal 2nd violin, National Orchestra 1955–57; NZBCSO/NZSO 1967–98; NYO tutor and auditioner.
35. Seamus Hogan is head of the department of economics and finance, University of Canterbury. 'In a non-musical career I occasionally jam string quartets for fun; but I'm hoping to re-live my musical career through my children.' Seamus Hogan, emails to author, 28 February and 25 March 2009.
36. Andrew Sewell, conductor of the Wisconsin Chamber Orchestra and the Wichita Symphony, has implemented Side by Side concerts with both the Wisconsin and Wichita Youth Symphony Orchestras.
37. Mary-Anne Sewell (née Owen), Schola Musica 1980–83 (and leader). Email to author, 13 February 2009.
38. Tim Young is executive director, Reno Philharmonic Association, Reno, United States, a regional professional orchestra with a budget of US$2 million. The orchestra has two youth orchestras and, Tim says, 'I often think of my NZYO experiences when I see them in rehearsal or performance. Three of my four boys play in these orchestras.' Tim Young email to author, 27 February 2009.
39. *Concert Pitch* 17, January 1985, p12.

40. *Concert Pitch* 18, June 1985, pp 20–21.
41. Ibid.
42. Ibid. 19, October 1985, p 20.
43. Ibid. 18, June 1985 p 20–21.
44. Alwyn Palmer, interview with author, 3 December 2008.
45. Alan Broadbent, New Zealand jazz composer, left for the United States in 1966, where he became well-known for his work with Woody Herman.
46. Alwyn Palmer, interview with author, 3 December 2008.
47. Michael Vinten, email to author, 13 April 2009.
48. Mark Sheppard is now an urban designer and plays in the Melbourne Sinfonia ('amateur but reasonably high level'). Email to author, 2 March 2009.
49. Palmer, email to author, 19 February 2009.
50. Hugh Rennie CBE, Queen's counsel, chairman BCNZ 1984–88.
51. NZYO programme, 1985.
52. Palmer, email to author, 12 June 2009.
53. Erica Challis plays in the Vector Wellington Orchestra and freelances.
54. *Concert Pitch* 23, January 1987, pp 20–21.
55. Lisa Egen, violin and viola, Schola Musica 1986–88; leader, NZSO 1988–.
56. Sarah Thompson studied horn in Germany, and then freelanced in Southern Germany and Switzerland, 1988–91. Sarah returned to New Zealand and trained and worked as an ambulance paramedic, and still 'plays when time permits'. Sarah Thompson, email to author, 27 February 2009.
57. Dr Calvin Scott is now strategy adviser, Creative New Zealand.
58. Craig Utting, Schola Musica 1988–89; MA in composition, Victoria University of Wellington. Craig is a violist in the Vector Wellington Orchestra, also currently a piano teacher, and administrator for a music school in Tawa. Email to author, 11 February 2009.
59. Stephen de Pledge, a solo pianist based in United Kingdom for seventeen years, performs and records internationally. In 2009 Stephen gave four piano recitals for Chamber Music New Zealand; his appointment as senior lecturer, school of music, Auckland University, was announced; and also his return to New Zealand. Email to author, 24 February 2009; *Cook Strait News*, 2 September 2009.
60. Advertisement, *Concert Pitch* 27, June 1988, p 18.
61. Te Rangatahi literally means, 'the new net', and members of the Māori cultural group represent the next generation of singers and dancers of their coastal village, Porangahau, in Hawkes Bay.
62. *Concert Pitch* 28, October 1988, pp 22–23.
63. Official programme, 'Queensland Youth Orchestra's International Festival of Youth Orchestras', p 34.
64. *Concert Pitch* 28, October 1988.
65. This award commemorates the NZSO's late assistant concertmaster, John Chisholm, leader of the National Youth Orchestra in 1967 and 1971.
66. Tom Warren's instruments are used by many professional players, including NZSO members.
67. Palmer to author.
68. *Concert Pitch* 29, November 1988.
69. Alwyn Palmer, interview with author, 3 December 2008.
70. His Excellency, the Honourable Sir Walter Campbell QC.
71. Anita Gude played in Auckland Philharmonia four years, and is now a freelance violist in various orchestras and active in chamber music ensembles in The Netherlands. In 2006 Anita set up 'Musical Mysteries' for primary- and intermediate-aged children, giving concerts at schools and other venues, in The Netherlands, Aruba, New Zealand, Australia, and England. Personal communication, 2 June 2009.

72. Alwyn Palmer had sent the orchestration in advance. Two verses were played of the Ashley Heenan arrangement, but no words were supplied for the second verse, which, as embarrassed New Zealand players discovered, few of them knew.
73. Programme, *Queensland Youth Orchestra's International Festival of Youth Orchestras*, 2 August 1988.
74. Craig Utting, email to author, 11 February 2009.
75. Ibid.
76. Ian Fraser, later commissioner general to Expo 92 in Seville; chief executive NZSO and TVNZ.
77. BCNZ magazine, *Talkback*, undated clipping; article also reprinted in other New Zealand newspapers.
78. Concert review, clipping from unknown Brisbane newspaper, date unknown.
79. *The Queensland Youth Orchestra's International Festival of Youth Orchestras* – New Zealand Youth Orchestra.
80. Alwyn and Gay Palmer to author, 3 December 2008.
81. Ibid.
82. Michael Vinten to author, 4 July 2010.
83. *Newcastle Courier*, 20 August 1988.
84. 'Dog' was on display at the NYO's 50th anniversary in 2009, and was then donated to the Salvation Army.
85. Michael Houstoun, email to author, 26 October 2009.
86. *Concert Pitch* 29, November 1988, p 19.
87. Michael Vinten, email to author, 13 April 2009.
88. Alwyn Palmer, interview with author, 12 June 2009.
89. In comparison, 24 New Zealand players played in the International Festival Orchestra in 1975.

Chapter 8: 'Cast adrift'

1. Palmer, interview with author, 13 June 2009.
2. 'The Company', *Concert Pitch* 30, June 1989.
3. Ibid.
4. James Loughran won the Philharmonia Orchestra's Conducting Competition in 1961, and has since conducted all leading British orchestras and opera companies. He was concurrently principal conductor and musical advisor to the Halle Orchestra (1971–83), principal conductor, Bamberg Symphony, 1979–83 and, from 1987, the Halle's conductor laureate. Loughran was then newly appointed chief guest conductor of the BBC Welsh Orchestra; and was a favourite conductor of the Henry Wood Proms in London.
5. *Concert Pitch* 30, June 1989, pp 26–27.
6. NZYO concert programme 1989.
7. Palmer, interview with author, 13 June 2009.
8. *Concert Pitch* 30, June 1989.
9. Palmer, interview with author, 12 June 2009.
10. Craig Utting, email to author, 11 February 2009.
11. Palmer, interview with author, 12 June 2009.
12. Ibid.
13. *Concert Pitch* 31, October 1989.
14. Victoria University School of Music, in Wellington.
15. Elizabeth Kerr, an inaugural member of the NZSO board, is now chief executive SOUNZ. Previous positions include chief executive Creative New Zealand; chief executive Historic Places Trust; chief

executive Relationship Services NZ; Arts Council of New Zealand music programme manager; lecturer in music Victoria University; manager Concert FM, Radio New Zealand.

16. Simon Tipping, associate professor and programme leader, Massey University Conservatorium of Music; conductor, writer on choral music and orchestras in New Zealand.
17. Michael Vinten, in Tonks, *Bravo, the NZSO at 50!*, p 179.
18. The Auckland Philharmonic, Vector Wellington, Christchurch Symphony, and Southern Sinfonia orchestras.
19. Michael Vinten, email to author, 13 and 20 April 2009.
20. Eugene Albulescu won TVNZ/NZSO Young Musicians Award 1986, aged sixteen, and first performed with NZSO in the Proms, 1987. He won the International Grand Prix di Liszt, for his debut CD recording of Liszt piano works, and also included Liszt in his recent début at Carnegie Hall. Albulescu is now associate professor of music, LeHigh University, in Bethlehem, Pennsylvania, where he uses an innovative programme, 'Inside the Piano'.
21. *Concert Pitch* 32, January 1990, pp 10–11. Philip Walsh was director of music, Wellington Cathedral of St Paul, 1989–99.
22. JM Thomson, *Biographical Dictionary of New Zealand Composers*, Victoria University Press, 1990.
23. Craig Utting, email to author, 11 February 2009.
24. Sharon Callaghan (née Tongs), orchestra trainee June–September 1987; NZSO 1987–92.
25. Michael Steer, orchestra trainee 1983–85; NZSO 1986–95.
26. Gareth Farr did not apply for NYO, having regular work as a percussionist with APO and NZSO.
27. *Concert Pitch* 34, 1990, p 28.
28. World Youth Festival programme, 29 August–22 September 1990.
29. Ibid.
30. World Youth Festival information.
31. Palmer, interview with author, 12 June 2009.
32. Hopkins, *The Point of the Baton*, p 118.
33. Karen Grylls ONZM, PhD, MMus Hons. Associate head Undergraduate Studies; associate professor in conducting and head of Choral Studies, University of Auckland. Musical director New Zealand Youth Choir and founder musical director Voices New Zealand.
34. World Youth Festival, Official Souvenir Programme, 1990.
35. Commissioned for the World Youth Festival by the Concert Programme of Radio New Zealand.
36. Philip Norman is a composer of music for stage, opera, ballet and orchestra. His works include *Footrot Flats*, *A Christmas Carol*, *Peter Pan*, and *The Juggler*. He is also an author, whose works include his distinguished biography *Douglas Lilburn: His Life and Music* (2006). Norman's current book is a general history of New Zealand compositions.
37. Reviewer for the *Press*, also musical director of *Praise Be* (TVNZ) in Christchurch.
38. Outer Control, from Hornby High School.
39. Philip Norman, emails to author, 26 January and 10 February 2009.
40. Peter Averi, email to author, 24 July 2010.
41. Kate Kingston, née Hansen, is a former music administrator at Victoria University School of Music, and currently 'a full-time mum'. Kate, a second generation NYO member, is the daughter of Alison McKenzie (Hansen), NYO cello 1960–66.
42. Sarah McClelland (Jacobsen), email to author, 13 July 2009; Jeunesses Musicales World Youth Orchestra 1993–95.
43. Granddaughter of Charles Nalden, daughter of David Nalden, NYO violin, 1959.
44. Matthew Ross, graduated Canterbury University, 1992. He studied at the Rotterdam Conservatorium and gained experience overseas, including Jeunesses Musicales World Youth Orchestra 1993–95. NZSO 1st violins, 1994–2002; concertmaster, Vector Wellington Orchestra, since 2002.

45. Joy Aberdein, NZSO publicity and PR manager 1985–2004, later NZSO marketing and communications manager 1999–2000, editor *NZSO Symphony Quarterly* 1994–2000 and *Notes* 2001–2005, is now a freelance classical music writer and editor *Ritmico Journal.*
46. Paddy Nash, administrator for NZ Youth Choir, 1955–58, NYO "Orchestra mum", 1990–93, 95.
47. Bridget Douglas graduated from Victoria University School of Music, and undertook further studies in the United States. She was appointed associate principal flute, NZSO, in 1997, and principal flute in 2000.
48. Houstoun, email to author, 26 October 2009.
49. *Concert Pitch* 32, January 1990.
50. A 10-page pamphlet, issued by Broadcasting Corporation of New Zealand.
51. July 1991 when Minister of Finance Ruth Richardson delivered her infamous 'Mother of all Budgets'.
52. *Concert Pitch* commenced in March 1980; its last issue was in July 1991.
53. *Dominion*, 22 October 1991.
54. Peter Nisbet was head of music, BCNZ/RNZ, 1970–77; general manager and artistic director, NZSO, 1977–92.
55. Tonks, *Bravo*, pp 62–64.
56. Russian conductors Kurt (1981) and Thomas Sanderling (1983, 1986) were the second father and son to conduct the NZSO. Another son, Stefan Sanderling (a half brother of Thomas) conducted the NZSO in 2005.
57. Nicholas Braithwaite: chief conductor, Adelaide Symphony (1987–91); principal conductor Manchester Camerata from 1984; is a frequent guest conductor of all major orchestras in the United Kingdom, Europe, Japan and Korea. He is a respected opera conductor, and also known for his work with youth orchestras, and his recordings, one of which, *Flute Concertos with Alexa Still* (NYO 1979–80, NZSO 1987–1999) and New Zealand Chamber Orchestra, earned a Grammy Award nomination in 1992.
58. *Evening Post*, 31 August 1992.
59. Paid from the reparations fund set up as a result of the bilateral resolution of the *Rainbow Warrior* bombing in 1985.
60. New Zealand Post NYO programme 1993.
61. Gary Brain conducts orchestras in London, and throughout Europe and Scandinavia. He conducted Philharmonia Orchestra in Aldeburgh (Snape Maltings), Athens, and Chichester festivals; Bamberg Symphoniker (Festival of Saint-Florent-Le-Vieil); and was musical director of the Festival of Fontainbleau, Paris, 2009. His recordings for various labels – with several world premiere works and first recordings among them – include works by Rossini, Truscott, Marek (Preis der Deutschen Schallplattenkritik 1997), Ippolitov-Ivanov, Collet, and Mysliveček.
62. Rita Paczian, MMus (conducting and organ), Lübeck Musikhochschule, was a musical assistant to Martin Haselböck at the Viennese Baroque Orchestra Wiener Akademie, and was organist and choirmaster at St Jacob (Hamburg). Rita emigrated to New Zealand in 1999. Now a freelance conductor and organist, she performs throughout the world, and is music and artistic director of Bach Musica NZ, in Auckland.
63. Peter Averi performed as organist in the NZSO performance of Saint-Saëns' *Organ* Symphony under chief conductor Gyorgy Lehel in Dunedin, 29 July 1989. (Averi, email to author, 24 July 2010). This was the final work and NZSO concert for Lehel, who died six weeks later on 23 September, and for Gary Brain as timpanist.
64. Dr Joe Harrop is music performance lecturer, University College Falmouth, Cornwall, United Kingdom.
65. Yid-Ee Goh, studied Victoria University School of Music; concertmaster Vector Orchestra 1998–2001; Studied Music Therapy in London; director and music therapist Raukatauri Music Therapy Centre; string teacher, concertmaster, in Auckland.
66. Paczian, emails to author, 15–26 July 2010.
67. Performing in this concert were forty surviving members of the Sarajevo Philharmonic Orchestra, the Sinfonica di Milano and soloists François Pollet and Simon Estes.

68. Hamish Keith, 'The Real Art Roadshow', *Listener*, 28 February 2009.
69. Alwyn and Gae Palmer, interview with author, 19 February 2009, and August 2010.
70. *Symphony Quarterly* 6, July 1994.
71. Mark Keyworth, an Australian, was deputy general manager of Queensland Arts Council for ten years; manager Royal New Zealand Ballet, 1986–92; chief executive NZSO, 1992–98. He then returned to Queensland.
72. 'What's On', *Dominion*, January 1995.
73. Allan Badley, NZSO artistic development and general manager New Zealand Chamber Orchestra, 1984–96.
74. *Symphony Quarterly* 6, July 1995.
75. Ashley Brown, Christchurch-born winner TVNZ Young Musicians Competition and a TVNZ Young Achievers Award, later won prizes at the ROSL Music Competition in London. Cellist of the New Zealand Trio (with Justine Cormack, and Sarah Watkins).
76. Philip Norman, email to author, 19 October 2009.
77. The Scott Report 1996 was commissioned jointly by the NZSO Board and shareholding ministers, 'to provide information on the financial needs of the Orchestra and any matters of operation that may require attention in the future'. 'Editorial', *Symphony Quarterly* 9, June 1996.
78. Sir Selwyn Cushing KNZM 1999, for services to business, sport and the arts, CMG, ACIS, CMA, FCA.
79. Dame Catherine Tizard (former Governor-General), Barry Dineen (company director formerly of Shell NZ), Joe Pope (chief executive Apple and Pear Marketing Board), Bronwen Holdsworth (*More* Businesswoman of the Year 1988), Elmar Toime (chief executive New Zealand Post and chairman NZSO Foundation), and Peter Walls (professor of music at Victoria University).
80. *Evening Post*, 14 May 1996.
81. Ibid.
82. New Zealand Post message, NZPNYO programme 1995.
83. 1996 National Youth Orchestra Report. NZSO.
84. John Dodds, NZSO violin 1955–57, principal 2nd violin, 1967–98.
85. This organisation was invited to take over advertising for the concert in return for all box office takings.
86. 1996 National Youth Orchestra Report. NZSO.
87. *Capital Times,* 10 September 1996.
88. The founding members of the NZSO Foundation were Elmar Toime (chair), Lloyd Morrison, Michael Stiassny, Patsy Reddy, Ruth Harley OBE, and John Allen. *Symphony Quarterly* 11, January 1997, pp 20–21.
89. *Capital Times,* 10 September 1997.
90. *Evening Post*, 1 September 1997
91. Dr Peter Ramsauer, former managing director of Salzburg Mozarteum Orchestra.
92. NZNYO internal report, based on comments from players, 29 October 1997.
93. Kirstin Eade is associate principal flute, NZSO.
94. Malcolm Mawhinney is a music teacher and freelance player in Shanghai, China. He has established a chamber music collective, and is a member of a core string quartet.
95. Lindy Tennent-Brown studied piano at Victoria University of Wellington and the Royal Northern College of Music; held junior fellowships at RNCM and Royal College of Music, London. Inaugural Wigmore Young Artist, 2003–95, and one-half of the prize-winning longfordbrown piano duo, Lindy now maintains a freelance career as pianist, music director and vocal coach, working for the Royal Opera House, Covent Garden, the English National Opera, and several West End musicals. Email to author, 11 August 2010.

Chapter 9: 'What a gift!'

1. Christiaan (Chris) van der Zee, BMus Hons, Victoria University of Wellington, postgraduate studies in Germany. Founder member Tasman Quartet, 2006–09: Anna van der Zee (née Broadbent), leader; James Andrewes and Jennifer Banks, violin; Christiaan van der Zee, viola; Miranda Wilson, cello (all alumni of NYO, late 1990s/2000).
2. Michael Joel, freelance orchestral and operatic conductor, viola player, Vector Wellington Orchestra, and teacher.
3. Lindy Tennent-Brown, email to author, 11 August 2010.
4. Ian Fraser, OBE, chief executive NZSO 1998–2003; New Zealand Commissioner-General, World Expo Seville (1992) and Brisbane (1988); executive officer performing arts Queen Elizabeth II Arts Council; television presenter, actor, musician; chief executive Television New Zealand. Emails and phone call, 26–31 August 2010.
5. The camp was postponed because of events in Tiananmen Square.
6. Yo Yo Ma, Chinese cellist born in France 1955. Moved to New York, and has given public concerts from the age of five, achieving international eminence as soloist.
7. Cho-Liang Lin, born in Taiwan, 1960, has performed with many major orchestras in a global career over 28 years, and performed with the Asian Youth Orchestra, March–April 2009.
8. Benjamin Zander studied composition under Benjamin Britten and Imogen Holst, aged 12. At 15 he began studies with the Spanish cellist, Gaspar Cassadó, in Florence, and at the State Academy in Cologne. On completing his degree at London University, Zander travelled to United States on a Harkness Fellowship. He was founding conductor of the Boston Philharmonic (1978), and guest conductor of many other orchestras, including the Philharmonia Orchestra. A much sought-after speaker to major international organisations, from the World Economic Forum in Switzerland, to the US Army, Zander brought 'his insights as the conductor of a symphony orchestra to leaders involved in transformation and change' (NYO programme, 1999).
9. 40th NYO anniversary programme, 1999.
10. Ibid.
11. Ibid.
12. Brigid O'Meeghan, report to author.
13. 'Nimrod' from Elgar's *Enigma* variations.
14. Amelia Giles was an intern with Auckland Philharmonia; she now teaches music and directs two string ensembles and a choir at St Cuthbert's College. Amelia also plays in two historically informed baroque ensembles and is a freelance violin teacher and violinist around Auckland.
15. Bruce McKinnon (NZSO principal percussion emeritus) says, 'Yes, but NZSO played it first, and that's always harder!' McKinnon, email to author. Gareth Farr says, 'I actually don't remember saying that, but it's exactly the sort of thing I would say!' Farr, email to author, 21 April 2009.
16. Malcolm Mawhinney, personal communication.
17. M Kartomi, 'The Australian Youth Orchestra Inc: Its National Identity and Role in the Transmission of Orchestral Music in Australian Society', draft manuscript, 10 December 2006.
18. Denis and Verna Adam were the inaugural recipients of the Arts Foundation of New Zealand Award for Patronage (2006). Their support includes the Adam Art Gallery and the Adam Concert Room at Victoria University of Wellington, the Adam Foundation Prize for Creative Writing, the Adam Portraiture Award and Exhibition, the Adam Chamber Music Festival, the NZSO National Youth Orchestra, and the Adam International Cello Competition. The Adams also fund Playmarket's Adam Playreading series at Downstage Theatre as well as providing funds for an extensive number of individuals and one-off events.
19. NZSO NYO programme 2000.
20. O'Meeghan to author, 30 March 2009.
21. Helen Clark, ONZ, the 37th Prime Minister of New Zealand, served three consecutive terms, 1999–2008; administrator, United Nations Development Programme, 2009–.

22. Mark Churchill was then associate conductor of the Boston Ballet, conductor and music director of Symphony Pro Musica, music director of the Salisbury Chamber Orchestra, and guest conductor of many orchestras including New England Conservatory's Youth Repertoire Orchestra. As Dean, his work involved overseeing gifted young musicians, continuing education, and a full-time music specialist music school. He was also heavily involved in developing new curriculum and music teacher training, through the Conservatory's 'Research Centre for Learning through Music'.
23. Marylou Speaker Churchill was also an active teacher. She had served on the faculties of the Preparatory School of the New England Conservatory, the Asian Youth Orchestra and the Carnegie Hall Solti Programme, and was violin sectional coach for the New England Conservatory's Orchestral Programme. She taught at Boston University Tanglewood Institute, Musicorda Summer String programme, and was then on the faculty of Tanglewood Music Centre.
24. O'Meeghan email to author, 30 March 2009.
25. Mawhinney, personal communication.
26. Ashley Brown won the Westpac National Chamber Music (twice), National Concerto, and TVNZ Young Musicians Competitions, and TVNZ's Young Achievers Award. Two years' study at Yale University followed, and then six months' study with William Pleeth in London.
27. The Turnovsky Trio (named after Fred Turnovsky) was founded in 1991 by Sam Konise (NYO violin, 1985–88), cellist Christopher Kane (NYO 1980, NZSO 1991–97, deceased), and pianist Eugene Albulescu. The Trio performed nationally for Chamber Music New Zealand and performed special school programmes. In 1998 the Trio (now Konise, Catherine McKay, and Ashley Brown) gained residency at the University of Waikato.
28. *Evening Post*, 5 September 2000.
29. *Dominion*, 2 September 1999.
30. Lutz Köhler, known for his special affinity with young musicians, was then director of studies with the European Union Youth Orchestra, director of orchestras at the Royal Academy of Music in London, and chairman of the jury at the Munich International Music Competition. Köhler had conducted all major orchestras in Germany, and in the United States, Europe, Great Britain, and many European festivals. He was professor at the Hanover Academy of Music and Theatre for 25 years, and was appointed professor at the Berlin Academy of Arts in 1999.
31. Justin Bird, a prize- and award-winner from the age of six, later represented New Zealand at the Australasian piano concerto competition. He was a member of the winning group in the Schools Chamber Music Contest in 1997 and 1999, and was awarded a new Kawai grand piano at the AMES Awards for young achievers in 1998. A semi-finalist in the New Zealand Young Musician of the Year Competition in 1999, Justin later won the Young Performer of the Year for pianoforte in 2000.
32. *New Zealand Herald*, 8 September 1999.
33. *New Zealand Herald*, 19 September 1999.
34. Wellington Friends of NZSO was founded July 2000, through an idea promoted by NZSO chief executive Ian Fraser. Leslie Austin was the first chairman. The Friends took over the NYO BBQ and NZSO Lunchtime Seminars, in 2002. Valerie Rhodes became chairman in 2003.
35. O'Meeghan, email to author, 30 March 2009.
36. Ibid.
37. Amalia Hall, NYO violin (1999–2004); associate concertmaster, 2006; co-concertmaster 2007, 2009; currently studying at the prestigious Curtis Institute of Music. Lara, violin (1992, 1993, 1995, 1997, 1999), concertmaster 2000, 2002–03, gained her masters and doctorate in violin performance at the University of Michigan. She was appointed lecturer in violin and viola at the University of Waikato in 2006, and is concertmaster of the Opus Orchestra and a member of New Zealand Chamber Soloists. Elroy, violin (1996–2000, 2002–04), concertmaster Auckland Youth Orchestra, 2002–03, is currently teaching violin in Auckland and Hamilton. Callum, cello, 2000, 2003–05, principal 2006, co-principal 2007; completed his masters degree at the University of Waikato, 2008, and is studying for a doctorate in cello performance at Michigan State University, United States.
38. O'Meeghan to author, 30 March 2009.

Chapter 10: 'Taste of the real thing'

1. Pascale Parenteau, NZSO NYO report to author, 14 April 2009.
2. David Gilling studied Royal College of Music, 1981–85; freelanced BBC Philharmonic; played in the Britten Pears Orchestra at Aldeburgh; co-leader Christchurch Symphony; NZSO 1987 to present, sub-principal 2nd violins.
3. NZSO, *Notes* 8, September 2004.
4. Parenteau, NZSO NYO report to author, 14 April 2009.
5. Alasdair Neale was previously associate conductor San Francisco Symphony, and music director, San Francisco Youth Orchestra (12 years). Neale's other guest conducting engagements included the New York Philharmonic, San Francisco Symphony, and Orchestre National de Lyon.
6. *New Zealand Herald*, 6 September 2004.
7. *Press*, 6 September 2004, p 4.
8. Robin Toan, BMus (composition and clarinet) 2003; significant prizes awarded 2004 include Philip Neill Memorial Prize and the University of Auckland Douglas Lilburn Composition Prize Concert, in both electronic and acoustic categories.
9. John Psathas, associate professor in composition, New Zealand School of Music, Victoria University; Arts Laureate 2003; composer of music for 2000 Olympic Games in Athens.
10. John Psathas, Mentor's Report, 2005.
11. *Dominion Post*, 25 August 2009.
12. *Press*, 26 August 2005.
13. *Capital Times*, 31 August 2005, p 9.
14. Tonks, *Bravo!*, pp 127–49.
15. Grant Gilbert, interviews with author, 14 January 2009.
16. Parenteau to author, 14 April 2009.
17. Claire Cowan studied composition at Auckland University. She had had work performed by NZSO, and also writes for film, theatre and dance, and television commecials. Also a performance cellist, Claire plays in Toad, an alt-Gothic folk band.
18. Ross Harris QSM, NYO French horn 1966, NZSO 1969–70. Studied composition with Douglas Lilburn, Victoria University, and taught there for 33 years. A prolific composer of over 150 works, including electronic, opera, symphonies, chamber music, klezmer and jazz. Won CANZ citation for services to New Zealand music 1990, and has been a frequent winner of the SOUNZ Contemporary Award.
19. Parenteau to author, 14 April 2009.
20. Nézet-Séguin was also artistic director of the Orchestre Métropolitain in Montréal, and the winner of three coveted Prix Opus prizes awarded by the Conseil Québécois de la Musique.
21. *Dominion Post*, 5 September 2007.
22. Parenteau to author, 14 April 2009.
23. President Rex Collins, Sharyn Evans, Gil Evans, Nancy Luther, Joy Tonks, Michael Cuncannon.
24. Jacques Lacombe, born in Quebec, is artistic director and principal conductor of the Ochestre Symphonique de Trois-Rivières; and was principal guest conductor, Montreal Symphony 2002–06. He made his Metropolitan Opera debut conducting *Werther*, and conducted the world premiere of *Fanny et Marius* by Vladimir Cosma with Angela Gheorghiu and Roberta Alagna at the Opera de Marseille, 2007/08; Lacombe has conducted Monte Carlo Opera, Deutsche Oper Berlin, L'Opera de Montreal, and Vancouver Opera.
25. Recording works by Lyell Cresswell and Beethoven for soprano and orchestra for the Naxos label.
26. Madeleine Pierard, BMus (Hons 1st class), Victoria University; began her vocal training in New Zealand Youth Choir, Voice New Zealand and the Tudor Consort. PGDip with Distinction, Royal College of Music; studied with Lillian Watson, Benjamin Britten International Opera School, London; many scholarships and awards, including the Great Elm Award, Wigmore Hall. Performances include Meleagro in *Atalanta*, London Handel Festival; Marzelline in *Fidelio* with the APO and the NBR

New Zealand Opera; appearances as a guest with Dame Kiri Te Kanawa and Jonathan Lemalu; as soloist with the NZSO on its tour to China; and for HRH Queen Elizabeth II at Westminster Abbey, for the Commonwealth Day Observance, 2008; premiered Ross Harris's Symphony no 2 with the APO.

27. Rod Biss, '"Access to all Areas": A rare glimpse behind the scenes with the National Youth Orchestra', *New Zealand Listener*, 17 October 2008.
28. David Sell, *Press*, 28 August 2009.
29. William Dart, *New Zealand Herald*, 1 September 2009.
30. Quesionnaires 2008.
31. Peter Walls, NZSO NYO programme, 2008, p 5.

Chapter 11: Celebrating 50 years, plus

1. Richard Gill is a pre-eminent and much-admired conductor in Australia, with an international reputation as a music educator, specialising in opera, musical theatre, vocal and choral training.
2. Vesa-Matti Leppänen, born Turku, Finland. Studied Sibelius Academy of Music, held leading roles in Turku Philharmonic. He became concertmaster NZSO in 2005. He is a featured artist for Naxos, and teaches at the New Zealand School of Music.
3. Pascale Parenteau, excerpts from official report 'NZSO National Youth Orchestra, 2009'.
4. Eyal Kless is a member of the Manchester Piano Quartet, professor in the Royal Northern College of Music, and Buchman-Mehta Academy in Tel-Aviv, and teaches at Chethams School of Music, in Manchester. He has taught at the Royal Irish Academy for Music in Dublin (8 years), the Summer Festival in Salzburg (6 years), and is regularly invited to be part of the jury panel for international competitions. Kless is the author of *Zen and the Art of Violin Practicing* (available from www.eyalkless.com).
5. Excerpts from official report by physiotherapist Greg King.
6. Peter Williams, musician and reviewer, is also NZSO's representative in Hawke's Bay.
7. NZSO IT administrator and accounts support.
8. NZSO Auckland regional representative.
9. David Pawsey died 1 December 2008.
10. Valerie and Alan Rhodes, email to author, 31 March 2009.
11. Edited extracts from a report on NZSO NYO national music camp. Valerie Rhodes, email to author, 31 March 2009.
12. Edited comments from the Conductor's Report, NZSO NYO national music camp, January 2009.
13. Amber Vickery, emails to author, 8 and 15 February 2009.
14. NZSO principal percussion.
15. Tim Myhill, letter to Pascale Parenteau.
16. *NZSO National Youth Orchestra Report*, 2009, p 23.
17. NZSO NYO pre-course report, undated.
18. Sarah Claman, email to author, 26 May 2009.
19. 'Education '09', NZSO brochure, 2009.
20. Beth Goodwin, email to author, 4 June 2009.
21. Paul Daniel also has conducted opera at the Royal Opera House, Frankfurt Opera, Geneva Opera, Bayerische Staatsoper, and Frankfurt Opera.
22. Ross Harris, Composer Mentor Report, 2010.
23. Angela Lindsay, composers John and Helen Rimmer, Dr Stephen Guest, and Edward Pople were interviewed by Robbie Ellis, *Upbeat*, RNZ Concert; Jane Freed and David Kempton were interviewed by Lynn Freedman, *Arts on Sunday*, RNZ National. Pascale Parenteau was interviewed by Eva Radich, *Upbeat*, RNZ Concert, 4 May 2009; John Hopkins, interviewed by Eva Radich, 6 July 2009.

24. Sharyn Evans née Green, formerly McKenzie, NYO 1972–73; trainee 1969–72; NZSO 2nd violins, June 1972–; Gil Evans, principal trumpet NZSO, 1964–96; Nancy Luther, NZSO flute/piccolo, April 1973–; Brigid O'Meeghan; Norbert Heuser, NZSO viola, 1975–; Alwyn Palmer; Joy Tonks; Hannah Anderson, NZSO development executive; Rachel Hyde, former NZSO manager artistic planning.
25. *Dominion Post*, 6 July 2009.
26. Gemma New received one of four places in the masters in orchestral conducting course, Peabody Conservatorium, Johns Hopkins University, Baltimore. *Dominion Post*, 19 August 2009.
27. See appendix F.
28. Marion Tulloch (Townend) NYO viola, 1964–65, played professionally in Auckland and Australia, married Hugh Townend, NYO viola 1964–67, and was active in teaching and promoting music in Rotorua; she was also a member of Lake District Strings and Opus Orchestra. Andrew Townend, NYO viola 2000, is her son.
29. Beth Goodwin hopes to teach music, 'especially to those who want to learn but can't afford it, both in New Zealand and my country of birth, Zimbabwe, where music tuition is only offered to the very rich. I'd love to be able to change this as several of my teachers have been able to do for me.' Beth Goodwin, emails to author, 3 June and 5 November 2009.
30. John Hopkins to Peter Walls, July 2009.
31. Pascale Parenteau to author, September 2010.
32. Claire Lewis studied music at Cardiff University before taking up a position as vocal animateur and project manager with Welsh National Opera. After several years coordinating chamber opera tours and community choirs of up to 300 individuals, Claire moved to the Royal Philharmonic Orchestra and managed orchestral education projects across the United Kingdom.
33. Rossen Milanov studied at the Julliard School, Curtis Institute, Duquesne University, and Bulgarian National Academy of Music – and conducts in the United States, Great Britain, and Europe. A committed supporter of youth, Milanov is music director of both the New Symphony Orchestra (a privately funded youth orchestra in Sofia) and Symphony C (a leading professional training orchestra in the United States).
34. In 2008, aged 16, Jason Bae won the Bradshaw & Buono International Piano Competition in New York, where he had a debut recital in Carnegie Hall's Weill Recital Hall. Jason Bae was winner of the New Zealand Young Performer of the Year Award in 2008.
35. Alexandra Hay graduated New Zealand School of Music (hons 1st class, 2007); and studied musicology at Freie Universität in Berlin under a DAAD scholarship. She was recipient of the 2008 NZSO Todd Corporation Young Composer Award, and her work has been performed internationally. Alexandra began her DMA as a Fulbright NZ Fellow at Stanford University in September 2010.
36. Claire Lewis, email to author, 13 September 2010.
37. Grant Cooper – rallying call prior to NYO's world tour in 1975.

Chapter 12: Future Proofing

1. 'Conductor of the People', *New York Times*, 28 October 2007.

Bibliography

Primary sources for this book were official files and records of New Zealand Broadcasting Service, New Zealand Broadcasting Corporation, Broadcasting Corporation of New Zealand and New Zealand Symphony Orchestra (held on site by NZSO, or transferred to Archives New Zealand) – unless otherwise stated.

Broadcasting House, 1963–1997: If these walls could talk ..., Radio New Zealand and Whitireia Publishing with Daphne Brasell Associates, 1997.

Buttrose, Charles, *Playing for Australia: A Story about ABC Orchestras and Music in Australia*, Australian Broadcasting Commission/The Macmillan Company of Australia, 1982.

Cottam, William, *John Hopkins: The Point of the Baton*, Lyrebird Press, School of Music, University of Melbourne, Australia, 2009.

Day, Patrick, *The Radio Years: A History of Broadcasting in New Zealand*, volume one, Auckland University Press, in association with the Broadcasting History Trust, Auckland 1994.

——, *Voice & Vision: A History of Broadcasting in New Zealand*, volume two, Auckland University Press, in association with the Broadcasting History Trust, Auckland 2000.

Downes, Peter & Peter Harcourt, *Voices in the Air, Radio Broadcasting in New Zealand: A Documentary*. Methuen Publications in association with Radio New Zealand, Wellington, 1976.

Heenan, Ashley, *NZBC Schola Musicum, a commentary & some personal reminiscences on the NZBC orchestral training scheme*, booklet, 1974.

Hollinrake, Roger, *The Life and Times of Horace Hollinrake 1904-55*, Mayfield Press, Oxford, UK, 2009.

Hurst, Maurice, *Music and the Stage in New Zealand, a Century of entertainment 1840–1943*. Charles Begg, Wellington, 1944.

Jensen, Owen, *NZBC Symphony Orchestra*, AH & AW Reed, Wellington, 1966.

Norman, Philip, *Bibliography of New Zealand Compositions, Editions 2 & 3*, Nota Bene Music, 1982, 1991

——, *Douglas Lilburn, His Life and Music*, Canterbury Press, Christchurch, 2006.

Renwick, William (ed.), *Creating a National Spirit, Celebrating New Zealand's Centennial*, Victoria University Press, Wellington, 2004.

Simpson, Adrienne and Newson, Geoffrey, *Alex Lindsay, the Man and his Music*, School of Music, University of Canterbury, Christchurch, 1998.

Thomson, John Mansfield, *A Distant Music: The Life and Times of Alfred Hill, 1870-1960*, Oxford University Press, Auckland, 1980.

——, *Into a New Key, the Origins and History of the Music Federation of New Zealand, 1950-1982*, The Music Federation of New Zealand, 1985.

——, *The Biographical Dictionary of New Zealand Composers*, Victoria University Press, Wellington, 1980.

——, *The Oxford History of New Zealand Music*, Oxford University Press, Auckland, 1991.

Tonks, Joy, *Bravo! The NZSO at 50*, Exisle Publishing, Auckland, 1996.

——, *The New Zealand Symphony Orchestra, The First Forty Years*, Reed Methuen, Auckland, 1986.

Recordings

The Best of National Youth Orchestra, 1972-74, NZSO 1975.

Michael Houstoun, piano. Ashley Heenan, conductor, Souvenir recording (box album) includes works by Bach, Brahms, Beethoven, Mahler, Tchaikovsky, Ravel.

National Youth Orchestra Return Concert, Christchurch, 1975, Radio New Zealand 1975.

Keith Spragg, clarinet, Ashley Heenan, conductor. Lilburn: Aotearoa Overture, Ritchie: Concerto for clarinet, other works by Haydn, Kodaly, Ho Ching-Chi, Ting Yi.

National Youth Orchestra in China, 1975 – Radio New Zealand (45 rpm) 1975.

New Zealand National Youth Orchestra and members Shanghai Philharmonic Soc, recorded in Peking by Radio Peking, 1975. Works include 'White-haired Girl' and 'Children of the Grasslands'.

National Youth Orchestra, NZ Post, NZSO Youth Orchestra – annual concerts recorded and broadcast by Radio New Zealand Concert, and its precursors.

Index

Italic page numbers denote images.

4YA Orchestra, 11
10th anniversary tour, 60–62
40th anniversary, 188
50th anniversary, 188, 198, 208–10, 212–13, 220–31
65th Regimental Band, 10

Abbado, Claudio, *78*, 80, 82, 83, 84, 99, 103
ABC *see* Australian Broadcasting Commission
ABC Training Orchestra, 70
Aberdeen, 77–78, 81, 105
Aberdeen City Police Pipe Band, 78
Aberdein, Joy, 164–65, 173
Aberystwyth, 84–85
Abreu, José Antonio, 234, 239
Academy of St Martin in the Fields, 205
Adam, Denis, 188, 209, 223, 225
Adam, Verna, 188
Adam Foundation, 188, 192, 223, 227
Adam International Cello Competition, 175
Adams, Glynne, 54
Adams, John *The Chairman Dances*, 228, 234
Adams, Juliana (Radaich), 2, 5, 34–35
Adams, Ron, 47, 48–49
Adelaide Festival, 51
Adelstein, Bernard, 84
Aim, Greg, *130*
Alard String Quartet, 235
Albulescu, Eugene, *159*, 159
Alex Lindsay Memorial Awards, 190, 191, 223
Alexander, Shelley, 137
Allen, Vivienne, 160
Alley, Rewi, 93
Allison, Mary, 83, 99
Allison, Megan, *195*
Alloway, Jessica, 229
alumni reunion, 212, 223–24
Anderson, Lesley, 27
Anderson, Lucy, 222
Anderson, Nan, 163
Andrew, Milla, 114, *115*
Andrewes, James, *following p 118*
Andrews, Ivan, 62, *64*
Andrews, R P, 49
Angus, Rita, 214
Ansell, Gillian, *94*
Anthony, Adele, *139*, 139, 141
APEC, 185
APEC Forum Leaders Dinner, 187–88
Arbroath, 80–81
Armstrong, Donald, 69, 76, *94*, 99, 113–14, 119
Arnold, Malcolm: Concerto for Clarinet and Strings, 129, 130; *English Dances*, 114; *Scottish Dances*, 127; *Three Shanties*, 215
Arts Advisory Council, 43
Asian Youth Orchestra, 175, 183, 184
Aspey, Vincent, 2–3, 4, *16*, 18, 21, 32, 41, 52, 58
Aspey, Vincent John, 1, 3–4, 21, 34, 42
attendance, 39
Auckland Festival, 66
Auckland Junior Symphony Orchestra, 56, 66, 234
Auckland Orchestral Society, 10
Auckland Orchestral Union, 10
Auckland Philharmonia, 164, 212
Auckland Savings Bank, 73
Auckland Symphonia, 56
Auckland Symphony Orchestra, 10
Auckland University College, 10
Auckland Youth Orchestra, 142, 234
auditions, 1, 29–30, 37–38, 42, 45, 54, 66–67, 124, 133–34, 209
Aunt Daisy, 35
Austin, Katherine, 134, *134*
Australian Broadcasting Commission, 50–51
Australian Training Orchestra, 63
Australian Youth Orchestra, viii, 27, 51, 64, 144, 188, 193, 234; exchange programme, 199; summer camp, 63, 193
Austrian Mozarteum, 237
Averi, Peter, 82, 89, 103–4, 111–12, 115–16, 118, *130*, *143*, 163–64; association with NYO begins, 30; auditions, 30, 124, 133, 143; concert manager, 71; and letter of complaint, 104–9; music coordinator, 160; tension in orchestra, 102–4; world tour 1975, 73–75, 77–79, 81–85, 83, 87, 89–91, 93, 95, 97–98
Averill, Beatrice, 131, 145
Averill, Joanne, 145
Averill, Nicola, 145
Awatere, Donna, 55
Awatere, Elsie, 56

Bach, Johan Sebastian, 215; Brandenburg Concerto no 6 in B flat, 66; Double Violin Concerto in D minor, 21; Toccata and Fugue in D minor, 137

Bae, Jason Jin-Hyung, 229, 234
Baillie, Isobel, 16
Ball, Eric, 78
Bank of New Zealand, 127
barbecue lunch, 190
Barber, Peter, 76, *86*, *90*, *94*, 99
Barber, Samuel: *Adagio for Strings*, 175; *Essay for Orchestra*, 177
Barnett, Maughan, 10
Barry, 84
Barry, Edward, *65*
Bartley, Bryce, 2, *6*
Bartok, Bela, 237; Concerto for Orchestra, 207
Barton, James, *48*
Bauer, Ingrid, 222
BBC *see* British Broadcasting Corporation
BBC Henry Wood Proms, 84, 174
BBC Northern Orchestra, 21, 22
BBC Scottish Orchestra, 22
BCNZ *see* Broadcasting Corporation of New Zealand
Beck, Harold, 11
Beeby, Clarence, 29
Beecham, Thomas, 17
Beethoven, Ludwig van, 214, 235, 239; Battle Symphony, 66–67; Concerto for Piano and Orchestra no 1, 178; Egmont Overture, 205; Overture *Coriolan*, 53, 125, 184, 186, 237; Overture *Leonora*, 58, 126; Piano Concerto no 1, 237; Piano Concerto no 4, 68; Symphony no 1, vii; Symphony no 1 in C major, 32; Symphony no 3 *Eroica*, 157; Symphony no 4, 157; Symphony no 5, 125, 131, 237; Symphony no 6, 237; Symphony no 7, 62, 215–16, 226; Symphony no 8, 67; Symphony no 9, 237
Beijing, 92, 105
Bellingham, WJ, 13
Belton, Lois, 40, 57
Bemelman, Stephen, *166*
Benfell, Tony, 114
Berg, Alban *Three Orchestral Pieces*, 81, 82
Berlin Symphony Orchestra, 132
Berlioz, Hector: *Beatrice and Benedict*, 159; *Carnival Romaine* Overture, 198; Overture *Le Corsaire*, 164–65; *Roman Carnival*, 197; *Symphonie Fantastique*, 139, 142
Bernstein, Leonard, 160, 175; *Chichester Psalms*, 161
Best, Donald, *48*, 213
Bicentennial Festival International Youth Orchestra, 149
Birch, Bill, 182
Bird, Justin, *following p 118*, 190–91, *191*
Bishop, John, 10
Bizet, Georges: *Carmen*, 39; Carmen Suite no 1, vii; *Jeux d'Enfants* Suite, 97; Symphony in C, 97
Black, Peter, *130*, 149, *151*
Bloy, Leela, 10
Blunt, Belinda, *60*
Bohemian Orchestra, 10
Bollard, David, 50, 70
Bond, Rupert, 77, 88, 99
Bond, Russel, 34
Bonelli, Aurelio, 215
Bonetti, Anthony, 4
Bonifant, John, *48*
Borodin, Alexander *Prince Igor*, 41, 42
Boulez, Pierre, 170, 238
Bournemouth Symphony Orchestra, 21
Bowcott, Alison, 69, 121–22
Bowles, Michael, 20, 23
Boyce, Raymond, 58
Boyes, Jane, 58
Bradley, Allan, 175, 181
Brady, Katherine, 149
Brady, Melvin, 133
Brahms, Johannes: *Academic Festival* Overture, 68, 147; Symphony in D major, 49; Symphony no 1, 197, 198, 237; Symphony no 2, 51, 52; Symphony no 4, 191, 237
Brain, Gary, 46, 59, 66–67, *169*, 169–72
Braithwaite, Nicholas, 80, 168, *168*
Braithwaite, Warwick, 20, 23, 44–45, 168, *168*
brass band movement, 239
Bremner, David, 213, 215, *218*
Brisbane Expo 88, *following p 118*, 143–50
British Broadcasting Corporation, 21
British Festival of Youth Orchestras, 161
British Youth Orchestra, 54
Britten, Benjamin: *A Charm of Lullabies*, 127; *Peter Grimes*, 135; *Soirées Musicales*, 131; *The Young Person's Guide to the Orchestra*, 168
Broadbent, Alan *Conversation Piece*, 137
Broadcast Communications, 155
'Broadcasting' *see* New Zealand Broadcasting Service
Broadcasting Act 1936, 14
Broadcasting Amendment Act 1937, 14
Broadcasting Corporation of New Zealand, 72, 155, 156, 157
Broadcasting House, 16, 46
Broadcasting Orchestral Consultative Committee, 24
Brooke, Rupert, *86*
Brown, Ashley, 165, 175, 189
Brown, Greg, *90*
Brown, Roger, 69, 76, 83, *94*, 99
Bruch, Max Violin Concerto no 1, 55
Bryer, Joy, 72, 74, 103
Bryer, Lionel, 72
Buchanan, Dorothy, *126*
Buchanan, Dorothy *Missa De Angelis – Pro Anno Infantantum*, 125–26
Bunz, Alfred, 11
Burry, Josephine, 53, *54*
Button, John, 190, 202, 207, 224

Buttrose, Charles, 50
Buxtehude, Dieterich, 215
Byrd, William, 215; *The Earl of Oxford's March*, 215

Campbell, Fiona, 171–72
Canadian Youth Orchestra, 211, 234
Canteloube, Joseph *Chants D'Auvergne*, 114, 210
Canterbury Trio, The, 235
Canton (Kwangchow), 89–91
Cappello, Roberto, 149
Cardiff, 84
Carr, Edwin: *A Blake Cantata*, 55; *Twelve Signs for Woodwind, Brass and Percussion*, 71
Carr, Miriam, 2
Carson, Bruce, 114
Carter, Winifred, *16*
Casa Fontana, 5
Castle, Olwyn, *48*
Cave, Caroline, *130*
Centennial Exhibition of New Zealand, 15
Centennial Festival Symphony Orchestra, *16*
Centennial Music Festival, 15–16
Centennial Orchestra, 15–16, 18
Central Band of the RNZAF, 165
Challis, Erica, 139
Chamber Music New Zealand, 196
Chan, Alex, 212
Chandler, Richard, 137
Chang Chun Chiao (Zhang Chun Qiao), 93
Chen, John, 201, *201*, 222, 224–25
children at concerts, 178–79
Children of the Grasslands, 91
China, 89–95, 100; ambassador to New Zealand, 74; world tour 1975, 89–97, 105
Chisholm, Alan, 49
Chisholm, John, 49, 64–66, 114
Cho-Liang Lin, 184
Chopin, Frédéric Variations on *La ci darem la mano*, 190–91
Christchurch Exhibition Orchestra, 12
Christchurch Orchestral Society, 11
Christchurch School of Instrumental Music, 2, 234
Christchurch Symphony Orchestra, 11, 56, 164, 212
Christiansen, Luke, 212
Chu Wei *The White Haired Girl*, 87, 89, 91
Churchill, Mark, 189
Churchill, Marylou Speaker, 189
Claman, Sarah, 221
Clare, Maurice, 15, *16*
Clark, Helen, 173–74, 188
Clarke, Owen, 165, *171*
Clinton, Bill, 187
Closer Cultural Relations, 193
Coates, Gordon, 13
Coca-Cola 1990 Rock Quest, 163
code of conduct, 204–5
Coker, Geoffrey, 179
Collins, Joyce, *45*, *48*
Columbia Recording Studios, 11
Comissiona, Sergio, 183
Composer-in-Residence Award, 198–99, 201–2, 222, 229, 238
Concert Artists Programme, 199, 201
Concert Pitch, 167
Concert Renaissance de Sarejevo, 171
conductor workshop, 199
Connal, Angela, vii, 1, 26–27, *44*, 45, 223
Conservatoire of Music, Brussels, 88
convents and musical teaching, 239
Coolahan, Kate, 58
Coombs, James, 11
Cooper, Grant, 69, 73, 74, 76, 83, *84*, 99, 127, 130–31
Copland, Aaron, 215; *Billy the Kid*, 60, 129; *El Salón México*, 179; *Fanfare for the Common Man*, 215; *Rodeo*, 179
Cottam, William, 227
Cowan, Claire, *207*, 222; *Trains of Thinking*, 205, 206
Cowdell, Alexander (Alex), *41*, *48*
Coxhead, Graham, 167
Craven, Glenda, 69, *94*, 98, 99, 121
Crawshaw, Sandra, 128
Creative New Zealand, 177
Cresswell, Lyell: *Ixion*, 161; *Salm*, 142, 143
Cross, Ian, 130
CSIM, 56
Cudby, Neville, *6*
Cultural Revolution, 75
Cumming, Christine, 57, *58*
Cuncannon, Michael, *90*, *94*, 99
Currie, Kevin, *90*, *94*
Cushing, Selwyn, 176, 182

Daly, Peter, *60*
Daly-Peoples, John, 225
Dam Xuan Linh, 49
Daniel, Paul, 199, 221–22, 224, 226, 233
Danish National Radio Symphony, 164
Darroch, Hannah, 222
Dart, William, 197, 225
Davies, Meredith, *129*, 129, 135, 237
Davies, Ralph, 58
de Couteau, Denis, 149
de Lisle, Ray, 229
de Mauny, Leon, 10
de Pledge, Stephen, 143, 148, *151*
Debussy, Claude: *La Mer*, 207, 208, 212; *Prelude à l' Après-midi d'un faune* , 57; Trio for violin, cello and piano, 214
Dech, Gil, 11
Decker, Franz-Paul, 122, 133–34, *134*, 135
Delius, Frederick: *Over the Hills and Far Away*, 39; 'The Walk to the Paradise Garden', 4, 32, 235

Department of Education, 4, 5, 6, 27, 28, 36–37
Department of Internal Affairs, 72
Deutsche Staatsoper, 132
Deutsche Symphonieorchester Berlin, 207
Diprose, Margaret, *48*
Dixon, Stacey, 190
Dodds, John, *following p 118*, 177
Dog, 153, *153*, 224
Dorati, Antol, 12
Douglas, Bridget, 165–66, *171*
Downey, Patrick, 76, 118
Dresden Staatskapelle, 207
dress code, 37
dress rehearsal, 41
Dukas, Paul, 129
Dunedin Civic Orchestra, 56
Dunedin Philharmonic Orchestra, 11
Dunedin Symphony Orchestra, 11
Dunedin Youth Orchestra, 122
Dutch National Orchestra, 103
Dvořák, Antonin: Symphony no 5 in F, 133, 135; Symphony no 6 in D, 58, 237; Symphony no 7 in D minor, 64; Symphony no 8, 41; Symphony no 9 *From the New World*, 18, 201

Eade, Kirstin, 179
East, Andrew, *166*
Edwards, Flora, 158
Edwards, Helen, 45
Egen, Lisa, *following p 118*, 139, 141, 145, 149, 160
El Sistema, 239–40
Elena *see* Houtman, Eleanor (Elena)
Elgar, Edward: Cello Concerto, 183; *The Enigma Variations*, 175, 197, 198; Introduction and Allegro for string quartet and string orchestra, 41, 42; *Nimrod*, 186
English National Opera, 221
Ensemble InterContemporain, 170
Ensemble Orchestral de Paris, 170
European Community Orchestra, 183
European Community Youth Orchestra, 234
European Union Youth Orchestra, 234
Evans, Kathy, *45*, *48*
Evans, Ruthchen (Ursula), 82, *94*, 99, *101*
Evans, Ursula (Ruthchen), 82, *94*, 99, *101*
Expo '70, 64

Farr, Gareth, 160; *Dua Lagu*, 214; *Te Papa*, 187
Fauré, Gabriel Pavane in F sharp minor, 47
Faust, 16
Fenwick, Diana, 224
Fernandes, Marcel, 198
Festival of Youth Choirs, 175
financial assistance, 208–9
Findlay, Gloria, *44*, 45
Finlayson, Christopher, 240
Fitzsimons, Jeremy, *171*
Forbidden City, 93
Foster, Roland, 12
Francis, Olivia, 229
Franck, César: Symphonic Variations, 157, 159; Symphony in D, 47
Fraser, Ian, *following p 118*, 148, 182, 187
Fraser, Peter, 17
Freed, Jane, 2, *3*, 5, *44*, 45, *45*, *48*
Freyberg, Bernard, 18
Friends of NZSO, 192
Friends of NZSO, Wellington, 216–17
fund-raising, 73–74

Gadd, Sharon, 76, *94*
Galbraith, David, 58, 59, *63*
Galway, Victor, 15
Gamba, Piero, *142*, *143*
Gane, Trevor, 61
Garth Williams Scholarship, 192
Gatun Lake, 22
Gergiev, Valery, 207
Gershwin, George *An American in Paris*, 60, 61
Gervis, Claude, 215
Gibb, Laurette, 55
Gibbs, Terry, 125
Gibson, Kurt, 216
Gibson-Cornish, Bryony, 212
Gilbert, Grant, 181, 205
Giles, Amanda, 186
Gill, Richard, 213–19
Gilling, David, 196
Gilling, Dominique Marcel, 196
Glen, Peter, *6*
Glinka, Mikhail, 114, 203; *Life for the Czar*, 32; *Russlan and Ludmilla*, 39, 40, 55, 201, 236
Glubb, Maurice, 37, 42–43
Goh, Yid-Ee, 170, 171
Gold, Helen, *44*
Goodwin, Beth, 221, 226
Goran, Eli, *48*
Graham, Douglas, 176
Grainger, Percy, 14, 238; *A Lincolnshire Posy*, 66; *Londonderry Air*, 215
Granwal, Ron, 2
Great Wall of China, 94–96
Grieg, Edvard Two Elegiac Melodies for Strings, 64
Grybowski, Tony, 193
Grylls, Karen, 161
Gude, Anita, 147
Guest, Stephen, 52
guest conductors, 123
Guild of Music Makers, 10
Guildhall School of Music, 83
Gunter, Angus, 11
Gustav Mahler Jugendorchester, 234
Gyde, Megan, 216

Haddo House Choral Society, 81, 82
Hair, 67
Hall, Amalia, 194, 222
Hall, Callum, 194
Hall, Elroy, 194
Hall, Lara, 194
Halsey, Simon, 175
Hamilton, David *A Song of Tamatea*, 144, 148–49, 153
Hammond, Joan, 128
Hancox, Nicholas, 222
Handel, George Frideric, 235; *Occasional* Overture, vii, 3, 32, 34
Hansen, Kate, 163–64
Harker, Stephen, 181
Harland, Bryce, 93
Harper, Arthur, vii, 28
Harris, Ambrose Reeves, 14
Harris, Josephine, 79, *84*, *94*
Harris, R, *45*
Harris, Rolf, 147–48
Harris, Ross, 205, 222
Harris, Walter, vii, 27–28, *80*
Harrop, Joe (Joseph), 170, 186
Harry Dexter Cello Scholarship, 83
Hartstonge, James, 23, 29, 42, 107, 109–10, 111
Hartstonge, Jean, 107
Harvey, Euan, *218*
Haydn, Joseph, 237; Mass, 158; Symphony no 100 in G, *The Military*, 114; Symphony no 103 *Drum Roll*, 89, 97; Symphony no 104 in D, *London*, 49, 237
Hazell, Chris, 215
health and safety, 209
Heathcoate, Karen, 179
Heenan, Alison, 76, *90*, *94*, 99, 112
Heenan, Ashley, 52–68, *53*, *55*, *64*, 74, 89, 102–22, 236–37; *Aotearoa* Overture, 85, 88; auditions, 30, 37; fund-raising, 74; health, 118–19; legal action against Broadcasting Corporation of New Zealand, 119–20; letter of complaint about, 104–9; *A Maori Suite*, 55, 67; *Nelson College* Overture, 127; orchestra trainees, 44–46; Schola Musica, 120; Schola Musicum, 44, 69–70; *Scottish Dances*, 78–79, 87, 89, 97; UNESCO fellowship, 46; world tour 1975, 75–79, 85–89, 93, 98–99, 105–7; and Zoltán Kodály, 50
Heenan, Joseph, 15, 44
Heinz, Bernard, 20
Heltay, László, 51
Hendy, Christie, 60, 61, 62, *63*
Heuser, Norbert, 226
Hickman, Murray, 165, *166*
Hight, James, 15
Hill, Alfred, 11–13
Hill, Beatrice, 4
Hill, Greg, *84*, 93, *94*, 95, 99
Hindemith, Paul: *Five Pieces for Strings*, 70; *Symphonic Metamorphoses on Themes by Weber*, 133, 135; Symphony *Mathis der Maler* , 125
Hinterhuber, Christopher, 179, 237
Hogan, Seamus, 135
Hohaia, Mark Te Tane, *148*, 153
Hollinrake, Horace, 15
Holst, Gustav, 86; *The Planets*, 157; *A Somerset Rhapsody*, 41; Suite in E flat, 215
Hong Kong, 89
Hong Kong Philharmonic, 183
Hopkins, Clare, 22
Hopkins, John, vii–viii, *3*, 3–4, 5, 6–7, 10, 21–29, *24*, 40–42, 44, *48*, 49, 64–66, 105–7, 115, 119, 120–21, 124, 129, 158, 199, 223, 224, 226–27, 234–37; ambitions, 37–38; auditions, 30, 38; contrast with Heenan, 105; legacy, 52–53; major goals in New Zealand, 50–51; manner with orchestra, 32; rehearsals, 47; Wellington Town Hall, *33*; World Youth Festival, 160, 161, 163
Hopkins, Rosemary, 21
Hopkinson, James, 19
Hopper, Derek, 133
Horsford, Shandelle, 211
Houstoun, Michael, *67*, 67–68, 71, 74, 131–32, 144, 146, 148, 153, 164–66, *167*, 239
Houtman, Eleanor (Elena), 69, 76, *94*, 112–13
Howarth, Elgar, 215
Hoy, Kenneth, *48*
Hummel, Johann Nepomuk Trumpert Concerto in E, 126–27
Hunt, Ann, *94*
Hunt, Jonathan, *following p 118*
Hunt, Natalie *Only to the Highest Mountain*, 222, 224–25
Hunter, Clive, 50
Hunter, Keith, 50

illness, 173
Inkinen, Pietari, 232
instrumental teaching, 21st century, 238–39
International Festival of Youth Orchestras, 72
International Festival Youth Orchestra, *78*, 79, 80, 102, 103
International Society for Musical Education, 69
International Year of Youth, 136
Ireland, Patrick, *48*
Isaac, Colin, 205
Italian International Opera Company, 19
Ito, Kanako, 169
Ives, Charles, 197; *Three Places in New England*, 191; *The Unanswered Question*, 123

Jack and Emma Griffin Trust, 191, 200
Jackson, Isaiah, 175, 176

Jacob, Gordon, 85–86, *86*, 238; *Fantasia on the Alleluia Hymn*, 87; *Sketches for Strings*, 87
James, David, 60, 61, 62, *63*, 86
Janácek, Leos Sinfonietta, 178
Jane, Catherine (Mountfort), 127
Jane, Philip, 99, 127
Japan, 97, 100
Jennings, Anthony, 69
Jensen, Gail, 42
Jensen, Owen, 32–34, 40, 53, 56, 57
Jeunesses Musicales World Orchestra, 164
Joel, Michael, *151*, 181
Johansen, Lars, *44*, 45
John Chisholm Award, 145, 191, 223
Johns, Graham, 79, *94*
Judd, James, 80, 103, 186, 190

Kabalevesky, Dmitry: Colas Breugnon, 62; Symphony no 2 in C minor, 61, 62
Kern, Jerome, 215
Kerr, Elizabeth, 158
Keyworth, Mark, 174
Khachaturian, Aram: *Gayaneh*, 57; Violin Concerto, 139
King, Edward, 222
King, Ruth (Railton), 27
Kingston, Kate (Hansen), 163–64
Kirkwood, Ruth, 226
Kleinsinger, George *Tubby the Tuba*, 60, 61, 62
Kless, Eyal, 213, 215, 218, *218*
Kloogh, Noeline, 45
Knight, Fiona, 58, 59, 62
Knight, Greg, 214, *220*
koauau, 144–45
Kodály, Zoltán: *Dances of Galanta*, 78, 89, 157; *Háry János*, 49, 50, 236
Köhler, Lutz, *following p 118*, 190, 192, 197
Kolloh, Evelyn, *48*
Kominik, Anna, 174
Kwangchow (Canton), 89–91
Kyung-wha Chung, 81, 82, 99

La Scala, 83
Lacombe, Jaques, *following p 118*, 199, *210*, 210, 211, 212, 233
Lalo *Symphonie espagnole*, 142
Lamb, Martin, 79, *94*, *following p 118*
Lambert, Constant, 238; *The Rio Grande*, 137
Laurian Club, 11
Lawson, Eric, 19
Lazarev, Alexander, 175
Leaso, Ferila, 58
Lees, Heath, 191–92
Lees-Jeffries, Susannah, *following p 118*
Leningrad Conservatoire, 132
Leningrad Philharmonic Orchestra, 132
Leo, Sister Mary, 239
Leppänen, Vesa-Matti, 213, 215, 218, *218*
Lewis, Claire, 228, 233–34
Lexus New Zealand International Violin Competition, 169
Lexus Song Quest, 210
Leyland, Coralie, vii, 26–27
Ligeti, György *Sechs Bagatellen*, 215
Lilburn, Douglas, 121; *Aotearoa* Overture, 47, 78–79, 81, 87, 89, 97, 131, 145, 236, 238; *Festival* Overture, 64, 175, 238; *Suite for Orchestra*, 57, 238; Symphony no 2, 114; Symphony no 3, 71
Lindsay, Alex, 18, 71, 205
Lindsay, Angela (Connal), 1, 26–27, *44*, 45, 223
Lion, Margaret, 68
Liszt, Franz *Totentanz*, 149
Loader, Linden, *128*, 128
London Philharmonic, 207
London Symphony Orchestra, 160, 205
Loughran, James, 156, *157*, 157
Lukáš, Zdeneck, 78

Māori creation, 202
Māori instruments, 144–45, 149 *see also* taonga puoro
MacFarlane, Norman, *94*
MacLean, Nigel, 130
Mahler, Gustav: Symphonic Prelude, 139; Symphony no 1 'The Titan', 68, 192, 197; Symphony no 5, 39, 178; Symphony no 6 in A minor, 149; Symphony no 7, 223, 224–25, 233, 235
Major, Dean, *94*, 99
Malcolm, Beverley (Bev), 64, 89, 103–4, 131; world tour 1975, 75
Managh, Stephen, *65*
Manawatu Youth Orchestra, 56
Manitoba Chamber Orchestra, 205
Mann, Athol, 158, 160
Mao, 95
Margertić, Karlo, *207*, 226; *Belt Sander*, 207
Marin Symphony, 197
Mark, Greta, 177, 178, 181
Marrier, Neville, 205
Martin, Mary, 82, 85, 99, 130–31 *see also* Martin, Marya
Martin, Marya, 82, 85, 99, 130–31 *see also* Martin, Mary
Mason, Bruce, 53
Mata, Eduardo, 174
Mathers, Rosemary, 64, *64*, 66
Matheson, John, 88
Matteucci, Juan, 51, 55, 56, 73, 74, *following 122*
Mawhinney, Malcolm, 180, 186, 189
McCarthy, Julia, *following p 118*
McClellan, Michael, 55
McClelland, Sarah, 164
McCracken, Sarah, *following p 118*

McDouall, Andrew, 226
McDouall Stuart (Securities Ltd), 192
McFarlane, Norman, 79, *80*
McIntyre, Michael, 7, 32, 37
McKenzie, A, *45*
McKenzie, Alan, 76, 79, *80*
McKenzie, Judith, 69, *94*
McKinnon, Bruce, 66, 219
McLean, Denis, 84, 87
McLeod, Jenny, 222; *Cambridge* Suite, 55
McNeill, Jeff, 125
McNeill, Marise (White), 88, *90*, *94*, 99, 112
McStay, Janetta, 39, *41*, 235
Meech, JV, 43
Meek, Alan, 174
Melbourne Exhibition, 11
Melbourne Symphony Orchestra, 83, 99
Melbourne Youth Orchestra, 27, 150
Mendelssohn, Felix, 235; Octet, 215; String Quartet no 4 in E minor, 222; Symphony no 9 in C minor, 70; Violin Concerto in E minor, viii, 32, 34, 61, 123, 124
Menuhin, Yehudi, 183
Menzies, Mark, 142
Metropolitan Opera, 221
Midsummer Common Leisure Fair, 85
Milanov, Rossen, 227, 228–29, 234
Miles, Bridget, *171*
Miller, Simon, 69, 82, *94*, 99
Mills, Richard: *Aeolian Caprices*, 147; *Festival Fanfare*, 147
Ministry of Cultural Affairs, 167
Ministry of Defence, 72
Ministry of Foreign Affairs, 72
Minnesota Symphony Orchestra, 12
Mobil Song Quest, 126
Modugno, Domenico, 215
Monde Marie, 5
Monteverdi, Claudio, 215
Montréal Symphony Orchestra, 210
Moon, Chloe *Episodes for String Orchestra*, 126–27
Morris, Michael, 156
Morris, Paul, 79, *94*
Morrison, Ben, *206*, 222
Moses, Charles, 50
Mountfort, Catherine, 127
Mountfort, Charles, 69
Mozart, Wolfgang Amadeus, 235, 239; *Don Giovanni*, 190; Flute Concerto no 1 in G, 179; *The Magic Flute*, 123, 125; Piano Concerto in E flat major (K482), viii, 33–34; Piano Concerto no 16 in D, 47, 53–54; Piano Concerto no 20 in D minor, 133; Piano Concerto no 23 in A, 66, 237; Piano Concerto no 24, 164, 165; *Sinfonia Concertante*, 215; Sonata in G minor for violin and piano, 214; Symphony no 39 in E flat, 78
Muir, Barry, 145
Mulligan, AW, 15
Municipal Orchestra, 10
Murray, Haydn, *16*
Music Bursary Committee, 43
Music Study Awards, 156
Musicians Union, vii, 19, 20, 43, 44
Muston, Colin, 10
Myhill, Tim, 219

Nalden, Charles, 4, *7*, 30, 56, 234
Nalden, Natalie, 164
Napier Junior Orchestra, 27
Nash, Olga, *48*
Nash, Paddy, 131, 165
'Nat Orch' *see* National Orchestra of New Zealand
National Band of New Zealand, 75
National Broadcasting Service (NBS), 13, 14, 15; string orchestra, 15; studio orchestra, 15–16
National Commercial Broadcasting Service, 14
National Concerto Competition, 175
national music camp, 213–21
National Music Conservatoire, 170
National Orchestra *see* National Orchestra of New Zealand
National Orchestra of Canada, 206
National Orchestra of New Zealand, 3–4, 5, 17, *18*, 18, 19–21, 168; cadets, 42–43; schools concerts, 27; touring, 19
National Orchestra Trainees, 42–46 *see also* Orchestra Training Scheme; Schola Musica; Schola Musicum
National Symphony Orchestra, Washington, 207
National Youth Band of New Zealand, 137
National Youth Brass Band of New Zealand, 160
National Youth Choir, 137, 160, 161, 179, 189, 237
National Youth Concert Band, 160
National Youth Orchestra of Great Britain, 27, 234
National Youth Orchestra of Wales, 234
National Youth Pipe Band, 160
Natzke, Oscar, 16
NBS String Orchestra, 16, 18
Neale, Alasdair, 197, 198, 237
Nees, Geoffrey, 58
Neumann, Geoff, 226
New, Gemma, 199, 226
New England Conservatory, 184
New South Wales State Orchestra, 12
New World Symphony, 197
New Zealand and South Seas Exhibition Orchestra, 11
New Zealand Broadcasting Board, 14
New Zealand Broadcasting Corporation, 46–47, 56, 103
New Zealand Broadcasting Service, 5, 6, 17, 20–22, 26, 28, 36, 43–44, 73–74
New Zealand Centennial, 14–15

New Zealand Choral Federation, 175
New Zealand Conservatorium proposed, 12–13
New Zealand Drama School, 158
New Zealand Federation of Chamber Music Societies, 29, 43, 47
New Zealand House, 21
New Zealand International Exhibition, 11
New Zealand Opera Company, 43, 114, 125
New Zealand Post, 156, 176–77
New Zealand Post Office, 139
New Zealand Post Office Awards for Excellence, 139
New Zealand Post Young Musicians Award, 179
New Zealand School of Dance, 136
New Zealand Secondary Schools Orchestra, 56
New Zealand Symphony Orchestra, 72, 80, 89, 99, 114, 124, 129, 131, 155, 156, 226; Artist Planning Forum, 232; Board of Directors, 158; overseas tour, 174–75; Play with the NZSO, 221; Players' Committee, 232; rural education, 239; solvency, 182; world tour, 230
New Zealand Trio, 165
New Zealand Women's Club of Great Britain, 74
New Zealand Yamaha Youth Jazz Orchestra, 137
New Zealand Youth Brass Band, 161
New Zealand Youth Jazz Orchestra, 160
Newcastle Youth Orchestra, 150
Newman, Helen, *48*
Newson, Geoffrey, 30
Newson, Gerald, 42
Nézet-Séguin, Yannick, 207, 207–8, *208*, 212
Ngāti Kahungunu, 153
nguru, 144–45
Niccolai, Otto *Merry Wives of Windsor*, 57
Nichol, Heather, *151*
Nisbet, Peter, 63, 72, 74, 119, 121, 124, 134, *143*, 155–56, 159, 167, 230–31
Noble, John, 149
Norman, Philip, 161, 162, 174–75; *The Ballad of Settler McGee*, 162–63, 164, 175
NZ Beer Band, 79
NZBC *see* New Zealand Broadcasting Corporation
NZBC Concert Orchestra, 46
NZBC Orchestra Trainees, 47
NZBC Symphony Orchestra, 47, 56, 59, 60, 66; Australian tour, 70–72
NZBS *see* New Zealand Broadcasting Service
NZSO, 232–40
NZSO Alumni Association, 209, 223, 226
NZSO Foundation, 178, 191
NZSO Foundation Trust Board, 190
NZSO Friends *see* Friends of NZSO
NZSO National Youth Orchestra Chair Endowment, 226
NZSO National Youth Orchestra Fellowship Programme, 220
O'Meeghan, Brigid, *following p 118*, 182–95, *195*, 230, 233
Orchestra Advisory Committee, 118
orchestra trainees, 68, 115–16; rift, 102–4
Orchestra Training Scheme, 121
Orchestral Society, 11
Orchestre National de France, 207
Orff, Carl *Carmina Burana*, 179, 180
Orpheus Choir, 159
Orr, Robert, 165, *166*
Ostrowsky, Avi, 78
Oue, Eiji, 160
Outwater, Edwin, 201, *201*
Owen, Mary-Anne, 135
Ozim, Igor, vii, 7, 32, 34

Pacific Music Festival, 160
Pacific Rim Youth Orchestra, 160
Paczian, Rita, 170
Page, William, 15
Palliser, Stefan, 1
Palmer, Alwyn, 63–64, 68, 72, *following p 118*, 131, 132, 134–35, 137, 145–46, 149, 155–56, 160–61, 164, 169, 172–73, 181, 205
Palmer, Gae, 131, 134, 145–46, 149, 172–73
Panama, 22
Panufnik, Andrzej *Sinfonia Sacra*, 170
Parenteau, Pascale, *following p 118*, 193, 196–212, 233, 238
Parry, WE, 15
Parsons Bookshop, 5
Pawsey, David, *following p 118*, 205, 216
Pearl, Ruth, 235, 236
Peking *see* Beijing
People's Republic of China, 87–88
Pergolesi, Giovanni Concertino in G minor, 70
Perks, Robert, 2, 234
Perks, Robin, 2, *3*, 4, 46, *48*, 49–50, 53, 56, 57, 234
Perry, George, 63
Persichetti, Vincent Serenade no 10, 222
Philadelphia Orchestra, 207
Philharmonic Society, 11
Philipson, Vicki, *94*
Phoenix Symphony, 177
Picasso Coffee Bar, 5
Pierard, Madeleine, *following p 118*, *210*, 210
Pilates, 214, 217, 219, *220*
Pitt, Wendy, *44*, 45, *48*
Pius XII Catholic Seminary, *following p 118*, 146
Pleeth, William, *48*, 83
Polglasse, Helen, *following p 118*
Pollock, Craig, 60, 61, 62, *63*
Pople, Edward (Ted), vii, 5, 57, 61, 62, 110–11, 119, 123, 124
Pople, Ross, vii, 5, 57
Porangahau Marae, 156–57
Post Primary Teachers Association, 29

Poulenc, Francis: Sextet for piano, flute, oboe, clarinet, bassoon, French horn, 215; Sonata for French horn, trumpet and trombone, 214
Pounamu Cultural Group, 163
Prankerd, Richard, *60*
press attendance, 37
Previn, André, 124
Priestman, Brian, 70, 71
profit, 40
programming, 232
Prokofiev, Sergei, 203, 237; *The Love of Three Oranges*, 192; Piano Concerto no 3, 71; Piano Concerto no 3 in C major, 201; *Romeo and Juliet* Suite no 2, 161; Symphony no 5, 190
Prouse, John, 11
Prouse, Lena, 11
Pruden, Larry *Soliloquy for Strings*, 170
Psathas, John, *following p 118*, 202
Public Broadcasting Fee, 166–67
Puccini, Giacomo *Turandot*, 114
pukaea, 144–45

Quebec Symphony, 205
Queen Elizabeth II Arts Council, 72, 74, 127
Queensland Youth Orchestra, 148
Quilter, Roger *A Children's Overture*, 61, 62

Rachmaninov, Sergei: *Paganini Variations*, 148, 153; Piano Concerto no 2 in C minor, 49, 64, 66, 213, 238; *Rhapsody on a Theme of Paganini*, 51; *Symphonic Dances*, 228, 234; Symphony no 2 in E minor, 178; *Valse and Romance*, 214
Radaich, Juliana, 2, 5, 34–35
Radford, Ross, *94*
radio broadcasting, 13–14
Radio Broadcasting Company of New Zealand Ltd, 13
Radio New Zealand, 17, 155
Railton, Ruth, 27
Ramsauer, Peter, 179
Rangitane, 22
Rattle, Simon, 78
Ravel, Maurice: *Albotada del Gracioso*, 210; *Daphnis et Chloe*, viii, 161, 163; *Introduction and Allegro*, 222; *La Valse*, 207, 208; Piano Concerto for the Left Hand, 224–25; Piano Concerto in G, 67; *Sonatine*, 215
Red Detachment of Women, 93
Reeves Harris Orchestra Fund, 190, 200
Reeves Harris Trust, 191
Regina Orchestra, 205
Registered Music Teachers Registration Board, 29
rehearsals, *38*, 54, *59*, 205–6; world tour 1975, 75
Rennie, Hugh, 139
Resphigi, Ottorino: *Fountains of Rome*, 148, 170; *La Boutique Fantasque*, 142
Rheidol Valley, 85
Rhodes, Alan, 216
Rhodes, Teddy Tahu, 179
Rhodes, Valerie, 216, 224
Riches, Sheila, *44*, 45
Rickard, Malcolm, 59
Ridding, Bert, 74
Ries, Ferdinand, 237
Rimmer, John *At the Appointed Time*, 71
Rimsky-Korsakov, Nikolai *Le Coq D'or*, 114
Ritchie, John, 74; Clarinet Concerto, 85, 87
Roberts, Gillian (Witton), 42
Roberts, Linda (Simmons), 49, 54, 57, 121
Robertson, James, 20, 23–24, *24*, 26, 28, 44, 88, 114–16, *115*
Rogers, Glenda, 124–25
Rogers, Murray, *94*
Rogers, Simon, 193
Ross, Matthew, 164
Rossini, Gioachino: *Barber of Seville*, 125; Duo for cello and double bass, 214; *The Italian Girl in Algiers*, 60, 61
Rotterdam Philharmonic, 207
Roude, Hayley, 212
Roussel, Albert *Bacchus et Ariane* 43 Suite no 2, 210
Royal Academy, London, 237
Royal Academy of Music, 88
Royal Ballet, 175
Royal Brussels Conservatoire, 125
Royal College of Music, London, 44, 88
Royal Concert for Her Majesty Queen Elizabeth II, 20
Royal Concert Orchestra, 56
Royal New Zealand Air Force Band, 18
Royal Overseas League International Competition, 131
Royal Stockholm Philharmonic, 207
Royal Wellington Choral Union, 10, 14
Royal Youth Concert for the Queen Mother, *following p 118*, 187–88
rural education, 239
Ruthchen, Ursula (Evans), 82, *94*, 99, *101*
Ryan, Paula, 58

Saffron Walden, 86
Saint-Saëns, Camille: Cello Concerto in A minor, 62; *Introduction and Rondo Capriccioso* for violin and orchestra, 41; Piano Concerto no 4 in C minor, op 44, 58; Symphony no 3 (*Organ Symphony*), 170; Violin Concerto no 3, 168, 169
Salamonsen, Anna, *94*
Salmon, Christopher, *48*
Salomon, Doron, *following p 118*, 137–39, 237
San Francisco Conservatory of Music, 197
San Francisco Symphony, 201
San Francisco Youth Orchestra, 201
Sanderling, Kurt, 132, 237

Sanderling, Thomas, 131–33, *132*, 135, 139, 141
Sandle, Nick, 64
Sargent, Malcolm, 12, 14, 15
satisfaction survey, 203
Savage, Michael, 12
Schaffer, Peter, *111*, 123, 124, *143*
Scharnke, Gudrun, *following p 118*
Scherek, Benno, 11
Schmitt, Karl, 10
Schola Musica, 111, 116, 122, 124, 131, 135, 136, 144, 155, 235, 236 *see also* Schola Musicum; demise, 158–59
Schola Musicum, 45, 79, 88, 110 *see also* Schola Musica; Australian tour, 69–70; International Festival Youth Orchestra, 102–3; rift with NYO, 105–6; world tour 1975, 81
Schools Music Contest, 196
Schroder, John, 22, 28, 29, 36, 40, 43
Schubert, Franz: Symphony no 8 *Unfinished*, 39, 177; Symphony no 9, 123
Schumann, Robert: Cello Concerto, 189; Symphony no 3 in E flat, *Rhenish*, 57, 237
Schwabe, John, *6*
Scotland, 99
Scott, Calvin, 142
Scott, Graham, 176
Scott Report, 176
Seaman, Christopher, *127*, 127, *128*, 135
Secker, Anthea, 69, 74, 89
Secondary Schools Festival of Music, 27
Sedares, James, *following p 118*, 177, 178, 179, 237
Seddon, Mary, 5
Segal, Uri, *126*, 135
Seggar, Matthew, *200*
Sell, David, 198, 202
Sewell, Andrew, 135
Sewell, Mary-Anne, 125, 134
Shakespeare, William *The Merry Wives of Windsor*, 158
Shanghai Philharmonic Orchestra, 92, 93
Shaw, Angela, 114
Shaw, Peter, 134
Shell New Zealand, 130
Shell Youth Scholarship, 130, 135
Shelley, James, 14, 15, 16
Shepherd, Neil, 54, 59
Sheppard, Mark, 138, *151*
Shipley, Jenny, 185, 187
Shostakovich, Dmitri, 237; Symphony no 1, 158; Symphony no 5, 184; Symphony no 10, 164, 165, 205
Showcase, 179
Sibelius, Jean: *Karelia* Suite, 175; Symphony no 3, 57, 89, 237, 238
Signor Squarise, 11
Siki, Bela, 47
Simenauer, Wilfred, 71, 114
Simmons, Linda, 54, 57, 121
Simón Bolívar Symphony Orchestra, 234, 239
Sinclair, George, 15
Sinclair, Hayden, 222
Slinn, Warwick, 48
Smale, David, *6*, 30
Smith, Ken, 75
Smith, Malcolm, 125–26
Smith, Wilma, 83, *94*, 99, 112, 184, 224
Smyth, Sonia, *44*, *45*, 45
SOUNZ, 196, 198
Southern Sinfonia, 212
Southgate, Brent, 31
Southgate, William, *40*, 48, 134, 136
sponsorship, 208–9
Spragg, Keith, 76, *79*, *83*, 83, 87, 93, *94*, 98–100
Squire, Tabea, *210*; *Feverdream*, 210, 211
SSL Spotless Services, 192
St Paul's schoolroom, Thorndon, 5
Stapleton, Alan, *90*, *94*
Steer, Michael, 160
Stiles, Winifred, 235
Stockhausen, Karlheinz, 238
Stokowski, Leopold, 175
Stone, Jacqueline, *66*, 237
Stossberg, Jochen, 216
Strauss, Richard, 215; *Der Rosenkavalier* Suite, 205, 233; *Don Juan*, 190, 233; *Don Quixote*, 71; *Four Last Songs*, 71; *Tod und Verklärung* op 24, Death and Transfiguration, 81, 82, 83; *Vienna Brass* Fanfare, 215
Stravinsky, Igor, 197, 214; Ballet Suite *Petrushka*, 126; Concerto for Piano and Wind Instruments, 227, 234; *Danses Concertantes*, 58; *The Firebird* Suite, 62, 138, 142, 143, 191, 210, 212, 233, 237; *Le Roi des Etoiles* for Male Chorus and Orchestra, 81, 82; *Pétrouchka*, 57, 138, 148, 168, 237; *Rite of Spring*, 137, 138, 237; *Scherzo à la Russe*, 53; Symphony in C, 215
Streatfeild, Simon, *following p 118*, 199, 205–6, *206*, 233
Strike, 165
Stronach, Marian, *48*
Stuart, Cameron, 211–12
summer tour 1970, 61–62
Sun Valley Summer Symphony, 197
Sutton, Reg, 121
swine flu, 220
SWR Radio Orchestra, 207
Sydney Conservatorium, 12
Sydney International Piano Competition, 201
Sydney Symphony Orchestra, 70, 213
Sydney Youth Orchestra, 27
Symphonia of Auckland, 73
Symphony 1997, *Heaven Earth Mankind*, 183
Symphony Quarterly, 173–74

taonga puoro, 149 *see also* Māori instruments
Tarrant-Mathews, Claudia, 229
Tarrant-Mathews, Sophie, 229
Taylor, Julie, 69, 70, 77, 88, 99
Taylor, Lindis, 179
Taylor, Penny, 164
Taylor, Richard, 226
Tchaikovsky, Pyotr Ilyich, 203, 204, 214; *1812* Overture, 137, 138, 148, 161; *Eugene Onegin*, 114; *Nutcracker* Suite, 47; Piano Concerto no 1 in B flat minor, 60, 61, 131, 135; Piano Concerto no 3 in E flat, 57; *Romeo and Juliet*, 184; *The Sleeping Beauty*, 67; *Swan Lake*, 51; Symphony no 4 in F minor, 201; Symphony no 5 in E minor, 53–54, 129, 177, 237; Symphony no 6, 215–16, 226; *Variations on a Rococo Theme for cello and orchestra*, 57, 175; Violin Concerto in D, 81, 82
Te Kanawa, Kiri, 71, 239
Te Rangatahi Māori Cultural Group, *following p 118*, 144–45, 147, *148*, 150, 156; *Te Ara Pounamu (The Greenstone Path)*, 145
Television One, 155
Television Two, 155
Tennent-Brown, Lindy, 180, 181–82
Thaxted, 86
The Best of National Youth Orchestra 1972–74, 74
Thomas, Gail, *94*
Thomas, Mark, *94*
Thompson, Chrisina, *following p 118*
Thompson, Jane, 99
Thompson, Jeremy, *65*, *94*, 99, *101*
Thompson, Sarah, 141
Thompson, Susan, *65*, 74, 99
Thomson, John Mansfield, 159
Tibbles, Margaret, *48*
Till, Maurice, 52, 68
Tilson Thomas, Michael, 160
Tintner, Georg, 122, 125–26, 237
Tippett, Michael *A Child of Our Time*, 159
Tipping, Simon, 158
Toan, Robin, *following p 118*, *201*, 201–2; *Tū-mata-uenga 'God of War, Spirit of Man'*, 201, 204
Tokyo Youth Symphony Orchestra, 97
Tongs, Sharon, 160
Tonhalle Orchestra, Zurich, 207
Townend, Hugh, 56
Towsey, Arthur, 10, 11
Trinity College, 88
Trussell-Cullen, Marcel, *following p 118*
Tulloch, Marion (Townend), 226
Turnbull, Elizabeth, 77, 78, 88, 99, 100
Turnovsky, Fred, 43
Turnovsky Trio, 189
Tyrer, Andersen, 15, *16*, 17, 18, 19, 23

Upton, Simon, 182
Ure, John, *94*
Utting, Craig, 142, 148, 157, 159

van der Zee, Christiaan, 181
van Drimellen, Glenda (Craven), 69, *94*, 98, 99, 121
Vancouver Bach Choir, 205
Vancouver Symphony, 205
Vanderwart, Marle, 235
Vaughan Williams, Ralph: *Fantasia on a Theme by Thomas Tallis*, 227, 234; *Folksongs of the Four Seasons*, 55; *Sir John in Love*, 158; Suite for Viola and Orchestra, 78, 85
Vector Wellington Orchestra, 212
Verbrugghen, Henri, 12
Verner, Amanda, *following p 118*, 193
Vickery, Amber, 218
Victorian College of the Arts, 124
Vienna Boys Choir, 125
Vinten, Michael, 118, *following p 118*, 124, 136, 138, 144, 148, 151, 153, 158, 172, 178; *Te Ara Pounamu (The Greenstone Path)*, 145
Vivaldi, Antonio Violin Concerto in A major, 70
von Alpenheim, Ilse, vii, viii, 7, 33, 237

Wagner, Richard: *Rienzi*, 49; *Tristan und Isolde*, 192
Wakem, Beverley, 111, 114
Walden-Mills, William, 4, 30, 37, 56
Wales, 85–86, 100
Walls, Peter, 49, 183, 212, 227, 229–30
Walsh, Philip, 159
Walters, Irwin, 27
Walton, Antony, *65*; Overture *Portsmouth Point*, 66
Walton, Mark, *65*, *99*, 99, 100, *129*, 130–31
Walton, Tony, 76, *94*, 99
Walton, William Overture *Johannesburg Festival*, 57
Warren, Allan, 145, 175
Warren, Tom, 145
Watson, Anthony *Prelude and Allegro for Strings*, 71
Watson, Helen, *130*
Watt, Peter, *94*
Webb, Ronald, 59
Webby, Helen, 149
Weber, Carl Maria von: Concertstück for piano and orchestra, 39; *Euryanthe*, 189
Welcome Home concert, 98
Wellington East Girls' College, 1–3
Wellington Orchestral Society, 10
Wellington Philharmonic Society, 10
Wellington Polytechnic Conservatorium of Music, 158
Wellington Professional Orchestra, 10
Wellington Sinfonia, 164
Wellington Symphony Orchestra, 10, 15–16
Wellington Youth Orchestra, 27, 56, 57, 136, 234–35
Welsh Youth Orchestra, 27
West Australian Symphony Orchestra, 222

White, Hugh Temple, 29
White, Julia, 69, 76, 77, 88, 99, 112
White, Marise, 88, *90*, *94*, 99, 112
Whitehead, Geoffrey, 111
Whitten, Ben, 212
Whyte, Sandy, 75, 89, 97, 131
Wieck, Michael, 235
Wielaert, Johannes, 10
Wiggins, Warren, *94*
Wigley, Richard, 127
Wilkinson, Farquhar, *48*, 74
Wilkinson, Jane, *94*
Williams, Garth, 200
Williams, Judith, *94*
Williams, Peter, 215
Wilson, Ken Quintet for flute, oboe, clarinet, bassoon, French horn, 214
Wilson, Ormond, 29
Wiltshire, Garth, 202
Witton, Gillian, 42
Wolf-Ferrari, Ermanno Overture, 85
World Festival of Youth, 64
world tour 1975, 75–102; Aberystwyth, 84–85; aftermath of world tour 1975, 102–22; Arbroath, 80–81; Barry, 84; Cardiff, 84; England, 76–77, 85–88, 100; Hong Kong, 100; Japan, 97, 100; letter of complaint, 104–9; London, 99–100; Peoples Republic of China, 100; Scotland, 99; tension in orchestra, 102–4; Wales, 85–86, 100; Welcome Home concert, 98
World Youth Festival, 160
World Youth Festival Orchestra, 164
Wright, AR, 14
Wright, Jane, 138

Yates, William, 6, 27, 28
Yendoll, Vyvyan, 54, 71
Yo Yo Ma, 183
Young, Jennifer, *94*
Young, Ken, 79, *80*, *82*, *84*, *94*, 95, 99, 117
Young, Tim, 135
Young Musicians Competition, 142, 179
Young Musicians Symphony Orchestra of Great Britain, 78, 80
Youth Arts 2000, 189
Youth Orchestra of Venezuela, The, 239

Zander, Benjamin, *following p 118*, 184, *186*, 186, 188, 191–92, 197, 237
Zwartz, Peter, 27